THE CENTRAL AMERICAN REPUBLICS

THE
CENTRAL AMERICAN
REPUBLICS

FRANKLIN D. PARKER

Associate Professor of History
University of North Carolina
at Greensboro

Issued under the auspices of the
Royal Institute of International Affairs
OXFORD UNIVERSITY PRESS
LONDON   NEW YORK   TORONTO
1964

Oxford University Press, Amen House, London E.C.4

GLASGOW NEW YORK TORONTO MELBOURNE WELLINGTON
BOMBAY CALCUTTA MADRAS KARACHI LAHORE DACCA
CAPE TOWN SALISBURY NAIROBI IBADAN ACCRA
KUALA LUMPUR HONG KONG

*Printed in Great Britain
by The Broadwater Press Ltd, Welwyn Garden City, Hertfordshire*

To

Dr Rafael Heliodoro Valle

1891 – 1959

Mid-twentieth century

Erudito de distinción

PREFACE

THIS five-in-one treatment of the Central American republics bears some special features of which the reader should be aware. They spring chiefly from the desire to speak meaningfully within small compass.

Five chapters of the book treat the area unitedly. The first four deal with matters which had their beginnings before the five states separated. The last discusses common attitudes and problems.

Chapters V–IX deal with the single countries. Here are presented the political, economic, and cultural characteristics which set one nation off from the other. The approach is meant to be analytical with some historical depth. The handling, for efficiency's sake, is strictly parallel republic by republic.

The footnotes are largely bibliographical in nature. Time after time the shortness of space precluded more than beginning the discussion of intriguing topics. It was felt that the least that could be done was to provide the reader with suggestions as to where he might probe farther. Where footnote remarks are appropriate in more than one place, especially from country to country, reference is generally made from the second to the first, again to conserve space.

Statistics are used profusely in the treatment of some topics. It may be argued that Central American statistics are unreliable; yet they suffice for the purposes at hand. They speak their story swiftly, and sometimes dramatically if followed with care. Tables of comparisons between the republics came constantly to mind, but, to have spoken the truth even as it was measured, they would have had to be riddled with notes of definition and exception. Besides, tables are not read; texts are, or may be.

Chapter X provides a 'postscript on politics', presenting the chief political occurrences from March 1961 to June 1962. Sections entitled 'Mid-Twentieth Century Politics' in the country chapters trace political events into 1961. Since judgements rendered in the earlier sections seemed to remain valid, it was decided not to disturb them when the manuscript proceeded slowly. The whole task of keeping up with the flow of events and statistics in five separate nations while writing progressed seemed as interminable as the painting of the Firth of Forth bridge.

Preface

The author has been intrigued by Central America since 1948. Two extensive visits by automobile have enabled him and his family to see much of the five republics. One year's study on the scene was financed by the Henry L. and Grace Doherty Charitable Foundation. Travel assistance was provided by the Southern Fellowships Fund during two summers five years apart. The Research Council of the Woman's College of the University of North Carolina helped to pay for one trip and purchased a large number of research materials for use in the project.

Although a great variety of sources has been tapped in the development of current events and statistics, the two most convenient have not been spurned when their aid was useful. These are the daily *New York Times*, with its good coverage in times of crisis, and the *Hispanic American Report* of Stanford University's Institute of Hispanic American and Luso-Brazilian Studies. The latter publication provides a month-to-month record which should be consulted by any user of this book who cares to follow the story to date.

No attempt has been made to duplicate the excellent treatment of Central American historical bibliography by R. A. Humphreys, in *Latin American History: a Guide to the Literature in English* (London, OUP for RIIA, 1958). Items there listed are mentioned here only when they served special purposes. In the sections here entitled 'Learning' and 'Art' there will be found a selection of books believed by the author to be among the most significant of Central American production.

Thanks are due to the many Central American friends from presidents to humble servants who helped me to understand the isthmian *ambiente*. Government publications were made generously available, and on occasion typewritten and handwritten information as well. The two persons who helped most of all—with research in newspaper files in every Central American capital, and back at home with critical reading and typing of the manuscript—were my wife Jennie and my daughter Ginger.

F. D. P.

6 July 1962

CONTENTS

Contents

CHAPTER I

BIRTH OF AN ISTHMUS

THE Central American republics number five. Together they constitute little more than one-hundredth part of the land area of the Americas and account for but one-fortieth of their population. Their weight in the Organization of American States is much greater; because they are five rather than one, they make up nearly one-fourth of this great international body.

Central America is as near the middle of the Americas geographically as one would expect from its name. The Americas stretch from 55° South Latitude to not quite 85° North. Costa Rica, Nicaragua, Honduras, El Salvador, and Guatemala are all included between the lines 8° and 18° North. The trend of the isthmus on which they are located is north-west and southeast, so that their range of longitude is almost precisely equal, lying between the lines 82° 30′ and 92° 30′ West. From one extremity to the other of these five lands taken as a unit is a distance of nearly 900 miles. But from any point on the coast of the Pacific Ocean, which lies to the south and west, one would have to fly less than 250 miles to reach the Caribbean Sea to the north and east.

Other American republics in or near the same latitudes are considered a part of the region called Middle America. This is a cultural rather than a political term, binding the five nations of Central America with other lands having some touch with the Caribbean. Central America consists specifically of those states which once formed the Provincias Unidas del Centro de América (1823–38). They are the same group which since 1955 have been members of the Organización de Estados Centroamericanos, though they have invited Panama (which has a quite different historical background) to join them. In estimated population at the middle of 1958, the Central American republics stood as follows, in order from north-west to south-east: Guatemala 3,546,000; El Salvador 2,434,000; Honduras 1,828,000; Nicaragua 1,378,000; Costa Rica 1,076,000. In area, Nicaragua is the largest (with 53,893 square miles to remain after an expected adjustment of her northeastern border); Honduras (43,277 square miles) and Guatemala

(42,042) are next; while Costa Rica (19,652) and El Salvador (8,164) are much smaller.[1]

FLORA AND FAUNA

During most of the long period of time known geologically as the Tertiary, a large part of Central America is believed to have been an island. Before the Tertiary (that is, before about 60 million years ago) a land bridge had existed between North and South America, across which passed many of the forms of terrestrial life which by then had developed. This connexion was broken for a very long time while South America developed its own species of both flora and fauna. Towards the end of the Tertiary, North America contained most of the plants and animals known there today in addition to native horses, camels, and mastodons. The contrasting mammal world of South America comprised several marsupials, some of them eaters of flesh; a large variety of bats; the hystricomorphic rodents, including porcupines and four-foot capybaras; the edentates—sloths, ant-eaters, and such; unique orders of grass-chewing ungulates quite different from any animal of to-day; and the remarkable marmosets and American monkeys. It is not certain that Central America was detached from the continent to the north during the Tertiary, but the likelihood is that Chiapas in Mexico, Guatemala, Honduras, and a part of Nicaragua constituted a large island, and that there were several other islets as well, the number of which varied from one geological epoch to another.

Somehow in the later Miocene epoch (about 15 million years ago) the racoon family of the North American carnivores (which until then were completely unknown in the southern continent) made their way to South America. Racoons can swim; but they must have arrived at a time when the gaps between the two continents were closing enough to make their passage possible. In the succeeding Pliocene epoch the gaps were completely closed. When that happened, Central America became the meeting ground of North and South American life (no one knows what forms she may have contributed of her own) in an exciting merger which is still in

---

[1] Official statistics as summarized in U.N., *Demogr. Yb.*, *1959*, pp. 114–15, except that 8,416 sq. km. have been subtracted from the area of Nicaragua (*La Prensa*, 19 Nov. 1960) and the area of El Salvador has been computed from departmental areas given in *Diccionario geográfico de la república de El Salvador* (San Salvador, Dir. Gen. Est. y Censos, 1959). National populations are discussed in chs v–ix.

progress.[2] Most of the story is unknown, but a rough-sketch record of the mammals is fairly clear.

Most South American marsupials died out before an onslaught of northern flesh-eaters; an exception was the opossum family, which thrived and made its own invasion of the northern continent from the southern. Several families of bats followed the same route, though not all reached that destination. Of the South American rodents the porcupines, capybaras, and agoutis made their way through the isthmus, but the capybaras did not last in their new homes; a family of spiny rats from the south reached as far as Nicaragua. Ground sloths measuring as much as twenty feet from head to tail and armoured glyptodons about half that size became familiar sights in North America long before they became extinct on both continents. Of their smaller cousins, the tree sloths reached Honduras, the ant-eaters Mexico, and the armadillos (which are yet on the march) still farther. Though the marmosets made it only to Panama (a part of the isthmus though not of Central America) four genera of monkeys spread beyond, two of them even to Mexico.

Migrations of mammals from the north were also remarkable. The shrew family and the cottontail rabbits found their way through to the south, as did the squirrels, pocket gophers, pocket mice, and other New World rats and mice among the North American rodents. The carnivores, except the racoons, came generally late in the Pliocene (which lasted until 1 million years ago) but made the greatest impression. One bear and several cats (the mountain lion, the jaguar, the ocelot, the margay, the jaguarundi, and a sabre-tooth) made the trek, though the bear has since disappeared from the isthmus and the sabre-tooths everywhere. Weasels, skunks, and otters followed; foxes too went all the way, but wolves and coyotes only to Costa Rica. Though no great variety of the larger species made their way to South America, the arrival of these newcomers doubtless helps to explain the disappearance of the southern ungulates as well as so many of the marsupials. Some new hoofed families came in from the north— the horses, which later became extinct in both continents; the tapirs, which lived on successfully in the isthmus and farther south but became aliens to the north; the peccaries, the northern range of which is likewise diminishing; the deer, which have continued

[2] Philip J. Darlington, Jr., in his *Zoogeography* (N.Y., Wiley, 1957), pp. 456–62, stresses the importance of this merger to future zoogeographical research.

everywhere; and the camels, whose modern descendants all live in the South American Andes. Bison of the cattle family once grazed as far south as Nicaragua. And finally, several mastodon species roamed southward through the two continents and survived (like the giant ground sloths who moved northward) until after the coming of man.[3]

In one manner or another, Central American vertebrate life came also to include a wide variety of birds, an inordinate number of reptiles, a fair share of amphibians, and a rather meagre assortment of fishes. A majority of Central America's bird families range widely in both North and South America as well. These are the grebes, cormorants, pelicans, hawks, falcons, ospreys, vultures, herons, ibises, ducks, quails, cuckoos, rails, oyster-catchers, plovers, gulls and terns, pigeons, owls, goatsuckers, kingfishers, swifts, humming-birds, woodpeckers, flycatchers, swallows, Old World warblers, thrushes, mocking-birds, wrens, dippers, vireos, New World warblers, tanagers, cardinal grosbeaks, finches, American orioles and blackbirds, and the jays. Many other bird families known on the isthmus are more familiar on the southern continent than to the north: the tinamous, storks, flamingos, guans, limpkins, sun bitterns, sun grebes, jacanas, thick-knees, parrots, potoos, trogons (the famed quetzal bird of Guatemala is a trogon), motmots, puff-birds, jacamars, barbets, toucans, tapaculos, ant birds, oven-birds and wood hewers, manakins, and the honey creepers. Only a few isthmian bird families—the turkeys, waxwings, creepers, and the titmice and chickadees—have their connexions solely to the north.

Central America has three families of turtles, seven of lizards (including the iguanas much seen on the highway, the geckos, and the skinks), and seven of snakes (the worm snakes, boas, common snakes, coral snakes, and pit vipers are all represented), as well as crocodiles from the north and caymans from the south. Amphibians include the South American caecilians, the lungless salamanders, and six families of frogs and toads. There are few strictly freshwater fishes in Central America, presumably because of the difficulty they have encountered in transferring from one river system to another across the young isthmus. From the south have come

---

[3] Recent reviews of mammalian species on the isthmus are provided by George G. Goodwin, 'Mammals of Honduras', *Bull. Am. Mus. Nat. Hist.*, lxxix (1942), 107–95; and 'Mammals of Costa Rica', ibid. lxxxvii (1946), 271–478.

several genera of characins, one family of gymnotid eels, and two families of catfishes; from the north only one family of suckers and one family of catfishes, and they only as far as Guatemala. Families which are more tolerant of salt water include the top minnows and killifishes and the viviparous minnows present on both ends of the isthmus, the rather numerous cichlids, which have come from the south, and the primitive gar-pikes, which have reached Lake Nicaragua from the north. Also present are a family of mud eels, one of catfishes which have come from the sea, and a unique species of shark which came from the Caribbean to make Lake Nicaragua its home.[4]

Among the vascular plants as among the vertebrate animals there is evidence of migration into the isthmus from both North and South America. Most isthmian plant families, however, are today well represented on both continents, only certain genera and species having a more localized distribution. The Dicksonia (tree fern) and polypody families are noteworthy among isthmian ferns, and the podocarp and pine families of the conifers. The pondweeds, grasses, sedges, palms, and aroids are prominent among the monocotyledons, as well as the families named for the pipewort, spiderwort, pineapple, lily, amaryllis, iris, canna, and the orchids. The wild pineapple itself is native to Central America, and probably nowhere else do orchids grow in greater profusion. Both Costa Rica and Guatemala have chosen particular orchids as their national flowers. The walnut, mulberry, nettle, buckwheat, goosefoot, amaranth, four-o'clock, and pink families are important among the apetalous dicotyledons. Polypetalous families include notably those of the custard-apple, poppy, saxifrage, witch-hazel, rose, legumes, oxalis, malpighia, spurges, soapberry, mallows, sterculia, dillenia, cacti, combretum, myrtle, melastoma, evening-primrose, water milfoil, and the carrot. The rose is the national flower of Honduras. The sympetalous dicotyledons are well represented by the families of the heaths, sapodilla, logania, dogbane, morning-glory, borages, vervain, mint, potato, figwort, bignonia, gesneria, acanthus, madder, gourds, and the composites. The heliotrope of

[4] Information concerning the land vertebrates has been gleaned from Darlington, pp. 102–22, 159–72, 206–30, 287–316, 371–406; the mammals being checked against E. Raymond Hall and Keith R. Kelson, *The Mammals of North America* (2 vols., N.Y., Ronald Press Co., 1959). Darlington expresses 'trepidation' in regard to details on the fishes (p. 74) but not as to the rest of the picture.

the borage family is the official flower of Nicaragua, while El Salvador has chosen from the madder family the non-native but widely seen white blossom of the coffee tree.[5]

WATER AND LAND

While these myriad forms of life—and a host of others representing the non-vascular plants and the invertebrate animals—made themselves at home on the Central American isthmus, the isthmus itself, in the late Pliocene and the Pleistocene epoch which followed, gradually assumed its modern configuration. Rising land to the north brought into being the Yucatan peninsula, which includes the Petén lowlands of northern Guatemala. To the east, submergence of ground delimited the extent of Mosquitia (north-eastern Honduras and Nicaragua) and left stranded the Bay Islands of Honduras. The Gulf of Honduras, with its Bay of Amatique, was defined between Yucatan and Mosquitia, and Lake Izabal detached from the bay. On the Pacific coast more explosive forces were at work. Close to the ocean and sometimes in it, probably no more than 2 million years ago arose a new chain of volcanoes ranging all along the isthmus. New land thus brought above sea level formed the Gulf of Fonseca, marine meeting-place of El Salvador, Honduras, and Nicaragua, as well as the Gulf of Nicoya and Golfo Dulce in Costa Rica. Most sensationally, a much larger arm of the Pacific in Nicaragua was cut off from the ocean completely. When rain falling into this detached basin had raised its waters to a level about 155 feet higher than its mighty parent and the 12-mile strip of land between them had not yet been topped, an outlet appeared to the east. Thus was born great Lake Nicaragua and the San Juan River which carries its now-fresh waters to the Caribbean.

The modern Lake Nicaragua is over 100 miles long and up to 45 miles wide. Its surface (lowered with the carving out of the San Juan channel) is 105 feet above and its bottom 125 feet below the level of the sea. Lake Managua, 20 miles north-west and 20-odd feet higher, flows into Lake Nicaragua through the Tipitapa River and is a part of the same detached basin. About 38 miles by 16, it is Central America's second-largest inland body of water. Lake Izabal of eastern Guatemala (about 30 miles by 15 but no more than 70 feet deep) lies at its surface only 26 feet higher than the Bay

[5] The English names of the plant families and their classification follow those in Earl L. Core, *Plant Taxonomy* (Englewood Cliffs, N.J., Prentice-Hall, 1955), pp. 215–428.

of Amatique to which it flows via the Río Dulce, 22 miles long. Guatemala's remarkable Lake Atitlán is Central America's fourth in lateral measurements (roughly 16 miles by 11) but stands over 1,000 feet deep at a surface altitude of some 4,500 feet, with mountains towering on every side. Lake Atitlán has no visible outlet; variations in its level are ascribed to blockages of the underground passage-ways through which its waters must escape. Twentieth-century residents of Central America are beginning to realize the recreational potentialities of these four large lakes, which certainly have an attractive future. But the margins of Lake Atitlán were long ago pre-empted by persons indigenous to the region, and Lake Atitlán will for some time retain the true indigenous flavour.

Much smaller but of some renown are Lake Amatitlán, the volcanic origin of which is attested by the steam rising from its warm waters, and Lake Coatepeque, nestled in a volcanic crater 3 miles in diameter. The former serves as a playground for residents of Guatemala City, the latter as a resort for the people of San Salvador and Santa Ana. Lake Ilopango, in a larger crater to the east of San Salvador, was popular until a volcano in 1880 reared its head in the very middle of the waters. Lakes Güija (on the Guatemala–El Salvador border) and Yojoa (away to the north-east in Honduras) are now being developed both as sources of electrical energy and as choice vacation spots for those who prefer a touch of solitude. Isolated in a world all its own is Lake Petén, far to the north in the Guatemalan lowlands, 15 miles long and less than 2 wide, yet great enough to contain an island holding the Petén's departmental capital.

For obvious reasons, Central American rivers are not long ones though they sometimes carry an impressive volume of water. The greatest river system to collect most of its waters in this area is the Chixoy-Usumacinta, which rambles some 250 miles through Guatemala as the Chixoy, the Río Negro, and the Salinas, and then as the Usumacinta takes its course another 350 miles along the Mexican border and through Mexican Tabasco to the Gulf of Mexico. Eight more rivers varying in length between 150 and 350 miles carry their waters towards or to the Caribbean. In order from north-west to south-east they are the Polochic and the Motagua of Guatemala; the Ulúa, the Aguán, and the Guayape-Patuca of Honduras; the Coco (or 'Segovia' or 'Wanks') on the Honduras–Nicaragua border; the Río Grande de Matagalpa of Nicaragua with its important Tuma tributary; and the Escondido (or 'Bluefields') of Nicaragua with either its Mico or Siquia head-branch. Only the Motagua of all these carries a railroad and modern highway along its banks. The Polochic (which flows into Lake Izabal) is used for the exportation of coffee, and the Ulúa and Aguán are familiar with the toot of the banana train, though much of the banana trackage along the Aguán has been allowed to lapse back into wilderness. The two longest, the Guayape-Patuca and the Coco, run most of their courses in grand solitude, though the latter holds along its banks a number of Indian villages. The Tuma is being harnessed for electricity; the Escondido is expected to become a bearer of ocean-going trade with inland highway connexions. South of the Escondido there is no river of consequence except the 120-mile San Juan (on the Nicaragua–Costa Rica border) which was once used extensively for commerce and is still considered the logical Caribbean gateway for a second trans-isthmian canal. The Pacific side of the isthmus, always more narrow from watershed to sea, contains only two rivers at all comparable—the Lempa, chiefly of El Salvador, and the Choluteca of Honduras.

The reason that Costa Rica's rivers are all short ones is quickly comprehended by the tourist who drives his automobile to the summit of Irazú volcano. This peak is easily reached on a good concrete highway, though at an altitude of 11,260 feet it is Costa Rica's highest volcanic eminence. There on a clear day, from the same vantage point and with hardly a turn of the head, one can view the waters of both Caribbean and Pacific. It is the way for the visitor to realize from first-hand experience the slenderness of the strand upon which he stands. At his feet, in the great crater still steaming and giant-bubbling with activity, he can see with equal wonderment some of the very forces at work which helped to build this isthmus. If he stops to meditate upon it all, as he should, the Pliocene and Pleistocene epochs will seem close at hand and the earth-shaking and isthmus-changing volcanic eruptions of 2 million and 1 million years ago seem but yesterday.

Without a doubt Central America's volcanoes are the most fascinating of her natural attractions. The isthmian line-up of volcanoes which began in the late Pliocene, but was still growing as late as the eighteenth century, now includes more than eighty important craters in the territory of the five Central American republics. The highest is Tajumulco, standing 13,816 feet above sea level in Guatemala only 10 miles from the Mexican border. Second is Tacaná,

8

13,333 feet in stature, only 15 miles from Tajumulco and immediately on the frontier. Neither of these, however, is so well known as Acatenango (12,992 feet), 25 miles west of Guatemala City; her near-by sister Fuego (12,582) with a continual wisp of smoke about her head; Agua (12,310) plainly visible from the Guatemalan capital; Santa María (12,362), which in 1902 wreaked havoc upon the city of Quezaltenango; and Atitlán (11,565), part of the beautiful backdrop for the lake of the same name. Of these seven giants, only Tajumulco is considered extinct. Five of them (Tajumulco and Acatenango excepted) have wrought tremendous death and destruction during the last half-millenium.

Costa Rica's four highest volcanoes, far to the south-east, are more mature in deportment though still far from dead. Their names are Irazú (11,260 feet), Turrialba (10,974), Barba (9,567), and Poás (8,930). All four lie within 25 miles north-east and north-west of the capital San José. Undistinguished in appearance, owing to their situation as part of a range of mountains rather than as isolated cones, they are noted instead for their accessibility. Both Irazú and Poás are much visited because of their continued crater activity. The highest peak in Costa Rica is the non-volcanic and quite inaccessible Chirripó Grande, 12,533 feet in altitude, 50 miles south-east of San José and only 40 from the border with Panama.

Honduras, so full of older mountains, has no remarkable volcanoes. In El Salvador and western Nicaragua, on the other hand, one is rarely out of sight of them. Though considerably lower in relation to sea level than those mentioned of Guatemala and Costa Rica, these often stand as high above the surrounding countryside and form a strikingly impressive view in their isolated splendour. Santa Ana (7,825 feet), San Vicente (7,132) and San Miguel (7,064), the three highest of El Salvador, are near the cities of the same names. San Salvador (6,400), once a mighty rebel but now lying dormant, has been made into a national park only 5 miles from the capital with hiking trails to the bottom of the vast crater. The youngest (born in the eighteenth century) and most active of all in Central America is Izalco (about 6,180 feet high) on the south shoulder of Santa Ana, often called the Lighthouse of the Pacific. Through most of her two centuries of history, Izalco's tongues of fire have been plainly visible by night, her incessant puffs of smoke by day.

Nicaragua's more noted furies include Concepción (5,577 feet) which rises out of the waters of Lake Nicaragua, joining bases with Madera (4,495) to form a two-headed island. Still smoky Momotombo (4,128) on the shore of Lake Managua proved too close a neighbour for Nicaragua's first capital in the early seventeenth century, and has shattered the quiet of the Nicaraguan countryside several times since. Little Cosigüina (2,776) has a peninsula all her own standing watch over the Gulf of Fonseca. To prove on one occasion (in the year 1835) that she was not to be outdone by the others, she blew her whole top to the four winds and the high heavens in an explosion which scattered ashes a thousand miles away.[6]

THE WEATHER

Most of Central America's volcanoes had become more sedate, and most of her flora and fauna, rivers and lakes quite well established before the fourth of the great ice ages which characterized the Pleistocene in the continent to the north had run its course. In all likelihood, it was not until the last North American glaciers had begun to recede (some 25,000 to 10,000 years ago) that Central American weather became roughly what it has been since. Central American temperatures run fairly even throughout the year, as is the case in most tropical climates. They vary much from one place to another according to altitude, with the coastal lands warm to hot and the tops of the mountains cool. (Ice was cut on Agua volcano in the nineteenth century, but snow has been very rare in the twentieth.)[7] The Caribbean side of the isthmus receives rainfall most of the year in rather heavy quantities, due to prevailing northeasterly winds during some months and a complex of thermal-heating and shore-breeze patterns during the remainder. The Pacific coast, sharing these same patterns but lacking the effect of the north-easterlies, has a marked wet season (roughly May to

[6] Central America's volcanoes have been the subject of extended comment ever since the days of Gonzalo Fernández de Oviedo y Valdés, who made a tour of western Nicaragua in 1528. See pt. iii, bk. iv, of his *Historia general y natural de las Indias, islas y tierra-firme del mar océano* (José Amador de los Ríos, ed., 4 vols., Madrid, 1851–5). A listing and interesting data concerning several were given a century ago by Ephraim George Squier in 'The Volcanoes of Central America', *Harper's New Monthly Magazine*, xix (1859), 739–62.

[7] '... The lake of water which fills the external crater is frozen in the months of December, January, and February, when the Indians of the neighbouring villages ascend it to fetch ice, and hoar frost, which falls so heavily as to resemble snow, for the supply of the capital. ...' Robert Glasgow Dunlop, *Travels in Central America* (London, 1847), pp. 91–92. Dunlop elsewhere (pp. 257–8) speaks of snow in the Quezaltenango region in December and January—'but it never lies on the ground'.

October) while the sun rides overhead, but very little precipitation the rest of the year (November to April) while the sun journeys into the southern hemisphere. The interior portions, particularly where the topography is most rugged, vary greatly from one locality to another in the amount of rainfall which they receive, with many areas drier than either coast and a few small districts nearly arid.

The traveller on the isthmus needs to go but a short distance to encounter all the variations in climate possible. From Retalhuleu, Guatemala, to Quezaltenango, for example, is but thirty miles by tortuous mountain highway. A weather station near Retalhuleu reported an average minimum temperature of $64 \cdot 4°$ and an average maximum of $80 \cdot 6°$ Fahrenheit for the year 1957. One near Quezaltenango reported a *mean* of $53 \cdot 8°$ for the same year. Retalhuleu, Escuintla, Guatemala City, Sanarate, and Quiriguá are stations on the Guatemalan section of the International Railways of Central America. The road distances between them, taken in that order, are about 84, 34, 43, and 112 miles respectively. In 1957 Retalhuleu had $136 \cdot 4$ inches of rain, Escuintla $72 \cdot 2$, Guatemala City $48 \cdot 5$, Sanarate $19 \cdot 5$, and Quiriguá $77 \cdot 8$. In September alone of that year Retalhuleu had $28 \cdot 4$ inches, Escuintla $15 \cdot 4$, Guatemala City $11 \cdot 9$, Sanarate $6 \cdot 9$, and Quiriguá $12 \cdot 2$. Just three months later, the totals for December were Retalhuleu $0 \cdot 2$ inch, Escuintla $1 \cdot 1$, Guatemala City $0 \cdot 02$, Sanarate $0 \cdot 00$, but Quiriguá still $6 \cdot 3$.[8] Quiriguá, just 50 miles from Caribbean waters, shares the rain habits of that side of the isthmus where seasonal variations are moderate. A few parts of that coast have seasons the opposite of the areas all about them. Everywhere else in Central America there is good reason why the people who live there call May–October *invierno* (winter, or one might say the season of inclemency) and November–April *verano*—summer, not a time of consistently warmer temperatures, but the season when sunshine exceeds showers.

THE COMING OF MAN

An isthmus well blessed with sun and showers and with the fruits of field and forest which such a combination encouraged was a likely spot for the development of America's first high civilization. Every evidence indicates that Central America's first human

[8] Temperatures and precipitation measurements as given in *Guatemala en Cifras, 1958* (Dir. Gen. Est.), pp. 15–18.

beings came at about the same time as its modern pattern of weather—at some time, that is, during the thousands of years when the last great glaciers of the continent to the north were giving up their hold of the land they had covered. Men moved first from Asia through Siberia and Alaska to occupy the great plains of western North America. From there some drifted into Mexico and the isthmus; from the isthmus South America beckoned still farther. Eventually the trek came to an end in Patagonia near the wastes of the Antarctic. Here a few persons made a meal of the flesh of the horse about 8,000 years ago and left bones and ashes behind them. Just how many hundreds or thousands of years earlier their ancestors had first penetrated the isthmus, no one can know as yet.

Three sharp cuts on a fragment of bone may constitute a clue. The cuts seem to have been made by man while the bone was fresh. The bone happens to be that of an ancient ground sloth. It was found in the same bed with petrified remains of camels, mastodons, and glyptodons along the Río de la Pasión, Guatemalan tributary of the Usumacinta, in 1948.[9] It strongly suggests that man the hunter has been in Central America much longer than 8,000 years.

Farther north, better evidence is available to show man's presence during such early times. Recent studies of this evidence from Mexico to Alaska have produced knowledge of several hunting cultures which coexisted or succeeded one another in the northern continent, each with its distinctive type of hunting equipment. One group followed herds of North American elephants for thousands of years, using a particular type of fluted stone point as its killing implement. One point of this type was picked up in Costa Rica in the year 1903 and identified as such in 1951.[10] But no one yet has found the bones of an elephant as far south as Costa Rica.

In time, some of Central America's hunters and food gatherers became her first farmers. The same men without doubt established Central America's first villages. The humble villages they built are not easy to locate today. Probable signs of one were found in 1946 at Copán, Honduras. Within a few square yards at the bottom

[9] Edwin M. Shook, 'Guatemala Highlands', in Carnegie Inst. of Washington, *Tb.*, xlviii (1949), pp. 219–24, reporting the discovery by Barnum Brown, palaeontologist. See also pp. 200–3 of the popular account of the expedition, Lilian Brown, *Bring 'em Back Petrified* (N.Y., Dodd, Mead, 1956).

[10] J. L. Swanger and W. J. Mayer-Oakes, 'Fluted Point from Costa Rica', *Am. Antiq.*, xvii (1952), 264–5. See also Michael D. Coe, 'A Fluted Point from Highland Guatemala', ibid. xxv (1960), 412–13.

of an excavation were some stones which may have been part of a hearth and some irregular stone flakes which were once used for tools.[11]

Seventeen primitive villagers literally left their footprints on the sands of time in what is now the capital city of Managua, Nicaragua. The footprints are today roofed over in a small park set aside for their study. The seventeen villagers walked across a flow of mud caused by the eruption of near-by Masaya volcano. The mud hardened into rock beneath new flows and the bare footprints were preserved. So were those in the same place of a large peccary, a bird, a lizard, and an otter. Some distance away, but in what is believed to be a mud-flow caused by the same eruption, are the tracks of a bison.[12]

Eventually, Central America's farmers learned to be potters. Only then did they leave behind them something easy to find and to study. At Islona de Chantuto, on the coast of Chiapas twenty-five miles from the Guatemalan border, scattered remains were found in 1948 of a people who did not use pottery, immediately beneath a residue left by persons who used a very coarse ware.[13] Other early pottery of more advanced design has been studied in Guatemala, El Salvador, and Honduras. The first of these finds to become established as of definitely great antiquity was reported from El Salvador in 1924. Sherds of pottery were found in a vein of black soil eight inches thick under *forty feet* of ash from Volcano Ilopango.[14] On top of the same ash, but entirely missing in the black soil below, lay pottery of Maya style, cultural remnant of the greatest of America's ancient civilizations. The Maya were Central Americans—the earliest Central Americans now recognizable by name. The pottery below Ilopango's ashes as well as the pottery above now gives some idea as to how human history in Central America began.

[11] John M. Longyear III, 'A Sub-Pottery Deposit at Copán, Honduras', ibid. xiii (1948), 248–9.

[12] Howel Williams, 'Geologic Observations on the Ancient Human Footprints near Managua, Nicaragua', *Contributions to American Anthropology and History* (Washington, Carnegie Inst.), xi/52 (1953).

[13] Philip Drucker, 'Preliminary Notes on an Archaeological Survey of the Chiapas Coast', *Mid. Am. Res. Rec.*, i (1948), 164–6.

[14] Jorge Lardé, *Arqueología cuzcatleca; vestigios de una población pre-máyica en el valle de San Salvador* . . . (San Salvador, 1924).

CHAPTER II

REMAINS OF ANTIQUITY

THE first slender threads of Central America's historical narrative appear in the second millenium B.C. The story as it is known today begins with two villages in Honduras and a town in Guatemala. The continuity of the record extending well over 3,000 years is dramatized by the fact that the ruins of the earliest known Guatemalan town lie today on the very edge of the busiest metropolis of the isthmus.

A very crude type of pottery has been found at Yarumela, a Honduran site on the Humuya River (tributary of the Ulúa), and in a pit at Los Naranjos on Lake Yojoa. Yarumela and Los Naranjos are evidently the sites of quite ancient agricultural villages whose inhabitants made good plates and jars but left them plain, and the jars without handles, feet, or spouts.[1]

Just as old as the crude kitchenware from Honduras (and quite possibly older) is a complex of remains, labelled Las Charcas, from the highlands of Guatemala. They were first located on a farm of this name, part of the large mound-site called Kaminaljuyú on the outskirts of Guatemala City. The Las Charcas rubble consists of several forms of pottery, many of them formally decorated; of small clay figurines modelled after people and monkeys; of small whistles made to look like various birds and animals; of clay stamps which were used in the marking of pottery; and of evidence in stone, adobe, and ashes that the Las Charcas people grew and ground maize, ate several varieties of fruit, and used woven mats and rope.[2]

The Las Charcas culture of the Guatemalan highlands gave way eventually to another called the Sacatepéquez. It is impossible to say now whether this change was accompanied by an incursion of new peoples. Kaminaljuyú in Sacatepéquez times became a

[1] Joel S. Canby, 'Possible Chronological Implications of the Long Ceramic Sequence Recovered at Yarumela, Spanish Honduras', in Sol Tax, ed., *The Civilizations of Ancient America* (Univ. of Chicago Press, 1951), pp. 79–85; William Duncan Strong and others, 'Preliminary Report on the Smithsonian Institution–Harvard University Archaeological Expedition to Northwestern Honduras, 1936', Smithsonian *Miscellaneous Collections*, xcvii/1 (1938).
[2] E. M. Shook and A. V. Kidder, 'Mound E-III-3, Kaminaljuyú, Guatemala', *Contributions to American Anthropology and History*, xi/53 (1953).

centre of genuine sophistication where stone was sculptured and jade carved and polished. People in the Honduran village of Yaru-mela, meanwhile, were experimenting with decorative techniques in pottery design and learning to put handles on their jars. Some of their work at this stage was like that found at Playa de los Muer-tos along the Ulúa River in company with clay figurines and beads, amulets, and pendants made of jadeite.[3]

At about the time of the Sacatepéquez and Playa de los Muertos cultures (probably still within the second millenium B.C.), persons at Uaxactún in the north-central Guatemalan Petén, 30 miles north-east of modern Flores, and at a spot to the east now called San José, British Honduras, began to design simple pottery and rather crude figurines. Their remains are called Mamom, and are generally taken to be the work of the ancestors of the Maya who in-habited these places a thousand years later. Some authorities teach that the magnificent Maya civilization, including the highly accu-rate and complex Maya calendar, developed entirely in this Petén region where its first great flowering occurred. If so, the makers of Mamom pottery may have possessed genius to which their remains do not testify. But many scholars now give credence to the theory that Veracruz in Mexico, home of the Huastec kin of the Maya, is the real mother of Maya culture. Proponents of this theory point to a jade statuette with a date inscribed in the Maya manner from 98 B.C. and a stone monument with a date reconstructed as from 291 B.C., both found in Veracruz.[4]

New pottery phases in the first millenium B.C. are tied together by a type called Usulután from eastern El Salvador, the first to be identified stratigraphically as older than the classic Maya. Usulu-tán ware was produced in abundance in the area for which it is named; it was widely traded and much copied by artists in other regions. It is found all the way from Lake Managua to the Guate-malan highlands. Little is known of the potters of El Salvador or of the circumstances under which they did their work, but in trading circles their artistic renown must have been high.

The influence of the Usulután techniques was felt by the last generations of folk who inhabited the village of Yarumela in Hon-

[3] Dorothy H. Popenoe, 'Some Excavations at Playa de los Muertos, Ulúa River, Honduras', *Maya Research (Mexico and Central America)*, i/2 (Oct. 1934), 61–86.

[4] Chronological references in this chapter, both specific and general, are based on the 12.9.0.0.0 correlation between ancient Maya and modern Christian dates, the preference for which is explained on pp. 31–32.

duras. The styles developed at the end of Yarumela's history were the first to be used in Santa Rita, village on the Comayagua River connecting the Humuya with the Ulúa. They are likewise found at the bottom of excavations in Copán with the splendours of a mighty Maya metropolis built over them. At this early stage in her history, Copán was without doubt a simple village inhabited by the same kind of non-Maya people as those who lived in Yarumela and Santa Rita.[5]

Usulután ware also made its way to Kaminaljuyú. There it is first found in association with the remains of a culture named Miraflores. During the long Miraflores period, which followed the Sacatepéquez, Kaminaljuyú became a centre of considerable size and achievement. The tombs of two Miraflores nobles excavated in the late 1940's contained finely wrought vessels of marble and jade along with other items indicating great wealth and position. The tombs themselves were located in a pyramid over sixty-five feet high. Miraflores remains are found in other highland sites but nowhere else so abundantly. When those at Kaminaljuyú are more thoroughly studied, its inhabitants of the first millenium B.C. may stand as civilizers whose influence spread over a very wide area.[6]

As Miraflores followed Sacatepéquez in Kaminaljuyú, so Chicanel followed Mamom in Uaxactún. The people who left the Chicanel remains were probably the Maya; their vestiges are found in northern Yucatan as well as the Petén. Chicanel pottery was more advanced than the Mamom in both execution and design. While it was still being made, a first stone pyramid was constructed in Uaxactún about the second century B.C. with various tombs, plazas, and temples to follow. All these were without inscriptions. The earliest Maya date now known from the Petén (found at Tikal, eleven miles south of Uaxactún, in 1959) was carved on a stone monument in the year A.D. 32, at the end of the Chicanel period. Did some fresh infusion of blood reach the whole Maya region at

[5] William Duncan Strong, 'The Archeology of Honduras', in *Handbook of South American Indians* (7 vols., Washington, Smithsonian Inst. 1946–59), iv. 71–120, provides a chronologically-oriented discussion of this interesting Maya fringe area.

[6] A paper presented at the 1959 meeting of the Society for American Archaeology (but as yet unpublished) suggested Kaminaljuyú as a mother of Maya culture, on the basis of a stela bearing an archaic inscription, which was found in a Miraflores context. Michael D. Coe, 'Cycle 7 Monuments in Middle America: A Reconsideration', *Am. Anthrop.*, lix (1957), 597–611, argues for the validity of very early Maya-type inscriptions from both Veracruz and Escuintla, Guatemala, the latter not so far from Kaminaljuyú.

about the time of Christ bringing ideas from outside essential to the building of the Maya civilization? Whatever the reason, in the years which immediately followed there developed a quickening of life in the central Petén such as the whole of the Americas had never experienced before.

The early monument at Tikal is but one of a memorable series. The Maya at Tikal and at Uaxactún (where the first known monument dates from A.D. 68) evidently raised such markers to commemorate notable occurrences. With the passage of time, for some reason, Uaxactún fell into the pattern of dedicating elaborately carved stelae at regular intervals. By the year 146 the practice had begun to spread to other towns; by 156 it was observed in Tikal. In the meantime a whole new pottery complex had evolved in Uaxactún, including painted designs in colour combinations far more sophisticated than anything to be found there previously, and experiments had begun with a new type of corbelled-arch roof construction which was to remain the distinguishing mark of Maya architecture for twelve hundred years.

Expansion both outward and inward characterized the next hundred years. By the year 205 the village of Copán, more than 150 miles to the south, was operating in the Maya tradition. Ten years after this a first date was carved in Oxkintok, Yucatan, nearly 250 miles north of Uaxactún. Twenty years later (in 235) came the first stela in Toniná, 175 miles to the west. By the year 264 there were four more important centres, Xultún and Naachtún in the central area, Piedras Negras on the Guatemalan side of the Usumacinta River, and Yaxchilán (Menché) on the Chiapas side of the same. After this there was a great lessening of activity. For nearly one hundred years there are no surely identified remains from the oldest centres in the Petén.

Through the centuries of Maya advance the people of highland Guatemala and El Salvador held distinction of their own. Some towns founded at this time, such as Zaculeu in western Guatemala near Huehuetenango, were able to survive for many centuries when centres of greater grandeur fell. More notable in the early centuries A.D. were Kaminaljuyú, in still another phase of its long history, and Tazumal, today an easily reached tourist marvel near Santa Ana, El Salvador. Remains labelled Esperanza from this period in Kaminaljuyú show such strong Mexican influence as to suggest that the Esperanza people or their rulers had come to this region from the north-west. Whoever they were, they traded from the first century to the fourth with the Maya of the Petén, the builders of the great pyramids at Teotihuacán (near the present Mexico City), and the equally remarkable people of Tajín (Vera-cruz) and Monte Albán (Oaxaca). Esperanza men of distinction were buried in tombs containing pottery of excellent design and quality, a great quantity of jade, vessels of marble, and mirrors or plaques of iron pyrites.[7] Tazumal, only 75 miles to the south-east, had for some reason little to do with Kaminaljuyú but traded in-stead with Copán. Tazumal's pyramids are more imposing than any structure so far unearthed in Kaminaljuyú.

In the middle of the fourth century the pace quickened again in the lowlands. The potters of Uaxactún developed a fresh variety of products making much use of pictorial representation. Sculptors and architects in many centres made new dreams come true, to the delight of those who today rediscover them. Astronomers, already well versed in the movements of sun and moon, plotted accurately the wanderings of the planet Venus. By the end of the fifth century, with the older settlements functioning brilliantly, eight new major centres were thriving—Naranjo, La Honradez, and Nakum in the Petén; Calakmul and El Palmar in Mexican Campeche; Cobá in north-eastern Yucatan; Palenque in Chiapas; and Quiriguá, a colony sent out from Copán, near the Motagua River in Guate-mala. Many Maya lived near smaller centres interspersed through the area. Some authorities do not hesitate to estimate their total number at a few million.

MAYA CULTURE

What is known today of the fifth-century Maya? Of their poli-tics, very little. Many, perhaps most, of their chief centres have been discovered, but few have been studied with care. Evidence indicates that they were not cities in the modern sense, where people live along streets, but nuclei of settlement around which families lived on small farms. Whether the whole Maya territory was divided into districts resembling city-states, as suggested by some, is not certain. Inscriptions which remain largely unde-ciphered may give the answer to this question, though most specu-lation is to the effect that their message is primarily not of this

[7] Alfred V. Kidder and others, *Excavations at Kaminaljuyú, Guatemala* (Washing-ton, Carnegie Inst., 1946) deals primarily with the Esperanza period. The exciting finds from earlier periods have come chiefly since the Second World War.

world.[8] At present, not even the names of the ancient centres are known as the Maya knew them (Copán is a possible exception) nor is there the slightest suggestion of a distinctive personality who played a role in Petén Maya history.

Concerning the economy, there are some facts. The Maya were farmers. Their chief crop was maize. Much of it was ground for meal, as testify the remains of many stone metates. Maize has constituted the backbone of the Central American economy ever since the days of the Maya. Already in their time it was cultivated from North America to Peru. It had been important in Guatemala since at least the second millenium B.C. It was known in northern Mexico and New Mexico a thousand years earlier. Much work remains to be done before the origins of maize are completely understood, but there is no doubt of its early importance to civilization in both Mexico and the isthmus. Speculation suggests that it may have been taken from here to Peru.

The Maya or their Central American contemporaries are given credit for the first cultivation of three other food plants. These are the cacao tree, provider of beans which produce the beverages cocoa and chocolate; the papaya tree, bearing a large yellow fruit good for cooking or raw; and the aguacate or avocado or 'alligator pear', the Guatemalan form of which has seen a rebirth in California in recent years. There is little doubt that many other fruits were grown or at least known by the Maya, who (or their neighbours) may also have tamed the kidney bean, the lima bean, and the more primitive of the squashes.

In addition to food, the Maya grew cotton. It is believed that Central American cotton (most of it closely related to the 'upland' variety of the United States) and all the types grown in ancient times in the western hemisphere were hybrids springing originally from a cross between a Peruvian wild cotton and a cultivated one from India.[9] How the Indian species arrived in the Americas is unknown; the cultivation and use of the hybrids were widespread among early peoples. Cotton garments worn by the Maya were breech-clouts or loincloths and capes for the men and dresses and skirts for the women. Depictions of clothing worn by the nobility

[8] Tatiana Proskouriakoff, 'Historical Implications of a Pattern of Dates at Piedras Negras, Guatemala', *Am. Antiq.*, xxv (1960), 454–75, explains evidence that the undeciphered inscriptions *do* contain historical data, a possibility which has long been put aside.
[9] Empire Cotton Growing Corporation, *The Evolution of Gossypium and the Differentiation of the Cultivated Cottons* (London, OUP, 1947).

show signs of great dexterity in weaving and considerable interest in brocade work. Simpler and perhaps more common garments were made of the inner bark of fig trees.

Most Maya houses were of little substance; their building must have required little industry. Apart from a few palaces and a vapour bath found in Piedras Negras, stone cut by stone seems to have been available only for the monuments of civilization and the dwelling-places of the gods. Monuments included the stelae already mentioned, colonnades, great carved stairways, reviewing stands and stadiums, ball courts, dance platforms, and even astronomical observatories, but most elaborate of all were the temples. The quarrying from the original bedrock, transportation by human strength alone, and the setting up of the huge blocks of limestone (at Quiriguá sandstone and at Copán andesite) used in these extensive building programmes must have called for considerable effort by a large number of people. Some of the most impressive buildings from the later centuries are of lime-concrete with stone facing. Allied industries in stucco and fine wood construction were important, but left fainter traces behind them.

The Maya made baskets, or at least drew pictures of them; wove mats, which have left their imprints in other remains; moulded pottery, figurines, and simple musical instruments from clay; cut, polished, and carved jade pendants in meticulous detail; wore mirrors of pyrites; and fashioned beads, ear-plugs, and spangles of diverse description. The costume of the Maya noble included a fanciful head-dress covered with elaborately worked feathers. Careful excavation will someday reveal how many of these items made their way by trade to high centres of culture in Mexico or to the less advanced peoples farther south on the isthmus.

What then of Maya science, apart from the knowledge required to carry on these industries? Until the sixteenth century, no other people of the Americas had greater skill in writing. Maya hieroglyphs are intricate in design; the greater part remain a puzzle to the men who know them best. Those deciphered thus far deal almost entirely with the heavens or the gods or the procession of time. Most of the known symbols are conventionalized drawings. Some of these serve as signs for two words, one concrete and the other abstract, the pronunciation of which was the same but the meaning quite different. New attempts are now being made to render a phonetic interpretation of the remainder.[10]

[10] Y. V. Knorozov, Russian epigrapher, announced in 1952 that the phonetic

Far more than any other people of ancient America, and probably more than any people anywhere in the world of their time, the Maya learned to express themselves numerically. The Maya system of numbers was vigesimal rather than decimal, with the count recommencing at twenty-one rather than twenty or ten, but it was a neat system which included the idea of numerical placement and the concept of a symbol for the completion of a count. The most ancient Maya numbers are expressed by bars and dots; after the third century A.D. there are also nineteen distinctive numerals which are sketches of human heads. A dot alone meant one. A dot above a count-completion symbol (there were a variety of these) meant twenty-one. By extension of the system, with positions standing for the units, 20's, 400's, 8,000's, and so on, the Maya were able to express the large numbers with which they worked and handle them with great dexterity. Their contemporaries the Romans, on another side of the globe, had a system most awkward by comparison.

Because the solar year does not conform to a vigesimal system, the Maya time counts were less simple. A Maya date from the year A.D. 60 (carved on a jade pendant from Tikal, it was until 1959 the oldest-known from the Petén) reads in its full Maya form 8.14.3.1.12 12 Eb 0 Yaxkin. The 12 Eb stands for a particular day in the Maya sacred year of 260 days called the tzolkin, Eb being one of twenty day-glyphs which were combined with the numbers 1 to 13 in such a way as to give 260 separate day-designations. Use of the tzolkin persists among some of the Maya to this day. The 0 Yaxkin denotes a particular day in the Maya year of 365 days called the haab, Yaxkin being one of eighteen months of twenty days each (another month had just five days), and 0 meaning the first day of that month (19 meant the last). The tzolkin count and haab count together gave the Maya a series of combinations which would not repeat itself until the end of 73 tzolkins, or 52 haab, or 18,980 days. This period of time was used in central Mexico as well as the Petén. Only the Maya, so far as is known, used the additional time count which set every day in their history apart from any other. The 8.14.3.1.12 of the illustration at hand means that 8 baktuns of

approach would work, though it had been abandoned decades earlier by other experts. See 'The Problem of the Study of the Maya Hieroglyphic Writing' (written by Knorozov, tr. by Sophie D. Coe), *Am. Antiq.*, xxiii (1958), 284–91. For a criticism of Knorozov's approach, see J. Eric S. Thompson, 'Systems of Hieroglyphic Writing in Middle America and Methods of Deciphering Them', ibid. xxiv (1959), 349–64.

144,000 days each, plus 14 katuns of 7,200 days each, plus 3 tuns of 360 days each, plus 1 uinal of 20 days, plus 12 more kins or days, had passed since the arbitrary date chosen for the beginning of the Maya calendar. This is a total of 1,253,912 days, a fraction more than 3,433 solar years. The latest certain Maya date is 10.4.0.0.0 12 Ahau 3 Uo. This is 214,888 days, or a fraction over 588 solar years, later.[11]

Other time counts which often appear are one based on moon phases and movements and one to reconcile the length of the haab (invariably 365 days) with that of the true solar year. The latter was figured by the Maya as 365·2420 days, a bit closer to the correct 365·2422 than the Gregorian reckoning of 365·2425. With no mechanical equipment, with atmospheric conditions generally far from satisfactory, and with no real conception of the solar system as it really exists, the Maya made remarkably minute observations of the coming and going of both sun and moon over a period of many centuries. With these calculations, the Maya were able to predict the days when solar eclipses might occur, and did occur somewhere in the world, though not often within their range of vision. Perhaps the highest achievement of all was the working out of the average length of time necessary for a synodical revolution of the planet Venus—that is, a period of 583·92 earth days which elapses between any two occasions (on the average) when Venus appears from the earth to be directly behind (or in front of) the sun.

Only a little of Maya art reaches the modern eye. Pageantry doubtless played an important role. Stone-paved ball courts found at Yaxchilán and Copán, like others at Kaminaljuyú, were the loci of ceremonialized sport. There were various games, with two teams playing with a solid rubber ball. Under one set of rules the object was to propel the ball without the use of hands through a hoop placed vertically in the side-wall of the court.

Maya architectural accomplishments are seen most magnificently in the ruins of Tikal, whose five pyramid-temples range in height from 143 feet to 229; at Copán, whose so-called Acropolis covers twelve acres with pyramids, temples, and terraces; and at Palenque in Chiapas, whose several pyramid-temples and Palace Group of buildings are counted among the most beautiful of the area.

The full story of the Maya mastery of sculpturing techniques is

[11] Since 1959, the time-span of *monuments* from the *Petén* extends over 596 solar years (A.D. 32–629). Until 1959 the first and last sure Maya dates from the general area were both carved on jade.

recorded in the stelae. The early ones, found especially at Uaxactún, represent the human figure awkwardly and lifelessly. Later examples, at Uaxactún and elsewhere, show much greater skill on the part of the artist. At Piedras Negras, Copán, and Quiriguá, by the sixth century, excellent compositions in stone were being produced with the model now portrayed from a front view with dimensional detail on either side.

Only recently has the high Maya skill in painting been recognized. Few examples of the amazing Maya work with murals are known even today. The best, from Bonampak near Yaxchilán, Chiapas, is a realistic depiction of Maya life. Finished in the sixth century, it remained hidden in modern times until 1946.[12] Other fine painting was done in parts of the Maya area on vases and bowls made of clay, themselves often distinguished works of art.

Did the ancient Maya have a literature? Yes, probably even this, if picture-book aids to memory and tables of astronomical observations may be counted as such. From these ancient times no Maya books are known. From later times there are three written by the Maya of Yucatan before the modern era, now found in European libraries. One of them, located in Dresden, was written about the eleventh century, but is believed to be a copy of a text several centuries older. The script deals chiefly with the eclipses and the movements of Venus.

Religion is believed to have played a most vital part in Maya life. The specifics of Maya religion during these earlier centuries are none the less very little understood. Of the later Maya deities, the corn god and the nine gods of the lower world have been found in the older inscriptions but others of equal or greater importance are missing. Until evidence to the contrary is located or better apprehended, it will be taken for granted that the more ancient Maya, like those of later centuries, thought of their gods chiefly as individuals to be propitiated by offerings. Around Piedras Negras and Yaxchilán, human sacrifice was a part of the propitiation. The mightier gods were doubtless addressed by the priests and the nobles—it is possible that the priests *were* the nobles—in large assemblies of people in the midst of great pomp. Lesser divinities, represented by figurines in the homes, were perhaps of equal or greater popularity.

---

[12] Copies are shown in Agustín Villagra Caleti, *Bonampak, la ciudad de los muros pintados* (Mexico City, Instituto Nacional de Antropología e Historia, 1949) and Karl Ruppert and others, *Bonampak, Chiapas, Mexico* (Washington, Carnegie Inst., 1955).

Did the gods demand only physical offerings? Did Maya priests teach morality? Too little is known of the Maya culture to vouchsafe an answer to these questions. Maya memorials are notably lacking in war scenes, though captives of some sort are depicted. In all likelihood this was not an egalitarian society. But for hundreds of years it may well have been one whose rulers valued what they had to the extent that they cared little to conquer what lay about them.

THE MAYA FADE-OUT

Came the year 500. Activity was rife in the Maya community. Copán had just added to her splendours two new temples on the Acropolis and a famous stairway leading to one of them, the stairway with the longest inscription (over 1,500 glyphs) so far found in the Maya area. . . . 511. Quiriguá dedicated a stela fashioned from a block of sandstone 35 feet long, 5 feet wide, and over 4 feet thick, weighing 65 tons. It was but one of at least ten raised in various centres on the same date. . . . 530. The next end of a katun, or Maya twenty-year period, was celebrated by no less than nineteen centres, an all-time record in stelae so far recovered. In all corners of the Maya realm, save possibly Yaxchilán and Palenque where no stone of this date appears, this must have been a time of great jubilation. . . . 550. Twenty years later, the known list of celebrants drops to twelve, with three more of the great names missing.

570. A tremendous date indeed, 10.0.0.0.0 7 Ahau 18 Zip, the beginning of a new baktun which would last 144,000 days. But only three markers have been found commemorating the occasion. From all appearances, eleven of fifteen major centres were no longer following the tradition. Two of the stones for this year were in the Petén, the other far over in Chiapas at a new and minor site, close to Toniná and Palenque—a refuge for harassed Maya? . . . 590. Five stelae were raised, date 10.1.0.0.0. All of them were in the central area. . . . 629. Uaxactún, on the basis of formal stone monuments clearly recognized, became on 10.3.0.0.0 Omega as she had come near being Alpha. Her first stela had been erected on 8.14.10.13.15, some 561 solar years earlier. Her last was one of three known of the same date, Xultún not far away and Xamantún, a minor centre in Campeche, closing their chapters simultaneously. Without exception, the major sites outside the central area had already been quiet for three-quarters of a century.

There are still, in the old Maya notation, a sure date carved on jade (10.4.0.0.0) from southern Quintana Roo, Mexico, and a less sure one (the same) carved on a stone marker from southern Campeche. Were the Maya then on their way from old homes in Guatemala, Honduras, and Chiapas to build a new civilization in northern Yucatan, as was widely believed only a few years ago? Certainly new civilizations were to blossom in northern Yucatan, societies which would hold on to much of the ancient Maya tradition and continue to express the Maya spirit. But evidence of a mass Maya migration to the north is mostly lacking. Maya civilization was well established in Yucatan long before it faded in Guatemala. If some persons left the Petén, especially those who watched the stars and knew the tables, others lingered on and scattered throughout the country. Nor did they all die childless, for the Maya tongue is spoken widely in Central America today, both inside and outside the forests where the Maya relics are picked up.

What had happened? No one knows. It seems well to remember, however, that this closing-up-shop of the Maya was not necessarily an isolated event. Whatever the cause, the great centres of Kaminaljuyú and Tazumal were now being humbled also. Simple kitchen pottery or no pottery at all is the extent of their historical record for the later ages. In Mexico, too, the great shrines of olden times were being put aside as memories. Teotihuacán and Monte Albán —and Tajín was to follow—were becoming ghost centres like Tikal and Copán. With other factors certainly involved—religious fatalism? soil exhaustion? proletarian revolution?—and with the complexities of the situation still far from worked out, it seems reasonable to assume that massive conquests of one kind or another were in process when the old way of life for so many came to an end.

Maya pottery, made by Maya or non-Maya people, continued to be produced in El Salvador and Honduras. Residents of Copán and Quiriguá, with the abandonment of those sites, may have simply moved to nearby villages where this pottery is now found. Santa Rita, the village site as old as Copán, seems later in its history, like many others, to have harboured over long periods of time some persons manufacturing Maya pottery and some producing styles quite different in design. Some of the latter were of traditions prevalent among potters of Nicaragua and Costa Rica and tribes on down into Colombia. These southern-oriented peoples of the isthmus, though they were villagers and farmers, had not shared the high intellectual attainments of the Maya. The precise condition of their culture in the early centuries A.D. is unknown because no chronological stratification of their remains has been worked out, even for their pottery. Baktun 10 without doubt brought the Maya much closer to the level of this remainder of the isthmus— but hundreds of years later the difference remained substantial.

MAYA STUDIES

The first renaissance of Maya culture occurred in north-western Yucatan, where many new cities blossomed and Uxmal grew to splendours commensurate with those of Tikal and Copán. New monuments were raised, but without the day count which distinguished one ancient Maya katun from the other. Uxmal was eventually humbled through conquest and the peninsula fell into the hands of the ruling house of Itzá. Chichén Itzá, the tremendous new religious centre which the Itzá made their capital, was both Mayan and Mexican in its inspiration. In time, very likely at the end of the twelfth century A.D., Chichén Itzá, like other centres before it, was forced to yield to the exigencies of the age. In its place in political importance grew Mayapán, which lasted in its turn until the middle of the fifteenth century. Spanish invaders from overseas became acquainted with Yucatan less than a hundred years later. By the time the Spaniards arrived, the ancient centres in the Petén, Chiapas, and Honduras had been deserted for 900 years or more. It was a long time before the newcomers even noticed most of the ruins.

The first report of Maya antiquities was an exceptional one. On 8 March 1576 Diego García de Palacio, a member of the governing body of the isthmus, wrote from the capital a report to King Philip II of Spain. His purpose was to describe some ancient provinces of the realm. In the letter he said, '. . . As one goes to the city of San Pedro, in the first place of the province of Honduras, called Copán, are certain ruins and vestiges of a great population and of superb edifices, of such art and magnificence that it appears they could never have been built by persons as barbarous as the natives of that province.'[13] Palacio's description which follows is an interesting one and apparently accurate though brief. A quarter of a millennium passed before Copán was described again by an eyewitness.

The ruins of Palenque in Chiapas, farther removed from human contact than those of Copán, were discovered quite accidentally in 1746. They soon became the object of many visits both private and

[13] Translated from p. 90 of 'Relación hecha por el Licenciado Palacio al Rey D. Felipe II . . .', *Anales*, iv/1 (Sept. 1927), 71–92.

official. The first great publicity they received abroad, however, was through a book (translated from the Spanish of Antonio del Río) printed in London in 1822.[14] This was the first book published on the ancient Maya culture, decades before the culture was clearly recognized as Maya. Other books which dealt with Palenque's ruins followed.

Quiriguá became the third site to attract attention. Frederick Catherwood, a British artist, made sketches of some of Quiriguá's stelae one day in March 1840; these were reproduced the following year in a book written by his travelling companion, John Lloyd Stephens of New York.[15] Stephens and Catherwood together visited Copán and Palenque, and through excellent word and brush depictions of their remains caught the fancy of a wide reading public in America and Europe. Stephens estimated correctly that these ruins were of much greater antiquity than those of Yucatan. But the origins and attachments of such an ancient culture remained mysterious. The mystery only deepened in 1848 when agents of the Guatemalan government examined the site of Tikal, first to come to light in the heartland of the Petén.

The unravelling of the puzzle began in 1864. Charles Étienne Brasseur de Bourbourg, French churchman and antiquarian, in that year published a two-hundred-years-old manuscript written by Diego de Landa, bishop of Yucatan in the sixteenth century. Landa had described the Maya calendar in its abbreviated Yucatecan form, had presented a Maya alphabet, and had given much solid information on the customs of the Maya as he knew them. All this information had lain hidden until Brasseur de Bourbourg brought it forth from the Royal Academy of History in Madrid. Landa's alphabet has not proved a simple key to an understanding of the ancient writing. His calendar presentation, on the other hand, has made it possible for deciphering to begin. Maya dates and matters intimately connected with them remain nearly a century later substantially the only Maya glyphs yielding data.

Twenty-three years passed before Ernst Förstemann, of the Royal Library of Dresden in Germany, first explained the Maya system of numbers (in 1887). Förstemann had made an intensive study of the oldest of the three extant Maya manuscripts, the one owned by his own library. He believed (as is accepted today) that

[14] *Description of the Ruins of an Ancient City, Discovered near Palenque, in the Kingdom of Guatemala.*

[15] *Incidents of Travel in Central America, Chiapas, and Yucatan* (2 vols., N.Y., Harper, 1841).

each number in the manuscript stood for a day in Maya history, all reckoned from the same chronological starting-point. By the time this discovery was made, a new Maya site had been uncovered at Yaxchilán by three separate visitors in two years (1881–2), and one of these, Alfred P. Maudslay of England, had undertaken a series of visits to the known Maya centres making the first intensive study of the monuments for scientific purposes.

Maudslay's work convinced him that Copán, Palenque, Quiriguá, Tikal, and Yaxchilán were all built by the same Maya people who lived in Yucatan, though their age was still uncertain. The results of his work were published from 1889 to 1902 as a large section of the monumental work then in progress on Middle American biology.[16] His unexcelled reproductions of the inscriptions on the printed page enabled a California newspaper editor, Joseph T. Goodman, to decipher from the monuments, as Förstemann had done from his codex, a series of dates which made sense together. Goodman's discoveries and his famous table, which for the first time presented the Maya cumulative count of days along with the correct tzolkin and haab designations, were published in 1897 as an appendix to Maudslay's work. In the same decade Teobert Maler, an Austrian archaeologist, had found Piedras Negras in the wilds along the Usumacinta, and Harvard University's Peabody Museum had begun the first institutional studies of the southern Maya area. Maudslay and Maler both joined in these studies as they progressed.

Nakum, first investigated in 1905 by the Frenchman Maurice de Périgny, was the last of the major sites to be revealed by a private explorer. Naranjo and La Honradez, in the same decade, were brought to light by the Peabody Museum expeditions along with quite a number of minor sites. The *Memoirs* published by this Museum added tremendously to the knowledge of the field. Charles P. Bowditch, chief sponsor of its Maya work, published in 1910 his own summary of the intricacies of Maya science.[17] Two well-known correlations had by this time been proposed between Maya and Christian chronology. Yucatecan manuscripts of the sixteenth century made it quite plain that a Maya katun ending with a tzolkin designation of 13 Ahau fell somewhere in the late 1530's. One suggestion was that 11.16.0.0.0 13 Ahau 8 Xul in the ancient

[16] *Archaeology* (5 vols., London), part of E. DuCane Godman and Osbert Salvin, eds, *Biologia Centrali-Americana* (1879–1915).

[17] *The Numeration, Calendar Systems and Astronomical Knowledge of the Mayas* (Cambridge, Mass., University Press).

Maya notation was the likely katun-ending. This meant that the monuments of the Petén would have been raised from the fourth to the ninth centuries of the Christian era. The next katun ending on a 13 Ahau was 12.9.0.0.0 13 Ahau 8 Kankin. A proposal to place it in the 1530's puts the age of the Petén civilization some 260 years earlier.

The second decade of the twentieth century witnessed the termination of the Peabody expeditions and the beginning of a long series of field studies by the Carnegie Institution of Washington. The Carnegie personnel with the help of native *chicleros* who searched the forests in the employ of the chewing-gum industry were able to report two new major sites, Uaxactún and Xultún. Sylvanus G. Morley, associated with the Carnegie Institution, published in 1920 a detailed study of the monuments of Copán which came near being a history of the ancient city.[18] Such a study, comprehending many remains the dates of which were illegible as well as others clearly marked, was made possible by an earlier chronological ordering of Maya art styles by Herbert J. Spinden, student at Harvard.[19] Spinden also interested the public in Maya-Mexican correlations, pointing out the similarities in earliest cultural remains.[20]

By the 1920's Maya studies were in high gear. The Carnegie Institution, busy with intensive work at Uaxactún and Chichén Itzá, located Naachtún and many smaller sites and learned the great antiquity of Cobá in north-eastern Yucatan. Tulane University of Louisiana extended the Maya area considerably with its discovery of Toniná and other sites in Chiapas.[21] On the other side of the Petén the British Museum studied several ruins in British Honduras, providing T. W. F. Gann with material for five popular books on Maya lore and excavations.[22] In the meantime, the pre-Maya cultures of Central America were beginning to be understood as distinct from those of Mexico by such men as Lardé in El Salvador;[23] Manuel Gamio, Mexican archaeologist, first to work in

[18] *The Inscriptions at Copán* (Washington, Carnegie Inst.).
[19] *A Study of Maya Art: its Subject Matter and Historical Development* (Cambridge, Mass., Peabody Mus., 1913).
[20] *Ancient Civilizations of Mexico and Central America* (N.Y., Am. Mus. Nat. Hist., 1917).
[21] *Tribes and Temples* (2 vols., 1926–7).
[22] *In an Unknown Land* (1924); *Mystery Cities* (1925); *Ancient Cities and Modern Tribes* (1926); *Maya Cities* (1927); *Discoveries and Adventures in Central America* (1928); all published in London.
[23] See ch. i, n. 14, p. 13.

Kaminaljuyú; and Samuel K. Lothrop, whose surveys and excavations ranged widely through the isthmus.[24]

Work went forward on several fronts in the 1930's. The Carnegie Institution continued its intensive study of Uaxactún, added Calakmul and El Palmar to the list of great sites discovered, and began a memorable series of publications on the Maya area. The latter included many full-length monographs on separate sites in addition to the Institution's *Contributions to American Anthropology and History* chiefly centred on the Maya. The University of Pennsylvania took a close look at Piedras Negras during this decade, and Morley wrote his monumental work which did for Piedras Negras, Uaxactún, and all the other sites in or near the Petén what he had already done for Copán.[25] The ruins of Copán became the first to undergo partial restoration. New pottery studies there and in Uaxactún, north-western Honduras, and the Guatemalan highlands began to suggest connexions between the Maya and their neighbours of many generations. And in the meantime T. W. F. Gann and his countryman J. Eric S. Thompson had published in 1931 the first general history of the Maya for non-specialists.[26]

The Second World War slowed the pace of Maya research considerably. The three most notable publications of the half-decade after its conclusion were all summations of data gathered over a period of time. Morley published in 1946 a new popular history of the Maya, much more elaborate than its predecessor in the field but placing great trust in literal interpretations of sixteenth-century Yucatecan manuscripts and somewhat misleading in its failure to place the Maya in their proper setting among other peoples.[27] Thompson, now also associated with the Carnegie Institution, reviewed the study of Maya hieroglyphics as it had progressed to 1950.[28] Tatiana Proskouriakoff performed the same type of service with the study of Maya sculpture.[29] The discovery of Bonampak's murals during this decade made up in excitement for the fact that no new sites of great size were reported.

[24] Lothrop's *Pottery of Costa Rica and Nicaragua* (2 vols., N.Y., Mus. of the Am. Indian, Heye Foundation, 1926) remained the standard work for this southern part of the isthmus until the late 1950's.

[25] *The Inscriptions of Petén* (5 vols., Washington, Carnegie Inst., 1937–8). Vol. i, pp. 76–102 details the history of Petén Maya studies from 1831 to 1937.

[26] *The History of the Maya from the Earliest Times to the Present Day* (N.Y., Scribner).

[27] *The Ancient Maya* (Palo Alto, Calif., Stanford U.P.).

[28] *Maya Hieroglyphic Writing* (Washington, Carnegie Inst., 1950).

[29] *A Study of Classic Maya Sculpture* (Washington, Carnegie Inst., 1950).

With the withdrawal of the Carnegie Institution, first from its studies in Guatemala and then from the whole Maya field, institutions with more limited objectives moved in. The University of Pennsylvania began in 1956 the first intensive study (and a restoration) of Tikal which has already yielded rich data. The very active Instituto Nacional de Antropología e Historia of Mexico has done some of the same for Palenque, where an interesting tomb find was made in 1952. The National Geographic Society and the Middle American Research Institute of Tulane have worked since 1957 in extensive ruins at Dzibilchaltún, ten miles north of Mérida, Yucatan, shedding important light on a long run of Maya history. In the remainder of the isthmus, the Museum für Völkerkunde in Hamburg, Germany, and the Institute of Andean Research have sponsored stratigraphic excavations in 1959 and 1960 which may reveal Maya and Mexican connexions far to the south. Investigations on earlier levels, partly under the auspices of the young Instituto de Antropología e Historia of Guatemala, have already revealed ancient commerce as far down the coast as Ecuador.[30] Two new summations of Maya civilization were made before most of these endeavours began. One, published by Thompson in 1954, is for the general reader the most pleasurable and provocative of the lot.[31] The other is a valuable posthumous edition of Morley's history, revised to bring it more into line with the thinking of other experts.[32]

The 'tentative' label is an important one for many lines of study. In a field so vast and still so largely unexplored as that of the Maya antiquities, the best conclusions of today may dissolve into the discarded theories of tomorrow. Occasionally too a fond thought of yesterday may be revived. The 11.16.0.0.0 Maya-Christian calendar correlation, most popular in the last few decades because it was thought to square better with pottery findings, now seems likely to give way to the 12.9.0.0.0 arrangement of dates (used in this chapter). Tests of dated organic materials by analysis of their radioactive carbon content seem to confirm the 12.9.0.0.0 hypothesis, as do the latest pottery studies at Dzibilchaltún.[33] If the 11.16.0.0.0

[30] Michael D. Coe, 'Archeological Linkages with North and South America at La Victoria, Guatemala', *Amer. Anthrop.*, lxii (1960), 363–93.
[31] *The Rise and Fall of Maya Civilization* (Norman, Univ. of Oklahoma Press).
[32] George W. Brainerd, ed., *The Ancient Maya* (Palo Alto, Calif., Stanford U.P., 1956).
[33] 'Notes and News', *Am. Antiq.*, xxv (1960), 626–37, p. 637. This chapter was written before the publication of Linton Satterthwaite and Elizabeth K. Ralph, 'New Radiocarbon Dates and the Maya Correlation Problem', ibid. xxvi (1960),

correlation does yield, there will be ample room in history for an Uxmal-centred Maya renaissance before the greatness of Chichén Itzá but *after* that of Tikal and Copán. Then too, Morley's faith (though not the *simplicity* of his faith) in sixteenth-century Maya manuscripts will have been somewhat vindicated. Another sixteenth-century manuscript, that of Diego de Landa, is also getting new attention since the announcement by Y. V. Knorozov in 1952 that the remaining Maya hieroglyphs can be read, that many of them must be interpreted phonetically by an *ancient* Maya tongue, and that Landa's imperfect alphabet *is* a beginning key. If Knorozov is correct, new light from the Maya inscriptions should soon make much of *this* presentation an antiquity of its own.

165–84, detailing seemingly incontrovertible evidence in favour of the 11.16.0.0.0 correlation. However, further doubts having been raised since that time, it was decided to leave the chapter in its original form.

CHAPTER III

THE INDIGENOUS POPULATION

NEARLY a millennium of Central American history stretches from the disappearance of high Maya culture to the arrival of Europeans. Only a small notion of what happened in the isthmus during this period is available. It was without doubt a time of warfare, when the foremost centres of civilization came to be hill-top strongholds surrounded by stone fortifications. There was also much movement of peoples; many tribes which inhabited the isthmus in the sixteenth century were not there in the seventh. But 900 years is a considerable time. During a great deal of it, Central America's villagers may have lived quietly. There were always lands to cultivate, and a great wilderness about each populated centre through which hunters roamed and traders carried their goods.

Most pre-Columbian villages of Costa Rica and Nicaragua, built of impermanent materials and now abandoned, have been lost to history. Many in Honduras, El Salvador, and Guatemala, where some people have stayed put and where stone was used during the nine centuries before Columbus in the construction of some edifices, are now known through living contact or archaeological study. Pottery reconstructions of this period have been slow to develop. Ceramic styles in highland Guatemala are identified by time but not by people. Others of north-western Honduras have highly tentative moorings with both time and people.[1] Some sequences for Salvadoran types have now been suggested.[2] Artifacts from the Pacific side of Nicaragua are associated with specific tribes. The sherds of the rest of the isthmus await further scrutiny.

More than humble remains await the archaeologist who enters the study of this period. The gleaming reconstructed temples and ball court of Zaculeu, so handily seen by the motorist as he enters Central American territory on the Inter-American highway, are mute testimony to this effect. Zaculeu became inhabited while the Maya still raised monuments in the Petén, but her period of great-

---

[1] Some of the tentative moorings have only recently been refastened. See Jeremiah F. Epstein, 'Dating the Ulúa Polychrome Complex', *Am. Antiq.*, xxv (1959), 125–9.

[2] Wolfgang Haberland, 'Ceramic Sequences in El Salvador', *Am. Antiq.*, xxvi (1960), 21–29.

ness came later.[3] Chutixtiox, 20 miles north of Santa Cruz del Quiché, Guatemala, was an important fortress late in this period; just *whose* fortress it was is not clear. Cahyup and Chuitinamit near Rabinal were, it is believed, the object of much contention; the identity of the contenders is not certain.[4] The ruins of Tenampua, a mound-site with many structures of stone, lie fifteen miles southeast of Comayagua, Honduras, with *no* tie-in with history at all.

The persons who lived near these more brilliant establishments, together with all the others of Central America, amounted at the beginning of the sixteenth century to somewhat less than a million in number.[5] They spoke, it is believed, some thirty-five 'languages', but with a good hundred variations mentioned by historians and ethnologists. Twenty-five of the languages have been grouped into six families, leaving ten for the moment unattached. More distant affiliations, with their inferences of blood ties for the peoples concerned, have been suggested for all.[6]

Eleven of the languages with twenty-one of the variations were of Mayan stock, divided into two families. The Mayoid family included the Maya language of urbanized northern Yucatan, spoken in the northern Petén; the Chol-Chontal spoken in a belt from Tabasco across Guatemala into Honduras; and the Chuj, Jacaltec, and Kanjobal on the Guatemala–Chiapas border. The Itzá tribe of this group (according to Maya records) left northern Yucatan only in the fifteenth century to live in Tayasal on the island in Lake Petén, whose antiquities include sixth-century stelae. The Quichoid family consisted of the Mam, Ixil, and Aguacatec languages of western Guatemala; the Quiché (with its well-known variations of Uspantec, Cakchiquel, and Zutuhil) just to the east; and the Quekchí and Pokom (Pokomam and Pokonchí) farther to the east and north, the Pokomam extending into El Salvador. In the fif-

[3] The story is told in Richard B. Woodbury and Aubrey S. Trik, *The Ruins of Zaculeu, Guatemala* (2 vols., United Fruit Co., 1953).

[4] Knowledge concerning Chutixtiox, Cahyup, Chuitinamit, and sixty-four other sites is discussed in A. Ledyard Smith, *Archaeological Renaissance in Central Guatemala* (Washington, Carnegie Inst., 1955).

[5] This is the conclusion of Angel Rosenblat, whose 'El desarrollo de la población indígena de América', first printed in *Tierra Firme* of Madrid, 1935, is reproduced in *Anales* xv (1939), 367–79, 486–503; xvi (1939), 114–31. See xvi (1939), 117, 121–2. Some sixteenth-century estimates were much higher.

[6] The speech classification presented here is that of J. Alden Mason, 'The Native Languages of Middle America', in *The Maya and Their Neighbors* (N.Y., Appleton-Century, 1940), pp. 52–87; delimited by Frederick Johnson, 'The Linguistic Map of Mexico and Central America', ibid. pp. 88–114; modified slightly by the use of Norman A. McQuown, 'The Indigenous Languages of Latin America', *Am. Anthrop.*, lvii (1955), 501–70. See also below, n. 7.

teenth century the Quichoid tribes were the most advanced in Central America. The ancient centre of Zaculeu was a stronghold of the Mam. The Quiché had their capital at Gumarcaah or Utatlán, near today's Santa Cruz del Quiché. About 20 miles to the south-east lay Yximché (Tecpán Guatemala or simply Tecpán), chief centre of the Cakchiquel. Mixco, another 20 miles to the north-east, was a strong place of the Pokomam, the inhabitants of which were later transferred to the Mixco of today near Guatemala City.

The Mayan stock is classified by some authorities as part of a great phylum of indigenous languages called the 'Macro-Penutian', spread out from western Canada to Panama. Five other languages of Central America with some fourteen variations may fit in this same broad grouping. Of these, the Xinca in south-eastern Guatemala and the Lenca covering most of central Honduras have as yet not been closely related to other languages. A second tiny pocket labelled Aguacatec in western Guatemala (the first was of the Quichoid family) contained a tongue related to that of the Mixe and Zoque people of Oaxaca and Chiapas. The Nahuat and Nahuatl were languages of the Aztecoidan family, Uto-Aztecan (from Idaho to Panama) stock. Nahuat was spoken by tribes which moved in from central Mexico, probably over a period of centuries, to four regions along the Pacific coast from Guatemala to Costa Rica. They included the Pipil, whose chief town was Antiguo Cuscatlán near San Salvador, but whose scattered holdings included Escuintla in Guatemala and Naco near San Pedro Sula, Honduras; and the Nicarao (whence the name Nicaragua) whose chief town has become the city of Rivas. Nahuatl was the language of the Aztec peoples themselves, spoken in Mexico as far south as Tabasco and Chiapas, in Central America at the mouth of the San Juan River (Nicaragua–Costa Rica), and in Panama on the Caribbean just below the Costa Rican border. The Nahuatl tongue came to Central America and Panama probably not long before Spanish.

Five languages of the south-eastern end of the isthmus with some twenty-eight known variations fit into the Chibchan stock, so named for the peoples of highland Colombia whose fifteenth-century culture was the most advanced of South America outside the Inca empire. Closest to the Colombian Chibcha speech, for some reason, was that of the Rama of southern Nicaragua. Guatuso and the Talamanca family (including Güetar, Talamanca, and

Boruca) plus several minor dialects in this same general category filled most of the linguistic face of Costa Rica.

The tribes of the great eastern portions of Honduras and Nicaragua spoke nine languages with twenty-nine variations, still closely enough tied to the Chibcha to be suggested as part of a great 'Macro-Chibchan' phylum extending from Honduras to Ecuador. Six of these—Ulva, Boa, Bauihca, Panamaca, Tauahca, and Yosco—were members of the Suman family occupying chiefly the interior of Nicaragua. The separate Matagalpa tongue was spoken in the same area, and the language called Tauira along the Caribbean coast. These eight are generally considered as of one stock. West of Tauira along the coast of Honduras, and also on the Bay Islands of Honduras, the Paya spoke a language believed to lean toward the Chibcha but as yet not classified with others.

Outside both Macro-Penutian and Macro-Chibchan (assuming that these two phyla do genuinely exist) remain five native languages of Central America with some ten variations. Jicaque was spoken on the north coast of Honduras, west of Paya and east of the Mayoid family. Choluteca was the speech of people living by the Gulf of Fonseca. Subtiaba, Mangue, and Orotiña occupied portions of the Pacific coast of Nicaragua and north-western Costa Rica. Of these, the Subtiaba tongue was very close to another spoken in the state of Guerrero in Mexico. It and Jicaque were quite different from all the other Central American languages, pertaining to the Hokan-Siouan phylum most prevalent in the area of the United States.[7] Choluteca, Mangue, and Orotiña were members of a family related to a speech of Chiapas (together they are called Chorotegan), more distantly with Otomí of northern Mexico, and possibly (more distantly still) through the suggested 'Macro-Otomangue' phylum with Mixtec and Zapotec of Oaxaca. This language phylum, if it can be said to exist, is the only one restricted to the area of Central America plus Mexico. It may represent the speech of the oldest isthmian settlers.

FIFTEENTH-CENTURY CULTURE

Sixteenth-century authors of the Quiché and Cakchiquel tribes wrote accounts of their legends and history. Two of these accounts tell of Central America's earliest historical personage. The Quiché and Cakchiquel believed that they had migrated to Guatemala

[7] Joseph H. Greenberg and Morris Swadesh, 'Jicaque as a Hokan Language', *Int. J. of Am. Linguistics*, xix (1953), 216–22.

from Tabasco, and that brothers of theirs had moved from Tabasco to Yucatan. Connexions between the kin were not broken. Instead, when the Quiché arrived in Guatemala they sent 'ambassadors to our father and lord Nacxit: that he will know the state of our affairs; that he will furnish us means so that in the future our enemies shall never defeat us; ... that he will designate honors for us and for all our descendants. ...'[8] 'Our father and lord Nacxit' was without doubt a ruler in Chichén Itzá, one of many who in the passage of time held the same title. His full appellation in Yucatan was Ah Nacxit Kukulcan, or in the speech of Central Mexico Topiltzin Acxit Quetzalcoatl. The first Quetzalcoatl or Kukulcan (both words mean 'feathered serpent') had been a monarch of Tula in central Mexico. He had become a legend, his memory attached to the wonders of the planet Venus; and his name forming a part of the titles of others with claims to similar brilliancy.

The most famed ruler of the Quiché was Quicab I, who flourished sometime in the fifteenth century. Under his leadership, the Quiché established hegemony over the other tribes of the Guatemala highlands, even the powerful Mam. It may have been at this time that the Nahua of central Mexico began to use the word 'Quauhtlemallan' or 'Guatemala', the Nahuatl translation of 'Quiché', for the name of this country.[9] By the time the Spaniards arrived, the Quiché 'empire' had dissolved, but without significant movement of peoples. The annals of those times lead one to believe that friendships and animosities between members of leading families were the controlling factor in decisions concerning war and peace, unity and separation. Inside the noble class, sons succeeded to privileges of their fathers; yet the councils of warriors often prevailed over the rules of simple inheritance in determining positions of great power.

As all Central American tribes made war, they also farmed. Maize was the first crop and was grown throughout the isthmus, though perhaps with less devotion by the peoples of the southeastern extremity. Highland folk could get but one crop a year, and that only with field rotation, while others in warm moist country

[8] P. 176 of Dionisio José Chonay and Delia Goetz, tr., *Title of the Lords of Totonicapán*. This English version of a Quiché manuscript forms an appendix (pp. 161–96) to Adrián Recinos and Delia Goetz, tr., *The Annals of the Cakchiquels* (Norman, Univ. of Oklahoma Press, 1953).

[9] Several other derivations of the name Guatemala have been suggested. The simple argument for this one is presented by Adrian Recinos, ed., *Popol Vuh: the Sacred Book of the Ancient Quiché Maya* (Norman, Univ. of Oklahoma Press, 1950), p. 77.

grew all they wanted with little trouble. Also of great importance among the tribes of northern orientation was the cultivation of cacao. In the Pacific lowlands from north-western Costa Rica all the way through Guatemala there was no crop more precious. The drink made from the cacao bean, called *chocolatl*, was served on the most formal occasions. The beans themselves were used as a standard of currency in business transactions.

Several varieties of legumes were grown now, especially the kidney bean and the lima bean, and a similar assortment of squashes. There was also the chilacayote, a watermelon-like fruit grown at higher altitudes, and the chayote or *güisquil* or 'vegetable pear', probably a native of Central America. The papaya and avocado were cultivated as far south as Panama. Another fruit, the ciruela or *jocote* or 'Spanish plum', was likewise so well known as to suggest a local origin. Chili peppers were grown widely, though they were likely immigrants from Mexico. Other domesticated plants were the *miltomate* or ground cherry (a small fruit used in sauces), the tomato (at that time little developed), probably the potato (a relative of the 'Irish' potato then evolving in Chile), the *guayaba* or guava (from Mexico to Peru, used today for making preserves), and tobacco called *piciete*, a type known widely on the American mainland in those days, stronger than the popular form of today which comes from the Caribbean islands.[10] From Mexico to southern Brazil, at least by mid-sixteenth century, grew the platano or plantain, its origins unsure, its banana cousins native only to the lands of another hemisphere.

Still other crops seem likely to have been tamed in South America and transmitted northward by the tribes of Chibcha affiliation. One of the oldest of these was the sweet potato, which spread as far as the Tropic of Cancer in Mexico. Sweet manioc or *yuca* or sweet cassava, another popular root vegetable, came later but reached the same northern limit. Pineapple culture extended into southern Mexico, but the fruits known as *guanábana* or soursop and chirimoya reached only to Costa Rica and Nicaragua. The latter was perhaps also the case with the two cultivated palms of South America, the coconut and the *pejibaye* or peach palm.[11]

Domesticated animals were fewer. There were two birds, the

[10] Felix Webster McBryde, *Cultural and Historical Geography of Southwest Guatemala* (Washington, Smithsonian Inst., 1945), pp. 134–44, reviews several native plants in his region.

[11] Carl O. Sauer, 'Cultivated Plants of South and Central America', in *Handbook of South American Indians*, vi. 487–543.

'Muscovy' duck from South America and the turkey from Mexico, both raised primarily for eating. Dogs lived with some of the tribes, but their role is quite unclear. The only other creature kept for eating was man himself, sometimes retained a short time after his capture to provide the *pièce de résistance* at a ceremonial banquet.

By far the most important crop not grown for food was cotton. Among the more advanced tribes enough was raised so that cotton garments were not unusual for anyone. In the warmer areas less cotton was necessary as garments were reduced to a minimum. Among the less advanced tribes cotton was also grown but not in great quantities. Here a cotton textile was a mark of rank, while the common people wore breech-clouts and occasionally short jackets made of bark cloth. Sandals, wherever they were worn, tended to be of deer hide.

Houses too, for ordinary persons, were as unsubstantial as those of earlier times. A dirt floor, a pole wall, and a thatched roof sufficed for most. In some regions the walls might be of dried mud instead of poles. For community houses, the tribes of Costa Rica, Nicaragua, and Honduras usually built larger wooden structures about a plaza of some sort. Others of El Salvador, Guatemala, and some parts of Honduras used stone for this purpose, in the building of what might be called palaces. In the Guatemala highlands it appears that the ancient stone industry remained active enough through all these centuries (seventh to sixteenth) to provide one centre after another with materials for long-lasting temples and paved ball courts. Utatlán, capital of the Quiché, had twenty-four 'large houses' for its nobles, a palace for the ruling families, a pyramid-temple, a sacrificial platform, a ball court, and fortifications—all built of stone.

Stone metates, often artistic in design, were used throughout the isthmus. Pottery was probably manufactured by every tribe though gourds called *tecomates* were raised in some places to serve the same general purpose. Baskets, mats, and hammocks were common everywhere, the hammocks serving as beds and the mats often assuming a role of considerable ceremonial significance. From Panama and the southern extremity of Costa Rica in the fourteenth and fifteenth centuries came gold, sometimes alloyed with copper, cast or hammered into a variety of objects of personal adornment— pendants shaped like animals, headbands, ear rods, nose rings, necklaces, bracelets, finger rings, even greaves. The golden objects were traded as far as the north coast of Honduras, where they met artifacts of copper and bronze moving from Mexico in the opposite direction. Most common of the latter were one- or two-inch bells with pebbles inside. Rarer finds indicate that both axes and fish-hooks were made of copper, perhaps even the soles of sandals.

These centuries were not, except for the new knowledge of metals, an age of scientific attainment. In northern Yucatan, new generations of star-watchers kept up with, but did not noticeably deepen, the ancient understanding of astronomy. The Maya of Guatemala did not even keep up with the old science, having left of the calendar by the sixteenth century only the 260-day tzolkin shared by other tribes. Neither were the glyphs used any longer. Stelae were few and unmarked by inscriptions. 'Books' seem to have been made, of accordion-folded bark cloth, but they contained only pictures. The whole Maya system of numerals disappeared save in Yucatan, where stelae with abbreviated dates continued to be erected.

One other ancient interest persisted. The tribes of Guatemala, enthusiastic warriors and persistent growers of maize and cacao, were like their forebears devotees of the ball game. Zaculeu, Utat-lán, the old Mixco, Chuitinamit, and Chutixtiox all had ball courts, along with at least thirty-five lesser sites in the highlands. So did Naco, the still largely unknown Tenampua in Honduras, and sites far to the east in El Salvador. When Hun-Hunahpú and Vucub-Hunahpú, god-heroes of Quiché legend, descended to the underworld of Xibalba, they did so to accept the challenge of the monarchs of the underworld to a game of ball. And long after Hun-Hunahpú and Vucub-Hunahpú had met disgrace and death, twin sons of Hun-Hunahpú infuriated the princes of Xibalba by playing a return engagement and winning the contest. This was definitely a sport of the aristocrats. 'Not for you shall be the ball game', the princes of Xibalba were told after their defeat. 'You shall spend your time making earthen pots and tubs and stones to grind corn.'[12]

There were well developed traditions of music and dance. Most of the old dances have been forgotten but a few still survive. One depicts in marathon fashion the age-old struggle between man and the wild animals. Another mimics the venerable fertility theme, with one dancer at a time seeking by suggestive motions to win the favour of a central person dressed as a woman. Music was available in the Guatemala highlands from the *caracol* (a large shell used as a wind instrument), the ocarina (made of stone or clay), the piccolo

[12] *Popol Vuh* (1950), p. 161.

(of cane or reed), and various drums and rattles. The musical pattern with its own five-tone scaling was restrained in nature. Its rendition today whether by native or European instruments seems gentle, almost melancholy, by contrast with the vigorous rhythms of the lowlands and Caribbean.

The town of Rabinal, near the ruins of Cahyup and Chuitinamit, has preserved the only example of sophisticated native theatre. The *Rabinal Achí* is a dance drama which was performed for centuries until 1856. It would have been lost to history but for the distinguished Frenchman who transcribed it—stage directions, costuming, and all—from the oral descriptions of a performer.[13] Its story is that of a brave prince captured in battle (the play is named for his captor). Condemned to be sacrificed, honoured during the preparation period, treated with ceremony and consideration, even allowed to gaze distantly at his homeland, the prince is finally led to the high altar where his heart will be offered to the gods. Startling drama this, presumably, only to the uninitiated; but engrossing, surely, even to those who knew its every line and movement.

In Cahyup and Chuitinamit such poetic composition was matched by that of the architect. Sketched reconstructions of their ceremonial centres, and of others like them, reveal that they were built in a manner very pleasing to the eye. The sculpturing art had not held its own, however, and such stone carvings as are found are usually crude in form. They are located all through the Pacific and highland areas of the isthmus, generally depicting persons or animals or both on one statue. The position of painting during the immediate pre-Columbian period is unknown.

Isthmian books, such as they were, doubtless contained meaningful literature. Early Spaniards reported the existence of such enterprise all the way from Guatemala to Nicaragua. When the Latin alphabet became available with the arrival of the Spaniards, members of the Quiché, Cakchiquel, Quekchí, Pokomam, and Pipil nations used it to compose sixteenth-century manuscripts expressing their own dialects phonetically. The Quekchí, Pokomam, and Pipil pieces are believed lost, but ten others (six Quiché and four Cakchiquel) have been published in European translation.[14]

---

[13] The transcriber was Brasseur de Bourbourg, who did so much for classic Maya studies with the publication of the manuscript by Diego de Landa. See 'Descubrimiento del Rabinal Achí', *Anales*, vi (1929), 197–201. The text with a commentary by Georges Raynaud is given in 'El varón de Rabinal', ibid. vi (1929–30), 45–51, 347–70, 481–91.

[14] Some of these documents are known only through references in the late

One, the Quiché *Popol Vuh*, is as notable a document of indigenous literary effort as any to be found in the Americas. Its sixteenth-century composer claimed only to be writing what had been written before: 'This is the beginning', he says, 'of the old traditions of this place called Quiché. . . . We shall bring it to light because now the *Popol Vuh*, as it is called, cannot be seen any more. . . . The original book, written long ago, existed, but its sight is hidden to the searcher and to the thinker'.[15]

Popol Vuh means *Book of the Community*; it was actually the name given to the original, which could not have included all that now goes by the title. The first *Popol Vuh* must have contained the story of the creation of men from maize—men, not man, for the Quiché believed in separate creation for the various tribes. In another obviously old story mannikins are made from wood but for a punishment turned into monkeys. Two narratives of the younger ball-playing god-men (which take up much of the book) are also of considerable vintage. Other accounts with a distinctly indigenous flavour are those of the gift of fire by the god Tohil who expected blood sacrifices in return; the dawning of the sun after a long residence of the tribes in rain and darkness; and the account of the nude bathing of two young maidens in an attempt to lure three young gods into captivity. An abridged version of the latter story in the *Title of the Lords of Totonicapán* more realistically speaks of three young maidens—but substitutes three imperturbable old men for three all-wise and unwilling young gods.

Tohil, the chief Quiché god, shared honours in temple worship with Avilix and Hacavitz. A prayer in the *Popol Vuh* calls them collectively 'Heart of Heaven, Heart of Earth, Bundle of Majesty. . . . Arch of the Sky, Surface of the Earth, the Four Corners, the Four Cardinal Points'.[16] Each tribe on the isthmus had its own pantheon, so that the total number of gods ran into the hundreds. Some of them demanded sacrifices of turpentine and grasses, or birds and deer; others were not satisfied without the pulsating hearts of slashed and dying men and women. A formal priesthood supervised the many offerings in parts of Guatemala. Elsewhere the shamans—*curanderos* or 'medicine men'—were important indi-

seventeenth-century work of Francisco Antonio de Fuentes y Guzmán; see the Second Part of his *Recordación florida* (3 vols., Guatemala, 1932–3). All ten of those published have now been edited by Adrián Recinos in Spanish; see his *Popol Vuh* (Mexico City, 1947), *Memorial de Sololá* (Mexico City, 1950), and *Crónicas indígenas de Guatemala* (Guatemala, 1957).

[15] *Popol Vuh* (1950), pp. 77–80.   [16] Ibid. p. 227.

viduals, making contacts with the spirits of the countryside and aiding in the concerns of everyday living.

Even the more structured religion of the north-western end of the isthmus was close to the affairs of daily life. Sacrifices were of one's self as well as other beings. Pilgrimages were made to holy places, and self-denial formed a part of personal codes of behaviour. A famed Spanish bishop who had early contact with the natives of Verapaz, Guatemala, testified that they observed quite well the last seven of the Ten Hebrew Commandments before knowing them.[17] An early Italian visitor said isthmian Indians were often bewildered when Europeans who *knew* the Ten Commandments observed them little better.[18]

THE SPANISH CONQUEST

The first Europeans to visit Central America came with Christopher Columbus. They were members of the great admiral's fourth expedition to Caribbean waters sailing under the flag of Spain. On his three previous voyages over a period of ten years, Columbus had discovered the great West Indian islands and the mainland of South America. His new probe farther to the west was prompted by his belief that just beyond the lands he had already found lay the Indies of Asia. The expedition sighted Guanaja, one of the Bay Islands, on 30 July 1502. On 14 August Columbus first set foot on the Central American mainland at nearby Cape Honduras. He took formal possession of the land three days later. From here he chose to sail east along the coast, though high and contrary winds made his passage very difficult. He named Cape Gracias a Dios (where he arrived on 14 September) because of his *thanks to God* for delivery from that situation. Either his or the next expedition (four years later) is believed to have used the name Honduras for some of this coast because of great *depths* of the sea (between high waves?) which were encountered. Sailing was much easier southward along the coast of Nicaragua. From 25 September to 5 October Columbus stopped at a place he called Cariay, believed to be Puerto Limón, Costa Rica. On the latter date he found Indians wearing tempting ornaments of gold at the Bay of the Admiral (Bahía de Almirante) now so named for him, in Panama near the Costa Rican border. From sights such as these, without much doubt,

[17] Bartolomé de las Casas, *Apologética historia de las Indias* (Manuel Serrano y Sanz, ed., Madrid, 1909), pp. 626–9.
[18] Girolamo Benzoni, *History of the New World* (W. H. Smyth, tr., Hakluyt Soc., 1857), pp. 161–2.

this land received its reputation as a *rich coast* (though the name Costa Rica is not found in documents until later). When Columbus learned there was no water passage through Panama, he spent several miserable months trying vainly to establish a gold-procurement colony before returning to Spain empty-handed. The discovery of Central America, though to him it was only a sort of obstruction, was the last of his great accomplishments.

From Hispaniola, which Columbus had settled in 1493, sallied the two streams of Spanish colonization and conquest which soon encompassed this isthmus. The earlier venture (1509) produced the first European settlement on the mainland of the Americas in Panama; the later (1511) brought about the conquest of Cuba. In 1513 the men of Panama reached the Pacific Ocean for the first time, under the leadership of Vasco Núñez de Balboa. In 1517 those of Cuba laid amazed eyes on the coastal cities of Yucatan and decided to investigate their phenomena more carefully. It was traffic in human beings which had brought the Spaniards so close to Yucatan. At some time between 1511 and 1517 ships had started carrying unwilling natives from the Bay Islands to work in Cuba. Thus the slave trade was the first real impact made by the white man's culture upon the people of Central America.

In 1519 (to the south-east of Central America) the city of Panama was founded. In the same year (to the north-west) Hernán Cortés and his band, coming from Cuba, entered the city of Tenochtitlán, the most powerful in Mexico. Within two years Cortés had conquered and razed Tenochtitlán and established Mexico City on its ruins. The mainland of Central America remained inviolate through all this activity save for smallpox, the white man's disease which travelled faster than the white man himself. The Cakchiquel suffered tremendously from this malady, against which they had so little defence.

Heavy shadows and black night enveloped our fathers and grandfathers and us also, oh, my sons! . . . The people could not in any way control the sickness. . . . After our fathers and grandfathers succumbed, half of the people fled to the fields. The dogs and the vultures devoured the bodies. . . . So it was that we became orphans, oh, my sons! So we became when we were young. All of us were thus. We were born to die![19]

The first overland contacts between Spaniard and Central American native came in 1522, from both ends of the isthmus.

[19] *Annals of the Cakchiquels*, pp. 115–16.

Neither was of a markedly violent nature. While his pilot Andrés Niño traced the Pacific shores as Columbus had done those of the Caribbean twenty years earlier, Gil González de Avila with 100 men and four horses marched from Panama along the west shore of Costa Rica into Nicaragua as far as the great lakes. González was exploring, and not disinterested in the gold ornaments which he found all about him; but he spent a major portion of his time, according to his own account, baptizing the natives into the Christian faith. He retired from the scene when his reception became less friendly. Meanwhile from the Mexican state of Oaxaca, Pedro de Alvarado, one of the captains of Cortés, sent two emissaries to the Cakchiquel in Yximché seeking a native–Spanish alliance.

Two years later (in 1524) no less than four Spanish expeditions found themselves in Central America all at the same time. González returned by sea from Hispaniola, landing in Honduras instead of Nicaragua, bringing with him Central America's first Spanish women and her first persons of African descent. Cristóbal de Olid came also to Honduras, by water from Mexico, and captured González; Olid made plain his intention to develop Honduras on his own without regard for the authority of Hernán Cortés, who had sent him. Francisco Hernández de Córdoba came to Nicaragua from Panama and established the cities of Granada and León, Central America's first permanent Spanish settlements. Pedro de Alvarado came from Oaxaca, with over 400 Spaniards and many more natives of Mexico, to fight out the year in Guatemala and El Salvador. Alvarado won all his battles but lost all the wars. To his own commander Cortés he wrote:

... We are in the wildest country and people one has ever seen, and so that our Lord may give us victory I supplicate Your Grace to ordain that a procession be held in your city of all the priests and friars so that our Lord may help us. We are so far from help that if He does not help us, nobody can.[20]

But though the going was rough, the Spaniards were here to stay. As if to symbolize the change in Central America's destinies, the first child of mixed American and European parentage was born in Utatlán on 22 March 1524. Her name was Leonor, daughter of Pedro de Alvarado and Luisa Xicoténcatl, princess of Tlaxcala in central Mexico.

Honduras, though its conquest proceeded most feebly, became

[20] Pedro de Alvarado, *An Account of the Conquest of Guatemala in 1524* (S. J. Mackie, ed., Cortes Soc., 1924), pp. 66–67.

the first Central American province recognized in Spain in 1525. Cortés appeared in Honduras the same year, after Olid had been murdered, and the city of Trujillo was founded on the coast. Two years later Guatemala and Nicaragua were made separate respectively from Mexico and Panama and granted their first royal governors; Pedro de Alvarado in the former, Pedrarias Dávila (under whose orders Hernández de Córdoba had conquered) in the latter. Only in this year (1527) was Spanish security in Guatemala (including El Salvador) an accomplished fact, due more to the efforts of Alvarado's lieutenants than to those of Alvarado himself. Santiago de Guatemala (on the site of today's Ciudad Vieja) was founded in 1527, San Salvador (named for the Holy Saviour) in 1528, San Miguel in 1530. Their Spanish inhabitants were interested in gentleman farming and whatever gold they could find. The natives would be the labourers, as in Trujillo, León, and Granada, held along with the land as the right of the conquerors. Many white residents of the three latter villages were gaining an extra livelihood by selling miscellaneous Indians to buyers from the Caribbean islands and Panama.

Attention was diverted from the isthmus in the 1530's as the Spaniards in Mexico began to look northward and Panamanians found excitement in Peru. The establishment of new governing bodies called audiencias with legislative and judicial authority left Guatemala half-subject to Mexico, Honduras to Hispaniola, and Nicaragua to Panama. Nevertheless in this decade Honduras became firmly Spanish with the settlement of San Pedro Sula, Gracias, and Comayagua. The discovery of gold in fair quantity gave a short spurt to Honduras' economy. Francisco de Montejo, would-be conqueror of Yucatan, and Alvarado vied for the Honduran governorship. Alvarado, also interested in Peru, founded Realejo as a port in Nicaragua on his way to South Sea adventures. Nueva Segovia was founded by the Nicaraguans. The older Spanish villages also survived—and began to look more like Spain as the first Dominican, Mercedarian, and Franciscan friars moved in (with 300 years of their own history behind them) and as bishops were appointed by the king and confirmed by the pope to live in León, Santiago, and Trujillo.

Four important developments took place in the 1540's: (1) As the labour supply in Honduras became depleted through sickness, warfare, and the kidnapping trade, Negro slaves were imported from Africa. This involuntary migration continued, bringing with it cultural and racial changes which are very difficult to measure. During the next hundred years, it seems certain, more Africans came to the isthmus than Europeans. They came through northern Honduras but spread (mixing with both Spaniard and Indian) through Honduras, El Salvador, and Nicaragua.[21]

(2) The remarkable New Laws of 1542 (published in Spain on 1 May 1543) proclaimed that the Indian in America was to be treated as a vassal of the Spanish king. As a vassal his property would not be inviolate, and he would still have tribute to pay. But he could no longer be taken as a slave, he could no longer be parcelled out with the land in encomienda as though he were a beast, he could no longer be forced to labour (except as an interpreter in properly authorized conquests!), and he was to have his rights in court like any other vassal. Of course many of the Indians had already been parcelled out or taken as slaves; their status was not to be affected, unless they were being held 'illegally' or in immoderate numbers. A decision of 1545 permitted those who were held in encomienda to be passed on from father to son. Nevertheless this proved the end of the Indian slave trade and left large numbers of Central American natives still outside the encomienda system. Much of the inspiration for the New Laws came from the pen of a Central American friar, Bartolomé de las Casas, whose book *Brevíssima relación de la destruyción de las Indias* portrayed (with exaggerated statistics) the enormities of the white man's crimes against the Indians, and whose Dominican brothers were at this very time in Verapaz, Guatemala, demonstrating a new way of extending Spanish power without resort to violence.

(3) Central America became unified politically as a new Audiencia de los Confines (Audiencia of the Boundaries) began functioning on 16 May 1544. Its original jurisdiction extended from Chiapas, Tabasco, and Yucatan through Panama. The first seat of the audiencia was the city of Gracias in Honduras; in 1549 a move was made to a new Santiago de Guatemala. The latter was today's Antigua, founded in 1543 after its predecessor of the same name (the Santiago of Ciudad Vieja) had been ruined by flood.

(4) Under the guidance of the new audiencia, many Indians who had been conquered but remained outside the encomienda system

[21] Julio Lang, 'Espectro racial de Honduras', *R. de la Univ.*, xvi/11 (Oct.–Dec. 1952), pp. 72–76. The colonial spread of Central America's Negro population seems well documented in the early nineteenth-century data of Domingo Juarros, *Compendio de la historia de la ciudad de Guatemala* (2 vols., Guatemala, 1936), i. 10–94.

were concentrated into new and larger villages. Such were Cobán, Santa Cruz del Quiché, Quezaltenango, Totonicapán, Sololá, and Escuintla in today's Guatemala; Ahuachapán and Santa Ana in El Salvador; Managua and Masaya in Nicaragua; and Nicoya in Costa Rica. In these villages at first there were no Spaniards except a few representatives of the government and church. It was in fact to facilitate management by these two institutions that the Indians were thus brought together.

Francisco Hernández Arana, grandson of Hunyg, a once-powerful Cakchiquel chief, chronicled these events quite faithfully as they affected his own people. He gave credit to the conquerors where he thought it was due, but made plain the suffering they brought with them. The terrible sickness—and perhaps all the régime that went with it—he eventually accepted as 'the will of our powerful God'.[22] Bernal Díaz del Castillo, Spanish veteran of the wars of conquest and now a resident of Guatemala, painted the natives' welfare in rosier colours:

... The Holy Gospel is firmly planted in their hearts.... They are very excellent craftsmen, also lapidaries and painters.... Many sons of Chieftains know how to read and write.... They have planted so many trees that, because the peaches are not good for the health, and the banana plantations give them too much shade, they ... are cutting down many of them and putting in quinces and apples and pears....[23]

By the time Díaz wrote these words (in the 1560's) the wars were indeed nearly over. Peaceful pursuits predominated even in the 1540's and 1550's, when only three Spanish towns were founded (San Jorge de Olancho, Honduras, for gold miners; Choluteca, Honduras, for farmers; and Sonsonate, El Salvador, for merchants interested in a growing export trade in cacao). The heartland of Costa Rica was invested with Spanish authority in 1561; and Cartago was founded there three years later, a lonely European outpost in a province still largely Indian. Through decisions in Spain the Audiencia de los Confines lost Panama in 1550, Tabasco and Yucatan in 1560, and its own life in 1565, but was replaced on 3 March 1570 by a new Audiencia de Guatemala, ruling the isthmus from Costa Rica through Chiapas. For two and a half centuries under this régime, Central America enjoyed the blessings of quiescence.

[22] *Annals of the Cakchiquels*, p. 143.
[23] *The True History of the Conquest of New Spain* (Genaro García, ed.; Alfred Percival Maudslay, tr.; 5 vols., Hakluyt Soc., 1908–16), v. 265, 268–9.

The Indigenous Population

The Spaniard ruled, but he formed a minority. The Indian lived on, and lives on still, in numbers greater than the conqueror. His standing has been obscured by the fact that he is often not counted an Indian if he wears European clothing or speaks the Spanish language. He is there, none the less, forming the preponderant strain in the three-way fusion of peoples (Indian, European, and Negro) which constitutes about half the isthmian population. He is there too forming by far the largest group of the three 'pure bloods' (Indian, European, and Negro) who compose the remainder.

The Spaniards mastered most of the isthmus politically in forty years; their cultural conquest has gone on over 400. A mid-twentieth century trip along the Inter-American highway reveals the whole range of the latter accomplishment still in progress. The tourist entering Guatemala from the north does so near Huehuetenango, rubbing shoulders at once with tribes whose ways have changed very little. In the high mountains north-west and north-east of Huehuetenango live 13,000 Jacaltec; 11,000 Chuj; 42,000 Kanjobal; and 25,000 Ixil.[24] These people's language, clothing, religion, calendar, customs, and beliefs are distinctively their own; what they have of Spanish civilization, one might say, are the bits they themselves have chosen.

Just east of Huehuetenango live 8,000 Aguacatec; west and south along the Mexican border, so that the highway penetrates their territory, dwell 178,000 Mam. The Aguacatec and the Mam (unlike for the most part the four tribes earlier mentioned) live in association with persons of other habits; they themselves remain in great numbers a people definitely apart. Farther along the highway, in Totonicapán, one is in Quiché country; about Chimaltenango live the Cakchiquel. There are 339,000 Quiché; 167,000 Cakchiquel; just south of them 19,000 Zutuhil; and north 12,000 Uspantec. These people have customs more modified; many are able to speak Spanish. Their religion is often a hybrid. Distinctive clothing habits are sometimes abandoned by the men. The Pokonchí (38,000) and Quekchí (134,000) in the mountains around Cobán share these general characteristics, though Spanish is less

---

[24] The criterion here is language spoken in the home by persons over 3 years of age. Figures are rounded to the nearest thousand from Guatemala's *Sexto censo de población: Abril 18 de 1950* (Guatemala, 1957), p. 169.

common among them. Along the highway after Guatemala City the Spanish language gains a definite ascendancy, though 11,000 Pokomam and 12,000 Chortí (of the Chol-Chontal language) live not far away.[25]

In Guatemala, the Indian who chooses to become Europeanized in both language and clothing is called a ladino. (The word, used in Spain during the Middle Ages for an Arab who spoke Castilian, means nothing but Latin or *latino*.) For such an Indian, the conquest is nearly completed. Actually, of course, in cultural accoutrements as well as in race the ladino bears for some time the strong mark of the Indian. The end product itself is a mixed affair, with Indian manners affecting the European while the latter gain the ascendancy. The predominance of European ways is most notable in the fact that Indians become ladinos but ladinos do not return to be Indians.[26]

Driving along the Inter-American highway east of the Guatemalan capital one passes the old habitat of the Xinca, a smaller tribe now on the edge of extinction. In El Salvador one finds communities of Pipil who are rapidly forgetting the old language; in Honduras not far away at this point live the Lenca, who remember in some communities and have forgotten in others. Both Lenca and Pipil still hold on to old customs but with less tenacity than the nations of Guatemala. The men no longer wear the old costume; some women do, some do not, depending upon the locality. The religion is quite clearly Spanish Catholic. Ladinos are many rather than few, but barriers against them (raised by Indians who have remained Indian) survive in some communities.

Along or near the highway as the tourist continues to the east and south through eastern El Salvador, southernmost Honduras, Pacific Nicaragua, and north-western Costa Rica, he passes the sections where once lived the Choluteca, Matagalpa, Subtiaba, Mangue, Nicarao, and Orotiña peoples—in that order—all of them now submerged in a mass of Spanish-speaking humanity. Many persons in this area are doubtless Indians in the fullest sense if one considers ancestry alone as the criterion, but culturally all are ladinos. The native languages are forgotten, the older garments are no longer worn (save occasionally at time of fiesta), and many

---

[25] See the map in Antonio Goubaud Carrera, *Distribución de las lenguas indígenas actuales de Guatemala* (Guatemala, 1946), facing p. 16.

[26] The various modifications of Spanish and Indian cultures are classified in Richard N. Adams, 'Cultural Components of Central America', *Am. Anthrop.*, lviii (1956), 881–907.

though not all of the old customs have now been discarded. Villages or zones of cities which because of some lingering traits are still counted 'Indian' become increasingly rare in this region as the traveller progresses southward. The last is the tiny hamlet of Matambú, thirty miles from the highway, near Nicoya, Costa Rica.[27]

As one drives up and over from Puntarenas to the tableland on which most of Costa Rica's cities are located, Indian lands seem to be left far behind. Here is definitely a European district where everyone, poor or rich, speaks Spanish and acts and lives like a Spaniard. The Güetar dwelt in this place, and have now disappeared. Yet even here where white faces are in a large majority, there is much Indian descent, scattered in smaller percentages through who-knows-how-much of the population. Costa Rica has a few thousand living Indians also, but they have been pushed off to the margins where their whole lives are their own, limited only by physical circumstances. The Boruca language thus survives near the Golfo Dulce; various dialects of Talamanca are spoken near the Panama border; and a few remnants of the Guatuso live on near Lake Nicaragua.

The Inter-American highway does not traverse the Caribbean coast or its hinterland. Here (tracing back again from Costa Rica) a few hundred Rama Indians live on an islet near Bluefields; a few thousand Sumo speaking the Ulva, Bauihca, Panamaca, and Tauahca languages (Boa and Yosco are forgotten) inhabit the river valleys of Nicaragua and eastern Honduras; several thousand Miskito, with varying degrees of Negro admixture, speak Tauira dialects along the coast; and a few hundred Paya have their own river towns in Honduras. The Jicaque have reached the edge of oblivion without quite succumbing.[28] The Maya language of Yucatan is still spoken by scattered folk of the northern Petén little troubled by modern ways.

With the linguistic submergences here recorded and the extinction of small pockets of Mixe-Zoque and Nahuatl speech from

[27] Ibid. pp. 896–7.
[28] Julian H. Steward, 'The Circum-Caribbean Tribes: An Introduction', in *Handbook of South American Indians*, iv. 1–41, and Frederick Johnson and others, 'Central American Cultures', ibid. pp. 43–296, provide a summary of knowledge to 1945 of the non-Maya tribes of Honduras, Nicaragua, and Costa Rica. Nicaraguan census takers in 1950 found 20,723 persons above the age of six speaking 'Miskito' in the home and 747 speaking 'Sumo'. See *Censo general de población de la república de Nicaragua: Mayo 1950* (17 vols., Managua, 1951–4), xvii. 126.

Mexico, the number of indigenous Central American languages has dropped from thirty-five to twenty-four; the number of significant variants remains about half the original hundred. There is little doubt that the process will continue; it is a tribute to the degree of pre-Columbian civilization in the isthmus that it has not already progressed further. Where that civilization was strongest, there are more Indians today than in the sixteenth century. Where it was weakest the race has lost its identity or been pushed off to the edges, whenever the white man has decided to take over.

INDIAN STUDIES

Individual Europeans have long been curious about the race their people were displacing. Scientific curiosity, nothing more, is needed to explain the ethnological writings of two Spaniards who came early to Central America. First was Gonzalo Fernández de Oviedo y Valdés, who lived in Nicaragua from 1527 to 1529 and later became a historian. Part of Oviedo's history was personal experience; included in the latter were his accounts of Nicaraguan Indians. Bartolomé de las Casas, who fought so hard on the Indians' behalf, lived in Nicaragua (1532–6), Guatemala (1536–9), and Chiapas (1544–7). He knew with particular intimacy the natives of Verapaz and described them in thirteen chapters. The missionary motive helped to prompt Las Casas' eager interest and that of several generations of friars who followed him. Their studies of the Indian languages (they prepared grammars and catechisms) have not lost their importance. But neither curiosity nor evangelism procured the printing of voluminous manuscripts. Oviedo's work was published in full only in 1855; Las Casas' had to wait until 1909.[29]

Just before and after the year 1700, three Guatemalan chroniclers took action to conserve valuable Indian lore. Francisco Antonio de Fuentes y Guzmán wrote a history of the parts of Guatemala with much reference to the natives. He made use of many documents which have since disappeared. Among them were native manuscripts, one of which gave him a Quiché history unlike the *Popol Vuh* in various aspects.[30] Francisco Vázquez found the manuscript *Annals of the Cakchiquels* in Sololá, used it a little, and placed it in the archives of his Franciscan order for safekeeping. Francisco Ximénez transcribed the *Popol Vuh* in both Quiché and Spanish, and used a free translation for twenty chapters of his own

[29] See ch. i, n. 6, p. 10, and above, n. 17.   [30] See above, n. 14.

great Dominican history of Guatemala.[31] But the *Popol Vuh*, the *Annals*, and the histories of Fuentes and Ximénez, like the works of Oviedo and Las Casas before them, all went unpublished through the eighteenth century and unnoticed by the rest of the world.

Books which did reach print—a Spanish history, an English travel account (most scarce until the nineteenth century), or a pirate's adventure story—provided brief titbits of information concerning the Indians. So did other odds and ends such as official reports and missionary accounts, which are useful today as they come to light. The first systematic account of all Central America, written by Domingo Juarros early in the 1800's, dealt chiefly with Spanish institutions, though the Indians were not neglected entirely.

In the mid-nineteenth century, persons from outside the isthmus provided the impetus for later studies. Ephraim George Squier, antiquarian and business man from New York, gave the first precise description of many Indian peoples in Honduras, El Salvador, and Nicaragua.[32] Carl Scherzer, a Viennese physician, published the first edition of the *Popol Vuh*, revealing the aboriginal attainments of Guatemala.[33] Brasseur de Bourbourg, the French enthusiast who did so much for Maya research, used the *Popol Vuh* and the *Annals of the Cakchiquels* to place the Quichoid peoples properly in the story of pre-Columbian civilization in both Mexico and Central America.[34] Hubert Howe Bancroft and his associates, writing in California in the 1870's, summarized quite ably almost all on this subject that had been written before. To them, the Central American Indian was part of a study which reached from Panama to Alaska.[35]

Isthmian linguistic studies, popular in early colonial times, were renewed in the 1870's. Since then an increasing number of ethnologists have become interested in obtaining vocabularies before languages become extinct, while (more recently) missionaries have again sought to contact peoples whose languages remain vigorous. After several more restricted studies (particularly in Guatemala

---

[31] *Historia de la provincia de San Vicente de Chiapa y Guatemala de la Orden de Predicadores* (3 vols., Guatemala, 1929–31).

[32] *Nicaragua* (2 vols., N.Y., Appleton, 1852) and *Notes on Central America* (N.Y., Harper, 1855).

[33] *Las historias del origen de los Indios de esta provincia de Guatemala* (Vienna, 1857).

[34] *Histoire des nations civilisées du Mexique et de l'Amérique–Centrale, durant les siècles antérieurs à Christophe Colomb* (4 vols., Paris, 1857–9).

[35] *The Native Races of the Pacific States of North America* (5 vols., San Francisco, 1874–5), i. 684–797; iii. 759–96; iv. 1–139; v. 540–613.

and Costa Rica) the first linguistic map to include all of Central America was published in 1911.[36] Walter Lehmann, a German scholar, later produced a classificatory analysis of work done in the entire isthmus to the year 1920.[37] The processes of emendation and new classification continue.[38] A most active role in Maya language study has been taken by the Wycliffe Bible Translators founded in 1942. William Cameron Townsend, chief organizer of this Protestant association, started his work in the 1920's with a translation of the Gospel of St. Mark into Cakchiquel. Wycliffe translators have now worked with at least 175 language groups in eleven countries, including most of those of Guatemala.[39]

Ethnological reviews of whole peoples of Central America were begun in the 1880's. Outstanding among earlier works was that of Otto Stoll on the living Maya of Guatemala.[40] Few works of this genre have been published, however, with the depth required for modern anthropological study. A 1932 review of the Miskito and Sumo tribes by Eduard Conzemius and a close look at the Chortí of Guatemala by Charles Wisdom (1940) are in a class by themselves.[41] A book on the Jicaque might be added.[42] Studies of particular Indian communities, which have become fashionable in recent years, are much narrower in conception. Unless more reviews of the broader type are undertaken soon, further population groups will become extinct before they are made objects of scientific study. Implied recognition of this point is made by Richard Adams, who has written an over-all review of the cultures of the isthmus (Guatemala to Panama, but omitting Costa Rica) presenting the modern Indian for the first time in proper perspective with those who live about him.[43]

Intensive work of anthropologists in individual Guatemalan communities, lasting six months or a year at a time, started in the 1920's. Much work has since been accomplished by both United

[36] Cyrus Thomas and John R. Swanton, *Indian Languages of Mexico and Central America and Their Geographical Distribution* (Washington, Smithsonian Inst.).
[37] *Zentral-Amerika* (2 vols., Berlin, 1920).   [38] See above, n. 6.
[39] See Ethel Emily Wallis and Mary Angela Bennett, *Two Thousand Tongues To Go: The Story of the Wycliffe Bible Translators* (N.Y., Harper, 1959).
[40] *Zur Ethnographie der Republik Guatemala* (Zurich, 1884).
[41] *Ethnographical Survey of the Miskito and Sumu Indians of Honduras and Nicaragua* (Washington, Smithsonian Inst.); *The Chorti Indians of Guatemala* (Univ. of Chicago Press).
[42] V. Wolfgang Von Hagen, *The Jicaque (Torrupan) Indians of Honduras* (N.Y., Mus. of the American Indian, Heye Foundation, 1943).
[43] See above, n. 26, and Adams, *Cultural Surveys of Panama–Nicaragua–Guatemala–El Salvador–Honduras* (Pan American Sanitary Bureau, 1957).

States and Guatemalan scholars. While the findings from many of these projects are available only on typescript and microfilm, books (of varying degrees of professionalism) have been published on several.[44] Despite an aura of objectivity in such work, each writer seems to have his own hobbies to ride and his own preconceptions. Each tries to comprehend a people not his own, in most cases without the people's language. Some seem to resent the intrusion of new forces, as though the Indian were intended for clinical study but should be isolated from contaminating modernity. Put all together, the community studies are a significant advance in scientific understanding. Taken separately, each must be accepted only on its own merits, the reader remembering that much of what is omitted from consideration may be important and that much of what is presented is debated by the anthropologists themselves.

Heritage of Conquest, a 1952 publication, is a record of a week-long discussion by thirty-two persons who had done field work among the Indians of Mexico and Central America. The discussion contains examples of the refutation of theses poorly stated. Other statements which are open to question go unchallenged in this record. In regard to the acceptance by the Indians of the culture of the Spaniards, for instance, one reads, 'The people who were most highly civilized were acculturated most rapidly', though the Quichoid peoples of Guatemala have accepted much less than the Pacific coast tribes of Nicaragua, who were their decided inferiors in civilization. Or again, 'From what we know of Central America, in the altitudes above 600 metres the acculturation of the Indians is much more progressed than in altitudes below 600 metres'; though the actual situation along the Pacific in Guatemala is just the reverse.[45] The value of *Heritage of Conquest* is that the seminar of which it is a record was designed to help cure the very maladies which it discloses, maladies derived in the main from the fault of

[44] Oliver La Farge and Douglas Byers, *The Year Bearer's People* (New Orleans, Tulane Univ., 1931), dealing with Jacaltenango; Webster McBryde, *Sololá* (New Orleans, Tulane Univ., 1933); Charles Wagley, *Economics of a Guatemalan Village* and *The Social and Religious Life of a Guatemalan Village* (Beloit, Wis., Am. Anthrop. Assoc., 1941 and 1949), which both treat of Santiago Chimaltenango; Oliver La Farge, *Santa Eulalia* (Univ. of Chicago Press, 1947); John Philip Gillin, *The Culture of Security in San Carlos* (New Orleans, Tulane Univ., 1951), in which 'San Carlos' is really San Luis Jilotepeque; Maud Oakes, *The Two Crosses of Todos Santos* (Pantheon Books, 1951); Ruth Bunzel, *Chichicastenango* (Tucson, Ariz., Am. Ethnological Soc., 1952); and Sol Tax, *Penny Capitalism* (Washington, Smithsonian Inst., 1953), a study of Panajachel.

[45] Sol Tax and others, *Heritage of Conquest* (Glencoe, Ill., The Free Press, 1952), p. 290.

overspecialization. Through the combined efforts of the anthropologists who carried on this dicussion, the linguists, who also have much to contribute, and the archaeologists, who as yet have done little to unravel the complicated Central American picture from the seventh century to the sixteenth, there is every assurance that some day the life of the pre-Columbian peoples of this isthmus, from the seventh century through the twentieth, will be much better understood than at present.

CHAPTER IV

THE ISTHMUS UNITED

The Spaniards whose Audiencia de Guatemala ruled Central America from 1570 to 1821 numbered only in the low tens of thousands.[1] Of a total population of about one and a quarter million at the end of the colonial period, well over half were Indians.[2] Most of the remainder were mestizos, mulattoes, or sambos of many degrees of intermixture. By this time the Negro population important in the first century of the colony had melted into the general stream. Those of the Spaniards who remained separate, though in great numerical inferiority, completely dominated the isthmian government and economy.

Only eight centres of population retained throughout the rule of the audiencia the attributes of a Spanish *ciudad* or *city*. The first of these and capital of all until 1776 was Santiago de Guatemala. By the late seventeenth century, with a new cathedral, magnificent establishments of the religious orders, and a university chartered by the king, this metropolis shone less brilliantly only than Mexico City and Lima in all the Spanish New World. Its near-destruction by earthquake in 1773 was followed by the building of a new Guatemala City (the present one) as the seat of the audiencia, the remnant of the old being designated the *villa* or *town* of Antigua. By 1821 Guatemala City contained over 30,000 inhabitants, while Antigua had slipped to about one-fourth that number.

The second city of the realm late in the colonial period was San Salvador, nearly half the size of the capital. Quezaltenango, with probably the third largest population, was only an Indian *pueblo* or *village* officially, though its Spanish residents had a recognized *cabildo* or council. Somewhere near the size of Antigua (roughly 6,000 to 8,000 inhabitants) were four cities (Comayagua, León,

[1] This seems the inescapable conclusion to be made from the Spanish city and town population data given by Juarros, i. 15–66. Rosenblat (*Anales*, xv (1939), 375), gives a much higher figure for *blancos*.
[2] The National Constituent Assembly of Central America in 1824 used population figures for assigning quotas to each state which totalled 1,217,491, not counting Costa Rica. See Alejandro Marure, *Bosquejo histórico de las revoluciones de Centro-América* (2 vols., Paris, 1913), i. 83–84, 189. The number of delegates to the first federal Congress (variously given as 39 or 40) multiplied by 30,000 inhabitants for each delegate gives a total of 1,170,000 or 1,200,000.

57

Granada, and Cartago), two other towns (San José and Heredia in
Costa Rica), and perhaps five pueblos (Totonicapán, Comalapa,
Cobán, Chiquimulilla, and Santa Ana). Somewhat smaller (about
4,000 to 6,000 persons) were the two remaining cities (San Miguel
and Ciudad Real, now called Ciudad de las Casas, in Chiapas);
likewise six towns (Sonsonate, Choluteca, and Rivas; San Vicente,
El Salvador; Tegucigalpa, Honduras; and Alajuela, Costa Rica)
and a few dozen pueblos including probably Sololá, Ahuachapán,
Cojutepeque, Managua, and Masaya. Five pueblos used as administrative centres (Mazatenango, Chimaltenango, Chiquimula,
Escuintla, and Nicoya) were even smaller, as were Chinandega
and Matagalpa (more notable in the twentieth century).[3]

All of the audiencia's cities except the late capital were founded
before the audiencia itself was established. Of the towns, Tegucigalpa was started as a mining camp in the 1570's; San Vicente as
an indigo centre in 1635; and Heredia (1707), San José (1736),
and Alajuela (1782) as new nuclei in a suddenly expanding Costa
Rican population. Six centres lost their early colonial importance,
San Pedro Sula and Gracias languishing in the sun when new trade
routes passed them by, Realejo suffering when coastwise shipping
entered a decline, San Jorge de Olancho sinking to insignificance
when its supply of easy gold was exhausted, Nueva Segovia being
battered by isthmus-traversing buccaneers, and Trujillo being
sacked by pirates.

COLONIAL GOVERNMENT

The government of colonial isthmian cities and towns differed
only in degree. Local policy decisions were made by the *regidores* or
councilmen, who varied in number from as many as twelve in the
capital city to as few as two in the lesser towns, with some towns
(the late ones and the most decayed ones) having no *cabildo* at all.
In early days the *regidores* were sometimes chosen freely by the
property owners of the municipality; with the passing of time,
their 'election' became generally a closed affair, power remaining

[3] These population figures are adjusted from two sources in Juarros, i. 15–66,
69–74. The latter consists of ecclesiastical reports from the late eighteenth century. An example of the adjustment follows: Totonicapán is said to have had
7,000 residents (p. 46) but 13,604 parishioners (p. 72). Cobán is mentioned as
having 12,434 parishioners (p. 72), but is grouped here with Totonicapán despite a statement elsewhere (p. 29) which equates parishioners with inhabitants.
All colonial cities and towns are mentioned, but only those pueblos which were
important administratively, which seem to have held over 6,000 population, or
which grew to 10,000 by the year 1950.

in the hands of a few families who often paid the crown for the privilege of retaining office. The *regidores* were usually natives of the localities they controlled, and did have the right to correspond directly with the king on matters of local concern. Their attention was of course focused most fondly upon those items which concerned their private interests, which might or might not coincide with those of the community. Administrative officials and two *alcaldes* or magistrates, who exercised primary jurisdiction over most suits in court, were all selected by the *regidores*. The controlled Indian pueblos had the same form of government, on a simplified plan, with the Indians themselves participants but a greater amount of supervision from outside. Petitions direct to the crown for the preservation of ancient rights for particular Indian families were not unknown in the sixteenth century. But as Spaniards, mestizos, and mulattoes became important elements in the population of previously all-Indian villages, the original inhabitants gradually lost control of all municipal decisions.

Authority superior to that of all *regidores* and local alcaldes was administered by the *corregidores* (in areas where the numbers of Indians were overwhelming), the *alcaldes mayores* (in regions with a sizable Spanish population but without separate government during the conquest), and the *gobernadores* or governors (whose offices had been created before the establishment of the audiencia). The provinces of these officials, known respectively as *corregimientos, alcaldías mayores*, and *gobiernos*, differed somewhat in rank and prestige, but were not subordinate in any sense one to the other. Governors and *alcaldes mayores* were usually appointed by the king, with the lowest salary of an *alcalde mayor* in the early seventeenth century one-tenth that of the best-paid governor.[4] These men were powerful each in his own province, controlling local troops wherever they were located, making policy decisions on the provincial level, often intervening in municipal matters as well, and acting as courts of appeal from the local alcaldes. *Corregidores*, generally chosen by the president of the audiencia, were paid small official salaries, but had the same powers as the governors and were able to extract from their subjects (the Indians) the extra emoluments which their offices entailed.

Beginning in the seventeenth century, the number of *corregi-*

---

[4] Salaries are given in Antonio Vázquez de Espinosa, *Compendium and Description of the West Indies* (Charles Upson Clark, tr., Washington, Smithsonian Inst., 1942), p. 285.

mientos gradually decreased from a peak of 19 (9 in modern Guatemala, 1 in Honduras, 5 in Nicaragua, 4 in Costa Rica) to a low of 2 (Quezaltenango and Chiquimula, both in Guatemala). Totonicapán, Sololá, Chimaltenango, Sacatepéquez (capital Antigua), and Escuintla were late *alcaldías mayores* formed from earlier *corregimientos*. Ciudad Real, Suchitepéquez (its late capital Mazatenango), Verapaz (capital Cobán), Sonsonate, San Salvador, Tegucigalpa, and Nicoya were *alcaldías mayores* through most of the colonial period. Soconusco (the Pacific coast of Chiapas), Comayagua, León, and Costa Rica (its capital Cartago) were the four *gobiernos* until 1786, when a major reorganization took place. Four *intendencias* or intendancies were then formed: Chiapas (to include Ciudad Real and Soconusco), San Salvador (a considerable step-up in rank for the *alcaldía mayor*), Honduras (Comayagua plus Tegucigalpa), and Nicaragua (León, Nicoya, and two old *corregimientos*). The intendants who ruled in these new provinces, with the sub-officials they appointed, tended to supersede all older officers, even on the municipal level. Costa Rica, Sonsonate, and the nine provinces in the area of present-day Guatemala, however, remained outside the intendancy system.

The positions of highest authority in this realm were those held by the members of the audiencia, five in number through most of the colony (the *oidores* or justices of the supreme court, so to speak), and the president (chief justice) who generally presided over their sessions. The justices were each paid the same salary as the best-paid provincial governor, in the early seventeenth century, while the president of the body received two and a half times that amount.[5] The Audiencia de Guatemala, as an area, was often called a *reino* or kingdom, suggesting the real autonomy it enjoyed, though technically it was a part of the Viceroyalty of New Spain governed from Mexico. The president of the audiencia, who also through most of the period held the titles of governor and captain-general, was in a very real sense the personal representative in the *reino* of its king who had to be absent. This royal agent was not always a wise man or a good one, nor was he inevitably either foolish or evil. His decisions counted for much, regardless of which direction they took, for high-level policies were usually of his determination, as well as most of the machinery for carrying them out. There were but three checks on his authority: the audiencia, highest court of appeal in judicial matters short of Spain itself and a power in ad-

[5] Vázquez de Espinosa, pp. 282, 285.

ministration (the audiencia sometimes argued successfully with its own president, though its victories were usually slow ones); the municipal *cabildos*, especially that of the capital, with the privilege of making their own complaints to the king; and the near certainty (until the eighteenth century) that at the termination of the president's employ an open hearing would be conducted regarding the manner in which he had carried out his duties. All the personnel of the audiencia, both regular and presiding, were normally natives of Spain. For better or for worse, their actions were those of the royal hand in Central America.

The first six presidents of the Audiencia de Guatemala, from 1570 to 1611, were appointed by King Philip II. These were true civil servants well educated in the law, with considerable judicial experience in the New World before coming to Central America. The appointees of Philip III and IV, holding the office from 1611 to 1668, were often men direct from Spain whose education mattered less to those whose choices they were than their standing at court. The first of these, who remained in Santiago for sixteen years, was actually an illiterate though he was designated a count during his residence on the isthmus. The sacking of Granada by English freebooters in 1665 and 1670, followed by greater depredations and a pirate crossing of the broader isthmus in the 1680's, encouraged from this point onwards the appointment of military men to the position, though both of the earlier types appeared from time to time. The replacement of the Habsburg line of Philip II by the Spanish Bourbons made little difference at first. After British government influence became strong along the Caribbean coast in the mid-eighteenth century, however, all the appointees (beginning in 1752) were men of considerable rank in the Spanish army or navy. Real warfare took place with the British during the term of office of Matías de Gálvez (1779–83). Later, officers past the usual military age, such as José Domás y Valle (1794–1801) who *retired* at the age of 100, were considered adequate to hold the land.

Some parts of the isthmus were in truth never occupied by the Spaniards. The last Spanish conquest in what is now Central America was that of the lowlands of the Petén, accomplished in 1697 by an expedition from Yucatan, but placed under the jurisdiction of the Audiencia de Guatemala. The Petén remained a frontier district uninhabited by Spaniards outside a fort built in old Tayasal. East of Tayasal, along the Caribbean coast, there appeared a few English settlers beginning in the 1630's. By the end of that century the English colony of Belize, nucleus of the area now called British Honduras, was exporting sizable quantities of logwood for use in the production of dyes. Negro slaves, and after a time Negro freemen, were prominent in the population of Belize.

Other Negroes in the same decades were escaping from the West Indies to freedom in eastern Honduras and Nicaragua, where they mixed freely with the Indians to form the Miskito peoples of the coast. West Indian buccaneers first, and the British government later, made overtures to these people, whose lands and hinterlands were called Taguzgalpa (in Honduras) and Tologalpa (in Nicaragua) by the Spaniards but had not been taken by them. The British situated themselves strategically in these areas in the 1740's, and took the Bay Islands of Honduras as well. British ambition in the region finally led to an unsuccessful attempt in 1780 to sever the Spanish hold on the isthmus at Lake Nicaragua. The Treaty of Versailles (1783) and subsequent Convention of London between Great Britain and Spain (1786) called for complete British evacuation of the Bay Islands and Mosquitia, but stipulated that British exploitation of the natural resources of a limited area around Belize might continue under Spanish sovereignty. A brief British repossession of the Bay Islands in 1796 brought a new population element—the so-called Black Caribs, an Indian–Negro mixture, transported thither from St. Vincent island in the Windwards—which soon became important on the Caribbean coasts of Honduras and Guatemala.

The people who lived in Central America were accordingly a most varied lot. In every part of the isthmus, their greatest freedom lay in comparative remoteness from control. The arm of the law could be strong in the Spanish-held portions, but it was almost invariably slow. There were many situations where man took advantage of man—the Indian was forced to labour, the mestizo and mulatto compelled to demean himself, the *criollo* or creole (white man born on the isthmus) often obliged to grant unearned privileges to the newcomer from Spain. Yet injustice did not breed mutiny during the long colonial period. Most inhabitants who had heard of the monarch across the ocean would probably have said, with one of the early conquerors, 'We all bow down . . . to our King and Lord, and place our lives and fortunes, whatever may happen, at the service of His Majesty.'[6] They could say this, after the first generation or two, knowing that the real state of their

[6] Díaz del Castillo (1908–16), v. 272.

affairs lay very much in their own hands and those of their more immediate neighbours.

Almost every inhabitant of colonial Central America was in one way or another a farmer. In this respect, the isthmus had not changed since before the Spanish conquest. The greatest crop of all, as for many centuries past, was maize, now accepted as the first food by Indian, Negro, and Spaniard. The crop of second widest distribution was probably the kidney bean, another indigenous standby accepted by the immigrant. Likewise of importance, though grown only in the cooler altitudes, was wheat, which the newcomers had brought with them. Sugar from cane of the warmer regions, its production impeded by the lack of equipment, slowly took the place of honey, which was early gathered in large quantities from the forests and produced by colonies of kept bees. Rice was eventually cultivated in quantity along the Pacific coast from Escuintla to Sonsonate and transported thence to the cities. Several other grains were raised, and a variety of vegetables, both native and imported (Spanish *garbanzos* or chickpeas were popular, for example), became the specialities of districts which catered to urban markets.

The isthmus, as always, abounded in fruits, but now more than ever before with European varieties added to pre-conquest favourites. Of the latter, the *jocote* was perhaps the best liked by the Spaniards, but many others were relished as well. Somehow bananas of several types appeared very early; the manner of their distribution is not at all clear, but they were cousins to the plantains which were probably already on hand. The apples and quinces mentioned by Bernal Díaz became plentiful in highland Guatemala; peach and other trees made their appearance; oranges and limes became common along the Pacific from Guatemala to Nicaragua.

Many estates in every province were dedicated to stock-raising. Cattle were pastured in wide areas, both the beef and the hides being valued. Pork was available from the swine raised in many parts. Horses and mules, important respectively for the transportation of man and his burdens, were bred and used in all areas where Spaniards lived. Sheep were also introduced in the cooler areas, where the meat provided variety and the wool made some impact upon the textile industry. There was perhaps no greater change in

Central America's mode of life from pre-conquest to colonial days than this first appearance on the scene of domesticated animals larger than the turkey. The number of poultry too was augmented with the importation and wide raising of chickens.

Cotton remained important as a non-food crop in several of the provinces. Though other textiles were now available, the demand for cotton clothing probably increased as the less advanced Indian tribes turned to styles of European dress. Henequen fibre was also produced from Honduras to Costa Rica. Enough tobacco was raised to satisfy local demand. Many roots and herbs were sought as medicinals, with one root, sarsaparilla, exported in quantity from Trujillo while that city lasted. Tree gums and resins were also employed, with pine pitch and tar a major export from Realejo to Peru. Balsam, mistakenly called balsam of Peru, went to Europe from Sonsonate.[7]

Beginning with the construction of Pedro de Alvarado's fleet on the Pacific, Central America had good sea connexions with North and South America. During the first century or so of audiencia government, these connexions were used for a notable exportation of cacao. This was the beginning of a world trade in cacao beans which has lasted ever since. Cacao was grown all along the Pacific coast of Central America, overland routes to Mexico providing an outlet for that of Soconusco and Suchitepéquez, Sonsonate serving as collection point for the very rich crop from Escuintla to San Salvador, and Realejo handling the more slowly developed business from Nicaragua. Good crops of cacao were also grown in Chiquimula, and in later times exports went out from the Caribbean coast. The great early trade in Central American cacaos went to Mexico, for only slowly did the taste for chocolate grow in Spain and the rest of Europe. Sonsonate was in those days the second largest community in Central America, entirely owing to her association with this business. In the seventeenth century cheaper beans from Ecuador began to drive out the competition in Mexico, while more favourably situated Venezuela supplied most of the European market. Cacao continued to be grown widely on the isthmus, but by the nineteenth century was also being imported from Ecuador.

The *jiquilite* plant from which *añil* or indigo dye was extracted,

[7] The colonial agricultural products mentioned here are those listed with greatest frequency by Vázquez de Espinosa, pp. 203–67, and Juarros, i. 15–66. Both are province-by-province accounts, Vázquez written in the early seventeenth century, Juarros in the early nineteenth.

also known in the isthmus before the Spanish conquest, provided Central America's second great export. Though it was grown quite widely in the earlier years of the colony, particularly in warm areas along the Pacific, it eventually became the speciality of the province of San Salvador (so much so that it was said the cultivation of other products of first necessity in San Salvador was sometimes neglected).[8] San Vicente was an 'indigo town', planned for Spaniards, in much the same sense as Sonsonate was 'cacao town'. Central American indigo was sold early to Mexico and Peru; later the principal buyers were Spain and Europe. The market was best in the mid-eighteenth century, after which the precariousness of Spanish commerce during the several wars allowed the British to enter the trade. Central American production had declined drastically by the end of the century, long before artificial dyes had replaced the natural. Annato dye from the fruit of the *achiote* tree, used in foodstuffs as well as textiles, made its way in early colonial years from Central America to distant China.

The appearance of gold in the streams, which so excited the Spaniards when they were new in the country, proved no indication of great mineral wealth on the isthmus. Silver was discovered a few decades later at several places in what became the *alcaldía mayor* of Tegucigalpa, but the amounts transported to Spain were trifling compared to those from Peru and Mexico. The industry lagged as the centuries went by, though there was enough of both silver and gold to allow the minting of coins in the capital after 1733. Such mining as existed under the Spaniards was a new occupation for the isthmus, as were also extensive shipbuilding operations set up at Realejo and Nicoya. Crown restrictions on intercolonial trade eventually made the shipbuilding business too an unprofitable one.

A commercial step backward was taken when Central America itself ceased to be used as a land bridge between North and South America. With the conquest, gold ornaments from Panama no longer made their appearance, nor did copper bells from Mexico, as Indian trade contacts were broken and old habits disappeared. Central American manufactures increased, however, as artisans of every race fashioned items of silver, wood, and stone and worked with iron and glazed tiles, both quite new on the isthmus. Stone continued in use for religious edifices and public structures, while silver was now employed in the furnishings. Wood, stone, iron, and

[8] Juarros, i. 24.

tiles were all utilized to make the homes of the wealthy more attractive. In the meantime, most of the people were satisfied with pre-
conquest living accommodation. The making of their jars, mats,
and baskets still occupied the attention of many.

Altogether, save for cacao and indigo, this was a static economy.
These two crops brought fortunes to some families but no better
living to most. Those Spaniards who owned the farms usually led
a comfortable existence, bothered only by the high prices on imported goods due to government levies and devious means of transportation. Their Negro slaves, wherever they lived, were less fortu-
nate. So were the masses of Indians who were either held in encomienda (until that institution died out after the first century or
so) or were 'free', but as free men had still to pay tributes and to
obey orders for compulsory labour when their services were needed.
Most persons of mixed blood, concentrated in the Spanish cities
and towns, performed their labours as servants or artisans for a
pittance. The crown, less enamoured of this *reino* than those which
produced more mineral wealth, may be partly blamed for conditions. In 1797 it could still be said, 'The roads are impassable, the
great rivers are crossed with danger, and in the uninhabited places
travellers are exposed to destruction by outlaws and wild beasts.'[9]
But Matías de Córdova, the friar who penned those lines, believed
that the real trouble lay in the unwillingness of the controlling
class to share its prosperity with the mass of the population. 'Each
Indian, Negro, mulatto, mestizo, and even the poor Spaniard', he
said, 'needs nothing more than his woman. She prepares him the
corn which he sows, and both inhabit a contemptible hut, denied
all civility, without requiring another person to clothe or sustain
them'.[10] Give this vast majority of the population a chance to respect itself, Córdova argued, and its requirements would make the
whole *reino* prosperous. His words constituted a lesson the significance of which Central America has not yet grasped.

COLONIAL LEARNING

Matías de Córdova won a prize with his remarks. They were
part of an essay he prepared for a contest; his idea was actually
suggested by the contest sponsors. The sponsors were the intellectual community of the Guatemalan capital, one of the most dis-

[9] 'Utilidades de que todos los indios y ladinos se vistan y calcen a la española y
medios de conseguirlo sin violencia, coacción, ni mandato', *Anales*, xiv (1937),
211–22, p. 213.
[10] Ibid.

tinguished of the late eighteenth century in all the Americas. All through the colonial period, while most of Central America's inhabitants could not read or write, some men in each of the cities maintained some kind of contact with European learning. In the capital, by the eighteenth century, the number of residents with university degrees was impressive.

The first Roman Catholic churchmen to come to Central America were all men of education. From the earliest years many of those who lived in Guatemala dedicated themselves to the study of the native tongues. Before long they were composing grammars of the dialects they knew best and simple catechisms for those who knew no Spanish. New alphabet characters were invented so that strange sounds might be expressed. A catechism in the Cakchiquel dialect was published in Mexico as early as 1556. Though such studies after the first century or so became rarer, a lengthy grammar in Cakchiquel, Quiché, and Zutuhil was printed in Santiago de Guatemala as late as 1753.[11]

Because the first churchmen brought their Latin with them, instruction in European courses of study was slower to develop. The Dominicans were first in the field (1556) when they established a chair of theology in Santiago and a course in the arts in Ciudad Real for the training of young Dominican friars. Other monastic orders followed suit during the next century and a half at sundry times and places. Seminaries for secular priests were established (the first in 1601) in the four cities which boasted cathedrals and bishops (Santiago, Ciudad Real, Comayagua, and León). In Santiago, classes open to laymen as well as priests were begun by the Jesuits in 1615. The Dominicans were then allowed to confer degrees in theology and the arts for a few years in the 1620's. The bishop conferred the same degrees upon graduates from the Jesuit college, 1640 to 1676. In 1681, the University of San Carlos was founded in Santiago with full courses in the arts, theology, civil law, canon law, and medicine. From its inception through 1821, this university granted 2,415 degrees of which 206 were doctorates.[12] Very late in the colonial period (1812) the episcopal seminary in León became the only other degree-conferring institution in this audiencia.

The chief contribution to knowledge made by isthmian resi-

[11] Ildefonso José Flores, *Arte de la lengua metropolitana del reyno Cakchiquel, o Guatemalico.*

[12] John Tate Lanning, *The University in the Kingdom of Guatemala* (Ithaca, N.Y., Cornell U.P., 1955), pp. 203–4.

dents during these two centuries and a half lay in the field of history. Here Bernal Díaz del Castillo (working from the 1550's into the 1570's) wrote his inimitable account of the conquest of Mexico by Cortés and his band and the subsequent march to Honduras. Here Antonio de Remesal, Dominican friar from Spain, began in 1615 a history of his order in Central America which ranks as a prime source for material on the life of Bartolomé de las Casas. Layman Francisco Antonio de Fuentes y Guzmán, in the 1680's and 1690's, wrote a detailed historical and geographical account of the territory included in today's Guatemala, using many references which have since been lost. A lengthy account of Franciscan work in Central America, written by Francisco Vázquez, was the first history to be published in Santiago, 1714–17. Immediately afterwards Francisco Ximénez, preacher-philologist-naturalist-historian extraordinary, wrote a Dominican history, most vigorous of the colonial productions.[13] Finally, the secular padre Domingo Juarros, in 1808–18, published comprehensive treatises on the history and geography of the entire audiencia, the first to be translated into a foreign language.[14]

In the last few generations before independence, intellectual life in the capital was especially strong. It had long since outgrown the bounds of the monastery halls and now affected much of the higher society. Despite physical and financial difficulties brought on by the ruin of the old capital in 1773, the university continued in business. An average of more than thirty degrees annually was granted after 1790; an occasional year's total reached over sixty.[15] A new plan of study, emphasizing eighteenth-century trends of European thought, came into vogue after 1782. José Antonio Goicoechea, a Franciscan from Cartago who presented the plan, was noted for his interest in experimental physics. José Felipe Flores of Chiapas, a contemporary, won such distinction in the field of medicine that he was called upon eventually for counsel to the king. Guatemala City was saved from a smallpox epidemic in 1804 when Narciso Esparragosa y Gallardo from Venezuela, a pupil of Flores

[13] The best originals of these works are reproduced in the series of the Guatemalan Sociedad de Geografía e Historia known as *Biblioteca 'Goathemala'*. Díaz del Castillo is vols. x–xi (1933–4); Remesal vols. iv–v (1932); Fuentes y Guzmán vols. vi–viii (1932–3); Vázquez vols. xiv–xvii (1937–44); Ximénez vols. i–iii (1929–31).

[14] J. Baily, tr., *A Statistical and Commercial History of the Kingdom of Guatemala, in Spanish America* (London, 1823). This is only a part of Juarros' *Compendio*, the 1936 edition of which is cited in ch. iii, n. 21, p. 47.

[15] Lanning, p. 201.

and noted surgeon and obstetrician in his own right, vaccinated thousands of persons with the new serum for the first time available. Guatemala opened a natural-history museum in 1796. But most significant were the organization of a Real Sociedad Económica de Amigos del País (1796–9 and again after 1811) which provided a forum for lively discussion of a wide variety of topics, and the establishment of a regular newspaper. The *Gazeta de Guatemala* (1794–1816; an earlier effort had been made in 1729–31) often took the critical approach to isthmian affairs, with an attitude clearly progressive.[16]

COLONIAL ART

Great changes took place in the realm of the arts under the colony. On the south-eastern end of the isthmus, high city culture appeared for the first time. On the north-western end, as the tastes of the Spanish aristocracy superseded those of the native hierarchies, one worthy tradition took the place of another. The ball game was no longer played; horse showmanship and the bull-fight were excitements of the new society. Native dances were forgotten, while European performances were accepted (such as that depicting the struggle of Christians and Moors for the mastery of Spain; in Guatemala one of these was composed to dramatize the struggle of Alvarado and the Quiché). Native theatre gradually disappeared, with nothing to take its place but fireworks and a rare Spanish comedy. Religious pomp and ceremony continued, with the Spanish Catholic tradition prevailing in the cities but a mixture of Catholic and pagan common in the countryside. The architectural grandeur of such centres as Cahyup and Chuitinamit was quite completely neglected, but in every Spanish part of the isthmus great churches were built, and some fine homes and public structures erected.

The architecture employed in the elegant edifices of the capital was distinct in some qualities from that of Spain, Peru, or Mexico.[17] The Spanish traditions in building from the sixteenth to the nineteenth century may nevertheless be followed in a study of isthmian constructions.[18] Colonial sculpture, such as the statues of Christ

[16] Copies of this *Gazeta* for 1729–31 and 1797–1816 are extant in Guatemala. Concerning the years 1794–6, see David Vela, *Literatura guatemalteca* (2 vols., 1944–8), i. 216–20.
[17] Sidney David Markman, 'The Architecture of Colonial Antigua, Guatemala, 1543–1773', *Archaeology*, iv (1951), 204–12.
[18] See J. Antonio Villacorta C., *Historia de la capitanía general de Guatemala* (Guatemala, 1942), pp. 306–34.

carved by Quirio Cataño, Portuguese resident of the capital in the late sixteenth century, was superior in every respect to that from just before the conquest. Designs in silver, iron, and tiles were of course entirely new to the isthmus. In music and painting, there were also notable advances—or so it seems in the absence of pre-conquest evidence to the contrary. Popular music was influenced, no one can say how rapidly, by the advent of the guitar, the harp, and the violin; though the old music was remembered wherever Indian customs prevailed. In the Spanish community, church organs and choirs were heard as early as the sixteenth century, string concerts somewhat later. The capital had a full orchestra by the end of the period. Outstanding artists painted scenes from the lives of Christ or the saints, several of which may still be viewed. The art of engraving was carried to a notable state of perfection by Pedro Garci-Aguirre (master of the mint) and his several disciples in the new Guatemala City.

Briefly in the sixteenth century Central America showed promise of producing a truly distinctive literature. When Bernal Díaz was an old man, he could truthfully say that many sons of Indian chieftains knew how to read and write. During the short time that this was true—before the padres had given up their fight to save the Indian from degradation—two notable works were written, others minor which are known, and a number more which have since been lost.[19] The modern *Popol Vuh* is a piece of real literary merit.[20] The *Annals of the Cakchiquels*, less interesting for its style, is a remarkable presentation of the immediate pre-conquest picture among the Cakchiquel people, the conquest itself as seen through the eyes of the conquered, and the gradual change-over to colonial ways of life in the village of Sololá where the manuscript was composed. One wonders what further word compositions might have been produced if the sons of the sons of the chieftains, like their fathers before them, had been encouraged to read and write.

The Spanish community, particularly after the establishment of the first press in the capital in 1660, was flooded with a host of printed sermons of isthmian authorship, and, as time went by, served some of its own needs for elementary grammars, arithmetics, catechisms, and almanacs. No one during the colonial period tried

[19] See ch. iii, n. 14, p. 41.
[20] A discussion of its pre-Columbian content was given in ch. iii; see above, p. 42.

his hand at prose fiction, but in keeping with Spanish tradition quite a number of persons turned to poetry. The most famed of these, Rafael Landívar (1731–93), was born in Santiago, became a Jesuit priest and teacher, did missionary work in Mexico (1750–60), and returned to Guatemala, only to be expelled in 1767 along with the rest of his order from all the Spanish dominions. *Rusticatio Mexicana*, the long poem in Latin on which his fame rests, was written in Bologna, Italy, and published in 1782. It speaks majestically of the everyday features of New Spain—the lakes, the valleys, the fruits of the field, the minerals, the cattle, the forests, the wild animals, the amusements of the people. The opening dedication, itself thirty-four verses in length, is to Guatemala, particularly to Santiago de Guatemala, which at the time of writing had just suffered its tremendous destruction by earthquake.[21]

Two other poets of the late colonial period are worthy of mention. Matías de Córdova (1768–1828), composer of the prize-winning essay, was a Dominican friar from Tapachula, Chiapas, who moved to Guatemala City, then to Madrid, and finally back to Chiapas. Somewhere along the way he wrote *La tentativa del león y el éxito de su empresa*, a moral tale which (though every detail of its theme seems to have been taken from a fable written by a Frenchman, Louis François Jauffret) is so well devised that one must admire its immediate creator. The young lion of the story decides to seek out a man, curious to see what manner of being it is which his mother describes as the controller of the world. He meets first an ox, then a horse, then a dog, conversing with each under the original impression that this creature might be the man for which he is searching. He finally meets a real man, only to be trapped by him into captivity. The poem ends as the young lion admits the supremacy of *inteligencia*, but is then set loose with a brief lecture on the even higher merit of *la clemencia*.[22] Simón Bergaño y Villegas (1781–1829) was a cripple, born in Escuintla of humble parentage, who lived for some time in Mexico, but was editor of the *Gazeta de Guatemala* from 1804 to 1807 and died in Cuba after forced exile caused by his own rashness in literary expression. Bergaño was no traditionalist, but an intellectual enthusiast for a new human society on the isthmus. His poems often expressed bitterness toward a

[21] A facsimile of the 1782 edition was published in Guatemala, 1950, with the same title, and an introduction by José Mata Gavidia.

[22] Text of the poem, *Anales*, viii (1931), 7–26. In ibid. pp. 62–67 (copied from *Electra*, Epoca 2, no. 4, 1920), Adrián Recinos under the title of the poem discusses the various appearances of its theme.

life which had mistreated him; they spoke also with contrasting excitement and surprising freedom of his lively interest in books and women. Only the new Guatemala, toward the end of the colonial period, could produce such a man as Bergaño, and even the new (or what was left of the old) could not endure his daring for long.[23]

COLONIAL RELIGION

The man responsible for Bergaño's exile was the archbishop of Guatemala, chief guardian of the morals of the entire audiencia. The Roman Catholic faith which he represented was throughout the colonial period the only Christian doctrine tolerated in Central America. There was paganism also, the slowly diminishing remnant of the pre-conquest religions, which from the mid-sixteenth century all the way through the eighteenth remained the object of attack by persuasion rather than by violence. The vigour of Catholicism in colonial Central America is attested by this prolonged missionary effort as well as by the remarkable church buildings which were erected in so many populated places.

Even well into the nineteenth century the ecclesiastical organization of the isthmus was as significant to its inhabitants as the political structure. The hierarchy of the church was more simple than that of the state, if the secular arm alone is considered, and correspondingly more effective in its operations. In 1570 there were five episcopal provinces, later reduced to four: Nicaragua (founded 1531, including Costa Rica); Guatemala (from 1534, including today's El Salvador); Chiapas (from 1538); Honduras (established in Trujillo in 1539, its seat transferred to Comayagua in 1561); and Verapaz (organized in 1559, its seat in Cobán, but annexed to Guatemala in 1607). Toward the end of the eighteenth century Nicaragua reported a total of 88 churches; Chiapas had 102; Honduras 145; and Guatemala 424, serving parishioners of more than a dozen languages.[24] The cathedral in Santiago became in 1743 the capital of the archbishopric of Guatemala covering the territory of the entire audiencia. Pedro Cortés y Larraz, third of the eight archbishops who presided until 1821, fought hard to prevent removal of the capital to the new site after the earthquake of 1773, excommunicating by his own edict all those (including the audien-

---

[23] Some of Bergaño's poems are given in Ramón A. Salazar, *Historia del desenvolvimiento intelectual de Guatemala* (Guatemala, 1897), pp. 206–23; reprinted in ibid. (3 vols., Guatemala, 1951), ii. 207–25.
[24] Juarros, i. 69–74.

cia and most of the people) who recognized the new order of the day.

Much of the work of the church was done by the several religious orders. The first of these to establish houses—Dominicans, Mercedarians, and Franciscans—remained dominant throughout the period, doing most of the work of teaching and baptizing the unlettered tribes. The Dominicans, with provincial headquarters in Santiago, were very active in the *corregimientos* to the west, took special pride in their peaceful conversion of Verapaz, and tried without success in the sixteenth and seventeenth centuries to repeat this performance with the less civilized peoples of the Petén. The Franciscans, with two provinces on the isthmus (centred at Santiago and León), were seen in every part but Verapaz and the Petén. The paganism of Taguzgalpa, Tologalpa, and the Talamanca of Costa Rica challenged many a valiant Franciscan in the seventeenth and eighteenth centuries, including even such a noted person in the intellectual community as Goicoechea. This work was managed after 1685 by the Recollects, Franciscan reformers, who established residence in Santiago and counted among their number Antonio Margil de Jesús (1657–1726), a Mexican much admired for his virtues and energetic missionary labours. The Mercedarians, a group of Spanish origin whose provincial headquarters in Santiago were the first of the order in the New World, were also spread through the isthmus though in smaller numbers. The Jesuits, from their arrival in 1582 until their expulsion in 1767, had but one house, including the college before mentioned, in Santiago. Restricted also to the capital were the Augustinians and the unofficial congregation of St. Philip Neri, the sixteenth-century saint of Italy. Brothers of the order of San Juan de Dios, dedicated to medical work since their sixteenth-century foundation in Spain, operated hospitals in the capital and five other urban centres.

Good works were performed not only by these groups of men but also by the nuns in a number of convents (most of them in the capital), who provided some education for members of their own sex. A Franciscan tertiary order (for laymen) also developed, and a host of *cofradías* or social brotherhoods, in Spanish city and Indian pueblo alike. The man who more than any other seems to have exemplified colonial isthmian ideas of saintliness was a humble Franciscan tertiary, Pedro de San José de Bethancourt, who came to the capital from the Canary Islands in 1651 and stayed until his death in 1667 aiding the poor, caring for the sick, and serving generally as an agent for miracles in the lives of others.[25] Rodrigo de Arias Maldonado, Marqués de Talamanca (1637–1716, native of Spain, and as a young man governor of Costa Rica, where he won his title), had his life touched by that of Bethancourt in 1666 at a critical moment brought on by an amorous escapade, and took a vow to carry on the charitable work his own benefactor had started. From his activities came a new order of friars, the Bethlehemites or Compañía de Belén, recognized fully by the Pope in 1710, whose first house was in Santiago but whose work spread rapidly to Peru and Mexico. The large establishment of this order in the new Guatemala City served as hospital, public school, and—as events worked out—meeting-place late in the colonial period of persons who were disaffected with the colonial régime.

The religion of the masses, though it is difficult to assess, rested probably (as in most times and places) well below the level set by Bethancourt or by Fray Rodrigo after his conversion. Archbishop Cortés y Larraz, after visits to parts of his own diocese in 1768–70, reported a lack of attention to church requirements and expectations:

... The women very frequently leave their husbands; live in concubinage with others; they become pregnant, but when the fancy strikes them, return to their husbands and former children; they return without shame; and the husbands admit them with all serenity. . . . They are careless in calling for the administration of sacraments to the sick, and . . . for this reason some have died without receiving them. . . . There is no class for the training of the children. . . .[26]

Still, religious devotion of a sort must have been present in those thousands of persons who walked annually from many parts of the audiencia to Esquipulas, Guatemala, to worship in the presence of Quirio Cataño's most renowned image of Christ. There were so many that the image was eventually (1758) afforded sumptuous housing. Some elements in the church which encouraged such devotion never ceased to emphasize morality. The very last president of the audiencia (Carlos de Urrutia y Montoya, 1818–21) even tried to legislate puritanism by issuing edicts against swear-

[25] The First Central American Congress for the Beatification and Canonization of Bethancourt was held under ecclesiastical auspices in Antigua, 14–16 Dec. 1960. José García de la Concepción, *Historia belemítica* (Guatemala, 1956) is the second edition of a work published in Seville with that purpose in mind in 1723.
[26] *Colección de documentos importantes relativos a la república de El Salvador* (San Salvador, 1921), pp. 293, 278.

ing, desecrating the Sabbath, the singing of indecent songs, and mixed dancing behind closed doors.[27]

Simón Bergaño, no puritan himself, complained of the sermons of his day. Too many of them, he said, were without method or unction or but vain repetitions of hell-fire warnings.[28] Bergaño won trouble for himself by such statements, not only with the archbishop but also with the Inquisition, whose total influence in colonial Guatemala had been rather slight. Bergaño's comment seems today, however, to have a double significance: (1) It makes clear that the church of his time, whatever its efficacy, had not quit its role of preaching. (2) If Bergaño was sincere, there was at least one man in intellectual society who cared what the church was thinking.

FROM INDEPENDENCE TO DISUNION

The beginning of the end of the Spanish colonial régime in Central America came in November 1796 when José Domás y Valle, aged ninety-six, the thirty-third president of the Audiencia de Guatemala, presided over the first public session of the Sociedad Económica de Amigos del País. This society, though it was temporarily suspended just three years later, gave the educated class of the isthmus its first effective medium in 300 years for discussion of a new régime which might lead Central America to some realization of the potentials that lay within her. The *Gazeta de Guatemala* served much the same purpose when the society was suspended. The talk was not of political independence, to be sure. But it embodied the kind of planning and public debate which would be necessary when self-rule did arrive.

Antonio González Mollinedo y Saravia, next to occupy the presidency (1801–11), was in office when news came from Spain (August 1808) of the invasion of the mother country by Napoleonic armies; when oaths of loyalty were taken (January 1809) to the Spanish junta resisting Bonaparte's domination; when the first isthmian delegate departed (November 1810) to attend the anti-Bonaparte Cortes of Spain; and when new tidings arrived from Mexico (January 1811) of the insurrection for independence led by Miguel Hidalgo y Costilla. The Guatemalan city council proposed that Mollinedo y Saravia should attempt to mediate the Mexican dispute. But Mollinedo, an army man, was ordered to

[27] Ramón A. Salazar, *Historia de veintiún años* (Guatemala, 1928), p. 202.
[28] Ibid. p. 93.

Mexico to suppress the rebellion and lost his life there when he was caught by the rebels.

José de Bustamante y Guerra, the next president in Guatemala (1811–18), had to deal with the first signs of rebellion on the isthmus. In his strong dedication to Bourbon autocracy, which from 1809 through 1813 disappeared save in spirit even on the Spanish peninsula, Bustamante was seconded by Ramón Casaus y Torres, who came in 1811 as the last of Central America's colonial archbishops. Insurrections against established authority arose in San Salvador (November 1811), where a segment of the populace was demanding a separate bishopric; in Granada (December 1811), where a wealthy group of citizens resented the political dominance of León; and again in San Salvador (January 1814), inspired now by the Mexican independence proclamations of José María Morelos. In Guatemala City (December 1813) a conspiracy hatched in and around the establishment of the Bethlehemites was discovered before it could come to fruition. The majority of the Spanish community in the capital were opposed to these disorders but enthusiastic about the Constitution of 1812 and other liberal measures by the Cortes in Spain, in the drafting of which isthmian delegates participated. For a time after resumption of Bourbon rule on the peninsula in 1814 the pace of events slowed while the monarch, and Bustamante and Casaus on the isthmus, held tight control. Even the *Gazeta* ceased its labours in 1816. Nevertheless Carlos de Urrutia y Montoya, the elderly and puritanical successor to Bustamante, was the last person designated by royalty to authority over the audiencia.

Central American independence came after a return to liberalism in Spain. News arrived in April 1820 of the revolution which had brought the peninsula back to constitutionality. Beginning from 24 July the isthmus had a newspaper again, *El Editor Constitucional* managed by physician Pedro Molina, the very first number of which delineated the words *liberal* and *servil* as designations for two attitudes found in isthmian society and sought to associate itself with the former. Molina's early arguments were for such causes as freedom of trade and greater representation of the Americas in the Spanish Cortes, but within a year he had moved to the thesis that America was entitled to freedom. José Cecilio del Valle, trained in the law, published *El Amigo de la Patria* starting on 16 October 1820, which stopped short of recommending a break with the crown but engaged in considerable profundity of argument for other liberal themes of the day.[29] On 10 March 1821 Urrutia y Montoya (ostensibly for reasons of health) delegated his authority over the audiencia to Gabino Gainza, army inspector from Spain. When news arrived from Mexico on 10 April of Agustín Iturbide's proclamation of independence, Gainza urged unswerving loyalty to Spain. But as Iturbide's power grew and his proclamation was seconded by authorities in Oaxaca and Tehuantepec, the Spanish communities in Chiapas decided (under the influence of Matías de Córdova in late August and early September) to subscribe to that movement. The post from Chiapas reached Guatemala City on 14 September. Gainza called a public meeting the next morning of the chief political and ecclesiastical officers in the city. Molina and friends brought a crowd to hear the speeches and to raise a cry for independence. Valle and many others spoke in favour of freedom, while archbishop Casaus and a few others were opposed. Gainza proclaimed provisional independence the next day with himself at the head of the Government, and with a call for a congress representative of the several provinces which would make the final decisions. The document which he used was composed by José del Valle, and dated 15 September.

The first Central American assembly met nearly two years later. Delay was caused by indecision as to where the future of Central America lay. As the tidings of independence spread throughout the isthmus, each city responded with its own resolutions phrased each in its separate way. Some favoured union with Mexico to preserve the nominal colonial tie; others were adamantly against such a connexion; several were opposed to Guatemalan domination; some were more concerned with rivals in their own or adjacent provinces. When Iturbide sent an army, sentiment in Guatemala City and many other communities swung towards union with Mexico. San Salvador resisted Mexican domination, even sending an agent to Washington, but from 21 February 1822 until 29 March 1823 no independent action was taken in Guatemala City. Then Vicente Filísola, the Mexican general in charge, hearing of the abdication of Iturbide and the break-up of his empire, called for the meeting of the Central American congress promised in the first declaration of independence. By this time the other cities of the isthmus, save those of Chiapas which continued to adhere to Mexico, were ready

[29] For the text of Molina's paper and many articles from Valle's, see *Escritos del Doctor Pedro Molina* (3 vols., Guatemala, 1954) and José del Valle and Jorge del Valle Matheu, eds., *Obras de José Cecilio del Valle* (2 vols., Guatemala, 1929-30), ii.

to co-operate with Guatemala. Since Gainza had left for Mexico, Central America was now in real possession of her own destiny without having had to resort to violence to effect separation from either Spain or Mexico.

The National Constituent Assembly met from 24 June 1823 until 23 January 1825. A second declaration of independence was issued on 1 July 1823, confirming the first and using the name *Provincias Unidas del Centro de América* for that of the country. The number of provinces or states was five—Guatemala, which had been created in 1812 to include the old *corregimientos* of Quezaltenango and Chiquimula, the district of the Petén, and the *alcaldías mayores* Totonicapán, Sololá, Chimaltenango, Sacatepéquez, Escuintla, Suchitepéquez, and Verapaz; San Salvador, made up of the intendancy of San Salvador plus the *alcaldía mayor* of Sonsonate; Honduras, the same area as the intendancy; Nicaragua, likewise at first the intendancy intact; and Costa Rica, the old *gobierno* plus (in 1825) Nicoya or Guanacaste, disaffected from Nicaragua.

The chief task of the National Assembly was the writing of a constitution. This document, when it was completed on 22 November 1824, said (Article 10): 'Each one of the states . . . is free and independent in its government and interior administration'. It also said (Article 69) that the federal Congress would have the right to legislate in matters of common interest. The federal Congress was given the privilege of choosing taxes for the support of the federal government but the states were expected to make contributions to cover any federal deficit. Members of the Congress would represent the states in numbers proportional to their populations. The president, the Senate (a small body to act as a brake on the Congress), and the supreme court were to be chosen by the citizens at large through a three-step electoral process. People were to be people in the new régime, special rights of nobility and clergy being abolished along with the institution of slavery. There were several guarantees of civil rights, though public worship was restricted to adherents of the Roman Catholic faith. The question of the location of the permanent capital was left for later decision.[30]

The first president of Central America (1825–9), elected by Congress after a questionable decision that José del Valle lacked one electoral vote of a majority, was Manuel José Arce, who had

[30] Text of the constitution, Miguel Angel Gallardo, comp., *Cuatro constituciones federales de Centro América y las constituciones políticas de El Salvador* (San Salvador, 1945), pp. 1–20.

figured prominently in the first insurrection against Spanish rule and led the fight of San Salvador against the Mexicans. Arce was at first supported by persons of diverse political viewpoints but was soon considered a disappointment by the more liberal faction. Quarrels arose over interventions by Arce in the affairs of the states of Guatemala and Honduras. Sporadic civil warfare raged for two years (1827–9) until Arce's régime collapsed and Francisco Morazán, a young military genius of liberal convictions from Honduras, stood triumphant in Guatemala City. Arce and his chief supporters were expatriated; so, after an argument, were archbishop Casaus and a large number of friars. The church was too closely identified with the Spanish colonial régime to wriggle its way through the revolution unscathed.

Morazán was elected president in 1830, with Valle running a close second. Liberalism and anti-clericalism now had their day in Central America as state and federal governments passed a mass of new legislation. The monastic orders were hard hit and obligatory tithes abolished, while freedom of worship was introduced and civil marriages made legal. Elaborate plans were made for a system of public education to provide elementary instruction for the masses. The jury system of trials was introduced in three states with a code of laws from Louisiana. Negotiations were conducted with Dutch interests for the building of an interoceanic canal through Nicaragua. British colonists were settled on the shores of Lake Izabal, where new developments in trade were expected.

In 1834, when the federal capital was moved to San Salvador, there were new presidential elections. José del Valle won, and there is every reason to believe that Morazán was prepared to give way as was proper. Valle, as a moderate liberal of superior learning, was widely respected and might have preserved the union.[31] Valle died, however, before the votes were counted. Morazán was then re-elected, and the personal animosities roused by seven years of his vigorous leadership mounted until words alone proved inadequate for their expression.

The war which ended the union began in Guatemala in 1837. In the midst of unrest caused by a cholera epidemic, illiterate Rafael Carrera rose in rebellion, finding support among conservatives in Guatemala City who evidently believed they could control him. Morazán took the field and won victories over Carrera but the

[31] Such is the argument of my own *José Cecilio del Valle and the Establishment of the Central American Confederation* (Tegucigalpa, 1954).

latter continued to bounce back from each defeat with a popular following. The turmoil spread, toppling state governments all the way to Costa Rica. The western part of Guatemala seceded and set up a new state called Los Altos which lasted two years. The federal Congress passed a resolution on 30 May 1838 to the effect that the states might do as they saw fit concerning their attachment to the union. Three of them disassociated themselves before the end of that year. Morazán's term expired on 1 February 1839 without new elections. Guatemala withdrew from the union two months later, leaving only San Salvador faithful. Morazán was driven from San Salvador by Carrera in March 1840 and forced to retire to Panama. He returned to Costa Rica in April 1842, seized the government of that state, and prepared an army on the Nicaraguan border. But soon the tables turned again, and with fortune against him Morazán was executed on 15 September 1842, the twenty-first anniversary of Central America's independence.

THE PROCESS OF REUNIFICATION

After nearly 300 years of unity under the Audiencia de los Confines, the Audiencia de Guatemala, and the Provincias Unidas del Centro de América, the five states of Central America were separate after 1839. The idea of federation persisted, however, and has affected their history ever since. Only slowly, beginning with Guatemala in 1847 and Costa Rica in 1848, did the states denominate themselves republics. Even then they continued to recognize a citizen of one as a citizen of another by simple change of residence, often giving political preferences, even the presidency, to migrants of such status. Politicians thought nothing of using the territory and resources of a friendly one of the five in order to gain power in another. In fact the chief reason why several nineteenth-century attempts at reunion failed is that the politics of any one state were so intertwined with the affairs of the others that the slightest shift in power in one spot was often enough to shatter the entire construction.

During the long régime (to 1865) of Rafael Carrera in Guatemala, that state remained opposed to union. El Salvador, Honduras, and Nicaragua tried to put together weak confederations in 1842–4 and 1847–52 but in neither case did they get far. The decision of William Walker, adventurer from Tennessee, to make himself president of Nicaragua in 1856 brought military co-operation from all five states against him, but when Walker was defeated each resumed its own way. Unity proposals made in the 1860's did not even get as far as the planning stage of a constitutional convention.[32]

Proponents of union took heart when revolutions of the year 1871 in Guatemala and El Salvador brought simultaneously into power régimes of a liberal cast, bent upon the building of a new Central America which would have railroads and telegraph lines to tie it together. Ideals were difficult to change to reality, however, especially when Justo Rufino Barrios, the new strong man of Guatemala, confused dedication to the union cause with the matter of loyalty to his own person. After earlier negotiations had proved frustrating, Barrios decreed Central American union unilaterally in 1885, set out to enforce the decree by conquering any state which objected to his methods, and promptly lost his life in battle.

Barrios' death, coming as it did in conflict with an administration in El Salvador which also favoured union, had something of a sobering effect. Several proposals for reunion came during the next decade, with the chief one of them in 1888–9 again reaching the stage of initial planning. Finally, the three middle republics set up a confederation in 1895, which then joined with Guatemala and Costa Rica in 1898 to write a constitution establishing the *Estados Unidos de Centro-América*. The capital was to be located in a district round the Gulf of Fonseca ceded by El Salvador, Honduras, and Nicaragua. Disappointment was great when a change of régimes in El Salvador displaced one of the cornerstones and quickly brought the whole project to naught.

The Partido Unionista Centroamericano, founded in primitive form the following year (1899), provided a new approach to the problem. This organization, which has functioned with varying degrees of enthusiasm ever since, has been an intellectual movement more than a party in the usual sense of the word, striving to point out the real hindrances to union in Central America and the means by which these might be surmounted. Grand leader of the movement until his death in 1958 was Salvador Mendieta, whose efforts were unceasing in this cause. Mendieta (born in Diriamba, Nicaragua, 1879) mixed without hesitation in the politics of his day, being at one time or another both a resident and an exile of each of

[32] Details of this progression are given in Thomas L. Karnes, *The Failure of Union* (Chapel Hill, Univ. of North Carolina Press, 1961); and in companion volumes by Alberto Herrarte, *La unión de Centroamérica* and *Documentos de la unión centroamericana* (Guatemala, 1955 and 1957).

the Central American states.[33] He was opposed to tyranny, either domestic or foreign, but believed that tyranny was a fate the Central Americans had brought on themselves. The isthmus has never had a more thorough going-over than at his hands. His *La enferme-dad de Centro-América* literally picks the whole people apart and puts them all together again, as a nation—not just a union of five states.[34]

The first twentieth-century move towards unity adopted a grad-ualistic approach quite in keeping with Mendieta's teaching that the people must want union before it could be successful. Had this attempt come without the involvement of the United States in Central American politics it might have cut fifty years off the uni-fication time-table. The United States took a deep interest in isth-mian affairs after her acquisition of the Panama Canal Zone in 1903. A short war between El Salvador and Guatemala in 1906 led to a pact signed aboard the U.S.S. *Marblehead* calling for a peace conference in San José. There plans were laid for a Central Ameri-can pedagogical institute to foster isthmian educational progress and a Central American 'international office' for the development of common interests. New hostilities and threats involving Nica-ragua, Honduras, and El Salvador then led quickly to the Washing-ton Conference of 1907, where the San José planning was extended. Central American institutes of agriculture, mines, and arts were recommended. For the slow attainment of economic unity, annual conferences were envisaged. And for the settlement of quarrels be-tween nations while the states remained separate, the Central American Court of Justice was established, its five judges to be elected by the legislatures of the states.

The decisions of 1906–7 had little permanent effect. The recom-mended educational institutes were not organized. The inter-national office was opened but obtained little influence. The con-ferences met annually for seven years, but their worthy agreements were not ratified. And finally, the Court of Justice collapsed when Nicaragua withdrew in 1917 following decisions which displeased that country and the United States. The controversy which brought about the judgments rested upon the contention of Costa Rica and El Salvador that the Bryan–Chamorro Treaty of 1916 between the United States and Nicaragua had adversely affected

[33] 'Testamento político del Doctor Salvador Mendieta', *DCA*, 23–24 July, 28–31 July, 4–9 Aug. 1958.
[34] The first volume of *La enfermedad* was published in Barcelona, 1910. Five volumes which Mendieta considered a unit, three by this title and two named *Alrededor del problema unionista de Centro-América*, were printed in Barcelona, 1934.

their rights. The gradualistic approach to Central American unity was now put aside until the 1950's, when all the same ideas were resurrected.

The old method of quick union through federation was now tried once more. Inspiration was provided by the approach of the hundredth anniversary of independence. Overthrow of a conservative régime in Guatemala seemed to open the way in 1920. A constitution for a *Federación de Centro América* was issued on 9 September 1921 just six days before the anniversary. Tegucigalpa was to be the capital. Nicaragua and Costa Rica had not taken part in the hurried constitutional assembly, however, and a new revolution in Guatemala brought an end to that country's support. The project died in January 1922.

A new conference in Washington devised new treaties in 1923. These were designed to maintain isthmian peace but contained little to encourage the advocates of union. An arbitration tribunal set up to replace the Central American Court of Justice was a matter of convenience only, to be used when both parties to a dispute desired its services. When even these treaties were denounced by El Salvador and Costa Rica in 1933, and in 1934 the same countries objected to new plans looking toward economic association, the whole unification movement went into abeyance for more than a decade.

The late 1930's and early 1940's in Central America were a time when *continuismo* (the technique of staying indefinitely in power through 'legal' means but without real reference to the people) ran rampant in four of the five republics. *Caudillos* ruled in Guatemala and El Salvador from 1931 to 1944. In Honduras and Nicaragua they started later (1933 and 1937 respectively) but lasted longer. Each strong man of the isthmus had his own personal reasons for maintaining the *status quo* in his relations with his neighbours. The post-*caudillo* régimes of Juan José Arévalo in Guatemala (1945–51) and Salvador Castaneda Castro in El Salvador (1945–8) expressed enthusiasm for renewed unity talks and made definite moves in that direction. But new disorders in Costa Rica, Nicaragua, and El Salvador in 1947–8 brought in provisional régimes in those countries so that not until late 1950 were conditions ripe again for isthmian conversations.

Jacobo Arbenz Guzmán (Guatemala 1951–4), Oscar Osorio (El Salvador 1950–6), Juan Manuel Gálvez (Honduras 1949–54), Anastasio Somoza (Nicaragua 1950–6), and Otilio Ulate (Costa

Rica 1949–53) were the presidents ready in 1951 to embark upon a new quest for Central American unification. Their foreign ministers met in San Salvador on 8–14 October of that year and wrote the Charter of San Salvador providing for a new isthmian organization.

Considering [says the Charter] that the Central American republics, disjoined parts of a single nation, remain united by indestructible ties which ought to be utilized and strengthened for the common advantage; that for the progressive development of their institutions and the common solution of their problems the organized and fraternal co-operation of all is indispensable; that it is necessary to eliminate the artificial barriers which separate the Central American peoples and to attain the united will to resolve their problems and defend their interests through collective and systematized action; that the procedures tried in the independent life of the Central American republics for restoration of their old unity have proved inefficacious; and that modern international law offers adequate formulas for this end through the institution of regional associations; *therefore*: The governments above mentioned are resolved to establish an *Organización de Estados Centroamericanos* for the co-ordination of their common efforts.[35]

ODECA, as the new organization is known on the isthmus, is not a federation. It is designed by its five members instead to 'fortify the ties which unite them'. Pacific settlements of disputes are envisaged, joint solution of common problems, and the promotion of isthmian economic, social, and cultural development. The organs of ODECA are the Meeting of Ministers of Foreign Affairs (to take place ordinarily at least once each two years), the permanent Central American Office (the secretariat, headed by a secretary general, to be housed in El Salvador), an Economic Council (supposed to meet at least once a year), and occasional meetings of the presidents and other ministers. Though a Meeting of Presidents, when one is held, is considered the 'supreme' organ, the 'principal' instrument of the organization is the Meeting of Ministers of Foreign Affairs, to which the Secretariat and the one council are responsible. Substantive decisions may be made by the foreign ministers only by a unanimous vote. The entire direction of ODECA thus depends upon these five, who are of course held accountable by their respective administrations.

[35] Translated from *Carta de la Organización de Estados Centroamericanos* (San Salvador, 1956), pp. 4–5. An unofficial translation of the entire Charter of San Salvador appears in Charles G. Fenwick, 'The Organization of Central American States', *AJIL*, xlvi (1952), 509–12; reprinted in *Ann. OAS*, iv (1952), 351–5.

Prompt ratification of the Charter of San Salvador by the five states seemed to bode well for ODECA at the outset. Though Panama was invited to join, her participation (which has not yet materialized) was not required for the charter to become active. The organization first breathed life on 14 December 1951, when the last ratification was deposited (by coincidence just one day after the charter of the Organization of American States entered into force). But the first regular Meeting of Ministers of Foreign Affairs, which was supposed to convene in Guatemala within one year, was postponed from September 1952 to May 1953. On 4 April 1953 Guatemala withdrew from ODECA, charging that the press and publicity organs of the remainder of Central America had joined in a defamatory campaign against the Arbenz régime and that an isthmian alliance had been formed without Guatemala's participation.[36] In meetings at San José (16 April) and Managua (10–12 July) the remaining foreign ministers decided that ODECA should continue as planned and invited Guatemala to reconsider her decision. Carlos Castillo Armas, master of Guatemala in July 1954 after revolution against Arbenz, soon took his country back into ODECA. One last postponement of the full-scale foreign ministers' meeting, from March to August 1955, was necessitated by the near-conflict in January of that year between the forces of Nicaragua and Costa Rica. ODECA began its real functioning when the meeting was finally held in Antigua on 18–24 August.

The first secretary general of ODECA (1955–9) was José Guillermo Trabanino. Holder of the doctorate in chemistry, Trabanino was known throughout the isthmus as the representative of a drug concern; he had also served as mayor of San Salvador and El Salvador's foreign minister. Trabanino organized the Central American Office in San Salvador on a $125,000 annual budget and proceeded to use his own gentle diplomacy in all efforts tending toward unity. A Cultural and Educational Council was formed as a subsidiary to ODECA in 1956. Meetings in a wide variety of endeavours were held with ODECA's sponsorship or encouragement.[37] In February 1957, when Trabanino helped to cool tensions between

---

[36] Guatemala's note and one response to it are given in the 1953 *Memoria* of the Nicaraguan Foreign Ministry, pp. 137–54.

[37] Such activity continues. No. 24 of ODECA's *Bol. Informativo* (15 Aug. 1960), for example, reports on the isthmus' *first* meeting of cattlemen, its *first* meeting of investors, its *second* meeting of municipal leaders, its *fifth* meeting of ministers of public health, and its *fifth* meeting of university rectors.

his own state of El Salvador and the government of Nicaragua consequent upon the assassination of President Anastasio Somoza which took place five months earlier, it seemed that ODECA had passed a real test successfully. Trabanino's term-ending brought another crisis, but his own service during four years did much to establish the organization on a firm basis.[38]

Side by side with the slow growth of ODECA until 1959 came developments on the economic front also working toward isthmian union. An initial meeting of the Central American Ministers of Economy was held in Tegucigalpa on 23–28 August 1952, in co-operation with the United Nations Economic Commission for Latin America. Meetings under the same auspices (called jointly the Central American Committee on Economic Co-operation) have been held every year since, except 1954. That of 1953 reached an agreement on tariff nomenclature and decided to establish a school of public administration in San José. The reunion of 1956 agreed that there should be a five-nation pact looking toward a Central American common market. Two years later (10 June 1958) such a treaty was signed (called the Multilateral Treaty of Free Trade and Central American Economic Integration) providing for free isthmian trade on certain goods and year-by-year tariff reductions on others. An additional convention of the same date was designed to encourage new industries which might serve more than one country on the isthmus.[39] The moderate and slow-working free-trade agreement was ratified by four countries within two years, while Costa Rica hesitated. On 1 September 1959 the Economic Co-operation Committee devised a new convention for the equalization of import duties.

In 1960 both ODECA and the Committee on Economic Co-operation were caught up in a new whirl of activity which may prove as substantial as it is unprecedented. When the term of Trabanino ended as secretary general of ODECA on 14 October 1959, no agreement had been made as to his successor. In the second regular Meeting of Foreign Ministers held at Managua on 12–14 October, the Guatemalan candidate held three votes for the position and proposed Costa Rican rivals two. In November a five-person administrative council was set up until the impasse could

[38] Prospects for ODECA at this point in its history were discussed in Norman J. Padelford, 'Cooperation in the Central American Region: the Organization of Central American States', *Int. Org.*, xi (1957), 41–54.

[39] U.N. Committee on Economic Co-operation in Central America, *Report* (1958).

be resolved. President Miguel Ydígoras Fuentes of Guatemala (1958–64) suggested in November that a Meeting of Presidents be held with the object of reconstructing ODECA. The proposed re-union was not held, but Ydígoras managed to meet individually with Presidents José María Lemus of El Salvador (1956–60), Ramón Villeda Morales of Honduras (1957–63), and Luis Somoza Debayle of Nicaragua (1956–63) on 9–11 January.

Through the press at the same time Ydígoras published his plan for the new ODECA.[40] Under it, there would be an Assembly with five delegates from each state which could make weighty decisions with a three-fifths vote. The Assembly would prepare agreements to establish a common market, to create a Central American bank, and to unify the currencies as well as to reach several other more general objectives. There would also be a new Court of Justice not only to help settle isthmian controversies but also to formulate a Central American federal constitution. Ydígoras next sought to arrange peace on the ODECA front by accepting Alvaro Montero Padilla of Costa Rica as the second secretary general. When Nicaragua refused to go along with this nomination, Ydígoras' *Diario de Centro América* even wrote, 'Luis Somoza . . . is losing the only governing friend he has in Central America.'[41] On 15 February, a compromise solution brought the election of Marco Tulio Zeledón Matamoros as the new secretary general (1960–4). Zeledón is well-known as an expert on constitutional law and was president of Costa Rica's Partido Unionista Centroamericano.

'*Lo principal es el aspecto económico*', said President Ydígoras when commenting on his plan.[42] On 6 February, the ministers of economy of Guatemala, El Salvador, and Honduras put force into these words when they signed a new Treaty of Economic Association. The object of this tripartite pact was to establish a common market within a much shorter time than before contemplated. The 'free circulation of persons, goods, and capital' was the goal, and a definite plan to reach it was agreed upon.[43] With this treaty in force in April, an amendment was added on 9 June providing for a common Development Fund to which the three countries promised to

[40] 'Texto del proyecto de Guatemala para la reestructuración de ODECA', *DCA*, 11–12 Jan. 1960; reprinted in ODECA, *Bol. Informativo*, no. 24, 15 Aug. 1960, pp. 17, 28–29.
[41] 'Somoza rehusa la política fraternal', 4 Feb. 1960.
[42] *DCA*, 15 Jan. 1960.
[43] *Tratado de Asociación Económica de Honduras, Guatemala, El Salvador* (Tegucigalpa, 1960), p. 5.

subscribe $5,500,000. Ex-president Otilio Ulate of Costa Rica, in travels to Miami and Guatemala in May and June, pushed the idea of a Development Bank for the entire isthmus to help spur a self-sustaining economy. At a meeting in Bogotá in September Ulate's idea received some approbation from the Central American ministers of economy. Consultations were held in Washington requesting support for such a bank in line with the United States' decision to set aside a special $500,000,000 fund for aid to Latin America. Such support was announced on 4 November. Four Central American countries had promised to contribute an initial $2,000,000 each in capital, and Washington to provide $10,000,000. The ministers of economy of Guatemala, El Salvador, Honduras, and Nicaragua meeting in Managua signed on 13 December a General Treaty of Economic Integration providing for a Central American Bank of Economic Integration and a quadripartite common market to be realized within five years of the date of the third ratification.[44]

ODECA, Secretary General Zeledón complained, was not being properly taken into account at the December meeting in Managua.[45] Costa Rican Minister of Economy Jorge Borbón Castro, who had refused to attend the meeting, spoke much more strongly. The administration of President Mario Echandi of Costa Rica (1958–62) had been hesitant to accept even the slower approach to isthmian unity. The events of 1960 proved much too fast for that part of the isthmus which was the least convinced of advantages for itself in the proposed economic integration. Costa Rica had already achieved a livelier trade and a higher standard of living than her isthmian neighbours, and was the only party which conceivably had anything to lose by the agreement. '*Gracias a Dios tuvimos dos años*' to meditate upon economic integration before plunging into it, said Borbón on 20 December.[46] Yet there was much disagreement with that viewpoint in his own nation, and the prospects seemed to be that Costa Rica would eventually adhere to a common market and the isthmian bank. In that event, the treaty finally promised, both institutions would be linked closely to ODECA. Whether the latter organization would move rapidly to-

[44] Text of the treaty, *La Nación*, 12–13 Jan. 1961.

[45] 'ODECA reclama voto en mercado común', *D. de Hoy*, 12 Dec. 1960.

[46] *La Nación*, 21 Dec. 1960. Borbón's viewpoints were explained at length in a series called 'Integración Económica de Centroamérica' in *La Nación* beginning 10 Jan. 1961.

ward the establishment of an Assembly and a Court of Justice seemed much less certain.

The Partido Unionista Centroamericano, whose leaders have provided some of the inspiration for recent unity moves, without in most cases being directly responsible, received advice from one of its members in 1953. The party ought to be one of combat, he said, prepared to take part in the politics of the day, supporting those who fight for its ideals, opposing those who deny them. The party must have a defined ideology, *un conjunto de aspiraciones*, to lead not back to the Provincias Unidas of Morazán but to a new Central America. The party ought to be one of revolution, not 'to produce a simple change in the ruling oligarchies, but a fundamental change in the social, political, and economic structure, so that Central America might emerge from the state of barbarism and prostration in which she finds herself and be a nation free and prosperous, an authentic democracy, a country in which, at the side of social justice, flourishes exuberantly respect for human personality'.[47] The reunification plans now afoot on the isthmus will either lead in this direction or give new advantage to a few families. Both the cause of unity and the destiny of a people seem dependent upon the wisdom of the planners.

[47] Herrarte, *La unión de Centroamérica*, pp. 568–75.

CHAPTER V

GUATEMALA

OF the million and a quarter persons who inhabited Central America when independence came, well over two-fifths lived in the state of Guatemala.[1] Of the more than 10 million Central Americans of mid-1958, Guatemala still contained over one-third.[2] The population total in Guatemala passed the 1 million mark before the end of the nineteenth century, reached 2 million in the 1930's, and 3 million in 1953.[3] The estimated total in mid-1958 (3,546,000) surpassed that of El Salvador, the nearest isthmian rival, by over a million. Guatemala's nationwide density of population was considerably lower than that of El Salvador, but at 84 persons to the square mile was nevertheless the second highest in Central America.

The vast majority of the Guatemalan people of today are descended from the Indians who once ruled the area. More than half (1,497,261 out of 2,790,868) were counted as *indigenas* or Indians in the 1950 census, on the basis of being known as such in their local communities. Of this number 1,010,051 above the age of three spoke a Maya language in the home, and 827,873 above the age of seven wore Indian clothing.[4] Of the remainder (called ladino, meaning simply non-indigenous, in the census) there may be persons of pure Indian stock biologically, there are others of unmixed European ancestry, and by far the largest number are crosses between Indian and white. An accurate determination of the numbers involved in the racial groups would be impossible; the census division between Indian and ladino along vague socio-economic lines was really the only one practicable. A Guatemalan racial heritage from Africa dating back to the colonial period is also present

[1] Guatemala sent 17 delegates to the first federal Congress, El Salvador 9, Nicaragua 6, Honduras 5 or 6 (sources vary), and Costa Rica 2—a total of 39 or 40 on the basis of one delegate for each 30,000 inhabitants. On this reckoning, the respective populations were Guatemala 510,000; El Salvador 270,000; Nicaragua 180,000; Honduras 150,000 or 180,000; Costa Rica 60,000. The figures cited in Marure, i. 83–84, 189 (see ch. iv, n. 2, p. 57) do not take into account the transfer of Sonsonate from Guatemala to El Salvador.

[2] See ch. i, n. 1, p. 2.

[3] U.N., *Demogr. Yb.*, *1952*, pp. 105–6; *1959*, pp. 134–7.

[4] *Sexto censo de población*, pp. xi–xii, 43, 169, 179. See ch. iii, n. 24, p. 49.

in the Pacific and Caribbean lowlands, but now thoroughly mixed with the Indian and European. Outside the capital there is little Negro blood in the highlands. The Black Caribs who arrived so shortly before independence still constitute a separate linguistic group (1,116 in number above the age of three in 1950) on the short Caribbean coast.[5]

Despite enthusiastic promotion in Great Britain and Belgium during the 1830's and 1840's, immigration to Guatemala has never developed on a large scale. When independence was new and still exciting, plans were made for colonies of Europeans to settle about Lake Izabal and develop the commercial potentialities of the route from the Caribbean to the highlands. These plans failed and only a trickle of foreigners has entered Guatemala since, though their economic importance outweighs their numerical standing in the population. Of the 30,266 residents of 1950 who were born outside the country according to census count, 17,282 came from other Central American nations, 4,870 from Mexico, 1,558 from the United States, 1,530 from British Honduras, 970 from Spain, 741 from Germany, 567 from China, 435 from Jamaica, 331 from Italy, and 264 from France.[6] Those from British Honduras and Jamaica are chiefly Negroes who have come to the Caribbean coastal region and the capital as farm or service labourers. Permanent residents from the United States, Europe, and China will generally be found in commercial and agricultural enterprises of some consequence.

LOCAL GOVERNMENT

Racial considerations are no longer, as in the colonial period, a criterion in the determination of the rank of a settlement. There are now five ranks in Guatemala rather than three, the *aldea* (next to the smallest) and the *caserío* (smallest) having been added to the *ciudad*, the *villa*, and the *pueblo*. The status of the settlement is generally in accord with size, though administrative importance makes a difference (all twenty-two departmental capitals are 'cities') and other factors such as the rate of literacy and the progress of sanitation are taken into account. Guatemala had 28 cities, 29 towns, and 266 pueblos in 1957.[7]

The largest city by far in all Central America is Guatemala City, which has remained the capital of the state since the dissolution of the United Provinces. In a manner reminiscent of its predecessor Santiago de Guatemala, the modern capital was nearly destroyed

[5] Ibid. p. 169.   [6] Ibid. p. 99.   [7] *Guatemala en Cifras, 1958*, p. 21.

by a series of earthquakes in December 1917 and January 1918. It was rebuilt in neat fashion on the same site, however, and by 1950 had grown to a population of 284,000.[8] The general aspect of the capital is modern and cosmopolitan, at least by contrast with other Guatemalan cities and towns. Here live the persons associated with several embassies, of course, and many permanent residents who have come from outside the country. The base of the capital's population remains the same as at its foundation, however, with the person of mixed Indian-European or Indian-European-African ancestry in greatest numbers and the unmixed Indian very much in evidence.

Quezaltenango, second city of the state, was important both commercially and politically in the nineteenth century, serving more than once as a focus of separatist movements in the western part of the highlands. Quezaltenango was hard hit by an eruption of Volcano Santa María in 1902 but like the capital has been rebuilt. Its population in 1950 was 28,000 with an indigenous flavour greater than that of the capital. Puerto Barrios, with 15,000 inhabitants, is Guatemala's chief Caribbean port, founded in the early 1880's and named for President Barrios. Its significance and size relate directly to the traffic borne by Guatemala's and El Salvador's only rail connexion with the Caribbean, of which it is the terminus. Fourth and fifth of Guatemala's cities, with 11,000 persons each, are Mazatenango, where commercial development has also occurred chiefly since independence, and Antigua, the old Santiago de Guatemala, which maintains a sizable tourist trade with its grand colonial ruins.

All five of the centres mentioned so far are departmental capitals, and there are seventeen more of these. In the population range from 10,000 to 8,000 in 1950 lay Escuintla, Retalhuleu, Chiquimula, and Zacapa; from 8,000 to 6,000 Cobán, Jalapa, Totonicapán, Huehuetenango, and Chimaltenango; from 6,000 to 4,000 Jutiapa, San Marcos, and Santa Cruz del Quiché. Still smaller are the remaining five, Sololá, Salamá, Cuilapa, El Progreso, and Flores, the last-named having less than 2,000. All of these seventeen

[8] To provide comparisons, city and town populations given for all Central America are from the 1950 census, since two of the five countries do not attempt city estimates between censuses. Population counts planned for 1960 did not materialize. Numbers over 10,000 are generally rendered to the nearest thousand, while those below that amount are given in categories. City and town figures for Guatemala are from *Sexto censo de población*, pp. 5–42, using the urban count for the corresponding *municipio*.

communities were in existence in colonial times and have grown rather undramatically since (Cobán and Totonicapán hardly at all). Guatemala had three other centres in 1950 in the range 8,000–6,000 and eleven from 6,000–4,000. (Comalapa and Chiquimulilla, of fair size in colonial days, stood at only 7,400 and 3,500.) San José (2,800), the principal port on the Pacific, and Matías de Gálvez, a new installation (open only since early 1959) close to Puerto Barrios, give the latter some competition. But apart from the capital and Puerto Barrios, he who would find the great increase in Guatemalan population since independence must look not to the towns and cities but to the thousands of successful *aldeas* and *caseríos*.

The local unit of government in Guatemala is the *municipio*, which may include just one city (such as the capital) but usually contains a miscellany of settlements (such as a town, some pueblos, and a goodly number of *aldeas* and *caseríos*) in addition to some *fincas* or country estates. There are 323 *municipios* in the country (1957).[9] There is no great attempt to keep them equal in size in regard to either area or population. Before 1945 *municipio* affairs were handled by officials appointed in the capital; influential *municipio* secretaries still come from outside the towns where they officiate. Since 1945 democratic forms prevail in the election of a mayor and council though the spirit is often lacking, with large Indian populations more often than not under the control of ladino minorities. The mayor and lesser administrative officials are paid while the councilmen serve without remuneration. Budgets are small to the extent that many *municipios* have nothing to spare for public works.[10] The policing, tax-collecting, and petty judicial functions of the *municipio* are nevertheless all the government which many Guatemalans ever come to comprehend.

The twenty-two departments of Guatemala constitute an administrative and judicial level of government between the *municipio* and the nation. Originally (in 1825) there were only seven departments, consolidated from the seven *alcaldías mayores*, two *corregimientos*, and one frontier district which made up the state; these have been reorganized and subdivided on several occasions since. No policies are decided on the departmental level, nor is there such an event as a departmental election. The officers are a governor (until

[9] *Guatemala en Cifras, 1958*, p. 21.
[10] K. H. Silvert, *A Study in Government: Guatemala* (New Orleans, Tulane Univ., Mid. Am. Res. Inst., 1954), pp. 76–91. presents case studies of four *municipios*.

1945 called the *jefe político*) appointed by the president; his staff, selected by the governor; and court officials chosen by the supreme court of the nation. All form a part of the national government operating within the departmental boundaries.[11]

The department of El Petén in the north, ancient heartland of the Maya, now contains only 1·5 persons for each of its 13,843 square miles, one-third of Guatemala's area. Izabal, with its monopoly of the nation's trade through the Caribbean, has a population density of only 21.[12] Alta Verapaz, El Quiché, and Huehuetenango are large departments in the northern highlands bordering on El Petén or Mexico, with densities of 70, 67, and 91; Indians constitute well over four-fifths of their population.[13] In the Motagua valley along the road from Izabal to the capital are Zacapa and El Progreso (densities 85, 83) with less than one-fifth of their population Indian. Standing guard on either side of the road and railroad are Baja Verapaz, Chiquimula, and Jalapa (70, 158, 122) with over half of their people counted Indian. Jutiapa, Santa Rosa, and Escuintla (148, 127, 93) are along the Pacific from El Salvador westward, more than four-fifths ladino in their composition. Suchitepéquez and Retalhuleu (153, 114) farther west along the same coast are over three-fifths Indian. The remaining departments— San Marcos, Quezaltenango, Totonicapán, Sololá, Chimaltenango, Sacatepéquez, and Guatemala (197, 300, 287, 236, 194, 399, 676) from west to east in that order in the southern mountains— contain 11 per cent of the nation's area but 44 per cent of its population.[14] Not counting the last department, where the nation's capital is located, over three-fourths of their people are Indians.[15]

DEVELOPMENT OF THE STATE

Guatemala as a nation—as one of America's essentially Indian nations—came only slowly into being. Recognition as a Spanish province came in 1812. Constitutional organization as a state in the

[11] See Silvert, *A Study in Government: Guatemala*, pp. 70–76, for a case study of one department.

[12] Departmental population densities given for all Central America are the number of persons per square mile, as computed from population estimates. To provide comparisons statistics were used as they were available from the beginning, middle, and end of the year 1958. Densities for Guatemala are of 31 Dec. 1957, computed from *Guatemala en Cifras, 1958*, p. 13.

[13] *Sexto censo de población*, p. xxxii.   [14] Ibid. p. xx.

[15] All of Guatemala's departments have the same name as their own capitals except El Petén (Flores), Izabal (Puerto Barrios), Alta Verapaz (Cobán), Baja Verapaz (Salamá), Santa Rosa (Cuilapa), Suchitepéquez (Mazatenango), and Sacatepéquez (Antigua).

Central American union was completed in October 1825. The régime of Mariano Gálvez (1831–8) was notable for its espousal of judicial, educational, and anti-clerical reforms which went beyond those of the other states, and for the degree of real democratic debate which momentarily flourished. After Gálvez, however, came constitutional confusion, as Guatemala withdrew from the federal union in April 1839 but continued the same forms of government as before, with Rafael Carrera, the real master of the state, hovering in the background. Carrera became president in 1844 and declared Guatemala a republic in 1847, but then was exiled in 1848. It was not until October 1851 that a constitution was adopted to provide the republic with legal standing. Under this constitution Guatemala's affairs were to be decided almost single-handedly by the president. A house of representatives to be chosen by the people formed part of an assembly of notables (including the archbishop) whose function was to elect the president for a term of four years. Three years after Carrera was again chosen president in 1851, he was made chief executive for life. The Guatemalan state originally organized by university graduates and zealous adherents of liberalism thus became an autocracy ruled by an illiterate, who for fourteen years provided internal peace but very little progress while he played a heavy hand in the affairs of isthmian neighbours. Carrera died in 1865. His system continued under President Vicente Cerna, one of Carrera's generals, until 1871.

The revolution which ended the Cerna régime was considered by its authors a restoring of the pre-Carrera liberal principles in government. In the hands of Miguel García Granados, moderate president from 1871 to 1873, it might have become just that. But Justo Rufino Barrios, his successor from 1873 to 1885, while very much interested in anti-clerical and administrative reforms, saw little advantage in the restoration of real parliamentary debate. His own presidential position was regularized only in 1880 after the adoption of Guatemala's third constitution in December 1879. This new charter, which with considerable minor amendment lasted for sixty-six years, provided ample guarantees of liberty in times of peace, separated church and state quite completely, and provided elections for national judges, a unicameral legislature, and a president with a six-year term. The form but not the spirit of the new constitution was observed by Barrios, who continued to do very much as he pleased with Guatemala until his death in 1885. Only when he attempted to do with the whole isthmus what he had been doing all along in his own country—administering its affairs as he saw fit without consultation with persons who felt differently —did he find the insurmountable obstacle to carrying out his will. His death on the field of battle for his private conception of the Central American union was a tragedy of his own making.

For a time after the death of Barrios, Guatemala's constitution took on some meaning, only to fall into the hands of two men in succession who could not bring themselves to renounce the presidential power. Manuel Lisandro Barillas, president from 1885 to 1892 (from 1886 by election), did not seek a second term but permitted a real campaign in which Lorenzo Montúfar, one of Central America's outstanding liberals of the nineteenth century, went down to defeat and José María Reyna Barrios, nephew of the renowned Justo Rufino Barrios, won the chair. Reyna Barrios was assassinated six years later as a consequence of one man's resentment against him, but at a time when he had already secured an extension of his term without re-election by the people. Manuel Estrada Cabrera, who succeeded to office when Reyna Barrios died and quickly consolidated his power, was the winner of farcical re-elections for terms beginning in 1905, 1911, and 1917, showing no sign of quitting as long as he lived. Only the dry bones of the constitution remained under Estrada Cabrera, as he dealt ruthlessly with those who opposed him and rendered ridiculously little service for a man twenty-two years in office. Just as Estrada Cabrera did not hesitate to shoot those who displeased him, he was a target for assassination several times himself as public life in Guatemala sank to its lowest level. After he had survived every such attempt, his final removal from office in 1920 came on a wave of public emotion which swept him out as a mental incompetent.

The governmental cycle of 1885–1920 was repeated in 1920–44 until the constitution of 1879 was finally discredited and discarded. Its own worst enemy was the liberal party which had written it but never wholeheartedly subscribed to its spirit. Carlos Herrera, the unionist president who followed Estrada Cabrera, was swept out of office by a new revolt in late 1921. Then for nine years under José María Orellana (1921–6) and Lázaro Chacón (1926–30) the nineteenth-century liberal constitution came its closest to genuine fulfilment. Without social revolution, which that constitution did not envisage, there was economic progress accompanied by some regard for democracy in government. Orellana's term ended when he died of a heart attack, however, and that of Chacón when he suffered a brain haemorrhage. Jorge Ubico, who followed in early 1931, showed every indication, like Estrada Cabrera, of remaining in office as long as he could. A yes-or-no plebiscite in 1935 extended his term from 1937 to 1943. A constitutional congress in 1941 stretched it six years longer, terminating in 1949. Ubico matched Estrada Cabrera in the use of brutality and censorship, though a more efficient handling of governmental business and a quite original pose of friendship for the much-maligned indigenous race helped to sustain his régime. By the 1940's, however, many thinking Guatemalans had become impressed with the social and economic revolution taking place in Mexico since the 1920's and with wartime Allied propaganda regarding a bright new world of the future. These were factors with which Estrada Cabrera had not had to contend. Because of such influences, one dictator tumbled in El Salvador in May 1944. Ubico's writing on the wall began on 24 June of the same year, when public readings of the Atlantic Charter were coupled with demands for his resignation. Ubico turned the government over to his friend Federico Ponce on 1 July after a general strike. Ponce was dislodged by force on 20 October 1944. Next a military triumvirate maintained order for five months until a new constitutional régime could be established.

MID-TWENTIETH CENTURY POLITICS: STRUGGLE FOR DEMOCRACY

Guatemala's fourth constitution lasted nine years, starting in March 1945. Under its terms the country saw a return to political liberties it had not known since the 1830's. But more than that, these nine years were the beginning of a social and economic revolution in Guatemala which, though several of its features were checked in 1954, seems bound to survive into the future. The 1945 constitution contained thirty-four articles devoted to 'individual guarantees' and thirty-three to 'social guarantees' relating to labour, public employment, family, and culture. The first statement under the title 'Economic and Financial System' read: 'The State will orient the national economy for the benefit of the people, for the purpose of assuring to each individual a dignified existence....'[16] Stipulations regarding the illegality of large estates, the government's powers of expropriation, and public ownership of natural resources gave teeth to the statement of principle. A presi-

[16] Russell H. Fitzgibbon, ed., *The Constitutions of the Americas* (Univ. of Chicago Press, 1948), p. 415.

dent elected by the people for six years (with immediate re-election forbidden), a Congress with half of its members to be elected every two years, and a national judiciary selected by Congress were to implement the aims and guarantees which the constitution set forth. Congress was to play an important role, since it could remove members of the national judiciary as well as appoint them (both the supreme court and courts of appeal) and could likewise insist by a two-thirds vote upon the resignation of a cabinet minister appointed by the president. The president remained the most important official. The only two men who held the office under this constitution made an honest attempt to carry out its provisions, and only partially failed.

Juan José Arévalo, president from 15 March 1945 to 15 March 1951, was a college professor with the doctorate and a reputation as philosopher in the field of pedagogy. He had spent the years of the Ubico régime teaching in Argentine universities.[17] In a free election after a free campaign, though with only literate males voting, Arévalo won the presidency by a vote of six to one over his combined opponents. Arévalo's governing philosophy, as he described it, was one of 'spiritual socialism'—that is, one which recognized the necessity of a new social and economic order in Guatemala but which did not assume that man's happiness springs from material possessions alone. The Guatemalan Institute of Social Security (Instituto Guatemalteco de Seguridad Social or IGSS, 1946), Guatemala's first labour code (1947), and her important Institute for the Development of Production (Instituto de Fomento de la Producción or INFOP, 1948) stem from the first four years of his administration. Labour unions showed a rapid growth during the same years and both education and sanitation programmes were greatly stimulated.[18] A free press was allowed to develop, and political parties representing diverse points of view. Later, as the shadow of elections for the next presidential term fell over the scene, dissension became the order of the day among government supporters in Congress while Arévalo spent much of his energy simply remaining in office. Critics both at home and

[17] The thesis written by this unusual president in obtaining his doctoral degree was published as *La pedagogía ae la personalidad* (*Eucken–Budde–Gaudig–Kesseler*) (La Plata, 1937). See also his *Escritos pedagógicos y filosóficos* (Guatemala, 1945).

[18] Two remarkable Master's theses published in mimeographed form by Colgate University in 1949 and 1950 deal with the first four years of Arévalo's régime in some detail. They are Leo A. Suslow, *Aspects of Social Reforms in Guatemala, 1944–1949*; and Archer C. Bush, *Organized Labor in Guatemala, 1944–1949*.

abroad were many. Tension with the United States concerning the leftist qualities of the régime and attitudes displayed by United States Ambassador Richard C. Patterson led to a request for the latter's recall in April 1950.[19]

Jacobo Arbenz Guzmán, president from 15 March 1951 to 27 June 1954, was a military man like most of his predecessors. His father had been a pharmacist and an immigrant from Switzerland; his mother was a mixture of Spanish and Indian. Arbenz was not generally accepted in high society before becoming president though his wife was from a wealthy family of El Salvador. Both were genuinely interested in radical reform and found pleasure in association with young persons of like points of view, some Marxist and others non-Marxist in their orientation. The assassination in July 1949 of Francisco Javier Arana, a chief contender for the presidency, left Arbenz the most likely man to win this position. Widely discussed reports said that friends of Arbenz had engineered the murder; no one was ever prosecuted for the crime. Nevertheless the election which took place in December 1950 showed quite clearly that Arbenz was the choice of the Guatemalan people. In what is generally conceded to have been a fair count, he won 65 per cent of the popular vote. The literate men and women who voted secretly gave Arbenz a clear majority. The fact that the percentage of illiterate men who voted for him was higher than that of the literate men and women may be taken as a reflection of governmental coercion in the campaign or as a recognition on the part of the Indian that his best opportunity for national recognition lay in the continuation of Arévalo's policies, with which Arbenz had identified himself.[20]

The chief goal toward which Arbenz strove during his three years in office was agrarian reform, with unused lands of wealthy

[19] Suslow, pp. 122–3, suggests that Arévalo's own dedication to democracy without the accompaniment of propaganda depicting himself as a 'savior or hero' had made his régime unstable. Press and magazine critics in the United States were answered by Samuel Guy Inman, *A New Day in Guatemala* (Wilton, Conn., Worldover Press, 1951). On pp. 35–43 Inman describes an interview with Arévalo touching on international questions.

[20] Several controversial matters concerning the Arbenz régime touched upon in this paragraph and others to follow have been studied most objectively by Ronald M. Schneider in his *Communism in Guatemala, 1944–1954* (N.Y., Praeger, 1958). Schneider does not deal with Guatemala's social revolution as such, nor does he attempt to explain the controversy with the United States. For an examination of the partisan literature dealing with every aspect of this régime and its overthrow see Julio Adolfo Rey, 'Revolution and Liberation: A Review of Recent Literature on the Guatemalan Situation', *HAHR.*, xxxviii (1958), 239–55.

holders being expropriated on a large scale and the acreage made available to landless farmers. This programme brought him into direct conflict with the United Fruit Company, a United States corporation and the largest landholder in Guatemala. The United States government, which had become disturbed about Communist influences in Guatemala as early as February 1950, supported United Fruit's financial claims against the Guatemalan government and carried its perturbations concerning Communist influence to the Organization of American States at a meeting held in Caracas in March 1954.[21] When the Arbenz régime came to an end in June of the same year, after a rebellion which was launched from the territory of Honduras, there were few persons on the Central American isthmus who were not convinced that the United States had liquidated the government it disliked.

Despite the murder of Arana, and though the masses of the people continued illiterate, Guatemala reached a high point in democracy under Arévalo and Arbenz (at least until 1953) which has left its impression for the future. While leftist policies prevailed during these eight years, conservative sentiment was not stifled. Magazines and newspapers in the United States often referred to the Arbenz régime as a Communist dictatorship; yet under both Arévalo and Arbenz there was freedom for the Guatemalan press, which criticized both administrations severely.[22] Opposition voices were raised in Congress, their presence in that body guaranteed by a system of proportional representation effective in the more populated departments. A tremendous interplay of competing philosophies took place, with an almost feverish building and abandonment of new parties and coalitions. Communists entered their tickets in Congressional elections, but so did a whole host of parties

[21] The case of the U. S. Department of State is presented in *Intervention of International Communism in Guatemala* (Washington, USGPO, 1954). Great Britain. Foreign Office, *Report on Events Leading up to and Arising out of the Change of Régime in Guatemala*, Cmd. 9277, 1954, does not dissent from this general point of view.

[22] An example of the United States press campaign against the Arbenz régime is 'The Red Outpost in Central America', *Life*, xxxv/15, 12 Oct. 1953, pp. 169–77, which pictures the then-unfinished National Library, Inter-American highway, Franklin D. Roosevelt Hospital, and model village of Poptún as 'revolutionary boondoggles'. All have since been completed and are in use. Contrast the British view taken in 'The Social Revolution in Guatemala', *World Today*, x (1954), 279–82, which poses (p. 281) the question whether Guatemala is Communist: 'The answer is no. Full liberty exists, and the Opposition newspapers sell 50,000 copies daily. The social provisions of the Constitution are, after all, not as radical as those of the New Deal in the U. S. A. or the Labour Government in Britain'.

ranging to one on the opposite extreme which had no platform except opposition to Communism. Indians and ordinary labourers were made welcome in political meetings for the first time in history, while the Indians in many communities were given back (through the right to vote) the sixteenth-century privilege of running their own local affairs.[23]

Why did such healthy developments as these come to an end? The first important determining factor was the tradition of revolt, a hangover from the past, which the opponents of Arévalo and Arbenz did not spurn despite opportunities for more peaceful expression of their sentiment. Elections for Congress and the presidency from 1944 through 1953 were all fair enough to provide dissident minorities with an opportunity to test their popularity. Nevertheless Arévalo alone had to face more than twenty uprisings by persons who were not content with the electoral process. Carlos Castillo Armas, a soldier who served the first four years under Arévalo, adopted this pattern of opposition in 1949. He and others were unsuccessful in a coup intended to block the 1950 elections. Friends of Castillo failed to unseat Arbenz in April 1953, when a formidable attempt was made, but did bring about a government trend toward more authoritarian methods. With perseverance, Castillo came back in 1954 to become the successor of Arbenz as president of Guatemala. His credentials were that he had led a ragged band of rebels whose appearance near the Honduran boundary on 18 June brought a crisis Arbenz could not handle. Arbenz resigned on 27 June before the first real battle was fought. The juntas which followed in rapid succession were arranged and rearranged until Castillo became the real ruler of the country. His movement was called a 'liberation' and his success a triumph of democracy; yet he had forcefully deposed Guatemala's elected president and himself offered no genuine presidential elections before his death in 1957.

A second determining factor in the ending of the Arévalo–Arbenz era was the new (in Guatemalan experience) but very real devotion to the Soviet Union and its tactics on the part of those who most consistently had the ear of President Arbenz. Communism was an inheritor rather than the begetter of the 1944 revolution,

---

[23] The impact of the Arévalo–Arbenz era on ten Indian communities is studied in Richard N. Adams, ed., *Political Changes in Guatemalan Indian Communities: a Symposium* (New Orleans, Tulane Univ., Mid. Am. Res. Inst., 1957). See also John Gillin and K. H. Silvert, 'Ambiguities in Guatemala', *Foreign Affairs*, xxxiv (1956), 469–82, dealing with San Luis Jilotepeque.

the Communist party being founded as a secret organization only in 1947. By the end of the Arévalo régime several individual Communists had risen to positions of influence in other revolutionary organizations. In 1950, two Communist parties came into the open —one led by José Manuel Fortuny, the other by Víctor Manuel Gutiérrez—and secured four seats out of fifty-eight in the 1951–2 Congress. By 1952, the General Confederation of Workers of Guatemala, chief labour organization of the country, was completely in Communist hands; by 1953, likewise the National Peasant Confederation of Guatemala, of great importance in the countryside. The 1953–4 Congress contained again only four Communist party members out of a total of fifty-six (all four from Fortuny's group, which by now had absorbed the other), but the Communist party line was by this time echoed constantly by other powerful members of the National Democratic Front coalition of parties which actually ran the Congress. When Gutiérrez was elected First Secretary of the Congress in 1954, he was in position automatically to succeed Arbenz should misfortune befall the president. There can be little doubt that many of the Communists (Gutiérrez is an excellent example) were sincere in their dedication to the workers' cause. It seems fair to say also that President Arbenz (a non-Communist himself, as were all his cabinet ministers) cooperated as closely as he did with the Communists because he found them more honestly devoted than other advisers to his programme of betterment for the farmers.[24] Until the ugly days after the rebellion of April 1953 (at which time began the trend which developed into a policy of severe repression), there was little in the Guatemalan situation to suggest totalitarian lock-step. A local observer could easily have become convinced that the Communists were in the vanguard of democracy, as they liked to proclaim. Had the Communist leaders not been so thoroughly oriented towards complete obedience to Moscow directives, they might have adopted suave and more sensible tactics in places where they clung to outworn slogans instead. The acceptance of their programme by workers and peasants seems to have blinded them to the fact that they were outrunning their bases of power. When Castillo invaded in 1954 the Communists demanded that the workers and farmers be equipped with arms to carry on the defence of the Arbenz régime. It was this insistence rather than the strength of the Castillo

[24] A discussion of the relations between the Communists and Arbenz is found in Schneider, pp. 186–202.

forces which persuaded the army to desert Arbenz and so brought about the latter's resignation.[25]

A third factor was this very power of the army over its commander-in-chief and the country, a remnant of past politics which the nation falsely hoped it had overcome with its constitution of 1945 and civilian president. Francisco Javier Arana's assassination in 1949 came when many were convinced that he was prepared to use his strength as Arévalo's chief of the armed forces to gain the presidency and undo the revolution. When Arbenz resigned in 1954, it was on the demand of Carlos Enrique Díaz, his own chief of staff, who in turn may have been impelled to such action by his officer corps. The army did not want to see weapons put in the hands of the masses in the Guatemalan countryside. And so the army took measures into its own hands, and in effect chose (through its willingness to support) the régime which would take the place of the one elected.

The fourth reason democracy suffered a setback in Guatemala, and perhaps the reason of greatest significance in the long view, is that the many sincere reformers in the country who were without Communist sympathies had few allies in the world. The Communists could receive encouragement, advice (sometimes to their own detriment), and even financial support from their friends in wealthier countries. The non-Communist reformers, who until the year 1952 could easily have managed the show, and who until June 1954 were still in a position to retrieve the controls they had lost, found bafflement and opposition wherever they looked. Foreign business firms seemed to see little difference between Communist and non-Communist labour leaders and fought them both with equal vigour. The United States government expressed concern about United Fruit interests and the Communist 'menace' but not about Guatemala's Indians or her half-starved labourers. The democratic socialist movements of the world were not organized to lend assistance. The labour unions of the United States stood ready to help fraternal organizations, but like the Communists of Russia, were rather set in their ways and unready to bend them to fit foreign situations.

The Communist menace was a real one to observers from outside. Guatemala, it seemed, might easily become the first Communist-ruled nation in the Western Hemisphere. Once the Communists had taken over completely, experience in every Communist

[25] Ibid. pp. 311–17.

country had proved, there would be no opportunity to dislodge them by popular vote. Guatemalan 'anti-Communists' for this reason won much support from abroad, though most who used this label until 1954 were quite totally opposed to everything that had happened in their country since Ubico. After Castillo's entry into Guatemala on 18 June 1954 the government sent a note to the United Nations Security Council asking it to 'put a stop' to the 'open aggression' which, it charged, 'has been perpetrated by the Governments of Honduras and Nicaragua at the instigation of certain foreign monopolies.'[26] On 20 June the Security Council unanimously adopted a resolution calling 'for the immediate termination of any action likely to cause bloodshed' and requesting 'all members of the United Nations to abstain . . . from giving assistance to any such action'.[27] On 22 June Guatemala listed a series of air attacks which had been made on her territory since the Council's decision and asked for further United Nations action. Henry Cabot Lodge, Jr., United States delegate and president of the Council for the month, did not call a meeting until 25 June and then led the fight against placing Guatemala's case on the agenda. Only the Soviet Union, the Lebanon, New Zealand, and Denmark voted to consider Guatemala's note, Lodge's oppositionist argument being that the Organization of American States should handle the matter.[28] The Inter-American Peace Committee of the latter body, its work opposed by Arbenz' régime from 20 to 26 June in the hope of getting fairer treatment from the United Nations, arrived in Mexico on its way to investigate the situation on 29 June, two days after Arbenz had resigned, and soon gave up its mission.[29] More active than the Peace Committee was United States Ambassador John E. Peurifoy in the Guatemalan capital and in San Salvador, where the agreement was made to bring Castillo into the junta. One United States magazine reported concerning Peurifoy, 'When asked for advice, he gave it. In important ways, his recommendations were heeded. Thus, he was in constant contact with developments. And his advice was based on a single, firm principle:

[26] *New York Times*, 20 June 1954.
[27] Ibid. 21 June 1954.
[28] The question of U.N. versus OAS in this case is studied by Charles G. Fenwick, 'Jurisdictional Questions Involved in the Guatemalan Revolution', *AJIL*, xlviii (1954), 597–602; and Philip B. Taylor, Jr., 'The Guatemalan Affair: a Critique of United States Foreign Policy', *Am. Pol. Sci. R.*, l (1956), 787–806. Copious documentation is found in Cmd. 9277; see above, n. 21, p. 100.
[29] 'Report of the Inter-American Peace Committee on the Controversy between Guatemala, Honduras, Nicaragua', *Ann. OAS*, vi (1954), 239–45.

"Communism must go", he said.'[30] Seemingly little attention was paid elsewhere in the world to the fact that the reforming element in Guatemalan society was losing and not only the Communists.

From 8 July 1954 Carlos Castillo Armas was the ruler of Guatemala as head of the fourth military junta in succession. From 1 September 1954 he held the position of president. This position was confirmed only by a yes-or-no plebiscite, Ubico style, in October. The 1945 constitution was scrapped by decree, a new one (Guatemala's fifth) going into effect on 1 March 1956. In the first elections held (December 1955) all parties of the left were banned, the ready excuse being the charge that they had been infiltrated by Communists. Centre and rightist parties outside the pro-Castillo coalition were also blocked in this election, which was not governed by the system of proportional representation. The outstanding party with Castillo's blessing was the National Democratic Movement (Movimiento Democrático Nacional or MDN), which remained important after the death of its hero. That death came on 26 July 1957, through assassination.

Despite the lack of democracy in the workings of his government, Castillo did not undo all the reforms of his predecessors. Like the two basic charters preceding it, the constitution of 1956 provided guarantees of freedom; like the one just abolished, it recognized social obligations of the government, though without reference to the illegality of large estates. Constitutional relationships between Congress, the president, cabinet ministers, and the judiciary were unchanged; likewise the provision of the franchise for men and literate women over 18. IGSS and INFOP remained as vital government agencies, dating from Arévalo. Labour unions were recognized after reorganization under non-Communist auspices, though they lost a few advantages formerly theirs. Agrarian reform continued though at a considerably slower pace and with the interests of the wealthy landholder held in much greater esteem. The revolution had made too much of an impression to be ruthlessly suppressed without public indignation. Castillo seemed well enough advised to recognize this fact and to restrain the forces about him which would have restored the old order entirely.[31]

[30] 'Middleman in a Successful Revolution', *U.S. News & World Report*, xxxvii, 9 July 1954, 46–49, p. 46.
[31] Ruben E. Reina, in *Chinautla, a Guatemalan Indian Community* (New Orleans, Tulane Univ., Mid. Am. Res. Inst., 1960) and 'Political Crisis and Cultural Revitalization: the Guatemalan Case', *Human Organization*, xvii/4 (Winter 1958–9), 14–18, shows the impact made by the successive decisions of Arévalo, Arbenz,

The motives behind the assassination of Castillo have not been assessed. Though pro-government newspapers proclaimed at once a Communist inspiration for the deed, the little evidence which has been published seems to point in other directions. A presidential campaign took place while Luis Arturo González López took care of executive responsibilities (26 July–24 October 1957), resulting in the announced election on 20 October of MDN candidate Miguel Ortiz Passarelli. Riots in the streets of the capital, chiefly by the adherents of second-runner Miguel Ydígoras Fuentes who made charges of fraud, resulted in the cancellation of those elections and the announcement of new ones. Because Guillermo Flores Avendaño (in office 27 October 1957–2 March 1958) provided an amazingly neutral administration through a new campaign, the vote of 19 January 1958 is of considerable meaning for the future of the country.

Four good-sized parties were in the field—the MDN, the Reconciliación Democrática Nacional (called Redención) of Ydígoras, the Partido de la Democracia Cristiana de Guatemala (DCG), and the Partido Revolucionario (PR). The MDN and Redención are essentially conservative groups which none the less maintain some devotion to principles of democracy and 'social justice'. Only the play of personalities differentiates them. DCG is a Catholic group holding the same principles as Christian Democratic parties in other lands. PR is a leftist group which was not allowed to register under Castillo, but which supported non-Communist Mario Méndez Montenegro for the presidency in 1958. Ydígoras received 190,972 votes in this election, a plurality due perhaps partly to the vigour with which he had expressed his determination to become president. MDN candidate José Luis Cruz Salazar received 138,488 votes, Méndez Montenegro 132,824, and the DCG candidate only 5,834.[32] The new Congress, half of which was elected the same day with proportional representation again in effect, contained 23 MDN seats, 16 Redención, 9 DCG, and 6 PR in a total of 66. Ydígoras was elected president by Congress, MDN joining with Redención to form his majority and Cruz Salazar bowing out of the

---

and Castillo on the inhabitants of a *municipio* next door to Guatemala City. Chinautla is essentially a Pokomam Indian village, but this study takes into account the varied effects upon the ladinos of the community, the conservative Indian families tied to old *cofradía* customs, the Protestants, and the 'new Catholics' associated with the tertiary Franciscan order.

[32] Report of the Comisión Extraordinaria de Escrutinio to the Congress, 9 Feb. 1958, provided by the Guatemalan Electoral Tribunal.

race. Whatever the wisdom of the electorate or the forces which had been brought to bear upon it, there was a renewal of democratic practice in Guatemala in January 1958 which seems to bode well for the future.

Miguel Ydígoras Fuentes, sixty years old at his inauguration on 2 March 1958, is another army officer in the presidency. Since he had been closely associated with the Ubico régime and was the chief opponent of Arbenz in the elections of 1950, many thought of him as an ultra-conservative who would take the country back to dictatorship. Ydígoras has insisted, however, on his dedication to democracy. Though he was responsible for the upsetting of the October 1957 elections, the circumstances surrounding them were indeed suspicious. Another election in December 1958, for the important post of mayor in the capital city, seemed to belie Ydígoras' words, when Luis Fernando Galich (PR) won but was declared ineligible on a technicality. With the technicality removed, however, Galich ran again, was elected in July 1959, and in August assumed the office. The Congressional election of 6 December 1959, though it gave the parties backing Ydígoras a healthy majority, showed a strong vote in Guatemala and Escuintla departments for the Partido Revolucionario and considerable sentiment for three new parties on the left.[33] The municipal elections of 8 January 1961, though they resulted in several charges of fraud, brought PR officials into office in other *municipios* including Quezaltenango; in addition Redención, MDN, and DCG candidates were favoured in a variety of localities under a complex array of local circumstances, and in still other centres the popularity of independent civic groups was recognized.[34] The trend toward fair counting evidenced by the success of opposition candidates seems to indicate that seeds of democracy planted in Guatemala have survived the trampling of 1954–7 and may be hardy enough to last and bear flower in the future.

In the freer atmosphere since 1958, comparable in some ways to that which existed in 1945–53, the growth of small parties representing fine divergencies of viewpoint has been tremendous. To bring some order out of the growing electoral chaos, Congress decreed on 28 April 1960 that a group must present the names of 10,000 affiliates (rather than 5,000 as had been the requirement), of whom at least 10 per cent must be literate, before it could be

[33] *DCA*, 8 Dec. 1959, gives the following incomplete totals for all candidates: Redención 80,458; PR 54,335; the three mentioned leftist parties 27,329; MDN 20,823; DCG 18,231; others 5,634.
[34] *Imp.*, 9–11 Jan. 1961.

inscribed as a party.[35] Even with this requirement there remained ten legal parties in October 1960.[36] The two largest were Redención and MDN, which by this time had moved closer together in support of Ydígoras (together they commanded a two-thirds vote in the Congress). DCG and PR remained the most significant of the others. Three leftist parties organized in 1958 (Unidad Revolucionaria, Auténtico Revolucionario, and Nacional Reivindicador del 44) were important chiefly in that they were allowed to be active despite occasional stands somewhat to the left of PR. Three splinter parties on the right served only to emphasize the conservative orientation of the post-Arbenz epoch. Two new rightist groupings of some size, whose future remains uncertain, were organized late in 1960. They are the Movimiento de Liberación Nacional, which apparently hopes to gain votes left behind when MDN moved closer to Ydígoras, and the Unión Democrática, which now includes a number of Congressmen elected by MDN and Redención.

The reputation for conservatism of the Ydígoras régime itself stems chiefly from the background of the president, the administration's continued political battles with PR, and its stand in international affairs. Ydígoras suspended diplomatic relations with the Cuban régime of Fidel Castro in April 1960. Through the remainder of that year and into 1961 his government was accused in the United Nations of harbouring anti-Castro persons who were training for an assault upon the island of Cuba. Ydígoras' close co-operation with the United States government during this period was obvious. Yet even that co-operation produced some move toward reform in Guatemala. A project for an income tax brought Ydígoras the strong support (on that issue) of the country's labour unions, for example, and seemed to place the United States (which was in favour) and Ydígoras considerably to the left of PR (which was opposed).[37] In assessing this administration, one cannot forget that it is likewise continuing many of the reforms begun in the Arévalo–Arbenz era. On the other hand, one hears much in Guatemala of secret government connivance against its enemies. In 1959

[35] See *Ley electoral* (Guatemala, 1957) and text of the decree, *El Guatemalteco* (Guatemala), 9 May and 9 June 1960.

[36] 'Brete de partidos por requisito de diez mil afiliados', *Imp.*, 13 Oct. 1960.

[37] The headlines in *DCA* regarding the labour unions' stand are impressive: 'Entusiasta pronunciamiento de los sindicatos: apoyan impuesto a la renta' (20 Jan. 1961); 'SAMFistas apoyan income tax' (24 Jan.); 'Sindicato Luz y Fuerza apoya income tax' (31 Jan.).

Guatemala

and 1960 there were many unexplained and seemingly senseless bombings in public places, as well as assaults upon persons critical of the régime. Méndez Montenegro was jailed in January 1960 and Guatemala's largest newspaper closed in November of the same year, when each incurred the president's wrath, but both were protected almost at once by the courts. The big test will of course come in 1964 when it may be seen whether a very un-neutral régime like that of President Ydígoras can provide the same atmosphere for a presidential campaign and election which prevailed when he was chosen in 1958. Perhaps this is not too much to expect from a man who has said that the major effort of his first two years was to seek peace for Central America and democracy for his own country.[38]

BOUNDARIES AND BUDGETS

The republic of Guatemala has thus slowly begun to assume true republican dimensions. Equally slowly, the area of its geographical jurisdiction has been settled until now only one problem of this genre remains. The adherence of Chiapas to Mexico and the inclusion of Soconusco in Chiapas were not considered final by Guatemala until 1882, when an agreement settled the present boundary with Mexico. The extent to which the Motagua valley belonged to Guatemala was ascertained with definitude only in 1933, when a special tribunal of arbitration settled the frontier with Honduras. The less controversial line with El Salvador was established in 1938. The *de facto* boundaries with British Honduras on the east are not recognized by Guatemala to this day, nor even the right to existence of the British colony in Belize.

The last treaty arrangement between Great Britain and Spain in regard to this territory was the Convention of London of 1786, which stipulated the British right to cut logwood and mahogany around the settlement of Belize as far south as the Sibun River, but specified the sovereignty of Spain. In 1859 President Carrera of Guatemala was willing to sign a treaty with Great Britain setting *boundaries* with British Honduras, admitting the British to new lands they had occupied from the Sibun to the Sarstún River, without reference to the previous stipulation of Spanish sovereignty. The

[38] 'En resumen, el mayor esfuerzo hecho por mi Gobierno durante los 24 meses de su existencia, fue buscar la paz, la paz, la paz, para tranquilidad y sosiego de guatemaltecos y demás centroamericanos y, la democracia, la democracia, la democracia, para felicidad de nosotros los guatemaltecos.' (*Mensaje del General e Ingeniero Miguel Ydígoras Fuentes, Presidente de Guatemala, al Honorable Congreso Nacional, 1º. de marzo* (Guatemala, 1960), p. 2.)

British position in regard to the colony, established officially in Belize just three years later, is that previous Spanish rights in the area (no longer asserted after 1821) did not necessarily devolve upon either Mexico or Guatemala at the time of independence; and that the treaty of 1859 with Guatemala and a similar one of 1897 with Mexico were a complete acknowledgement by those nations of Britain's sovereignty in the defined region.

In Article 7 of the treaty between Great Britain and Guatemala, the two governments agreed to take 'adequate means for establishing the easiest communication (either by means of a cart-road, or by employing the rivers, or both united, according to the opinion of the surveying engineers), between the fittest place on the Atlantic coast, near the settlement of Belize, and the capital of Guatemala'.[39] The cart road or its equivalent was never built. A railway and highway which have been constructed more recently were done without aid from the British government. Various compromise offers have been made by both countries to resolve the lack of realization of the agreement, generally concerning an amount of money to be paid by Great Britain in lieu of her promise of assistance, but none has been accepted by both parties. Guatemala has for this reason insisted in recent years that the treaty of 1859 has lost its validity, and that she is entitled to the same sovereignty in Belize as was once exercised by Spain. (Mexico had held to the same claim for the district north of the Sibun River until 1897.) Great Britain offered in 1946 to let the International Court of Justice interpret the validity of the Treaty of 1859, but Guatemala declined arbitration unless it dealt on a basis of equity with the entire question of the ownership of Belize. Neither country now seems interested in pressing its case in the Court's direction.[40]

Since 1938, when this issue was revived, the Guatemalan press has frequently been whipped up to a passion on the subject of 'nuestro Belice', and several books have been written on the sub-

[39] *The Annual Register* (London, 1860), Chronicle, p. 223.

[40] R. A. Humphreys, 'The Anglo–Guatemalan Dispute', *International Affairs*, xxiv (1948), 387–404, succinctly reviews the chief arguments presented on both sides. These are developed more fully, and the British position defended, in the same author's historical treatment of the territory's status entitled *The Diplomatic History of British Honduras, 1638–1901* (London, OUP for RIIA, 1961). New complexities striking at both countries' contentions are dealt with by Wayne M. Clegern, 'New Light on the Belize Dispute', *AJIL*, lii (1958), 280–97, and 'A Guatemalan Defense of the British Honduras Boundary of 1859', *HAHR*, xl (1960), 570–81, D. A. G. Waddell, *British Honduras: a Historical and Contemporary Survey* (London, OUP for RIIA, 1961) provides a well-balanced picture of attitudes and situations within the colony.

ject.[41] The British Hondurans themselves have shown more interest in self-rule than in attachment to Guatemala. But if complete self-rule should come, such attachment or more likely inclusion as a distinct part of a Central American union cannot be ruled out as a possibility.

How does the republic of Guatemala, perturbed by the question of democracy and excited about the matter of Belize, get and spend its money? Public finance in Guatemala as in many other countries has become big business indeed during the last twenty years. Government receipts in the fiscal year ending 30 June 1939 were only 12 million quetzales; in 1944, 17 million; 1949, 45 million; 1954, 66 million; 1959, 90 million.[42] Expenditures have generally kept pace; in the years 1956–9 they surpassed receipts by more than 14 million quetzales annually. (In United States dollars the figures are the same, the dollar and Guatemalan quetzal having been traded at par since 1926.) A large share of the revenue (46 per cent in 1939, 47 per cent in 1959) comes from customs duties on imports and exports, with the former about three times the latter. A consumption tax on alcoholic beverages and tobacco brings in nearly 20 per cent of the total; other excise taxes and stamp taxes about 10 per cent.[43] A profits tax established in 1938, though somewhat broadened since 1944, brought in only 9 per cent of the total in 1959, compared with 6 per cent under Ubico. This means that the tax structure of the old régime in Guatemala has remained relatively untouched by the governments since 1944. The income-tax proposal under discussion in 1961 would change this situation.

From the United States Guatemala received $9 million in grants in the period 1946–50, $6 million in 1951–5, $16 million in 1956, $19 million in 1957, $17 million in 1958, and $12 million in 1959 and again in 1960. Of the total since World War II ($93 million, 1946–60) the sum of $57 million was for economic and technical assistance, $29 million for road-building, and $3 million for urgent relief in 1955–6.[44] The rise in United States assistance after the

---

[41] The opening charge was Guatemala. Secretaría de Relaciones Exteriores, *Libro blanco* (Guatemala, 1938); Eng. tr. *White Book* (Guatemala, 1938). Continuations have been published in succeeding years.

[42] U.N., *Stat. Yb.*, *1951*, pp. 480–1; *1958*, p. 471; *1959*, p. 498. Figures are rounded to the nearest million.

[43] U.S. Bureau of Foreign Commerce, *Investment in Central America* [*Investment in C.A.* in subsequent footnotes] (Washington, USGPO, 1956), gives more detailed tax information on each of the Central American countries in sections headed 'Public Finance' and 'Taxation'.

[44] *Foreign Grants and Credits by the United States Government* (U.S. Office of Business

advent of Castillo to power was quite notable, and contrasted rather sharply on a per capita basis with programmes in neighbouring countries. (In 1956–8, Guatemala received from this source nearly $16 per resident, Honduras a little over $3, El Salvador less than $2, and Mexico 12.5 cents.) In the period 1954–8, Guatemala was also the recipient of aid amounting to $1 million each from United Nations technical-assistance and children's-relief programmes and of substantial loans from the International Bank for Reconstruction and Development and the United States Export-Import Bank.[45]

The Guatemalan executive organism contains ten ministries. Of these, Communications and Public Works was apportioned 23 per cent of the nation's $102,433,788 budget for the fiscal year 1960–1, Public Education 13 per cent, Public Health and Social Assistance 10 per cent, National Defence 9 per cent, Finance and Public Credit 5 per cent, Government 5 per cent, Agriculture 3 per cent, Foreign Relations 2 per cent, Economy 1 per cent, and Labour and Social Welfare 1 per cent. Other large items were the public debt 9 per cent, the presidential office 5 per cent, agrarian reform 3 per cent, pensions 3 per cent, the judicial organism 2 per cent, and the University of San Carlos 2 per cent.[46] Current expenditures for education, health, and social welfare occupied the same relative position (21 per cent of the total) in the budget of 1939 as in that of 1959, though the outlay for defence dropped from 17 per cent under Ubico to 10 per cent under Arbenz.[47] Save for the item of defence, the régimes of Ubico, Arévalo, Arbenz, Castillo, and Ydígoras, gauged by their uses of money rather than their attitudes toward labour or agrarian reform, had indeed much in common. The economic realities of their nation are such as to have given them little other choice.

SUBSISTENCE AGRICULTURE

The basic economic structure of Central America has not changed in 140 years of independence from Spain. Guatemala like all her isthmian neighbours remains dependent upon agriculture for a

---

Economics; quarterly), June 1957, pp. S–23, S–24, S–25; June 1959, pp. S–26, S–27; June 1960, pp. S–36, S–40, S–41. Figures are rounded to the nearest million and represent U.S. fiscal years ending on 30 June of the years indicated.

[45] U.N., *Stat. Yb., 1959*, p. 423.

[46] *Presupuesto general de ingresos y egresos, 1960–1961* (Guatemala, 1960), pp. 8–9.

[47] U.N., *Stat. Yb., 1959*, p. 498.

living. In 1950 two-thirds of the Guatemalan people making a direct contribution to the economy were agriculturists, while others laboured in closely related food-processing industries.[48] Nevertheless only 5,086,000 acres, or less than one-fifth of the nation's total land area, was then being used for pasture or cultivation.[49] Though Guatemala is known to outsiders as a 'coffee republic' and has well-recognized banana interests, over nine-tenths of her farming area, now as in colonial and pre-colonial times, is devoted to production to meet her own immediate needs for food and clothing.

Maize, chief stand-by of the people for a few millenia past, was harvested from 1,361,000 acres or 27 per cent of the active farming area in 1950. Two-thirds of this crop was grown on farms of less than 10 *manzanas* or 17·26 acres each, testimony to the subsistence nature of the operation.[50]

Maize is grown in all parts of the country, a second harvest annually amounting to about one-sixth of the first. Very little is exported, and in poor crop years (such as 1955) there have been considerable imports. Increases in production have been accompanied by augmentation of the space devoted to the crop, the nation-wide yield in 1958 remaining at 600 lb. to the acre. The south-western departments of Quezaltenango, Retalhuleu, and Suchitepéquez have raised their own production per acre to twice the national level.[51]

Beans of several varieties (including black beans in abundance) were likewise grown widely in 1950, their harvest amounting to 184,000 acres. In 1958 half the acreage produced the same number of beans, with Jutiapa department in the south-east specializing in this product. The highlands of San Marcos and Quezaltenango produced more than half of the nation's 76,000 acres of wheat in 1950; much wheat and wheat flour are imported. Widely raised sorghum and *habas* or broad beans occupied about 50,000 acres

[48] *Sexto censo de población*, pp. 219–20, 261.

[49] Inter-American Statistical Institute, *La estructura agropecuaria de las naciones americanas: análisis estadístico-censal de los resultados obtenidos bajo el Programa del Censo de las Américas de 1950* [*Estruct. agr.* in subsequent references] (Washington, 1957), p. 131. 'Superficie total informada' less 'tierras con montes, bosques y breñales' and 'tierras de otras clases (no utilizables)'.

[50] Ibid. p. 186. No allowance is made for acreage duplication in the two harvests of maize.

[51] *Estimaciones de la producción agropecuaria de la república de Guatemala para el año agrícola 1957–58* (Guatemala, Dir. Gen. Est., 1958): 'Superficie cosechada y producción obtenida de maíz de primera y segunda siembra en la república, por departamento, año agrícola 1957–58'. One *quintal* in Central America equals 100 Spanish pounds or 101·4 lb. avoirdupois.

each in the census year. There were also 38,000 acres of sugar-cane (of which Escuintla provides one-third of the nation's production) and 19,000 acres of rice (Jutiapa and Santa Rosa predominating). Other ground crops grown in some quantity (in decreasing order according to the space devoted to their cultivation) were potatoes, tobacco, garden vegetables, cassava, sesame, henequen, peanuts, oats, green peas, chickpeas, and barley.[52] Cotton has assumed some importance since 1950, chiefly as an export commodity.

The area covered by Guatemalan tree and bush crops in 1950 was 443,000 acres, almost all of it planted in coffee.[53] Bananas, though important in trade, occupied only 42,000 acres. Other tree and bush crops (named in decreasing order according to the number of farms reporting them) were oranges, avocados, peaches, plantains, pineapples, apples, plums, coconuts, cacao, cinchona, and grapes.[54]

Guatemalan farmers in the same year reported 1,440,000 acres of land in natural pasturage; 1,060,000 acres at rest or with failing harvest; and at least 339,000 acres in seeded pasturage.[55] The 1950 inventory of domestic animals ran as follows: 919,000 cattle; 716,000 sheep; 424,000 pigs; 186,000 horses; 79,000 goats; 59,000 mules; and 10,000 donkeys. There were also 4,260,000 chickens; 236,000 turkeys; 58,000 ducks; 13,000 geese; and 121,000 swarms of bees.[56] Guatemala imports cattle and exports a few pigs, but livestock, poultry, and bees alike are basically for the Guatemalan people. Nowhere else in Central America are there comparable numbers of sheep and goats.

EXPORTS AND IMPORTS

With Central America divided, each part has had to look out not only for its immediate subsistence but for its own foreign exchange. From the decline of the Central American cacao trade in the seventeenth century until the coming of independence, the area of

[52] *Estruct. agr.*, p. 186; *Censo agropecuario: 1950* (3 vols., Guatemala, 1954–5), i. 118, 139, 157, 171, 233; *Estimaciones para 1957–58:* 'Frijol', 'Arroz en granza', 'Trigo', 'Caña de azúcar'.
[53] *Estruct. agr.*, pp. 131, 235. 'Tierras con cafetales, frutales y viñedos' of Cuadro 65 plus 'Superficie cosechada' of Cuadro 129. See Cuadro 65, note *a*.
[54] Ibid. p. 235.
[55] Ibid. pp. 131, 186, 235. The last figure is 'Tierras de cultivo cosechadas' of Cuadro 65 less 'Total superficie cosechada' of Cuadro 94 and 'Superficie cosechada' of Cuadro 129. The amount of seeded pasturage is uncertain because of the unknown factor of acreage duplication in the two harvests of maize.
[56] Ibid. p. 289.

the state of Guatemala had contributed much less to the colonial export trade than El Salvador and Nicaragua. From the 1820's until the 1860's Guatemala relied almost entirely on one commodity to provide her with purchasing power abroad. This was *cochinilla* or cochineal, a scarlet red dyestuff prepared from the dried bodies of insects of the same name which feed upon various species of tuna and nopal (prickly pear) cactus. The cultivation of cochineal was introduced from Mexico in early colonial times but did not then become commercially important. Only after 1811, when the Real Sociedad Económica took its second lease of life and displayed an active interest in the matter, did the industry really begin. When independence came, exports began on a large scale. Though production was erratic, due perhaps chiefly to varying political conditions, the sales trend was upward for nearly four decades, with the countryside about Antigua and Lake Amatitlán specializing in the trade. The production of synthetic dyes in Europe, beginning in the late 1850's, undermined the market rapidly, however, and Guatemala had to look for other earnings.

Coffee stepped in where cochineal stepped out. Coffee had been known in Guatemala for a century before this happened, but there had been little of it, and none had been grown for export. Justo Rufino Barrios was interested in the cultivation of coffee on his farms in San Marcos department in the 1860's, before he became president. Later he gave every encouragement both private and governmental, including free coffee plants, to persons interested in growing the crop. From the 1870's production grew almost steadily until the 1910's, after which it resumed its climb only in the 1950's. Only one isthmian nation (El Salvador) exports more coffee than Guatemala. In the four-year period 1956–9 its value constituted 76 per cent of the total value of the nation's trade to the exterior.[57] Guatemalan coffee, like that of the remainder of the isthmus, commands relatively good prices because of its mild flavour.

Coffee cannot be grown everywhere in Guatemala, but some of it is grown in nearly every department. (El Petén is the chief exception.) The bulk of the quality export comes from the populous strip along the face of the mountains toward the Pacific (San Marcos to Santa Rosa) and from another excellent area in Alta Verapaz. Since the successful planting of coffee requires a longer-term

[57] U.N., *Yb. Int. Trade Stat., 1959*, i. 250. In computing the percentage, the total export-trade value was taken from Table 4.

investment than the cultivation of maize or beans, the trend from the beginning has been toward larger coffee estates or *fincas* managed by wealthier persons. In the twentieth century, the small foreign community increased its holdings of coffee until only one-twentieth of the production remained in Guatemalan hands. Germans or persons of German descent alone held about two-thirds of the total, by contrast. The holdings of German citizens were expropriated in 1944 and 1945 and organized as the Fincas Nacionales managed by the government, providing about one-third of the nation's production. During the Arbenz régime, some of these estates were distributed to landless peasants, but under Castillo they were taken back by the government. The common labourer on the *finca*, whether it was run by private parties or the government, earned in recent years a money wage varying from 18 cents to 39 cents a day.[58] The average monthly earnings of *all* workers on the Fincas Nacionales outside Guatemala department was $18.18 in 1956.[59]

Guatemala's second most valuable export in the period 1956–9 was bananas, which made up 13 per cent of her trade.[60] Some bananas were shipped from Guatemala as early as the 1880's. The trade became significant after the United Fruit Company obtained its first concession in 1906. From that time until 1929 the business grew steadily and mightily. Then, after some fluctuations due to global conditions, a high peak was reached in 1947, when Guatemala was the second nation of the world (Honduras the first) in banana sales. After 1947 Guatemalan production dropped; in 1958 her position among world exporters was only ninth. United Fruit had all its early Guatemalan plantations in the Motagua valley near the Caribbean, where the village of Bananera (Izabal department) was its headquarters. Since the late 1930's a Pacific coastal area around Tiquisate in Escuintla has been more important. In the 1950's the Standard Fruit Company, a competing United States corporation, began significant banana operations around Retalhuleu. Standard Fruit in this area buys bananas from independent producers, to whom the company supplies various services; United Fruit has some similar arrangements.

---

[58] See p. 44 of Elizabeth E. Hoyt, 'The Indian Laborer on Guatemalan Coffee Fincas', *Int. Am. Econ. Aff.*, ix/1 (Summer 1955), 33–46, a study covering fifty farms, four of them Fincas Nacionales.

[59] See p. 476 of 'Minimum Wage Problems and Policy in Guatemala', *Int. Lab. R.*, lxxix (1959), 459–86.

[60] U.N., *Yb. Int. Trade Stat., 1959*, i. 250.

The United Fruit Company is the largest single agricultural enterprise in Guatemala, though it obviously has no monopoly position. Its size, the fact that it is foreign-owned, and its control of Guatemala's chief railroad and port facilities have combined to bring it much criticism in the country. When Ubico was president, the government and United Fruit worked hand in hand, both profiting at the expense of the labourer in the fields. During Arévalo's administration great labour troubles arose but were settled with gains for the workers. Arbenz moved to expropriate idle United Fruit properties which the company was holding for future reserves. These properties were returned by Castillo, though the company found much land it was now willing to donate toward agrarian resettlement. United Fruit points out that the wage it pays today is about twice as high as the coffee worker's wage, and at the same time admits that a man working for United Fruit produces two or three times as much wealth as the man on the coffee *finca*.[61] There is no doubt that, because of pressures from organized labour and more enlightened policies developed in Boston headquarters, United Fruit pays much better wages and provides much better facilities for its employees now than a generation ago. There is no indication, on the other hand, that either coffee or banana producers who have their employees in Guatemala and their customers abroad feel any special responsibility for lifting the economy of the Guatemalan nation anywhere near the level of the international economy of which it is a part.

The new cotton harvest composed 4 per cent of the nation's exports in 1956–9; a remaining miscellany of relatively minor items took up 7 per cent. Chicle from the forests of El Petén for use in the making of chewing-gum was important until 1948, when labour troubles and synthetic products reduced the trade tremendously; a volume worth $2,700,000 in 1959 suggests it may now be experiencing a revival. Citronella oil and lemon-grass oil together make up the only other item producing over a million dollars a year through most of the late 1950's. Guatemala's total exports in 1956–9 averaged $107,700,000 annually, 67 per cent going to the United States, 14 per cent to West Germany, 5 per cent to the Netherlands, 3 per cent each to Sweden and Belgium-Luxembourg, and 2 per cent to El Salvador.[62]

[61] Stacy May and Galo Plaza, *The United Fruit Company in Latin America* (Washington, Nat. Planning Assoc., 1958), p. 169.

[62] U.N., *Yb. Int. Trade Stat., 1959*, i. 250. The average value of total exports is computed from Table 4.

In the early years of Guatemalan independence, Great Britain quickly took Spain's place as the chief provider of the nation's imports. British trade declined and the United States took the lead in the earlier twentieth century, the First World War making the transition decisive. In the period 1956-9, Guatemalan imports averaged $142,200,000 annually, coming 61 per cent from the United States, 9 per cent from West Germany, 6 per cent from the Netherlands Antilles (petroleum products), 5 per cent from the United Kingdom, 3 per cent from Mexico, and 2 per cent each from Canada, the Netherlands, Belgium-Luxembourg, and Italy. From items reported by Guatemala as her imports of 1958, sorted for purposes of rough comparison into categories adopted by the Standard International Trade Classification, the following picture emerges: Manufactured 'goods' (as distinct from 'articles') made up 32 per cent of the total, with 'iron and steel and manufactures' purchased in excess of $11 million; 'piece goods and trimmings' over $9 million; 'paper, pasteboard, cardboard, and manufactures' over $4 million; rubber manufactures over $3 million; and 'thread, yarn, cordage, &c.', 'hand tools', and 'glass and glass manufactures' over $1 million each. Machinery and transport equipment was the second highest category (28 per cent of the total), machinery amounting to over $21 million; road motor vehicles over $5 million; and tractors and parts over $2 million. Chemicals constituted 14 per cent, with 'chemical products' over $6 million; medicinal and pharmaceutical products over $3 million; fertilizers over $2 million; and 'soaps, candles, dyes, &c.' and 'perfumery, essential oils, cosmetics, &c.' over $1 million each. Fuels and lubricants were another 10 per cent, with gasoline over $4 million; fuel oils over $3 million; and lubricating oils and greases over $1 million. Food and edible animal fats made up 8 per cent, with 'cereals', 'flour', and 'meat and edible animal fats' over $2 million each, and live animals over $1 million. Manufactured 'articles' other than machinery and transport amounted to 7 per cent, with 'made-up articles of textiles' over $6 million, and 'scientific and optical apparatus' over $1 million.[63]

[63] U.N., *Yb. Int. Trade Stat., 1959*, i. 249-50. In computing the percentages, the total used was that of the individual items listed. The minor items omitted from the listing would doubtless change the picture to some extent; so might also a more precise description of the items given, Guatemala being the only one of the Central American countries not yet to have adopted the Standard International Trade Classification.

NON-AGRICULTURAL OCCUPATIONS

Guatemala's list of imports is a reminder that, while two-thirds of her economically active people are devoted to agricultural pursuits, the remaining third are also important. The census of 1950 found 11·5 per cent of the economically active group engaged in some kind of manufacturing, 9·9 per cent employed in service occupations (domestic, governmental, and commercial), 5·4 per cent active in trade, 2·7 per cent in construction, and 1·6 per cent in transport.[64] A goodly portion of the manufacturers are craftsmen who work in the home, producing items which were already popular in colonial and precolonial epochs. Indian towns often specialize in certain articles of this type, much of whose distribution is effected by human burden-carriers using lines of commerce which still ignore the Spanish conquest.[65] More modern manufacturing has developed around the capital, Quezaltenango, and a few rural areas.[66]

An industrial census of 1953 showed a total of 20,567 persons working in 1,072 industrial establishments hiring three or more workers each. Of these, 3,737 were employed in 249 firms engaged in the processing of foodstuffs, especially coffee and wheat. Shoes and wearing apparel occupied the attention of 2,946 persons in 218 businesses; the shoes are made chiefly by hand, and much of the apparel in private homes connected with the establishments. The manufacture of textiles was in third place, with 2,558 workers in 45 plants, though 'piece goods and trimmings' are the largest single item on Guatemala's import list. The beverage industry (beer, *aguardiente*, and soft drinks) employed 2,021 persons in 43 plants. Other manufacturing industries employing more than 1,000 persons each were the making of non-metallic mineral products (there is one cement plant outside Guatemala City), the lumber industry, and the making of chemical products, especially soap and matches. Of the 20,567 persons included in the census, 660 were owners or associates without salary; 599 were managers at an average salary of $241.70 monthly; 2,549 were administrative workers paid an average of $87.12 per month; 15,849 were production workers at $43.54 per month; 597 were workers at home at $28.73; and 313

---

[64] *Sexto censo de población*, pp. 261–3.
[65] Felix Webster McBryde, *Cultural and Historical Geography of Southwest Guatemala*, provides an intimate look at the separate Indian economy.
[66] Manning Nash, *Machine Age Maya: the Industrialization of a Guatemalan Community* (Am. Anthrop. Assoc., 1958) studies the impact of a large textile factory on the *municipio* of Cantel.

were relatives who worked without remuneration.[67] The only significant new industry since this census is a rubber-tire company founded in 1958.

Mining has been of little consequence in Guatemala although zinc, lead, and a few other metals have been exported on a small scale. Neither has lumbering developed in proportions to match those of Honduras and Nicaragua, although the resources are present. The possibility of the existence of petroleum in commercial quantities in El Petén caused much stir in the capital in the late 1950's. The first oil drill was located on Guatemalan soil in January 1958, concessions having been granted to several United States firms. A first strike was made on 17 July 1959 near Chinajá, Alta Verapaz, on the border of El Petén. President Ydígoras announced there was well-founded hope that 1960 would be the year of petroleum in Guatemala.[68] But disappointment with short runs and dry wells proved to be the nation's lot for the time being.

The establishment of reliable communications systems, power facilities, and banking conveniences are of course essential to further industrial development in mining or manufacturing on the entire Central American isthmus. The Guatemalan government has paid attention to these necessities since the régime of Justo Rufino Barrios, and considering the difficulties a great deal has been accomplished in providing the basic requisites. The problems involved in providing transportation facilities have been the mountainous terrain, the country's basic poverty, and the unwillingness in repeated instances of contractors and concessionaires to put the interests of the country above the desire for immediate profits.

At the end of the Carrera–Cerna era in 1871, cart roads were as scarce as railways in Guatemala, there being none at all of either. The first of the cart roads were built by the Barrios régime, uniting the capital with both Caribbean and Pacific. Their condition remained bad, however, and many other roads unbuilt, until the 1920's. Since then every departmental capital except Flores in El Petén has been tied to the others by all-weather road. Stretches of asphalt were laid in the 1940's and 1950's, until by the end of 1960 Guatemala had four main arteries nearly completed.

The route best known in the exterior, because it carries the name of the Inter-American highway, runs near or through the departmental capitals Huehuetenango, Quezaltenango, Totonicapán,

[67] *Guatemala en Cifras, 1958*, pp. 78–80.　　[68] *Mensaje del Presidente, 1960*, p. 3.

Sololá, Chimaltenango, Antigua, Guatemala, Cuilapa, and Jutiapa, providing a most scenic drive through rough countryside from
the Mexican state of Chiapas to the Salvadoran department of
Santa Ana. The Inter-American highway in Guatemala, with short
side-trips along the way (to Zaculeu, Lake Atitlán, and Antigua,
for example) will be a tourist's delight for many years to come;
though to North Americans it is scarcely known as yet, its first 50
kilometres south-east of Mexico remaining difficult because of fre-
quent landslides and washouts. This short stretch, known locally as
El Tapón (the plug), was the last link missing in the highway from
Canada to Costa Rica until the first traffic passed through in 1957.
A roughly parallel route in the Pacific coastal lands promises to be
even more important for commerce. Retalhuleu, Mazatenango,
and Escuintla with their rich fields lie on this smooth connexion,
which runs from Chiapas to the Salvadoran department of Ahuachapán. When Chiapas finishes the coastal route on which it is
working and a bridge is built to provide fast passage to the Salvadoran littoral highway, inter-American autoists and truckers pre-
ferring speed to scenery will surely drive this way. Paved highways
paralleling rail lines now also connect Guatemala City with San
José on the Pacific and Matías de Gálvez–Puerto Barrios on the
Caribbean. Taken jointly, these two routes provide a 250-mile
journey passing through or near Escuintla, El Progreso, and Zacapa, the only paved highway crossing the isthmus between Mexican
Tehuantepec and Panama. In 1959 a river and earth road connexion was opened to Flores; other roads are planned to Belize and
frontier points with Honduras. In 1937 Guatemala licensed 2,500
passenger cars and 1,600 commercial vehicles; in 1957 there were
19,900 cars and 9,500 commercial vehicles.[69]

Guatemala's first railway lines were built in the early 1880's to
connect the capital and Retalhuleu with their respective ports San
José and Champerico. The important line from the capital to
Puerto Barrios was begun at the same time but not completed until
1908. In 1912 the International Railways of Central America
(IRCA) was formed through the consolidation of these three lines
and their connexions, reaching to a Mexican line at Ayutla or
Tecún Umán near the Pacific coast. Rails from El Salvador were
linked at Zacapa in 1929. There was much duplication of financial
interest between the new railway company and United Fruit.
(Minor Cooper Keith, for example, was for nine years president of

[69] U.N., *Stat. Yb.*, *1951*, p. 317; *1959*, p. 333.

IRCA while vice-president of the banana firm.) In 1936, when IRCA was in trouble financially, United Fruit obtained a controlling share of the railway's stock and introduced close operating agreements. To aid the railway, United reneged (with the co-operation of President Ubico) on a promise to build Guatemala a good port on the Pacific. To aid the fruit company, IRCA charged less for long hauls than for shorter ones where Pacific port competition would not enter the picture. San José (with an IRCA pier and IRCA connexions) is now coming into its own as a receiver of imports, however, and the new paved highway to new government port installations at Matías de Gálvez may reduce complaints concerning IRCA's service and rates to the Caribbean. There is a short railway in Alta Verapaz connecting coffee lands with the Polochic River, originally built by a German firm but taken over by the government in 1942. An electric railway operated in the 1930's between Quezaltenango and IRCA's Pacific coastal line but proved economically unfeasible. No railways have been built since, save those on fruit-company premises, designed only to get out the bananas.

Most passenger and freight traffic moving to and from Guatemala is conveyed by air or sea in carriers of foreign ownership. Guatemala began to develop a small merchant marine in 1959, however, and for fifteen years before that operated the Empresa Guatemalteca de Aviación or Aviateca, an airline of its own, which has provided service to Florida and Louisiana. Aviateca's chief importance is that it offers flights to most parts of the Guatemalan nation.

Greater weaknesses appear when one turns from transportation facilities to telecommunication and electric power. The telegraph came to Guatemala in the 1870's, the telephone a decade later. The telephone is used chiefly in local conversation; telegraph service is inexpensive and the more common of the two outside the capital. Electric power appeared in Guatemala City during the 1880's and has since become fairly widespread through the development of municipally owned stations utilizing the current of the streams. But production is small, only 39 per cent of the urban homes in the nation being served with electricity in 1949. Consumption in the vicinity of the capital alone advanced from 25 million kilowatt hours in 1937 to 124 million in 1957, however, and more progress is envisaged.[70] The United States-owned American

[70] U.N., *Stat. Yb.*, *1951*, p. 278; *1959*, pp. 283, 543.

& Foreign Power Company provides the current in the capital, which is more than that used in all the rest of the country.

Since the time of Arévalo and Arbenz, Guatemala's banking facilities seem ample. Reasonably stable currency has been available since 1926, when the quetzal came into being and was pegged at par with the dollar. The central bank formed in 1926, now called the Banco de Guatemala, has provided the core of native production investment ever since. The Crédito Hipotecario Nacional was created in 1929 to grant government loans to private agricultural enterprises. INFOP, organized in 1948, is intended to spur subsistence agriculture in crops now unnecessarily imported, to lessen the dependence of the country on two crops for export, to encourage the growth of new manufacturing enterprise, and to promote the building of much needed low-cost housing. The Banco Nacional Agrario was formed in 1953 to assist farmers who were being relocated under the agrarian-reform measure. Eight private banks also operate in the country.[71]

ECONOMIC OUTLOOK: SHOES FOR THE SHOELESS?

Midway through the twentieth century, fewer than one-fourth of the Guatemalan people aged seven and over wore shoes. Most of those who did were ladinos. Among the ladinos, to be more precise, the census of 1950 found that 46·4 per cent of the men and 51·9 per cent of the women wore shoes; 13·1 per cent of the men and 2·5 per cent of the women wore sandals; and 40·6 per cent of the men and 45·6 per cent of the women went barefooted. Among the Indians, constituting over half the population, 3·4 per cent of the men and 1·8 per cent of the women wore shoes; 27·4 per cent of the men and 5·2 per cent of the women wore sandals; and 69·3 per cent of the men and 93·0 per cent of the women went barefooted. Alta Verapaz, a very Indian department and the least accessible by car save for El Petén, counted 88·8 per cent of all its men and 94·9 per cent of all its women barefooted.[72]

The census takers also ascertained that in Alta Verapaz only 8·6 per cent of the males and 8·8 per cent of the females over seven

---

[71] *Investment in C.A.* gives more detailed banking information on each of the Central American countries in sections headed 'Money and Banking'. For developments since 1955, see the 'Banking' sections of *World Trade Information Service* (U.S. Bureau of Foreign Commerce and Bureau of International Programs), pt. i, nos. 59–56 (El Salvador), 59–59 (Costa Rica), 60–47 (Guatemala), 61–16 (Nicaragua), 61–71 (Honduras).

[72] *Sexto censo de población*, pp. l–li.

years of age habitually ate wheat bread. In the whole republic of Guatemala, 37·1 per cent of the males and 39·4 per cent of the females over seven included this item regularly in their diet.[73] In assessing the value of this measure, some argument may of course be made for a personal preference for maize cakes over wheat bread, though circumstantial evidence seems to indicate that the people of Central America who can afford wheat bread buy it. There is very little doubt that in the Guatemalan terrain the great majority of people prefer shoes to bare feet or the rough sandals which are worn. In the 1960's, it seems likely, more Guatemalans will wear shoes each year than did the year before. Guatemala is emerging, but is really just beginning to emerge, from a near-feudalistic economy into which she was locked tight until 1944. Her town and country workers, and especially her Indians, have yet a long way to go to achieve a minimum of economic dignity.

Slavery was prohibited in Guatemala and in all Central America starting in 1824. Compulsory labour for the Indian, however, continued until the 1880's, enforced by the departmental *jefes politicos* as by the *corregidores* of old. 'Debt slavery' became general practice in Guatemala in the 1870's, the law working hand in hand with owners of the new coffee *fincas* to keep most humble folk on the job through contracted labour to pay never-ending obligations. Money wages under this system at the dawn of the twentieth century ran from about 4 cents to 24 cents U.S. per day.[74] Forty years later in many parts of the country they were not significantly higher. The nineteenth-century liberal programme, supposed to be that of Guatemala's rulers from Barrios to Ubico, thus included even less attention to the needs of the masses than it did to genuine democracy. The late-colonial essay contest won by Matías de Córdova showed that some leaders at the time of independence comprehended the importance of the Indian community as something more than a slave labour market; such understanding had disappeared by the time of Barrios. Ubico, the last of those who flew the Barrios liberal colours, changed the system but not the status of the workers. A vagrancy law passed in 1934 stipulated that the Indians must work, if not for themselves then for another, and that they must carry labour cards on their persons to prove they were meeting the

---

[73] *Sexto censo de población*, p. xlvii.

[74] Chester Lloyd Jones, *Guatemala Past and Present* (Minneapolis, Univ. of Minnesota Press, 1940), pp. 154–5, quotes a report of 1902 from the Guatemalan Dirección General de Agricultura to this effect.

law. The incentive of a decent wage, which might have made all the rest unnecessary, was in most parts of the country as disregarded as ever.

Since 1944 some changes have been made, though in the early 1960's the Guatemalan social revolution was still far from effected. City workers were assisted by the institution of IGSS in 1946 and the nation's first recognition of organized labour in 1947. Social security has grown slowly. In 1957 only 11,000 workers were contributors to a plan providing cash benefits for sickness or maternity, and none to old-age pensions, though 256,000 were protected against employment injury.[75] A minimum-wage plan was given careful study in 1951–2 by an International Labour Office technical-assistance mission; its procedures were adopted for textiles in 1953 but have spread to no other industry.[76] Guatemala's labour unions, however, have attained some vigour and have achieved some gains for city and transport workers.

The first union activity in the country came in the later 1920's, when workers in various small industries combined to press their cause. Ubico permitted no unions, but they were revived when his régime was over. The non-Communist Trade Union Federation of Guatemala represented most railway and factory workers from 1946 to 1951, when the General Confederation of Workers of Guatemala was formed under Communist leadership. The workers gained victories under both types of guidance while employers fought hard against unions in general. After the turnover of 1954 President Castillo permitted the unions to reorganize under non-Communist auspices, and they slowly regained their previous power. The Trade Union Council of Guatemala formed in 1955 is affiliated with the International Confederation of Free Trade Unions through its Latin American regional organization, but only ten trade unions are members (1960). Fourteen smaller unions belong to the Autonomous Trade Union Federation of Guatemala organized in 1954 and reorganized in 1957, which has shown strong sympathy for the Castro régime in Cuba. The largest unions in the country, however, belong to neither of these associations. SAMF, the Sindicato de Acción y Mejoramiento Ferrocarrilero or Syndicate of Railwaymen's Action and Betterment formed in 1944, proved its strength in a contest with IRCA in 1959. United

[75] *Yb. Lab. Stat., 1959*, p. 453.
[76] Even the study was timid. See René Roux, 'An Approach to Minimum Wage Fixing in Guatemala', *Int. Lab. R.*, lxxi (1955), 1–33.

Fruit workers have separate unions centred in Tiquisate and Bananera.

Guatemalan city industry will doubtless grow. The production curve has little place to go except upward. A 1951 study mission of the International Bank for Reconstruction and Development felt that particularly the food-processing industry of Guatemala held promise for the future. High costs for raw materials, the low productivity of labour, technological deficiencies, the shortage of capital and credit, inadequate transportation, and government import controls were all listed by the mission among the drawbacks to industrial production. Another factor mentioned was unprogressive management, which 'has not yet been won over to the economy of high wages and low prices'. The small size of the domestic market, said the mission, was 'probably the greatest obstacle of all to the development of industry', and might be improved through increased agricultural and industrial productivity, improved transportation, the elimination of excessive profit margins, and a rise in real wages.[77] The government since 1944 has (through INFOP and health, education, and public works programmes) sought to increase productivity and improve transportation. Private management, if it is to survive, will have to cut the profit margins and make possible the rise in real wages.

Farm workers in Guatemala's banana areas controlled by United Fruit live about as well as their city cousins. Company housing and stores, and even schools and hospitals, have long been a part of this industry's offering to its workers. Most banana workers' families, however, are forced to lead a very humble existence, some sharing with other country workers real degradation and misery. It is the country worker in general who has suffered most from the steps taken in 1954 to undo partially the Arévalo–Arbenz revolution. Guatemala's poor farmers were organized first by the Communist-led Confederation of Workers of Guatemala in the late 1940's, then by the more important National Peasant Confederation (organized 1950) also controlled by Communists after 1953. The great hope of the peasants seemed to become reality in 1952, when the Arbenz régime began its programme of agrarian reform. The census two years earlier had indicated that 72 per

[77] IBRD, *The Economic Development of Guatemala: Summary* (Washington, 1951), pp. 27–31. Compare manufacturing wages (note 67 of this chapter) with 1958 nation-wide average prices of 11·7 cents a pound for rice, 10·8 cents for black beans, 4·0 cents for maize, and 8·6 cents for potatoes. *Bol. Est.* (G.), *1959*, nos. 11–12 (Nov.–Dec.), pp. 29, 31, 33.

cent of the nation's farm land lay within 2·17 per cent of the nation's *fincas*, those of one *caballería* (110·46 acres) or more in extension.[78] Much of this land was unused, though many landless Indians were half-starving. In a period of twenty months (17 June 1952–20 February 1954) the Arbenz government expropriated over a million and a quarter acres, most of them idle. By 1 March 1954 some 55,734 persons, most of them heads of families, received the use of shares of the land the government thus had at its disposal.[79] A few months later President Castillo returned titles for the expropriated properties to their original owners, and many private owners proceeded to dispossess the farmers of the lands they had occupied.

A new agrarian statute of 1956 nevertheless holds some promise for the future. There is continued provision for expropriation of idle properties, though with more generous remuneration for the holder. There is a new tax on idle lands, designed to put the land to work either through use or sale. There is provision for outright possession of the soil by the farmer, rather than his holding it under lease from the government as was done in 1952–4. Credit is offered, and technical assistance and education, so that the farmer may reap real rewards from his labours. Inexpensive housing is planned to attract the Indians from the mountains, where they have long lived by preference, to the lowlands, where farm land is more plentiful and productive. In its first three years of operation, this law did little to resolve the problem. The several thousand Indian families moved were virtually all 'resettled'—that is, simply transferred from one place secured under Arbenz to another supplied by Ydígoras. Most of the scores of thousands of families whose lives remained untouched by the programme in 1954 still waited in 1960 for their turn to contribute meaningfully to the national welfare. But the statute continues as law and will be further implemented.

There is a prejudice in Guatemala against the Indian who is the country worker, a prejudice which forms part of the concept called 'the Indian problem'. Most persons who own money and property of any dimensions in the republic share the prejudice which takes as elementary the notion that the Indian of Guatemala wants very little. It is true that the Maya-Quiché and their kin, like all other men, are seldom willing to give up a life they count their own until they comprehend that another is distinctly to their advantage.

[78] *Censo agropecuario: 1950*, i. 19; *Estruct. agr.*, p. 30.
[79] *New York Times*, 14 July 1954, p. 8.

But, as another commentator has come close to putting it, the real problem in Guatemala lies not with the Indian but with the propertied ladino.[80] The most basic step needed to spur Guatemala's economy is the acknowledgement on the part of those in a position to direct business affairs that the Indian of the country *wants* shoes —and is entitled to have them. When the day of that acknowledgement arrives, Guatemala's society too will have been reborn.

LEARNING

The mass of the people in republican Guatemala, concerned with the day-to-day struggle for existence, have paid little attention to the worlds of learning and the arts. The few who have engaged their energies in intellectual endeavours have made some noteworthy contributions. Guatemala's continuing inadequacy in the intellectual realm stems from the blockage of most of her talent at its start.

Guatemala alone of the Central American republics suffered intellectual catastrophe after independence. Only in Guatemala, that is to say, was it possible for the state of learning to go backward, since university life existed nowhere else on the isthmus. Guatemala's short-lived egalitarianism of the 1830's brought promise of a system of primary instruction which might have done wonders for the nation at large. But with the coming of an illiterate to power—Rafael Carrera could scarcely write his own name— popular education was forgotten, while the university sank to only a shadow of its former self. With the passage of time Guatemalan society was reduced to that low level where it was the exceptional person who could be called well-informed on any subject. Only very slowly since the 1870's have the cities of the nation risen from this dark period. The rural folk and a large proportion of the urban remain to this day illiterate.

The moral fibre and enthusiasm which characterized Guatemala's liberalism in the 1830's must have owed much to the pre-independence atmosphere at the University of San Carlos. By the time of Barrios, Guatemala's less-trained liberals of another generation persuaded themselves that the faith of their fathers was restored by the simple adoption of anti-clericalism and bureaucracy to replace conservative peremptoriness. The university itself was

[80] Melvin Tumin, 'Cultura, clase y casta en Guatemala: una nueva evaluación', in Seminario de Integración Social Guatemalteca, *Integración social en Guatemala* (2 vols., Guatemala, 1956–60), ii. 97–108; synthesis of a paper read in 1956 and given in full in ibid. i. 163–91.

allowed to pass out of existence in 1882, the state having no substitute for teachers who were eliminated when instruction was divorced from the church. The faculties of civil law and medicine, however, continued in being, and in 1927 the university was recreated. A reorganization in 1944 enabled it finally to earn twentieth-century prestige.[81] The venerable Faculties of Legal and Social Sciences and of Medical Sciences had been joined by that time by the Faculties of Engineering, Chemical Sciences and Pharmacy, Economic Sciences, and Odontology. Humanities (1945), Agronomy (1950), and Veterinary Medicine and Zootechny (1957) have been added since. Three of the faculties have branches in Quezaltenango.[82] A modern campus or 'university city' is being erected on the outskirts of the capital. There were living in Guatemala in 1950 some 5,203 men and 845 women who had attended university classes. The University of San Carlos enrolment in 1955 was 3,244.[83]

Only since 1944 has there been a real attempt to chop away at Guatemalan illiteracy. Every régime since the 1870's has built some schools but has needed to build many more. Propaganda for popular education is now incessant, though there are those in high society who are still not convinced that the Indians should share in the experience. The chief difficulties have been lack of funds and a shortage of talent for dealing with the many groups whose native language is not Spanish and whose opportunities are limited by custom. From 1944 to 1957 daytime primary school enrolments increased from 135,150 to 249,832; while the numbers in postprimary schools below the level of the university grew from 6,963 to 20,545.[84] But the magnitude of the task is seen in the fact that in 1950 only 28·1 per cent of the population over the age of seven (including only 32·0 per cent of those aged 15 through 19) could read and write. This was the lowest national literacy figure in Central America. To compound the problem, schooling was very unevenly divided between ladinos and Indians, the basic skills having been acquired by 49·1 per cent of the former over the age of seven as compared with 9·7 per cent of the latter.[85]

[81] J. Daniel Contreras R., 'Vicisitudes de la Universidad de Guatemala en la época republicana', *Univ. de San Carlos*, no. 52 (Sept.–Dec. 1960), 51–58, traces name and other changes in detail.
[82] *Guía orgánica de la Universidad de San Carlos de Guatemala* (Guatemala, 1958).
[83] *Sexto censo de población*, p. 153; U.N., *Stat. Yb., 1959*, p. 556.
[84] *Guatemala en Cifras, 1958*, p. 139.
[85] *Sexto censo de población*, pp. xli, 112–13.

For those who could read, Guatemala has not been without a newspaper since the days of Molina and Valle. The state itself has published a gazette since its foundation in 1824, with only one year (1840) unrepresented in its issues. Other papers have come and gone, with a few showing real literary merit. The oldest daily newspaper on the isthmus is the *Diario de Centro América*, founded by Mark Kelly from the United States in 1880, which has since become a Guatemalan government organ. Well-known are *El Imparcial* (founded 1922) and *Prensa Libre* (1951), both independent in politics and able to survive the crises. Altogether, there were six daily newspapers in the country in 1957 with a total circulation of 104,000, or 30 papers for every 1,000 inhabitants.[86]

Guatemala's chief efforts in the applied sciences have been in the fields of medicine and engineering. Through the nineteenth century most medical work was directed towards saving the cities from the greater epidemics which from time to time swept the countryside. Beginning in the twentieth, mass campaigns were undertaken to abolish smallpox and yellow fever and to combat malaria and hookworm. The International Health Division of the Rockefeller Foundation lent great assistance here, and in all Central America, from 1915 to 1928 in the control of hookworm and from 1918 to 1925 in the fight to eliminate yellow fever. The death-rate in Guatemala in 1958 remained very high—213·3 deaths for each 10,000 inhabitants. Among the chief causes remaining in that year were gastro-enteritis and colitis (27·4 deaths for each 10,000 inhabitants), pneumonia and bronchitis (21·7), malaria (17·6), influenza (14·8), worms (13·6), whooping-cough (12·4), measles (10·3), dysentery (8·6), infections of infancy (8·3), lung tuberculosis (3·4), and malignant tumours (2·5). There were 45 institutions with highly variant standards functioning as hospitals in 1957, with 9,743 beds and cradles. They were situated in Guatemala City (15 with 3,983 beds and cradles), in nearby San Juan Sacatepéquez and Amatitlán, in nineteen of the remaining twenty-one departmental capitals, United Fruit's Quiriguá and Tiquisate, Coatepeque in Quezaltenango department, and the new village of Poptún in El Petén. In 1957 there were 542 physicians (nearly one for every 6,300 people) and 130 dentists.[87] Native engineering skills, here and in all Central America, through providing access roads,

[86] U.N., *Stat. Yb.*, *1959*, p. 578.

[87] Ibid. *1958*, pp. 26, 541; *Guatemala en Cifras*, *1958*, p. 151; *Bol. Est.* (G.), *1960*, nos. 3–6 (Mar.–June), 86–88, 94, 133.

sewage systems, and better drinking water, are now making some dent in the walls of primitiveness and isolation which must crumble before medicine can be highly successful.

Guatemala's chief contribution to knowledge in the republican as well as the colonial period has been in the field of history. Alejandro Marure (1806–51), liberal statesman and teacher of law, provided the first example of perspicacious historical writing after independence when he reviewed the turbulent events of his own time from 1811 to 1828.[88] Lorenzo Montúfar y Rivera Maestre (1823–98), flaming liberal and anti-clerical, continued in detailed but very partisan manner the story of Central America to 1860.[89] José Milla y Vidaurre (1822–82), conservative statesman, journalist, and novelist of genuine distinction, undertook a modern study of the colonial audiencia, which was completed by Agustín Gómez Carrillo (1838–1908) when death overtook its designer.[90]

Ramón A. Salazar (1852–1914) after retirement from life as a physician, journalist, and diplomat dealt with the cultural development of the colony as Milla had treated its politics and economy.[91] Salazar showed the important role ideas played in the unfolding of Central American independence, a theme since expanded by Virgilio Rodríguez Beteta (b. 1885).[92] José Antonio Villacorta Calderón (b. 1879) has dealt ably with every phase of Guatemalan history, writing voluminously on topics from Maya archaeology and linguistics to early twentieth-century tumult.[93] From 1924 to 1942 Villacorta directed the publication of the *Anales* of Guatemala's Sociedad de Geografía e Historia, a historical journal of real merit.[94] This society, founded in 1923, began also in 1929 a memorable series of reprints and first prints of colonial manuscripts which in 1958 reached its twentieth volume.[95] Villa-

[88] *Bosquejo histórico de las revoluciones de Centro-América* (Guatemala, 1837; 3rd ed., 2 vols., Paris, 1913).
[89] *Reseña histórica de Centro-América* (7 vols., Guatemala, 1878–88).
[90] *Historia de la América Central* (5 vols., Guatemala, 1879–1905; 2nd ed. of the first 2 vols., Guatemala, 1937). For a study of Milla with his complete bibliography, see Walter A. Payne, *A Central American Historian* (Gainesville, Univ. of Florida Press, 1957).
[91] See ch. iv, n. 23, p. 72; (2nd ed., 3 vols., Guatemala, 1951).
[92] See ch. iv, n. 27, p. 75; Rodríguez Beteta, *Ideologías de la independencia* (Paris, 1926) and *Evolución de las ideas* (Paris, 1929).
[93] His chief summary volumes are *Prehistoria e historia antigua de Guatemala* (1938); *Historia de la capitanía general de Guatemala* (1942); and *Historia de la república de Guatemala, 1821–1921* (1960); all published in Guatemala.
[94] i/1, July 1924; xxxii/1–4, Jan.–Dec. 1959.
[95] See ch. iv, nn. 13 and 25, pp. 68, 74. Vol. xx was the first of Pedro Cortés y Larraz, *Descripción geográfico-moral de la diócesis de Goathemala* (Guatemala).

corta was president of the Sociedad de Geografía e Historia from 1936 to 1942. José Joaquín Pardo, who held the same position in the years 1946–50, has served through varied political régimes as director of the national archives, organizing them to the point where they have become a Mecca for the study of Spanish colonial life.[96] Adrián Recinos (1886–1962), successor of Pardo in the presidency of the society, distinguished himself with translations of Quiché and Cakchiquel manuscripts and carefully written historical monographs.[97] David Vela (b. 1901), an associate and well-known journalist, has meantime specialized in the history of literature and high-quality biography.[98]

With all this commendable activity, Guatemalan historians have been notably reluctant to bring their subject down to date.[99] Hubert Howe Bancroft and his associates of California were the first to do this for the entire isthmus in their remarkable volumes of 1882–7, treating colonial and republican history with the same thoroughness they had applied to their survey of the native races.[100] A generation later Dana Gardner Munro in study as a doctoral candidate reviewed the political and economic conditions of all Central America into the early twentieth century.[101] Chester Lloyd Jones, professor of economics and political science at the University of Wisconsin, in the time of Ubico made a careful economic and social study of Guatemala alone, tracing his diagnosis all through her colonial and republican history and terminating with prescriptions under the heading of 'If I Were Dictator'.[102] Monographic treatments of Central American history in the United States are recently on the increase; several have been prepared by graduate students under the guidance of William J. Griffith at Tulane University.

The noteworthy studies pursued by foreigners in Guatemala relative to her Indians and ancient remains have already been discussed.[103] Guatemalan interest in the ancient lore has been en-

---

[96] The *Boletín del Archivo General del Gobierno*, published quarterly by Pardo (1935–46), is itself a storehouse of colonial information.

[97] See ch. iii, n. 14, p. 41; also, for example, *Pedro de Alvarado* (Mexico City, 1952).

[98] *Literatura guatemalteca* (2 vols., Guatemala, 1943); *Barrundia ante el espejo de su tiempo* (2 vols., Guatemala, 1956–7), a good look at the generation after independence.

[99] See William J. Griffith, 'The Historiography of Central America since 1830', *HAHR*, xl (1960), 548–69, a review of publications since 1920.

[100] *History of Central America* (3 vols., San Francisco); see ch. iii, n. 35, p. 53.

[101] *The Five Republics of Central America* (London, OUP, 1918).

[102] See above, n. 74.   [103] See chs ii and iii.

couraged by an excellent museum collection in the capital and by
the formation of an Instituto de Antropología e Historia (1949)
with its headquarters in the museum building and a publication of
its own.[104] The situation and peculiar problems of present-day
Indians are the subject of study of the Instituto Indigenista Nacional, an office of the government created in 1946 and reorganized in
1954.[105]

The Guatemalan Sociedad Económica of late colonial times
was active through much of the nineteenth century, but with the
advent of Barrios saw its functions taken over by the government.
It had much earlier ceased to serve as a nucleus for liberal ideas.
Studied economic and social analysis of the contemporary scene
has been rare even in the mid-twentieth century, much of the important work again having been done by outsiders—the International Bank for Reconstruction and Development;[106] a private
group invited to study the nation's public finance;[107] and Nathan
Laselle Whetten, professor of sociology at the University of Con-
necticut.[108] Mario Monteforte Toledo (b. 1911) recently contributed the first extensive study of this sort done by a Guatemalan.[109]
More generalized interpretations of the scene abound in the literature for and against the Arévalo, Arbenz, and Castillo régimes. Of
this, the pro-Arévalo and pro-Arbenz presentation by Arbenz'
foreign minister Guillermo Toriello Garrido (b. 1910) is the most
careful and telling. More meticulous studies of the Arévalo and
Arbenz régimes are limited to selected aspects.[110]

No one has experienced the geography of Guatemala more intimately than Karl Theodor Sapper (1866–1945), who came from
Germany to Cobán to live with his brother in 1888, but spent almost all his time in scientific travel until 1900, when he returned to
Germany to teach. His articles in the German language on Guatemalan and Central American volcanology, meteorology, eth-
nology, and general geography were legion; he also produced

---

[104] *Antropología e Historia de Guatemala*, i/1, Jan. 1949; xii/2, July 1960.
[105] Its *Boletín*, Epoca 2, i/1–4 (1955), explains its near-demise after Castillo's
advent to power.
[106] *Economic Development of Guatemala: Report* (1951).
[107] John H. Adler and others, *Public Finance and Economic Development in Guatemala* (Palo Alto, Calif., Stanford U.P., 1952).
[108] *Guatemala: the Land and the People* (New Haven, Conn., Yale U.P.,
1961).
[109] *Guatemala: monografía sociológica* (Mexico City, 1959).
[110] Toriello Garrido, *La batalla de Guatemala* (Mexico City, 1955); see above,
nn. 18 and 20.

several notable books.[111] Sapper's friend Franz Termer, also well acquainted with the local scene, began publication of a Guatemalan geography in 1936.[112] The only comparable work done by a non-German has been the study of the south-western part of the republic by Felix Webster McBryde of the United States.[113]

It would be wrong to think of educated Guatemalans as having abdicated all responsibility for their own country's scholarship (aside from the field of history) to outsiders. Textbooks by native authors are growing in number.[114] Theses of varying degrees of significance are from time to time published. The university review, issued three times a year, contains a wide range of articles which prove the readiness of their authors to deal in precision and profundity.[115] It must be remembered that in today's Guatemala even the average university graduate has to devote virtually all his time to the struggle for existence. Only when a happier economic day arrives will he be free to exercise his skill at making learned presentations.[116]

ART

The world of art like the world of learning suffered a setback in Guatemala with the coming of independence. In the field of general literature as in history, nevertheless, each generation has supplied some unforgettable legacy. The twentieth century has brought a renaissance in painting and sculpture, and on every side, without doubt, lies talent waiting to be awakened.

Mass recreation in the Guatemalan countryside has changed but little since colonial times. Feast days bring out the statues from the churches, the rented costumes of dancers, the fireworks, the intoxi-

---

[111] Sapper's chief Central American studies were summarized in his *Mittelamerikanische Reisen und Studien aus den Jahren 1888 bis 1900* (Braunschweig, 1902). His travels are sketched in Franz Termer, 'Carlos Sapper', *Anales*, xxix/1–4 (Jan.–Dec. 1956), 55–101; see also Franz Termer, 'Bibliografía de Carlos Sapper', ibid. pp. 102–30.

[112] *Zur Geographie der Republik Guatemala* (Hamburg).

[113] See ch. iii, n. 10, p. 38.

[114] For one in a new field, see Jorge del Valle Matheu, *Sociología guatemalteca: manual introductorio* (Guatemala, 1950); for one in an old field, consult S. Aguado-Andreut, *Campaña del año 56 de Julio César* (Guatemala, 1950).

[115] *Univ. de San Carlos*, no. 1, Oct.–Dec. 1945; no. 52, Sept.–Dec. 1960.

[116] Other periodicals containing a variety of Central American contributions to knowledge and thought are listed in Irene Zimmerman, *A Guide to Current Latin American Periodicals: Humanities and Social Sciences* (Gainesville, Fla., Kallman, 1961), pp. 92–96 (Costa Rica), 116–21 (El Salvador), 121–5 (Guatemala), 128–32 (Honduras), 163–5 (Nicaragua).

cating beverages, the crowds, marimba bands (these possibly are a new element), and a touch of the old music.[117] Apart from the feast days there is no real recreation for many of the people—small wonder that they deem these important!

Residents of city and town have become accustomed to something more. The first baseball club was organized in Guatemala City in the year 1880. The sport spread, and was joined by others after the turn of the century. By the 1930's *futbol* or soccer was becoming more popular than baseball; basketball and boxing were also attracting attention. Leagues and championships developed as accoutrements to the three ball games, while these and bicycling (at which Guatemalans have done well) carried over into international competition. Guatemala City still offers bull-fights in season, but these are now a sideline compared to the newly developed interests.

Dancing and attendance at the cinema are also common pastimes. The moving pictures come from abroad—chiefly the United States, Mexico, and western Europe. The dances are a wide variety with hemispheric background, as interpreted by the marimba and other instruments or on records. The marimba, a single or double keyboard using gourds or tubes made of fine wood as resonators, has become the musical trademark of Guatemala, used in both town and country; it plays all types of music, including a few indigenous songs which give it special distinction. The deep-throated and resonant quality of the Guatemalan marimba band (composed of seven members) sets the republic's music off from that of neighbours on both sides who also use the marimba. Home music is often heard on Guatemala's 32 radio stations, of which 21 are in the capital.[118] There are also two television transmitters.

Musical concerts were presented in Guatemala City even in the time of Carrera; the compositions were European, with Italian and Spanish tastes predominating. Travelling theatre groups occasionally provided entertainment as well. George Washington Montgomery of the United States saw one performance in honour of Saint Isidro in the country near Gualán (Zacapa department) in 1838:

[117] The history of the Guatemalan marimba has been the subject of much discussion, but remains largely unexplored. Early travellers in republican Guatemala say little or nothing of the instrument.

[118] Radio information for all Central America is for the year 1958, as given in *World Radio Handbook* (published in Copenhagen) *1959*, pp. 137–44. Guatemalan call letters have the prefix TG. Only one station uses 10,000 watts power.

The title of this performance was *El enamorado pobre,* or the Poor Lover. The plot turns upon the rivalship of two gentlemen, who aspire to the hand of a fair lady: the one exceedingly amiable, accomplished, and handsome, but very poor; the other, destitute of every advantage, except that he is very rich. . . . It was amusing to observe how much regard was paid by the people to the character represented, and how little to the manner of performance. The poor lover, as an actor, was decidedly inferior to the rich one; yet he was the favourite of the public, who were lavish in their praise of him, while the other, whenever he came on the stage, was received with murmurs, and ran the risk of being hissed. . . . The only person who did not enjoy the fiesta was my English friend. The play, he said, was a bore, St. Isidro a humbug, and the people all fools. . . .[119]

In 1896 Guatemala's first symphony was written. The composer was Jesús Castillo (1877–1946) who studied Maya music all his life, writing an opera called *Quiché Vinak* and a' musical suite *Popol Buj* containing some notable piano pieces. Julián Paniagua Martínez (b. 1856) was a composer of popular music; his nephew Raúl Paniagua (1898–1953) wrote *The Mayan Legend,* a symphonic poem introduced in New York. José Castañeda (b. 1898) experiments with ultra-modern music.[120] Guatemala City now has two symphony orchestras, a municipal chorus, a modern ballet group, and a little theatre production, all of them products of the most recent generation.

An art renaissance began in Guatemala as early as the 1920's.[121] Its most original manifestations have appeared in painting and sculpture. Influence from revolutionary Mexico has been strong but not always overriding. Humberto Garavito (b. 1897), the most popular resident artist, paints Indian landscapes and portraits realistically as he finds them. Carlos Mérida (b. 1891), the only Guatemalan painter well known internationally, studied in Europe and has lived in Mexico since 1919. Mérida, himself a mixture of Maya and Zapotec, works in water-colours to produce his own painted symbolisms related to Maya thought and life.[122] Gua-

[119] *Narrative of a Journey to Guatemala, in Central America, in 1838* (N.Y., 1839), pp. 72–73.

[120] Reviews of musical developments in Central America are given in Nicolas Slonimsky, *Music of Latin America* (N.Y., Crowell, 1945), pp. 173–8 (Costa Rica), 200–7 (Guatemala), 212–13 (Honduras), 254–8 (Nicaragua), 279–81 (El Salvador).

[121] Constance Allen Ward, 'The Guatemalan Art Renaissance', *Bull. of the PAU,* lxxv (1941), 282–90.

[122] Photographic reproductions of recent Guatemalan art are shown in José Luis Cifuentes, *Algunos pintores contemporáneos de Guatemala* and *Algunos escultores contemporáneos de Guatemala* (both Guatemala, 1956).

Guatemala

temala's aesthetic sense is revealed also in the beauties of a few buildings and boulevards in the capital city, the picturesque cobble-stoned streets of many a village, and the often intricate designs found on colourful textiles woven by persons frequently of humble origins.

Each score of years since 1780 (Matías de Córdova of Chiapas was born in 1768) at least one birth has occurred of a Guatemalan person who came to be known in literary circles outside the isthmus. Antonio José de Irisarri, born in 1786, left Guatemala in 1807 (he returned 1827–30) to live in six countries of South America, Curaçao, London, and Paris before spending his last thirteen years (until 1868) as Guatemalan minister to the United States. Irisarri liked to found literary periodicals (he founded fifteen altogether) to which he contributed a variety of items showing insight into his times. He also wrote two novels portraying thinly-disguised characters from his own experience, and many articles on philology.[123] José Batres Montúfar was born in San Salvador of Guatemalan parents in 1809; he contracted malarial fever working with John Baily on his Nicaraguan canal survey in 1838 and died in 1844. 'Pepe' Batres wrote poetry which has been highly praised; the most noteworthy his *Tradiciones de Guatemala*, three tales in verse which at times are rich in local colour.[124]

The compiler of Batres' verse for its first publication one year after his death was José Milla y Vidaurre, later an outstanding figure as both historian and novelist. Milla was born in 1822, one year after independence, and lived through the time of Carrera and well into that of Barrios. During the conservative régimes he served the state. In the first three years of the liberal triumph (1871–4) he travelled abroad, but then returned home to continue literary activities until his death in 1882. Throughout the 1860's and again late in life he proved his skill as a *costumbrista*, a depicter of local customs. Even his *Un viaje al otro mundo*, three volumes (1875) describing his travels, is a commentary on customs—those of other peoples as seen through Guatemalan eyes. Before his long trip, Milla published three historical novels in romantic vein: *La hija*

[123] Antonio Batres Jáuregui, *Literatos guatemaltecos: Landívar e Irisarri* (Guatemala, 1896; 2nd ed., Guatemala, 1957) comments on his life and works. The two novels are *El cristiano errante* (2nd ed., Santiago de Chile, 1929) and *Historia del perínclito Epaminondas del Cauca* (2nd ed., 2 vols., Guatemala, 1951).
[124] His *Poesías* were published in Guatemala, 1845; 13th ed., 1952. Three editions appeared abroad. See also José Arzú, *Pepe Batres íntimo* (Guatemala, 1940).

del adelantado (1866) dealing with the life of Doña Leonor, daughter of Pedro de Alvarado; *Los nazarenos* (1867) relating events in Antigua of the mid-seventeenth century; and *El visitador* (1869), placed earlier in the seventeenth century. In later life he contributed two more, showing the influences of literary realism: *Memorias de un abogado* (1876) telling a story from late colonial times in the new Guatemala City; and *Historia de un pepe* (History of a Foundling, 1882) dealing most effectively with the circumstances of the same time and place.[125] Milla was without doubt Central America's greatest prose writer of the nineteenth century.

Antonio Batres Jáuregui (1847–1929) wrote voluminously as a literary critic, philologist, and disorganized historian. A lawyer and many times over representative of Guatemala abroad, he also taught literature and proved himself a significant commentator on the work of others in both prose and poetry.[126] Widely-travelled Máximo Soto Hall (1871–1944) wrote political novels to portray the threats he saw in the United States involvement in Nicaragua.[127] Enrique Gómez Carrillo y Tible (1873–1927), son of Agustín Gómez Carrillo the historian, liked Paris better than Guatemala. He went there at the age of eighteen and returned only once to the land of his birth. A devotee of 'art for art's sake', Enrique Gómez Carrillo wrote amoral stories of love, war, and travel enough to more than fill twenty-six volumes.[128] He is praised for his fine style in the tradition of the *modernista* school of expression set by Rubén Darío of Nicaragua. In addition, his observations on art and travel are valued: 'There is an art of travel and of enjoying

[125] *Obras completas de Salomé Jil (José Milla)* (12 vols., Guatemala, 1935–7) includes four of the five novels, the two volumes of history, the three of travels, and three of customs sketches called *Libro sin nombre*, *El canasto del sastre*, and *Cuadros de costumbres*. For comment on the five novels, see T. B. Irving, 'Las dos maneras de Pepe Milla', *Univ. de San Carlos*, no. 52, pp. 111–33. See also above, n. 90, p. 131.

[126] Martin E. Erickson, 'Antonio Batres Jáuregui: Guatemalan Critic', *Hispania*, xxv (1942), 343–50. Batres' most important books were collections of articles; for example, *Literatura americana* (Guatemala, 1879) and *Vicios del lenguaje y provincialismos de Guatemala* (Guatemala, 1892). The posthumous third and last volume of his *La América Central ante la historia* (Guatemala, 1916–49) has some value as a personal memoir.

[127] *El problema* (San José, 1899) deals with the isthmus as it might appear after a digging of the Nicaragua canal. *La sombra de la Casa Blanca* (Buenos Aires, 1927) is concerned with the marines.

[128] *Obras completas* (26 vols., Madrid, 1919–23) are not complete. See Juan M. Mendoza, *Enrique Gómez Carrillo: estudio crítico-biográfico* (2 vols., Guatemala, 1940). Two of the war books were translated into English and French as *Among the Ruins* (London, 1915); *Parmi les ruines* (Paris, 1915); *Au coeur de la tragédie* (Paris, 1917); *In the Heart of the Tragedy* (London, 1917).

travel', he said, 'as there is an art of love'.[129] Gómez Carrillo travelled in nearly every corner of the earth.

More recent generations have provided further activity. Rafael Arévalo Martínez (b. 1884) secured literary notice by depicting human personalities in terms of animal behaviour; his genre is the short story and novelette.[130] Flavio Herrera (b. 1895) has written much verse in the *haiku* tradition of Japan and presented a series of novels.[131] César Brañas has also attracted attention with his short novels.[132] Raúl Leiva (b. 1916) is noticed for his poetry.[133]

The strength of new forces in Guatemala is revealed in the literary work of Miguel Angel Asturias (b. 1899) and Mario Monteforte Toledo (b. 1911). Asturias has won praise for both his poetry and prose. He first attracted attention with a book of Guatemalan legends printed in three languages in Europe.[134] His poems are done in a variety of moods.[135] His first novel, written soon after the fall of Ubico, dealt with the corruptness of *caudillo* rule in an unnamed country of the hemisphere; two later ones, which are widely discussed, pose the fruit companies against their workers. Still another widely read work reflects through a series of pictures the new interest of the Arévalo–Arbenz era in the ordinary Guatemalan Indian.[136] Mario Monteforte Toledo began writing novels during the same era and continued with labours in straight sociology. In 1948 he presented two major works, one depicting the struggle of man against nature in the Petén, the other expressing the feelings of the coffee worker toward the employer of German extraction.[137] The novels of Asturias and Monteforte Toledo give small comfort to the outsider making his living in Guatemala. Their significance,

[129] From *La psicología del viaje* as quoted in Max Henríquez Ureña, *Breve historia del modernismo* (Mexico City, 1954), p. 389.

[130] A recent collection is *El hombre que parecía un caballo, y otros cuentos* (Guatemala, 1951). See *Juicios sobre Rafael Arévalo Martínez y lista de sus obras* (Guatemala, 1959).

[131] His best-known novel is *El tigre* (Guatemala, 1934), republished in Santiago de Chile, 1942. *Cosmos indio: Hai-kais y tankas* (Guatemala, 1938) is a collection of verse.

[132] Several have followed *Alba emérita* (San José, 1920), which was longer.

[133] *Oda a Guatemala, y otros poemas* (Guatemala, 1953).

[134] Spanish, French, and German; the first, *Leyendas de Guatemala* (Madrid, 1930) was republished in Buenos Aires, 1948.

[135] Those of thirty years are collected in *Poesía: sien de alondra* (Buenos Aires, 1949).

[136] *El señor presidente* (Mexico City, 1946); *Viento fuerte* (Buenos Aires, 1950); *El papa verde* (Buenos Aires, 1954); *Hombres de maíz* (Buenos Aires, 1949).

[137] *Anaité* deals with the Petén, *Entre la piedra y la cruz* with life on the coffee *finca*; both were published in Guatemala. See above, n. 109.

however, lies not in simple expressions of nationalism but in the sympathetic comprehension they display of the cause of the common labourer. The new Guatemala would have been only half-born without them.

RELIGION

The changed position of religion in Guatemala since independence is seen in the fact that this land which was sending out Christian missionaries in the eighteenth century was receiving them in the twentieth. The religious allegiance of the people has not changed drastically. Those who declared themselves Roman Catholic in the census of 1950 were 96·86 per cent of the population.[138] But in many instances churches which had been prosperous during the colonial period became poor in the nineteenth century and unattended by priests. Laymen whose understanding of Catholic doctrine was slight and whose worship practices were a blend of Christianity and paganism often came into complete charge of their own religious destinies. Rank superstition and negligence eventually prevailed in rural areas, while religious folk of the city often substituted interest in imagery and processions for a concern for humanity. Only in mid-twentieth century, with influences from abroad, have conventional religious groups begun to stem this tide. And in the meantime some persons interested in the well-being of society have turned to non-Christian, non-Jewish founts of inspiration.

The expulsion of archbishop Casaus and a goodly number of friars from Guatemala in 1829 did not of course aid the work of the church. The charges against them, however, were that the friars had become an incubus upon society, more concerned with the acquisition of worldly possessions than with the missionary, educational, and welfare work which had once been in their charge; and that the archbishop had interfered in the world of politics on the side of the conservatives. The ban against the archbishop and the larger orders lasted only ten years, though Casaus did not return before his death in 1845. With the beginning of Carrera's period in 1839, the Roman Catholic church was restored to its former privileged position with the exception of some limitations upon the power of the clergy and the re-acquisition of lost properties. Relations with the papacy were formalized in 1852, as early as those of any other western-hemisphere sovereignty. Despite these arrange-

[138] *Sexto censo de población*, p. liii.

ments, the church did not revive. The Jesuits returned, along with other orders, but their efforts were not enough to outweigh the general negligence. In 1871, with the triumph of the liberal revolution, relations with the papacy were broken, another archbishop expelled along with the Jesuits, and the other orders disbanded. Guatemala has since this date been a land of officially complete religious freedom as between Catholicism and other faiths.[139]

Apart from a missionary district of El Petén and the still-popular shrine of Esquipulas, both of which are separate, the archdiocese of Guatemala is now synonomous territorially with the republic of Guatemala. The nation contains 1,229 Catholic churches—a great number more than in the last days of the colony—but staffed with only 279 priests or one for every 11,100 Catholics.[140] Six bishoprics have been organized or reorganized in the twentieth century—Quezaltenango and Verapaz in 1921 and Jalapa, San Marcos, Sololá, and Zacapa in 1951—while the remainder of Central America has been subtracted from Guatemala's archdiocesan jurisdiction. The much-strengthened hierarchy may be taken as an indication of the church's decision to renew its effort in these parts.

Despite old restrictions, nearly two-thirds of the Catholic clergy are members of religious orders. Many are from Europe and North America. In 1943 President Ubico allowed the Maryknoll Fathers of New York to open missionary work in the very neglected department of Huehuetenango. By 1960 there were 41 Maryknoll Fathers in the department; also 19 Maryknoll Sisters who had come since 1953, and 3 Christian Brothers engaged in educational work. (Eleven Franciscans from the United States also work in Guatemala.)[141] The change in religious habits brought to some villages by these outsiders is striking. One enthusiastic report reads, 'In one town which not long ago had only 35 communions at Christmas, a thousand Indians now receive every Sunday. In another town, there wasn't a confession during the first six months after the

[139] Mary P. Holleran, *Church and State in Guatemala* (N.Y., Columbia U.P., 1949) traces the details régime by régime.
[140] Catholic statistics for all Central America are taken from *Basic Ecclesiastical Statistics for Latin America, 1960*, pp. 34–37, 42–43; this is a biennial publication of World Horizon Reports, Maryknoll, New York. The reporting year for 18 of Central America's 27 ecclesiastical circumscriptions is 1959, for 1 1958, for 5 1957, for 2 1956, and for 1 1955.
[141] *U.S. Catholic Overseas Missionary Personnel, January 1, 1960* (Washington, 1960), pp. 92–93, 95. Guatemala has 37 religious houses for men and 35 for women. *Basic Ecclesiastical Statistics, 1960*, p. 42.

priest's arrival; today there are 500 confessions a week.'[142] In addition to the usual activities connected with missionary enterprise, the Maryknollers have trained lay catechists to carry on work in a sort of twentieth-century adaptation of the Lancasterian system. The duty of these persons is to visit the many Catholics the missionaries cannot reach personally, explaining in effect the vast difference between Catholic doctrine and the behaviour pattern of so many rural Guatemalans. The catechists have already made a real impact in many communities of this nation. Their work, though under different sponsorship, is remarkably similar in some respects to that performed by a growing body of Protestants; both groups face the same opposition from tradition-minded elements.

The first Protestant worker to enter Guatemala came in 1841 from British Honduras as joint preacher-teacher for a mixed colony of Europeans settling near the Polochic River. His name was Frederick Crowe; he was an Englishman born in Bruges, Flanders, and converted to the Baptist faith in Belize. From 1844 to 1846 Crowe taught classes in English and French in Guatemala City until forced to leave the country. One of his students was Lorenzo Montúfar, whose later writings sometimes revealed Crowe's influence.[143] The first organized Protestant missionary effort came many years later, in 1882, only after President Justo Rufino Barrios had extended a personal invitation to the Presbyterian Board of Foreign Missions of New York.[144] Since that invitation, some fifteen Protestant churches and agencies have entered the Guatemalan field to establish over 1,000 regular places of worship (organized churches plus other preaching stations).[145] With all this activity, only 1·47 per cent of the nation was counted Protestant in 1940; this figure nearly doubled, to 2·80 per cent, in 1950. The mid-century count showed that 4·27 per cent of the ladinos were

---

[142] From 'Maryknoll in Guatemala', one of several pamphlets provided along with typewritten information by a number of Catholic missionary groups doing work on the isthmus.

[143] See Montúfar's argument for separation of church and state, 'El Evangelio y el Syllabus y un dualismo imposible' (1884) republished in *R. de la Univ.* (Tegucigalpa), viii–x (1916–20). Crowe's autobiography appears in *The Gospel in Central America* (London, 1850).

[144] *Justo Rufino Barrios: a Biography* (Philadelphia, 1926) was written by Presbyterian missionary Paul Burgess.

[145] Protestant statistics are taken from *Protestant Missions in Latin America: a Statistical Survey* (Evangelical Foreign Missions Association, 1961); checked against *World Christian Handbook 1957*, a British publication; and supplemented by pamphlet and typewritten information of recent dates sent by many Protestant missionary agencies.

Protestant and only 1·53 per cent of the Indians. The highest relative numbers of Protestants by department were in Izabal and Zacapa (not quite 7 per cent each).[146] The Protestant work in Guatemala has continued to grow rather dramatically since 1950. A seventy-fifth anniversary celebration in 1957 brought an impressive parade of combined Protestant strength to Guatemala City. Only in Nicaragua of all the Central American states has Protestantism reached such proportions.

Guatemala is the only isthmian country to boast a large national church, called the Iglesia Evangélica. About one-fourth of the nation's Protestants belong to this group, an outgrowth of the activities of the Central American Mission though designed to include other Protestant bodies. The Central American Mission is a non-denominational fundamentalist group formed in Texas in 1890. Guatemala was next to the last of the Central American countries it entered, in 1899, but is now its strongest field by far. Some 52 United States missionaries work for the Central American Mission in Guatemala, assisted by national ordained pastors who in time to come will completely lead the Iglesia Evangélica.[147]

Four denominations which have a considerable history in Guatemala have divided much of the country between them. Together they account for nearly half of Protestant membership. In addition to the Presbyterians, who came in 1882 and now concentrate on work in the capital and among the Mam and Quiché Indians, they are the Church of the Nazarene (1901) now in Alta and Baja Verapaz and the Petén; the California Yearly Meeting of Friends (1902) in Jalapa, Chiquimula, Zacapa, and Izabal; and the Primitive Methodists, a British group transplanted to North America who came to Totonicapán and El Quiché in 1922. In the early 1960's the Presbyterians had 26 missionaries in Guatemala, the Nazarenes 17, the Friends 11, and the Primitive Methodists 10, with an emphasis in every case upon the training of national leadership. Any or all of these groups may become part of the Iglesia Evangélica; they already present themselves in most instances to the Guatemalan populace as 'evangelicals'.

Seven more sizable groups have entered this field more recently. They are the Seventh-Day Adventists (1927); the Assemblies of God, a Pentecostal body (1937); the Southern Baptist Convention

[146] *Sexto censo de población*, pp. liii, 192–3.
[147] Mildred W. Spain, '*And in Samaria*' (2nd ed., Dallas, 1954) is the story of the Central American Mission, which also publishes the bi-monthly *Central American Bulletin* (no. 361, Apr. 1962).

(1946); the Missouri Synod of the Lutheran Church, following Guatemalan Germans who had spent the war years in the United States (1947); the International Church of the Foursquare Gospel from the religious ferment of Los Angeles (1955); and two more Pentecostal organizations (the Church of God and the Church of God of Prophecy) both from Tennessee. Each of these groups has its own special message and considers any part of the country its domain. Also represented in Guatemala are the Protestant Episcopal Church, the Wycliffe Bible Translators, and two remaining small missionary agencies from the United States.[148]

The organized religious groups of Guatemala include besides Catholics and Protestants a fast-growing adherence to the Church of Jesus Christ of Latter-Day Saints (though work began only in the 1950's, Mormon missionaries numbered 85 in 1961);[149] and a small Jewish community.[150]

There seems little doubt that the activities of Catholic, Protestant, and Mormon missionaries and their associates the *catequistas* and the national preachers are making a real dent in the casualness of the average rural Guatemalan toward the concept of religion-derived obligations. The humbler social strata of the cities have likewise been affected. There is little evidence, on the other hand, that this religious renaissance has made much impact upon the more well-to-do families in society. Each generation has included some persons in these families who were conscious and devoted Catholics; others throughout republican history have scorned the teachings of the church in one way or another, in most cases without professing a substitute creed. The upsurge in religion largely misses this group and to quite an extent passes by the university.

A matured national church, either Catholic or Protestant, could supply much of the moral fibre which must constitute the backbone of a renovated Guatemala. The present management from Rome (for the Catholics) or from the United States (for both Catholics and Protestants) falls short of perceiving Guatemalan problems as Guatemalans must see them. Persons interested in solving these problems frequently turn to the secular philosophies current in mid-twentieth century as their chief source of inspiration. Moral fibre can be theirs too. It remains to be seen whether the future of Guatemala will be moulded by the one type of faith or the other.

[148] See ch. iii, n. 39, p. 54.

[149] Mormon statistics for Central America were provided by letter.

[150] There were only 829 persons of the Jewish faith in 1950. *Sexto censo de población*, p. 192.

CHAPTER VI

EL SALVADOR

SINCE the dawn of independence, El Salvador has made up in population growth for what she lacked in size. With roughly a quarter of a million persons in 1821, she had about half as many as Guatemala. El Salvador reached the 1 million mark at the end of that century and 2 million in 1953.[1] Her mid-1958 estimate of 2,434,000 was over two-thirds that of Guatemala. Because people in many parts of El Salvador do virtually cover the countryside, and because this republic contains no expanse of nearly uninhabited wilderness as do all its isthmian neighbours, its population density (298 persons per square mile in mid-1958) is by far the highest in Central America. There is in fact only one republic in all the Americas (Haiti) which is more crowded.

Most of the people of El Salvador are generally considered mestizos.[2] The census of El Salvador contains no data concerning racial ancestry. Persons of pure European stock must be as rare as in Guatemala. The chief difference between the two is that in El Salvador the full-blooded Indian is not everywhere in evidence. This difference may be partly illusory, since an Indian without distinctive garb is indistinguishable from a mestizo whose ancestry is preponderantly indigenous. Certainly the Indian strain in the mixed population is the dominant one, most of all in the western part, where many Indian communities cling to old patterns of life. There are also Spanish and Negro strains from colonial times (the latter probably the more prevalent) which are both widespread and now quite thoroughly submerged in the general stream of population. The word mestizo properly describes the vast majority of El Salvador's people, one feels confident, if it is taken to include three racial origins rather than only two and to cover persons with hardly perceptible fractions of the blood of any one of the three.

Immigration to El Salvador since independence, like immigration to Guatemala, has been small. There were only 19,291 residents in 1950 who were born outside the country, the smallest

[1] See ch. v, nn. 1–3, p. 90.
[2] Rodolfo Barón Castro, *La población de El Salvador* (Madrid, 1942), pp. 523–8, speaks only of mestizos, Indians, and whites in the present population, and leans toward a 75 per cent–20 per cent–5 per cent distribution in that order.

number on the isthmus excepting that of Nicaragua. Of these, 15,856 (or nearly all) came from the other Central American nations, 576 from the United States, 489 from Spain, 437 from Palestine, 385 from Mexico, and 324 from Italy.[3] The economic resources of El Salvador, much more than those of Guatemala, have remained in native hands, with the few foreigners fitting in here and there and controlling no particular aspect of the nation's production.

LOCAL GOVERNMENT

El Salvador counts among its settlements 63 cities, 78 towns, 119 pueblos, and 3,275 *caseríos*.[4] Greatest city of the state and second largest of Central America, as at the time of independence, is San Salvador. This city was the capital of the United Provinces from 1834 to 1839 and has since remained the capital of El Salvador save for brief periods when catastrophe laid it low. Earthquakes in 1854 and 1917 wrought great devastation, and large sections of the city have also been hard hit by fire. San Salvador's growth was not rapid in the nineteenth century but has been remarkable in the twentieth, the population in 1950 amounting to 162,000. (By the middle of 1958, the figure was an estimated 222,000.)[5] Much of the city has a modern appearance due to its successive rebuildings and the readiness of its inhabitants in recent years to construct taller structures designed to resist earthquake shock. The population of San Salvador, apart from the foreigners assigned here by their governments and business firms, is comparable to that of the country at large. Many families live in elegant homes, many more in quite inadequate structures or in new housing provided by recent administrations.

Santa Ana, with 52,000 population (71,000 in 1958), is the second city of El Salvador and the largest in Central America apart from the five national capitals. Santa Ana (like only one of the capitals, Managua) had its origins as an Indian village and was counted a pueblo until very late in the colony. Made a town in 1811 and a city soon after independence, Santa Ana grew so rapidly during the nineteenth century that for a time its size exceeded that

---

[3] *Segundo censo de población: Junio 13 de 1950* (San Salvador, 1954), p. 83.

[4] *Diccionario geográfico*, p. 75.

[5] City and town population figures for El Salvador are from *Segundo censo de población*, pp. 2–8, and (given only for those above 10,000 in 1950) 1 July 1958 estimates from *An. Est.* (El S.), *1958*, i. 15–21; in both cases using the urban count of the corresponding *municipio*. See ch. v, n. 8, p. 92.

of the capital. No other city on the isthmus owed so much to coffee. San Miguel, on the other side of the capital, has developed less sensationally but none the less quite notably. Third largest in El Salvador, with some 27,000 residents (33,000 in 1958), San Miguel ranks with the second cities of Guatemala and Honduras (Quezaltenango and San Pedro Sula) and is nearly double the size of any apart from the capital in Costa Rica. Cotton is now important to San Miguel. Santa Tecla (18,300 in 1950; 25,000 in 1958) and Sonsonate (17,900; 22,000) are El Salvador's fourth and fifth cities. Santa Tecla or Nueva San Salvador was founded in 1854 as a refuge for the residents of the capital so hard hit by earthquake. Its fortune survived the rebuilding of nearby San Salvador; its fine homes are impressive today. Sonsonate has grown steadily without regaining its early colonial pre-eminence, its connexions with Acajutla still serving to bring commerce its way.

Villa Delgado (13,000 people in 1950; 18,000 in 1958) is a suburb of San Salvador organized in 1935, one of only three communities in all Central America which had reached the population of 10,000 by 1950 but were not departmental capitals. El Salvador has fourteen departments altogether, five of whose capitals have already been listed. San Vicente (11,000; 14,000), Ahuachapán (10,300; 12,600), and Cojutepeque (10,000; 12,800) are next in size. In the range from 10,000 to 9,000 in 1950 were Usulután and Zacatecoluca; La Unión had nearly 8,000 residents; Chalatenango a few more than 4,000; between 4,000 and 2,000 were Sensuntepeque and San Francisco Gotera. Seven of these places were Indian pueblos during colonial times, San Vicente a Spanish town, and La Unión a tiny port village with another name. La Unión has grown most, as the eastern terminus of El Salvador's cross-country railway. (Cutuco, two kilometres farther east, is now technically the port.) Passengers from the United States and Canada can ride this far on rails toward Panama, though very few do so. Two other ports, Acajutla and La Libertad, have had little growth as communities, though Acajutla has recently received new facilities. El Salvador in 1950 had two centres in the range 10,000–8,000 which were not capitals, two from 8,000–6,000, and seven from 6,000–4,000. Her cities are an important part of national life, though as in the other states of the isthmus the population remains predominantly rural.

There are 260 *municipios* for local government in El Salvador (1958), playing the same semi-autonomous and democratic role as in Guatemala.[6] The spirit of democracy on this level (national politics permitting) has prevailed to a greater degree in El Salvador, there being virtually no caste problem to complicate matters. The system of *municipio* elections is much older than in Guatemala, though from the 1930's to 1952 it was abandoned in favour of appointments. El Salvador has a *distrito* level of government above that of the *municipio* (there were thirty-nine districts in 1958), but it is of little consequence. The fourteen departments in the country are, as in Guatemala, simply agencies of the national government. There were only four of them originally (in 1824), grouped around the state's four ranking communities—San Salvador, Santa Ana, San Miguel, and San Vicente.

Today El Salvador's departments are arranged in three zones— Western, Central, and Eastern. Ahuachapán, Santa Ana, and Sonsonate (with population densities of 260, 358, and 336 persons per square mile) make up the Western zone.[7] The first two border on Jutiapa department in Guatemala, which has by contrast only 148 persons to the square mile. The Central zone has seven departments. Chalatenango, between the Honduran border and the curving Lempa River, is the most sparsely settled of El Salvador with a density of 168. San Salvador and Cuscatlán in the centre (1,176; 401) are nearly surrounded by La Libertad, La Paz, San Vicente, and Cabañas (291, 277, 244, 242). On the other side of the Lempa as it takes its course from the Honduran border to the Pacific is the Eastern zone consisting first of Usulután and San Miguel (276, 269) and finally Morazán and La Unión (190, 195) shading off in population toward Honduras.[8]

DEVELOPMENT OF THE STATE

When Central American independence arrived, El Salvador had not yet completely emerged as a separate isthmian entity. The first big step in that direction had come in 1786, when San Salvador attained equal political rank (as an intendancy) with Honduras and Nicaragua. Ecclesiastical rank was just as important in those

[6] *An. Est.* (El S.), *1958*, i. 11. The territory of the *municipio* outside the city, town, and pueblo is subdivided into units called the *cantón* for administrative purposes.

[7] Departmental population densities for El Salvador are computed from population estimates for 1 July 1958, from ibid. i. 15, and areas given in descriptions of the departments in *Diccionario geográfico*. See ch. v, n. 12, p. 94.

[8] All of El Salvador's departments have the same name as their capitals except Cuscatlán (Cojutepeque), La Libertad (Santa Tecla), La Paz (Zacatecoluca), Cabañas (Sensuntepeque), and Morazán (San Francisco Gotera).

days, however, and this San Salvador lacked to the end of the colonial period. In this province rose the first movement for independence from Spain in 1811, involving Manuel José Arce and his uncle José Matías Delgado, a priest who hoped to become San Salvador's first bishop. Here stood the most determined opposition to Central American union with Mexico in 1822. Here lay jealous concern lest Guatemala take upon herself the direction of isthmian affairs when the connexion with Mexico was broken. San Salvador became the first organized state of the isthmus, her own constitution taking effect in June 1824 before that of the federation was finished in November. Delgado and Arce both played important roles in the federal government (Delgado as chairman of the National Constituent Assembly, Arce as the first president of Central America) and the city of San Salvador became the federal capital in 1834. Yet there was no bishopric in the state until 1842, and three times during the years 1832–40 San Salvador had to submit to outside intervention (twice by Morazán, once by Carrera) effecting changes in her régime. There was no real opportunity in these early decades for San Salvador to enjoy self-composure or to develop an experience of democracy.

After Morazán's departure in 1840 San Salvador became the plaything of Francisco Malespín, *comandante de armas* introduced to the state by Carrera, and her first bishop, Jorge Viteri y Ungo. A new constitution was adopted in February 1841 still providing for existence as a state in a union, though an assembly the month before had called the state the republic of El Salvador. A two-house legislature was to be chosen by democratic processes and presidential elections were to be held every second year; but affairs were not regularized immediately. In 1846, with Malespín murdered and Viteri exiled, a series of two-year terms began under moderate or liberal auspices. Political storms continued to swirl over the isthmus, with El Salvador now considered a friend to ideas repugnant to the neighbouring régimes. Doroteo Vasconcelos (president 1848–51) tried unsuccessfully to force political union with Guatemala and lost his own post as a result. In 1856 the state started referring to itself regularly as a republic. In 1859, after a revolution and constitutional amendment, Gerardo Barrios began a six-year term as president. But in 1863 Rafael Carrera of Guatemala, engaging in his last intervention, deposed Barrios and left Francisco Dueñas in his place.

Constitutions came and went rapidly during the following

twenty-three years—technically there were six new ones put into effect through that time—but presidents changed less rapidly and the nation saw its first real economic advancement. Dueñas held office until 1871, under a conservative constitution adopted in March 1864 to bring El Salvador's ideology more into line with that of her neighbours. This was the first basic charter which labelled El Salvador a republic. A liberal revolution in 1871 brought Santiago González into office three months before the similar liberal triumph in Guatemala. While Guatemala waited eight years after this change to rewrite her constitution, El Salvador adopted a democratic charter in October 1871 and rewrote it (calling for a four-year presidential term) in November 1872. González served out his one term, but new intervention by Guatemala (this time by Justo Rufino Barrios) soon deposed Andrés Valle, his successor. Rafael Zaldívar, considered a conservative but a unionist and good friend of Barrios until the latter's last days, then served as president for two terms (1876–84) during which there were two minor rewritings of the basic law (February 1880 and December 1883). Zaldívar began a third term but soon suffered a break with Barrios, who died on Salvadoran soil in the battle between them. Zaldívar resigned after the battle and Francisco Menéndez took his place, calling for another new constitution. El Salvador had not experienced anything more than the forms of democracy during this period, but with all the forced changes in power (1863, 1871, 1876, 1885) there were considerable intervals of tranquillity during which coffee engaged the attention of a people hitherto tempestuous.

Tranquillity with economic progress has been El Salvador's keynote ever since, though some notable lapses have occurred; relatively little attention has been paid to the concept of rule by the people. The constitution of August 1886, which lasted until 1939, provided for governmental democracy in all of its aspects—rights and guarantees for the citizens, a unicameral legislature to be renewed every year by the people, a president and vice-president popularly elected to serve four years, and a supreme court to be chosen by the legislature. In reality, however, through all this time the president (not the people) ran the country and the president was chosen by himself or by his predecessor in office. Francisco Menéndez (1885–90), Carlos Ezeta (1890–4), Rafael Gutiérrez (1894–8), and Tomás Regalado (1898–1903) all came into power by force, the last-named being he who dashed isthmian hopes for the Estados Unidos de Centro-América. In each of these four cases a vote was taken confirming the man in office once he had made clear his determination to hold it. Pedro José Escalón (1903–7), Fernando Figueroa (1907–11), and Manuel Enrique Araujo were all 'elected' to office with the blessings of the men who preceded them, but without the use of force; Araujo was assassinated in 1913. Carlos Meléndez, first-designate to the office who came next, served his own term from 1915 to 1919; his brother Jorge Meléndez followed (1919–23), then his brother-in-law Alfonso Quiñónez Molina (1923–7). The backing for all came from the coffee plant-ers' aristocracy, which believed in order and economic progress but saw no reason to cater to the masses in either economic or governmental planning.

Restlessness under the long rule of the Meléndez–Quiñónez family, coupled with the belief of some individuals that El Salva-dor should render more than lip-service to democracy, now brought a change in affairs. Pío Romero Bosque, president from 1927 to 1931, had been chosen for the office by his predecessor Quiñónez but once in office asserted his own independence. In January 1931 he sponsored El Salvador's first genuine elections. The result of his own fairness was that there were too many candi-dates, leaving no one a chance to become a majority president. Ar-turo Araujo was elected by the legislature but had little popularity in the country. An uprising in December forced him to flee. Gener-al Maximiliano Hernández Martínez, his constitutional successor, cared little for the democracy which Araujo might have defended or even for the constitutional niceties which had for some time pre-vailed, and El Salvador quickly sank into a dictatorship which showed no sign of ending.

Hernández Martínez ruled until August 1934 as Araujo's legal successor, though through that time the other Central American republics and the United States refused to recognize his succession. From 1935 until 1939 he served a term of his own. A new constitu-tion adopted in January 1939 provided that he should remain in office until 1945 without further election. This régime in El Salva-dor matched that of Ubico in Guatemala in time, in its determina-tion to prolong its own life, and in the use of brutality and censor-ship wherever resistance appeared. The most notable instance of brutality was the cold-blooded murder of a few thousand peasants in early 1932 when they became involved in a movement led by a few early Communists. Truckloads of workers who had nothing to

do with Communism were shot in just as savage a manner only a
month before Hernández left office in 1944. The constitution of
1939 contained promises to labour, but the president allowed no
organization of labour; his was but a continuation of the old régime
in El Salvador under less rather than more gentlemanly auspices.
There was efficiency in other matters than murder, but efficiency
was no innovation for El Salvador. Roads were constructed, and
state assistance given to coffee growers along with greater state
controls. An independent international note was struck with the
recognition of the Japanese puppet state of Manchukuo (1934)
and the Franco régime in Spain (1936) at a time when more democratic governments elsewhere were declining to make the same
moves; during the Second World War, nevertheless, the Allies received El Salvador's co-operation. In February 1944 a new constitutional assembly extended Hernández' term to the end of 1949.
In April a vigorous protest against this move was put down with
great bloodshed. But a general strike brought the resignation of
Hernández Martínez on 8 May.

MID-TWENTIETH CENTURY POLITICS: PREROGATIVE OF ARMY AND ARISTOCRACY

Guatemala's revolution which began in June 1944 was stabilized
in direction within a year. That of El Salvador beginning in April
1944 ran a faltering course for six years and has never become so
ambitious. The place of Hernández Martínez was first filled by the
legal designate for the office, Andrés Menéndez. A new revolt on 21
October 1944 put Osmín Aguirre y Salinas in power, over the
opposition of liberal forces which had fought to get rid of Hernández. In the election which followed, five candidates withdrew after
accusing Aguirre of unfair practices to ensure the success of his
candidate. Salvador Castaneda Castro 'won' and was inaugurated
president on 1 March 1945. In November of the same year the
country returned to its 1886 constitution providing the traditional
four-year presidential term instead of a six-year span stipulated in
the 1939 document. On 13 December 1948 an obeisant legislature
decided that Castaneda, having been elected under the 1939 constitution, was entitled to six years in office. On the following day a
military junta took his place. Castaneda was placed in prison.

After twenty-one months of junta rule during which (1949) El
Salvador received its first social-security legislation, a new constitution (technically El Salvador's tenth) became effective on

14 September 1950. Liberal enough in text, it nevertheless contained no revolutionary principles, apart from a recognition of the state's obligation to render public-health and social-security assistance. A Legislative Assembly would be elected every two years, with the suffrage granted to men and women over eighteen years of age. The president would be elected by the people for a six-year term with no immediate re-election possible. The national judiciary, structured like that of Guatemala, would be chosen by the Legislative Assembly, but the latter body would not have the privilege accorded the Guatemalan Congress of dismissing a presidential cabinet appointee by a two-thirds 'lack-of-confidence' vote. One continuing feature of Salvadoran political life was not defined in the constitution. Every chief executive of El Salvador since 1931 had been an army officer. The 1950 charter says, 'The Armed Forces are non-political and essentially obedient. . . .'[9] Yet nothing is plainer about the politics of the country since 1948 than that the army retains control, regardless of the means through which manipulation takes place, and that whatever obedience it has rendered has been to the interests of El Salvador's aristocratic society rather than to the country at large.

Major Oscar Osorio became head of the military junta in January 1949. In March a year later he was elected president of the country with an announced 56 per cent of the vote. Osorio's political grouping was the Partido Revolucionario de Unificación Democrática (PRUD), manufactured especially for his campaign. The Partido Acción Renovadora (PAR) supported his one opponent, another army officer named José Asencio Menéndez. Osorio (inaugurated 14 September 1950) was young and liberal in the sense that he was not afraid to move in new directions. He did not intend to undo the old régime, however, by undermining the strength of the army or the planter aristocracy. An extensive housing programme was begun (the Instituto de Vivienda Urbana, 1950). Labour unions were legalized (1951). Processing industries were encouraged (1952). New social-security legislation was passed (1953). A government project harnessing the power of the Lempa River was completed (1954). A Salvadoran Institute for the Development of Production (Instituto Salvadoreño de Fomento de la Producción or INSAFOP) was planned (1955). But agrarian reform, without which the mass of the people would remain impoverished, was not even suggested. And democracy in govern-

[9] PAU, *Constitution of the Republic of El Salvador, 1950* (Washington, 1953), p. 24.

ment, which seemed possible in 1950, was under Osorio quite completely forgotten. PRUD had charge, PRUD would choose its own people, and PRUD would see them elected without minorities to stand in the way. This was politics in El Salvador in 1955–6.

One civilian ran for the presidency. He was Roberto Edmundo Canessa, until 1954 Osorio's foreign minister, popular but without backing in the army. Canessa's support was his own Partido Acción Nacional (PAN). But in February 1956, one month before the elections, Canessa's candidacy was banned, as were those of Colonel José Alberto Funes and Major José Alvaro Díaz, on legal technicalities. Two other candidates, Lt.-Colonel Rafael Carranza Amaya (Partido Auténtico Constitucional or PAC) and Enrique Mazaña Menéndez of PAR (active six years before) withdrew from campaigning shortly before the vote, charging that the election was already rigged for PRUD's candidate, another army officer and Osorio's Minister of the Interior, Lt.-Colonel José María Lemus. The announced vote was 93 per cent for Lemus over his combined opposition, the withdrawals of Carranza and Mazaña not having removed their names from the ballot.

Until the anti-climactic finish, with Lemus the only candidate active in the field, the presidential campaign of 1955–6 with its six contending parties might have seemed an awakening of democracy in El Salvador's politics. Such a judgement would have been mistaken on two scores. First, the overwhelming dominance of the Salvadoran army in the electoral decision was obvious from the beginning. Canessa, a civilian without military support, had no chance for the presidency, though he was well known both inside and outside the country and though he had the financial resources needed for a vigorous campaign. (When he needed a newspaper to press for his cause, he simply purchased *Nueva Patria*, for example.) The real choice between all the candidates lay with the armed forces—or more properly speaking, with the officer corps rather than the forces at large—without whose prior approval the people had no opportunity to express either pleasure or displeasure. As the campaign developed and major opponents of PRUD were marked off the ballot, the army's control became ever more glaringly evident.

Secondly, it would be fair to say that even if all six parties had run down to the finish line, the electorate of the nation would have had little alternative. In a country where the masses live as poorly as in El Salvador, a real opening of politics to the sentiments of the people is sure to produce lively divergences in opinion on some very basic matters. Lemus and his opponents all planned a continuation of Osorio's social-welfare programme. They were also all agreed not to rock very violently the mid-twentieth century structure of Salvadoran society, not greatly changed from the nineteenth. One might say they all stood for what a fairly progressive aristocracy believed correctly 'modern' for the six years ahead. (Under such reasoning, for example, social security is approved not because of the plight of the people but because it is embarrassing to be listed in world reports as one of the few countries on the globe which do not have it.) No party representing a more revolutionary viewpoint was in existence. Yet it seems certain that El Salvador has more to argue about politically, when her gates of debate are opened, than the here-today gone-tomorrow fortunes of six men in substantial ideological agreement.

José María Lemus took office peacefully on 14 September 1956, and ruled for more than four years. PRUD managed somehow in the elections for the Legislative Assembly in 1956, 1958, and 1960 to provide him with unanimous backing in that body, barely dented in May 1960 when two disgruntled persons elected by PRUD turned to PAR while in office. PRUD swept all local elections also in 1956 and 1958 (having virtually no opposition in the latter year) but PAR won six mayoralties in 1960, including those of San Salvador, Santa Tecla, and Villa Delgado. Besides political rigidity, Lemus' régime was characterized by the continuation of public-works projects begun before his time, notably the building of works at Lake Güija to regulate the flow of its waters and provide new power for two countries, the erection of new port facilities at Acajutla, and the construction of a new highway on the Pacific littoral. In his speeches, the president liked to emphasize industry rather than politics: 'We are not yet in a political year', he said in September 1959, 'but in a year of hard work, of intense effort, of struggle destined to be fruitful. . . .'[10] But no politics seemed like unfair politics to those whose own ambitions had been thwarted by PRUD's continued command of the nation. Demands which were being raised by 1958 made it impossible for Lemus to neglect politics altogether.

The chief clamour of the opposition parties was for a new electoral law. Plain honesty, they felt, was needed in the counting of

[10] José María Lemus, *Mensajes y discursos* (5 vols., San Salvador, 1957–60), v. 158.

votes, and a representation of minorities in the Legislative Assembly seemed also desirable. Lemus suggested at the end of his second year that the electoral law, the administrative-probity law, and the civil-service law needed discussion and revision.[11] But when a new electoral law was passed by an all-PRUD Assembly over a year later (November 1959) it only inflamed the feelings of many persons of other parties whose recommendations had been flouted in its construction. Protest mounted into tumult, backed by all of PRUD's enemies on right and left, until Lemus was finally unseated by force on the morning of 26 October 1960.

The Partido Revolucionario Abril y Mayo formed in 1959 (PRAM, the name referring to the months of the year 1944 when Hernández Martínez was deposed) formed an important body among Lemus' opposition in 1960. Composed of students, intellectuals, and workers, it was sympathetic to the revolutionary programme of the Castro régime in Cuba and prescribed a programme of like vigour for El Salvador. PRAM was of course labelled Communist by the Lemus régime. Its membership was diverse, however, and it was accepted as a home product by Lemus' more conservative opposition as long as he remained in power. Ex-president Oscar Osorio, breaking with Lemus in 1959, founded his own party (called at first PRUD Auténtico) with a reform programme more moderate than that of PRAM. A Partido Radical Democrático (PRD) organized in 1959 joined with PRAM, PAN (from 1956), and PAR (from 1950) in a coalition to contest the April 1960 elections; but the union broke up before the voting took place, PRAM not fitting well with its allies. Street demonstrations against Lemus grew in volume and violence after May 1960, with university students playing the most active role but carrying with them the sympathy of many parties. When national police broke into the university on 2 September, Rector Napoleón Rodríguez Ruiz was taken prisoner along with a body of students; Roberto Canessa was seized and gravely injured by government agents the same day. (Canessa died in New Orleans 27 January 1961).

The forces against him were described by Lemus in his fourth annual message to the Assembly (14 September 1960) as a 'hybrid of Communists and reactionaries'.[12] He depicted his own programme as one which would better the lives of the workers and

[11] Lemus, *Mensajes y discursos*, iii. 281.

[12] 'Mensaje pronunciado por el señor Presidente de la República ante la Asamblea Legislativa el 14 de septiembre en curso con motivo de su cuarto año de gobierno', *D. de Hoy*, 17 Sept. 1960.

maintained that his reactionary opponents were so bent upon destroying his own proposals that they were willing even to league themselves with Communist subversion to accomplish their ends. When he was arrested and deported to Costa Rica just six weeks later, Lemus expressed complete surprise at his removal.[13] A statement which followed blamed the event on elements opposed to his liberal policies, 'egoists who feel not the slightest preoccupation for popular interests'.[14] Another suggested a 'curious coincidence' in the fact that the Legislative Assembly was due to consider a minimum-wage law the day its activities were ended along with those of Lemus.[15] The Junta de Gobierno which replaced Lemus, however, seemed not to be characterized by reactionary forces. The army was well represented, to be sure, by three men including Colonel César Yanes Urías, chairman of the group. The three civilian members of the body, however, were Fabio Castillo Figueroa, René Fortín Magaña, and Ricardo Falla Cáceres, all holders of the doctorate (one physician and two lawyers aged 42, 29, and 30 respectively) and connected closely with the university. It was the stand of this junta that the insurrection against Lemus was in accord with the 1950 constitution (Articles 112 and 175). Their declared intention was to put this constitution into full operation through the holding of genuine free elections. They took no stand on social issues, asserting only that viewpoints on the council ranged from moderate right to moderate left and that there were no ties with foreign ideologies or régimes. Apart from the establishment of an elected régime, only education was to get special attention.[16] It seems fair to say that the Salvadoran coup of 26 October 1960 was simply directed toward the elimination of a quite arbitrary administration in the hope of giving El Salvador a chance at democracy.

Seriousness about the matter of democracy promoted an immediate political vitality. In an interview on 9 November Rector Napoleón Rodríguez Ruiz spoke of the necessity of a basic plan of social and economic reform to include a labour law, agrarian reform, a reorganization of the tax system, a minimum wage accompanied by measures to ensure its practicability, steps to eliminate usury, and a number of other items. Rodríguez' programme was designed to strengthen and modernize El Salvador's capital-

[13] 'He sido el más sorprendido', *La Nación*, 28 Oct. 1960.
[14] 'Lemus reconoce causa de su caída del poder', *D. de Hoy*, 31 Oct. 1960.
[15] 'Lemus atribuye su caída a Ley del Salario Mínimo', ibid. 4 Nov. 1960.
[16] 'Gobierno garantizará unas elecciones libres', ibid. 29 Oct. 1960.

istic system, not to replace it with socialism, but nevertheless called for a series of measures quite unprecedented in El Salvador's history.[17] The party most interested in the reforms he suggested was PRAM, whose position was legalized in December by a Supreme Court chosen by the junta. The court expressed clearly the opinion that speeches made by party members expressing sympathy for the revolution in Cuba could not be taken as an indication that PRAM was an international or foreign party (prohibited by law), and that the ideology of a Salvadoran was no cause for a deprivation of his rights of citizenship.[18]

A new Partido Social Demócrata (PSD), founded on 29 December with the assistance of ex-president Oscar Osorio, spoke more vaguely than PRAM of social reform but stated that the nation has an obligation to procure the best utilization of the soil and that idle lands ought to be expropriated 'when the general interest demands it'.[19] By 23 January 1961 El Salvador had nine parties legally inscribed including the two just mentioned (PRAM and PSD), one from the campaign of 1950 (PAR), two from that of 1956 (PAN and PAC), the PRD constituted in 1959, the Partido Unionista Centroamericano (PUCA, organized long before but not accustomed to presenting candidates for office), and two very new ones, Partido Demócrata Cristiano (PDC) and Partido Acción Democrática (PAD). These nine parties and six non-political organizations from the legal profession were the participants in a congress inaugurated that day to draw up the new electoral law under which they would later compete for office. René Fortín Magaña, addressing the group for the governing junta, said, 'We have believed simply that a man can be revolutionary in his aims without being turbulent in his means and we have wished to leave to the people themselves, through their representatives freely elected, the solution of their own problems.'[20] Such thinking was not to prevail. Two days later (25 January) a new Directorio Cívico Militar proclaimed itself in charge of the country. Fortín Magaña and Ricardo Falla Cáceres were exiled to Guatemala, the other four members of the old junta were placed under arrest, and the pre-electoral congress was dissolved while the new ruling group prepared to reorient the election machinery.

The new change in government was a violent one, accomplished

[17] 'Rector propone plan de reformas sociales', *D. de Hoy*, 9 Nov. 1960.
[18] 'Corte ordena se inscriba al PRAM', ibid. 8 Dec. 1960.
[19] 'Integran el Partido Social Demócrata', ibid. 31 Dec. 1960.
[20] 'Instalado el Congreso pre electoral ayer', ibid. 24 Jan. 1961.

only over the protests of a large number of persons, a few of whom were killed and many wounded.[21] The armed forces, directly responsible for the new order of events, explained their actions thus: 'There was anguish and concern among the people over the visible and accelerated advances of the forces of *osorismo* and *comunismo*. The people were threatened and in danger of losing their most genuine democratic values, of seeing their economic structure upset, and of being led to chaos when the *comunista* and *osorista* forces entered into open clash with democratic institutions.'[22] The directory itself said, 'The Armed Forces as well as the widest and most honourable sectors of public opinion saw with misgiving and fear the growing influence of Communism and of persons and political cliques apparently determined to bring about a climate of unrest, agitation, and disorder. . . . Never will we permit that liberty be used by the bad sons of El Salvador to force the country into political, social, and economic chaos.'[23] The real import of these words was seen in the fate of the political parties. Five of the nine were asked for advice, while on the other hand the leaders of PRAM were arrested, Osorio of PSD was sent out of the country, and PRD and PAD were ignored. Nothing seems plainer than that the elements in society which had long run the country were fearful that in the full play of democracy envisaged by the deposed Junta de Gobierno the forces of the left would win and the structure of the past would crumble. Democracy (in the judgement of these elements) would have to be restricted to those parties which would not upset the established order, and the best time to do it would be 25 January 1961, before an electoral law fair to all could be composed and put before the public.

The Directorio Cívico Militar was composed of five persons—two military men (Aníbal Portillo and Julio Adalberto Rivera), two lawyers (José Antonio Rodríguez Porth and Feliciano Avelar), and one physician (José Francisco Valiente). Thus the civilians, all of whom again held the doctorate, outweighed the army. The moves of the directory toward elections were more rapid than those of the junta it displaced. The favoured parties (PAC, PAN, PAR, PDC, and PUCA) established a council on 13 February to help write a provisional electoral law, which would rule the elections for a new Legislative Assembly, which would then choose a pro-

[21] A full account was not published in El Salvador. See instead *Imp.*, 26–28 Jan. 1961, and *El Día* (Tegucigalpa), 26–28 Jan. 1961.

[22] 'Tres civiles y dos militares en Junta', *D. de Hoy*, 26 Jan. 1961.

[23] 'Directorio integra el nuevo Gabinete', ibid. 27 Jan. 1961.

visional president to fill out the term of José María Lemus until 14 September 1962. But the prospects of a genuine electoral alternative for a people who have long suffered a lack of representation in the determination of both their government and economy seemed very dim indeed.

El Salvador's frontier problems have been minor by comparison with those between her isthmian neighbours. As with Guatemala, however, there remains one border unsettled. As mentioned before, the short border between Guatemala and El Salvador was established in 1938. The longer stretch between Honduras and El Salvador is not marked, though most of it (along rivers) is not the subject of controversy. Various attempts have been made to settle the small arguments which have arisen. All-encompassing boundary conventions were drawn up in 1895 and 1918 but did not take effect, the first because the work was not done which the convention set forth, the second because El Salvador did not ratify it. The disagreements which thus stand (but cause little trouble) pertain to the allotment of lands between a few nearby villages of the two countries and the ownership of some sparsely inhabited islands in the Gulf of Fonseca.[24]

The revenues of the government of El Salvador have grown tremendously in the last twenty years, even to the point where sizable surpluses were accumulated in 1953–7. Receipts in the calendar year 1939 were nearly 20 million colones or $8 million (1 colón equals 40 cents U.S. since 1934); in 1944, they were $11 million; in 1949, $28 million; 1953, $56 million; 1957, $77 million.[25] As in Guatemala, a great share of the revenue comes from customs duties (60 per cent in 1939, 61 per cent in 1957). Until the 1950's, almost all of this was a tax on imports (in 1939, 55 per cent on imports, only 5 per cent on exports). Now one is almost as important as the other, with the government collecting for each bag of coffee which leaves the country. Consumption taxes account for about 15 per cent of the total. An income tax on both persons and business firms, together with inheritance and gift taxes, brought in about 10 per cent of the total in 1957; similar taxes accounted for 7 per cent of

[24] Details of this and other unsolved isthmian boundary controversies may be found in Gordon Ireland, *Boundaries, Possessions and Conflicts in Central and North America and the Caribbean* (Cambridge, Mass., Harvard U.P., 1941).

[25] U.N., *Stat. Yb.*, *1951*, pp. 478–9; *1959*, p. 497. Figures are converted to the nearest million dollars.

the budget under Hernández Martínez.[26] Wealthy persons in El Salvador, though they are obliged to pay more than they would elsewhere on the isthmus, pay far less through this variety of taxation than persons similarly situated in the United States and Great Britain.

Whatever the mode of procuring revenue, El Salvador has largely paid her own way in the world, even since the Second World War when foreign aid has become widespread. United States grants amounted to $1·5 million in 1946–50, nearly $3 million in 1951–5, and have averaged over $1 million a year since, making the 1946–60 total $10 million.[27] Practically all of this money was for economic and technical-assistance programmes; less than $1 million of it was for road construction, though El Salvador has the best highway system on the isthmus. Technical assistance and children's relief from the United Nations amounted to $1,500,000 in 1954–8.[28] Loans have been received from the International Bank for Reconstruction and Development, and from the Rockefeller-backed International Basic Economy Corporation for the development of the Valle de la Esperanza region (San Miguel department) hard hit by earthquake in May 1951.

The bulk of El Salvador's $72,400,000 general budget for the calendar year 1960 was funnelled through her twelve executive ministries. Culture (Education) received 18 per cent, Public Works 15 per cent, Public Health and Social Assistance 10 per cent, National Defence 9 per cent, Finance 8 per cent, Interior 6 per cent, Economy 5 per cent, Public Security 3 per cent, Agriculture and Livestock 3 per cent, Foreign Relations 3 per cent, Justice 2 per cent, and Labour and Social Welfare 1 per cent. Other large items were pensions 4 per cent, the public debt 4 per cent, the judicial power 2 per cent, the presidency 2 per cent, and legal assistance for the poor 2 per cent.[29] From 1938 to 1957 expenditures for education, health, and social welfare rose from 14 per cent of the total to 26 per cent, while the amount spent for defence dropped from 18 to 11 per cent.[30] El Salvador has a tradition of public-works expenditures extending back into the earlier years of this century. Her willingness to spend for social services in the years since Hernández Martínez, despite the lack of democratic controls over the

[26] See ch. v, n. 43, p. 111.   [27] See ch. v, n. 44, p. 111.
[28] U.N., *Stat. Yb., 1959*, p. 423.
[29] *Presupuesto del fondo general y presupuestos de instituciones autónomas, 1960* (reprinted from *Diario Oficial*, San Salvador, 23 Dec. 1959), p. 10047.
[30] U.N., *Stat. Yb., 1959*, p. 497.

government, is an indication of her aristocracy's understanding of the nation's sad economic realities. Increased outlays for education, as in many other lands, will sooner or later force radical revisions in the economic world as well.

SUBSISTENCE AGRICULTURE

Both human and land statistics show the dependence of El Salvador's economy upon agriculture. Nearly two-thirds of her economically active citizenry were engaged in farming pursuits in 1950.[31] Almost three-fourths of her land was marked off in farms, a high proportion for a country where mountains abound. Some 3,085,000 acres, three-fifths of the nation's soil, were in service for pasture or cultivation.[32] Though El Salvador is noted for her exports of coffee, seven-eighths of this active farm land, a fraction only slightly less than that of Guatemala, is used for immediate subsistence.

Maize, grown alone or in company with other crops, was harvested from 436,000 acres or 14 per cent of the area used for farming in 1950.[33] Though the average yield in 1958 was 900 pounds per acre, half again as high as that of Guatemala, El Salvador imports maize regularly because her own supply does not meet the domestic demand. Through the decade of the 1950's acreage devoted to the crop remained about the same from year to year.[34] Sorghum is a major second crop in El Salvador; in 1950 it was grown either alone or with other crops on 202,000 acres, nearly half the number devoted to maize. Sorghum is used for food by both people and animals, and has grown in production during the 1950's.[35] Both maize and sorghum are grown in all parts of El Salvador, but Usulután department in the east and centrally-located La Libertad are very important for maize, while San Miguel and La Unión in the east and Chalatenango in the north are notable when maize and sorghum are considered together. Both are chief interests of the smaller farmer, nearly two-thirds of the maize and over two-thirds of the sorghum having been raised on plots of less than 10 hectares or 24·71 acres each in 1950.[36]

Cotton, which has gained importance in El Salvador's export trade, ranked fourth among the nation's ground crops with 42,000

[31] *Segundo censo de población*, pp. 413–16.   [32] *Estruct. agr.*, p. 123.
[33] Ibid. p. 179. No allowance is made for acreage duplication with other crops.
[34] *An. Est.* (El Salvador), *1958*, i. 255.   [35] Ibid.; *Estruct. agr.*, p. 179.
[36] *Primer censo agropecuario: octubre-diciembre de 1950* (San Salvador, 1954), pp. 155, 163, 191; *Estruct. agr.*, pp. 179–80.

acres in 1950 but has since been planted in more than twice that area. Beans have dropped from third to fourth place, having been grown (alone or associated) on 72,000 acres in 1950 but on fewer since that time. Beans are grown widely, but about one-third of them are raised in La Libertad and Santa Ana departments. Sugarcane was harvested from 39,000 acres in 1950; rice from 28,000; hay 21,000; sesame for export 14,000; and henequen for bags 12,000. The first four of these crops were grown widely, though, among the departments, San Salvador had a wide lead in sugarcane, San Vicente held the same position with rice, and San Miguel grew nearly half the sesame. Almost all the nation's henequen was raised in San Miguel and Morazán in the east. Other ground crops grown in some quantity (in decreasing order according to the space devoted to their cultivation) were tobacco, garden vegetables, peanuts, and wheat.[37] Virtually all of El Salvador's wheat is imported, there being few zones in the country suited climatically for its production.

Some 378,000 acres of El Salvador's land in 1950 were devoted to tree and bush crops, with at least 285,000 of them planted in coffee. Widely grown bananas and plantains occupied 27,000 acres, though El Salvador does not raise bananas for export. Other crops of this sort (in decreasing order according to the acreage involved) were coconuts, pineapples, citrus fruits, and cacao. The small cacao crop, no more than a reminiscence of early colonial times, comes appropriately almost all from Sonsonate department. Sonsonate and adjacent La Libertad also continue to provide balsam for the export trade as they have since the colonial epoch.[38]

Farmers of the nation reported 1,308,000 acres of natural pasturage in 1950 and 432,000 of cultivated pasturage. Of domestic animals, there were 810,000 cattle; 389,000 pigs; 115,000 horses; 35,000 mules; 19,000 goats; 6,000 sheep; and 4,000 donkeys. El Salvador carries on a lively trade in cattle, both import and export, and imports large numbers of pigs. Domestic fowls in 1950 included 2,490,000 chickens; 162,000 ducks; and 78,000 turkeys.[39]

EXPORTS AND IMPORTS

Indigo, so important to the province of San Salvador during Central America's colonial period, remained a chief source of

[37] *Estruct. agr.*, p. 179; *An. Est.* (El S.), *1958*, i. 255–6; *Prim. cens. agr.*, *1950*, pp. 80, 103, 119, 127.
[38] *Estruct. agr.*, pp. 123, 230; *Prim. cens. agr.*, *1950*, pp. 227, 235, 243.
[39] *Estruct. agr.*, pp. 123, 287.

outside revenue for the state throughout the nineteenth century. The sales decline brought about by British competition before independence was halted when the British themselves began making purchases. The usual trade route lay overland to the Motagua River at Gualán in Guatemala, thence by water to Omoa in Honduras, where the indigo was reshipped to Belize and from there to Great Britain. Synthetic dye production in Europe in the second half of the century affected the indigo trade less precipitately than the Guatemalan business in cochineal, but the end result was the same. One student of Salvadoran affairs stated in 1911 (on one page) that in this republic 'next to indigo, coffee ranks second in importance'; and contrarily (on another page) that 'indigo . . . for long constituted the chief article in the exports of the country, but in point of importance it has had to give place to coffee'.[40] The latter statement is the correct one for the time when the observations were made; the former serves to emphasize how long indigo had remained supreme.

Coffee production on a commercial scale in El Salvador antedated that of Guatemala by a decade or so, Gerardo Barrios (president 1859–63) being given credit for the initial impulse to the industry in the same manner as the president of the same family name in Guatemala (Justo Rufino Barrios, 1873–85). Coffee exports exceeded indigo exports in value, it seems likely, by the 1880's. Production increased quite steadily until the 1920's, when market uncertainties appeared and brought about a more erratic sales index. In the late 1940's there was another push forward to the high plateau where El Salvador's coffee now stands. No Central American country exports more coffee than El Salvador; in the whole world only Brazil, Colombia, and (since the late 1950's) some African nations are significantly ahead. In the period 1956–9, its value was 76 per cent of the total worth of El Salvador's trade to other nations, 73 per cent of this in coffee beans and 3 per cent in coffee extracts as it left the country.[41]

Some coffee is grown in every department of El Salvador, but in 1950 five departments—Santa Ana, Ahuachapán, and Sonsonate of the Western zone, adjacent La Libertad, and more easterly Usulután—produced more than five-sixths of the total. The 1950 census showed also that 72 per cent of El Salvador's coffee is grown on estates of 30 hectares (74·13 acres) or more, comprising only

[40] Percy F. Martin, *Salvador of the Twentieth Century* (London, 1911), pp. 234, 232.
[41] U.N., *Yb. Int. Trade Stat., 1959*, i. 184.

7·5 per cent of the farms from which coffee was reported; or, to narrow the matter still further, that properties of 50 hectares (123·55 acres) or more, making up only 4·6 per cent of the nation's coffee farms, raised 62 per cent of the nation's production.[42] Thus, in El Salvador as in Guatemala, the growing of coffee is largely in the hands of relatively few families. The difference is that in Guatemala in the twentieth century most of the holdings came into the hands of persons of foreign extraction. In El Salvador the producers are nearly all native, the sons of families who have long held title to their lands.

Both the government and the private producers of El Salvador have taken an active role in defending her coffee interests; they were the first on the isthmus to form associations for the regulation and promotion of the trade. San Salvador is the seat of FEDECAME (formed in 1945 as the Federación Cafetalera Centroamérica-México-El Caribe, reorganized in 1955 as the Federación Cafetalera de América) which comprises such associations in all the Middle American countries. The FEDECAME nations participate in international coffee agreements setting quotas for each participant. Their special position derives from the fact that many of their coffees find preference in the world market because of their flavour. Ready acceptance of the varieties grown on the isthmus and a willingness to pay a premium price do not of course guarantee the kind of profit the Central American republics need in order to lift their economies. One solution for this problem is being sought in the opening of new markets, particularly in Europe. But large consuming nations have recently begun to comprehend that lands to whom coffee means as much as it does to El Salvador require at least a programme of price stabilization.

Only very recently has coffee in El Salvador shared the spotlight in exports with any other crop. In 1940, however, a cotton co-operative association was founded in the country. The growing of cotton has since increased so tremendously that in 1956–9 it provided 16 per cent of the total value of El Salvador's exports.[43] Cotton is important not only in reducing El Salvador's dependence upon the fluctuating price of coffee, but in providing a good source of foreign exchange from the nation's warmer agricultural lands where coffee could never have been grown. Nearly all of the nation's production in 1950 came from the departments of Usulután

[42] *Prim. cens. agr., 1950*, pp. 209, 217.
[43] U.N., *Yb. Int. Trade Stat., 1959*, i. 184.

and San Miguel in the east and La Paz in the centre.[44] The new cotton crop like coffee is in the hands of wealthy producers, who use the most modern devices to assure the high quality which guarantees the sale. Thus, while ox-teams fill the streets of Usulután or San Miguel to bring the white harvest to storage, aeroplanes have carefully dusted the crop to keep it from insect damage.

A miscellany of minor items comprised the 8 per cent of El Salvador's exports in 1956–9 remaining after coffee and cotton. Included were four items averaging near $1 million a year, live cattle, oil-seed cake and meal, sugar, and textiles, the latter two of which grew steadily in value through the four years. El Salvador's total exports in 1956–9 averaged $120,200,000 annually, going only 42 per cent to the United States, 30 per cent to Germany, 10 per cent to Japan, 3 per cent to the Netherlands, and 2 per cent each to Guatemala, Honduras, Italy, and the United Kingdom.[45]

In the 1820's the indigo-prosperous families of El Salvador were quick to purchase goods from countries other than Spain whose produce independence had made legally available. British traveller George Alexander Thompson thus referred to a shop in Ahuachapán just four years after the ties with Spain were broken: 'Mixed with China crapes and India Bandanas were Irish linens and Manchester cottons; and Birmingham cutlery was exposed to sale on the same counter with the coarser implements which the forges of the natives could produce.'[46] As indigo gave way to coffee, and as coffee has made some room for cotton, the still-prosperous chief families have found the means to purchase a continuing supply of goods produced outside the country, with early British predominance in the trade giving way gradually to the lead of other nations, especially the United States. In the period 1956–9 Salvadoran imports averaged $106,800,000 annually, coming 49 per cent from the United States, 9 per cent from Germany, 7 per cent from the Netherlands, 5 per cent from Honduras (chiefly food to make up domestic deficiencies), 5 per cent from Japan, 4 per cent each from the United Kingdom and Belgium, 3 per cent from Guatemala, and 2 per cent each from Mexico, Canada, and Italy. Placed in the categories of the Standard International Trade Classification, El Salvador's imports in 1959 ranged as follows: manufactured goods constituted 23 per cent of the total, with over $6 million spent for textile yarn and fabrics; over $4 million for metal

---

[44] *Prim. cens. agr., 1950*, p. 80.   [45] U.N., *Yb. Int. Trade Stat., 1959*, i. 184–5.
[46] *Narrative of an Official Visit to Guatemala from Mexico* (London, 1829), p. 94.

manufactures; over $3 million for paper products; and over $2 million each for iron and steel and for rubber manufactures. Machinery and transport equipment made up 21 per cent of the total, more than $7 million being spent for road motor vehicles; over $4 million for electric machines and appliances; and over $1 million for agricultural machinery. Food was the third largest category (17 per cent) with over $6 million for cereals; over $3 million for fruits and vegetables; over $2 million for dairy products; and over $1 million for livestock. Chemicals accounted for 16 per cent, with over $4 million each for fertilizers and for medicinal and pharmaceutical products, and over $1 million for cosmetics and soaps. Manufactured articles other than machinery and transport (11 per cent) included over $2 million for clothing and over $1 million each for prefabricated buildings and furniture. Lesser categories were fuels and lubricants 7 per cent (over $6 million for petroleum products); beverages and tobacco 2 per cent; and inedible crude materials other than fuels 2 per cent.[47]

NON-AGRICULTURAL OCCUPATIONS

The occupational distribution of the slightly more than one-third of El Salvador's economically active population not engaged in farming pursuits in 1950 varied but little from that of Guatemala. El Salvador's census found 11·9 per cent of her people engaged in service occupations (2 per cent higher), the difference being chiefly a greater proportion of domestic servants. Aside from this, there were 11·4 per cent of the group in manufacturing, 5·5 per cent in trade, 2·8 per cent in construction, and 1·5 per cent in transport.[48] The village crafts so important to the Guatemalan economy are noteworthy only in the Western zone of El Salvador. The bulk of manufacturing is nevertheless done at present in quite small establishments, which pervade El Salvador's cities.

El Salvador has taken two censuses of manufacturing industry and commerce, the first covering activities of the year 1951 and the second those of 1956. In the latter year 45,448 persons were found working in 2,472 establishments hiring five or more workers each. Of these, 28,580 were employed by 1,656 firms in the food-processing industry, sugar and coffee occupying the attention of most. The making of shoes and wearing apparel busied 3,347 persons in 272 workshops; the fabrication of textiles 3,116 persons in

[47] U.N., *Yb. Int. Trade Stat., 1959*, i. 183–4.
[48] *Segundo censo de población*, pp. 413, 417–18.

60 mills dealing with cotton and henequen. Other industries employing more than 1,000 persons each were the preparation of non-metallic mineral products (there is a cement plant in Acajutla) and the beverage industry. The same census (1956) located 18,168 people engaged in manufacturing in establishments employing only from one to four persons; 26,651 individuals engaged in the retail trade; and 8,247 busy with personal services other than domestic labour.[49] El Salvador witnessed the beginning of a small steel industry in 1958, the only one on the isthmus.

Of the 45,448 people employed in 1956 in manufacturing establishments hiring five or more persons, 1,981 were proprietors; 3,303 were administrative employees who earned an average of $1,094 for the year's work; 215 were workers in the home whose year's earnings averaged $285; 38,413 were production factory workers with an average for the year of $253; and 1,536 were members of the family who worked without remuneration. These compensation figures, though higher than in 1951, are considerably lower than comparable ones shown for Guatemala in 1953. The 8,247 individuals engaged in personal services were paid even less, their year's wages amounting to only $157 each.[50] Pay was highest in the capital city, but in 1958 the average hourly manufacturing wage in the vicinity of San Salvador was only 24·8 cents U.S. as compared to 32·5 cents in Guatemala City.[51] The willingness of Salvadoran men of wealth to invest in domestic agriculture may lead to a readiness to develop home manufacturing as well. Since mining and lumbering have no importance in El Salvador, and no one at present is looking for petroleum, the smallest state of the isthmus may one day need an abundance of factories to keep pace with her larger neighbours. But if private enterprise is to do the job, it will have to take the human factor sharply into account in a way these figures reveal has not been done to the present.

The first poor cart roads were built between Salvadoran cities during the second half of the nineteenth century. In the first decade of the twentieth, an extensive road construction programme was undertaken to make the connexions usable in all weathers. Earlier than any of her immediate neighbours, El Salvador then proceeded to lay asphalt over the earth foundations. All the departmental capitals have long been connected by all-weather roads, and all but

[49] *Segundo censo industrial y comercial: 1956* (2 vols., San Salvador, 1959), i. 24–33, 158; ii. 16, 107.

[50] Ibid. i. 52, 58–59; ii. 107. See ch. v, n. 67, p. 120.

[51] *Yb. Lab. Stat., 1959*, p. 289.

three of them are now united by pavement. The chief artery of commerce is the all-paved and busy Inter-American highway, from the Guatemalan department of Jutiapa through or near Santa Ana, Santa Tecla, San Salvador, Cojutepeque, San Vicente, and San Miguel to La Unión or the Honduran department of Valle. A paved coastal route roughly parallel to the Inter-American runs near or through Sonsonate, the ports of Acajutla and La Libertad, Zacatecoluca, and Usulután to La Unión, and at the end of 1960 promised soon to connect with other pavements along the Pacific through Guatemala and Chiapas. Both of these roads in El Salvador provide excellent tourist and commercial attractions. There are four paved connexions between them, and a paved side road to Ahuachapán from Santa Ana. Another paved stretch leads northward from the capital toward Nueva Ocotepeque in Honduras, and is planned to be continued through this corner of Honduras into Guatemala, providing easy access by highway to Matías de Gálvez and Puerto Barrios. El Salvador's remaining northern border is as yet little developed. There were 2,400 passenger cars and 800 commercial vehicles in the country in 1937; in 1957, the counts were 14,300 cars and 6,300 commercial vehicles.[52]

El Salvador has two railways, covering an extensive part of the country. The first line was opened between Sonsonate and Acajutla in 1882. Extensions brought a continuous track from Acajutla to Santa Ana by 1896 and to San Salvador by 1900. This network constitutes the British-owned El Salvador Railway Company, which owns the port installations at Acajutla and which in 1909 gave El Salvador her first regular steamship connexion with the rest of the world, service across the Atlantic being carried out by connexions with the Tehuantepec railway in Mexico. In 1910 a rail line was begun to connect La Unión with San Miguel and the capital. This enterprise was taken over by the International Railways of Central America, representing the interests of Minor Keith, and building continued until 1929, when the line extended through the capital to Santa Ana and Ahuachapán and connected the nation with Puerto Barrios through a Guatemalan junction at Zacapa. IRCA's Salvadoran business through Puerto Barrios is considerably less than that at La Unión. In the past, shipment to dockside at both Acajutla and La Unión had to be by rail though good highways were available. La Libertad, only 25 miles by paved road from the capital, offered some competition; but Acajutla with a

[52] U.N., *Stat. Yb., 1951,* p. 317; *1959,* p. 332.

new dock and other facilities now promises to take first place. Indeed, Acajutla, the point from which Central America's first notable export departed (Sonsonate's sixteenth-century trade in cacao) seems destined to become the major point on the Pacific, save for Panama, in the entire isthmus.

Several shipping lines make calls at El Salvador's ports, though none of them is owned in the country. The same may be said for the airlines, though one of these, Transportes Aéreos Centro-Americanos (TACA) is incorporated under the Salvadoran flag. TACA is the chief regional airline on the isthmus, to be contrasted on the one hand with the larger international companies for whom Central American business is but a small part of the total, and on the other hand with the domestic companies which do most of their flying within the boundaries of one state. Smaller El Salvador with her superior highway and railway networks is the only nation on the isthmus without at least one domestic airline.

Telegraph service covering the entire country and telephones in the larger cities are controlled by the state. Until the 1950's the power situation in El Salvador was not unlike that of Guatemala, with several municipal plants in operation throughout the country, and the capital and its vicinity served by a subsidiary of a foreign-owned concern, in this case the Canadian International Power Company. Power distribution has remained in the hands of the previous entrepreneurs, but power production since 1954 is largely a function of the government. The Lempa River through the dam at Chorrera del Guayabo (on the Cabañas–Chalatenango border) supplies the energy. A project undertaken at the outlet of Lake Güija (after joint understandings with Guatemala) regulates the flow of the Lempa waters so that El Salvador will have a dependable year-round surplus of electricity for her expected industrial development. With lower rates, more of El Salvador's homes will be electrically lighted as well. Only 39 per cent of the nation's urban residences were supplied with electricity in 1950, the same proportion as in Guatemala. Total production of electric current for public use advanced from 48 million kilowatt hours in 1948 to 178 million in 1957.[53]

El Salvador's banking has traditionally been handled by private interests, with the coffee growers' association playing the dominant role and the government involved chiefly as a granter of permissions. The colón, created in 1920, was stabilized at 2·50 to the dol-

[53] U.N., *Stat. Yb.*, *1959*, pp. 283, 543.

lar in 1934 when the Banco Central de Reserva and the Banco Hipotecario de El Salvador were formed, and has been kept there ever since. The government participated only in a small way in the management of these banks until 1960, when it took over the Banco Central de Reserva. The Banco Hipotecario lends chiefly to the wealthy but has invested some of its funds in recent programmes of public housing for lower-income groups. The Federación de Cajas Rurales de Crédito was organized by the state in 1943 to assist with smaller loans, but has never become important. INSAFOP, created only in 1955, has sought to expand Salvadoran enterprise in a greater variety of industries. Seven banks completely in private hands conclude the roster for the country.[54]

ECONOMIC OUTLOOK: PROMISE OF NEW LIVELIHOOD?

Most families in mid-twentieth century El Salvador eked out a bare existence. A studied estimate suggests that in 1946 only 20,000 five-person families of the republic enjoyed incomes of more than $960 each; another 20,000 families had from $480 to $960 each; 120,000 families had from $240 to $480 each; and 240,000 families (three-fifths of the total) had less than $240 each. Bare subsistence for a family of five was believed to cost slightly below $240.[55]

Twelve years later, with general conditions somewhat improved (though to what degree is uncertain), the government studied working-class expenditures in the capital and two suburbs, Villa Delgado and Mejicanos. Here, where conditions for the workers are as good as any in the republic, it was found that the average family of five in this class of society spent $81·52 per month in 1958 for its living. Over half ($44·17) went for food, including $15·57 for bread and cereals; $10·12 for dairy products, cooking fats, and eggs; $8·17 for meat and fish; $6·32 for tubers, vegetables, and fruit; and $3·99 for miscellaneous. Rent and the lighting of the home cost the same family $9·67, fuel $2·96, articles for the home $2·29, articles of personal use $3·41, and clothing $8·51. 'Cultural' expenditures were $3·69, medical care $2·92, transportation $2·31, and all else $1·59. Are prices then so low in the vicinity

[54] See ch. v, n. 71, p. 123.

[55] The study was made on the basis of a population of 2 million divided equally into 400,000 five-person families. Henry C. Wallich and others, *Public Finance in a Developing Country: El Salvador—A Case Study* (Cambridge, Mass., Harvard U.P., 1951), pp. 325–8.

of San Salvador that such spending is sufficient? A look at four food products alone is enough to give the answer. The average retail price of rice in 1958 was 12 cents U.S. per pound; that of beans 11·5 cents; that of maize 5·8 cents; should a rare family choose potatoes, it paid 8·2 cents per pound.[56] One need but compare with one's neighbourhood grocer.

Presidents Osorio and Lemus, though their party (PRUD) was labelled revolutionary, brought no more revolution to El Salvador than that associated with the United States term 'New Deal'. Except in the fields of housing and trade-union organization, even their moves in New Deal directions left but small impact in their decade. The social-security programme instituted in 1949 included in 1957 only 37,000 contributors toward sickness and maternity benefits, old-age pensions, and protection against employment injury.[57] Minimum-wage legislation was discussed but not passed before the fall of Lemus. Labour unions were formed, however, on a large scale in the 1950's. A General Confederation of Salvadoran Workers was organized in 1957 (with ten labour unions as members and a pro-Castro orientation in 1960), and a General Confederation of Syndicates in 1958 (forty-one members) having affiliation with the International Confederation of Free Trade Unions. A large Union of Railway Workers is separate. San Salvador was chosen in late 1961 as the seat for a new Central American Trade Union Coordinating Council. As for the housing situation, Lemus was able to say with pride in his annual report of 1959:

The Instituto de Vivienda Urbana worked arduously.... Nineteen multi-family edifices were built of four stories, with 296 apartments. ... In the said living-quarters there were lodged 1,776 persons. ... The one-family dwellings constructed total 275. ... The number of persons lodged was 1,650.[58]

Public housing was not new in El Salvador with Osorio and Lemus, but most of their progress reports were similarly impressive.

With powerful assistance from the government in the provision of highways, electric power, and such undertakings as the new port facilities at Acajutla, men of wealth in El Salvador in the early 1960's had the way better prepared for extensive industrial investment than any other group on the isthmus. Whether El Salvador, seizing this advantage, will assume at least a limited role of provid-

[56] *An. Est.* (El S.), *1958*, ii. 169, 171, 174–5.
[57] *Yb. Lab. Stat.*, *1959*, p. 453.   [58] *Mensajes y discursos*, v. 117.

ing factory-made materials to other isthmian peoples in exchange for food and raw materials remains to be seen. Except for one factor, her long-range potentialities as a manufacturing state are essentially no greater than those of her neighbours. The one factor is her surplus population which will have to turn somewhere. Emigration to nearby states for field labours has already provided one alternative to increased urbanism. In the event of closer union between the states, El Salvador will have to choose between steady depopulation, with her workers leaving to enrich other areas, or the provision of city job opportunities at home.

The mass of country workers in El Salvador, though race attitudes constitute no great factor, find themselves in the same plight as those in Guatemala. Farms in tiny El Salvador do not average as large, but it was still true in 1950 that 2·38 per cent of the nation's estates—those containing 50 hectares (123·55 acres) or more—held 59 per cent of the nation's farm land within their borders. Add to this the fact that the *rural* population estimate at the end of 1958 ran at 191 persons for every one of El Salvador's square miles, or about 30 persons for every 100 acres, and the magnitude of the problem will be realized.[59] Agrarian reform involving expropriation of large estates is no more popular with the landowners of El Salvador than it is with those of any other state. Expropriations in Guatemala were directed first towards land owned by Germans (while Guatemala and Germany were at war) and later towards both foreign-owned and native-owned properties which were not being cultivated. El Salvador has no large foreign interests in real estate and can point to much less land which is idle over a period of years. The only argument left for agricultural reforms is that the ordinary (now often landless) labourer is entitled to a better standard of living for the wealth his labour produces. A satisfactory system of reform for El Salvador's case has yet to be worked out.

The economy of El Salvador, perhaps more than that of any other isthmian nation, stands in a state of crisis. The hungry mouths are there to feed—66,000 more in 1952 than in 1951; 83,000 more in 1958 than in 1957.[60] Power and transportation facilities are available; the soil remains as rich and the weather as favourable as in cacao and indigo times. Those who own the land and fluid wealth of the country have now to decide whether they care to

[59] *Estruct. agr.*, p. 28; *An. Est.* (El S.), *1958*, i. 14.
[60] *An. Est.* (El S.), *1958*, i. 13.

share their gains through industrial investment and radical agricultural adjustment. Their fathers and grandfathers have often shown wisdom in the past in planning an economy among the most forward on the isthmus. Will they now lead the way in planning new livelihood for the masses? If they do not, it seems likely that the way will nevertheless be found without their assistance.

LEARNING

To enter the modern world, especially the world of industrialization, El Salvador needs one ingredient more than power facilities and communications. She needs most desperately to educate her people, though she has been slowly working at it since independence and though her literacy rate is the second highest of Central America.

Educated persons living in San Salvador, Santa Ana, and San Miguel at the dawn of nationhood were mostly individuals who had studied in the University of San Carlos in Guatemala City. In the middle of political chaos, as a part of their assertion of self-sufficiency, these men were interested in the creation of a Salvadoran system of higher learning. A Colegio de la Asunción was founded in the capital in 1841, teaching Latin. Theology courses were added in 1844 and medicine in 1847, at which time the school became the national university. The institution has functioned most of the time since. With reorganizations in the twentieth century, it has come to include the Faculties of Jurisprudence and Social Sciences, Medicine, Engineering and Architecture, Chemistry and Pharmacy, Odontology, Economics, and Humanities. A new campus is being brought into existence on the edge of the capital city. Some 3,815 men and 361 women living in El Salvador in 1950 had attended university classes. The total enrolment of the national university in 1958 was 1,624 men and 274 women.[61]

As in Guatemala, a real effort to educate the masses has been made only since 1944. Primary school enrolment advanced from 127,300 students in 1948 to 262,500 in 1958; secondary from 8,400 in 1950 to 27,300 in 1958.[62] The 1950 census showed that 39·1 per cent of the Salvadoran population over the age of ten (including 42·2 per cent of those aged 15 through 19) could read and write. In that year 170,219 of the children of the nation aged 6 to 14 were

[61] *An. Est.* (El S.), *1958*, i. 165; *Segundo censo de población*, p. 382. A history to 1930 is given in Miguel Angel Durán, *Historia de la Universidad de El Salvador* (San Salvador, 1941).

[62] *Hechos y Cifras de El Salvador, 1958* (Dir. Gen. Est. y Censos), pp. 21-22.

in primary school (according to census count) and 244,304 were not attending. Of the latter, according to report, 54,984 were at work, 88,202 were not attending because of parental negligence, and 64,609 had no school to attend.[63]

The first newspaper appeared in El Salvador in 1824. A government gazette has been published most years since 1847. *Diario Latino* is the oldest of the commercial dailies, founded in 1890. *La Prensa Gráfica* (1915), which supported PRUD and President Lemus, and *El Diario de Hoy* (1936), which provided Lemus' chief journalistic opposition, are the most widely read. There were seven dailies in the country in 1957, five of them alone having a total circulation of 104,000 or 44 papers for every 1,000 inhabitants, a figure significantly higher than that of Guatemala.[64]

Medical science has followed the same course in El Salvador as in Guatemala but has gone further. The death-rate in 1958 was 135·0 per 10,000 inhabitants, to be compared with Guatemala's 213·3. Among the principal known causes of death in El Salvador in 1958 were gastro-enteritis and colitis (16·6 deaths diagnosed as such for each 10,000 inhabitants, but with a much higher percentage of deaths than in Guatemala undiagnosed as to cause); pneumonia and bronchitis (6·9); infections of infancy (4·1, but with nearly five times that number of infant deaths undefined); malaria (2·9); whooping-cough (2·4); malignant tumours (2·0); lung tuberculosis (1·6); worms (1·6); and measles (1·5). Death from intentional personal violence (2·9) was greater than six of these other causes, but probably only because it was more clearly recognized. The government supported 14 hospitals in 1960–5 in San Salvador, 1 in Soyapango nearby, and 8 in departmental capitals. In 1955 there were 396 physicians (nearly one for every 5,500 persons) and 129 dentists.[65]

Salvadoran scholars have paid less attention to their nation's history than those of any other Central American republic. The first real attempt to write a separate history of the area was made just before his death by lawyer Santiago Ignacio Barberena (1851–1916) who covered only the pre-colonial and colonial epochs.[66]

---

[63] *Segundo censo de población*, pp. 87, 164, 298. *Hechos y Cifras, 1958*, p. 21, gives a 1950 primary matriculation figure of 145,200. The literacy–illiteracy count missed 3·2 per cent of the population.

[64] U.N., *Stat. Yb., 1959*, p. 578.

[65] Ibid. *1958*, p. 541; *Presupuesto del fondo general: 1960*, pp. 10304–18; *An. Est.* (El S.), *1958*, i. 15, 46–48, 82.

[66] *Historia de El Salvador* (2 vols., 1914–17).

Four significant pieces of work have been performed since. One is a monumental collection of source materials drawn from a most impressive variety of hiding-places by Miguel Angel García (1862–1955) to form his *Diccionario histórico-enciclopédico de la república de El Salvador*. The collection is arranged alphabetically by subject, though several special volumes have been published out of order. The design was too grand for one man to complete in his lifetime— the first thirteen volumes in order take the alphabet only to COL —but they are certainly a reminder of the vast amount of documentation awaiting the historian who cares to unravel the confused threads of El Salvador's past.[67] José Figeac in 1938 wrote a careful presentation of that past through the nineteenth century.[68] Rodolfo Barón Castro contributed a comprehensive study of El Salvador's demography in 1942.[69] Jorge Lardé y Larín has made the meticulous investigation of his nation's local history from pre-conquest times to the present his speciality, producing Central America's most outstanding work in this genre.[70] For other broad-scope contributions to El Salvador's historiography one must look to the work of foreigners dealing with the whole of Central America.[71]

Lengthy but general descriptions of the contemporary scene are the closest El Salvador has to a comprehensive geography.[72] A careful look has been taken at her public finance, but once again by outsiders.[73] Evidence of Salvadoran talent in the field of law is seen in the careers of Héctor David Castro (b. 1894), who served as president of the Council of the Organization of American States in 1953–4, and José Gustavo Guerrero (1876–1957), president of the Tenth Assembly of the League of Nations in 1929, of the Permanent Court of International Justice 1937–40, and of the International Court of Justice 1946–9. Talent in a wide variety of fields has been demonstrated by briefer contributions in writing; some significant examples have appeared recently in the university re-

[67] An idea of the scope of this work is provided by the space devoted to one president, Gerardo Barrios: iii. 394–571; iv, all; v. 1–300. The thirteen volumes in order were published in San Salvador, 1927–51. At least eleven others appeared in San Salvador, 1933–55.

[68] *Recordatorio histórico de la república de El Salvador* (San Salvador).

[69] See above, n. 23.

[70] *El Salvador: historia de sus pueblos, villas y ciudades* (San Salvador, 1957).

[71] See ch. v, nn. 99–101, p. 132.

[72] See for example David Joaquín Guzmán, *Apuntamientos sobre la topografía física de la república del Salvador* (San Salvador, 1883); or the item cited above, n. 40, p. 164.

[73] See above, n. 55.

view.[74] One has but to see how the average university professor in El Salvador works day and night just to keep living to comprehend why current productions do not reach further.[75]

As with education in general, El Salvador had an artistic base somewhat smaller than that of Guatemala at the dawn of independence. Instruction in music and the visual arts was slow in its beginnings. Except for the organization of an orchestra by Italian immigrants—which soon resolved itself into a military band—recreation in town and country alike changed little during the nineteenth century.

On New Year's Eve at the beginning of 1901 there was dancing in the streets of the capital until 2 a.m.—led by the Band of the High Powers which marched up and down. Twenty youths on bicycles raced about at midnight sounding their horns and cornets. A merry-go-round by the Parque Bolívar provided pleasure 'equally for the old and the young'. Other band concerts followed, almost one each night, and a social dance was held indoors on 12 January. A paper on the latter date commented on *el juego llamado* 'Base Ball'—'it is so popular in England and the United States, that it can almost be said that it forms part of the athletic education of masculine youth'. Ten years later a group had formed a baseball club—'already they have begun to practise the game'—but this was three decades after its introduction to Guatemala.[76] By the 1940's, nevertheless, Salvadoran addiction to both sports and cinema varied little from that of Guatemala. And by the late 1950's El Salvador had 21 radio stations, of which 12 were in the capital—one, La Voz del Trópico, was the only 50,000-watt transmitter in all Central America.[77] Two television stations provide additional entertainment.

El Salvador dances and sings the rhythms of the tropical Caribbean. María de Baratta (b. 1894), herself a Salvadoran mestiza, after studying in Europe and the United States composed a ballet called *Nahualismo* to capture some of her own country's Indian

[74] *La Universidad*, founded in 1875 but not published regularly; Año 84, nos. 1-2, Jan.-June 1959.
[75] See ch. v, n. 116, p. 134.
[76] *Diario del Salvador* (San Salvador), 2-12 Jan. 1901; 3 July 1911.
[77] See ch. v, n. 118, p. 135. Salvadoran call letters have the prefix YS. There are also three stations using 10,000 watts power.

spirit.[78] There are two symphony orchestras in San Salvador. There is also a new school of painters who have international connexions. José Mejía Vides (b. 1903), best known of the Salvadoran artists, studied in Mexico but returned to paint the life of his own land in an appealing style free from affectation.

A quartet of men born in the third quarter of the nineteenth century in El Salvador made an impression on isthmian letters. Francisco Castañeda (b. 1856) wrote a variety of essays including many on literary subjects.[79] Francisco Antonio Gavidia (1863–1955) wrote poetry inspired by French models, sometimes as drama; it was he who initiated the only slightly younger Rubén Darío of Nicaragua (of later great fame) in the study of French verse.[80] Alberto Masferrer (1868–1932) wrote both poetry and thoughtful prose, applying himself to social and spiritual matters. His is the plan called *mínimum vital* whereby the rich should limit themselves to that which they can amass without thriving upon the hunger, the health, or the blood of their fellows, while the poor should rely upon their own individual endeavours once they have reached a minimum of water, roof, coat, recreation, light, and bread.[81] Manuel Quijano Hernández (b. 1871) wrote essays and poems, his favourite topic being the countryside of El Salvador.[82]

Salvadoran authors of more recent birth have won less distinction. Some of their work appears in literary magazines of which El Salvador has her share—especially the quarterly *Ateneo* founded in 1912;[83] *ECA* (the letters stand for Estudios Centro Americanos), begun by the Jesuits of Central America in 1945;[84] and *Ars*, an annual publication of the Ministerio de Cultura since 1951.[85]

RELIGION

Neither paganism nor Protestantism carries quite the influence in El Salvador that it has in Guatemala. Salvadoran religion has nevertheless followed the same general trends as in the larger coun-

---

[78] See ch. v, n. 120, p. 136.

[79] *Estudios y artículos literarios* (San Salvador, 1890); *Nuevos estudios* (2 vols., San Salvador, 1919).

[80] *Poesía* (San Salvador, 1884); *Obras* (San Salvador, 1918) includes 'Poemas y teatro' and 'El libro de los azahares'.

[81] *La doctrina del mínimum vital* (San Salvador, 1948) is the first volume of his collected *Obras*. See Matilde Elena López, *Masferrer, alto pensador de Centroamérica: ensayo biográfico* (Guatemala, 1954).

[82] *De alma en alma* (San Salvador, 1911); *Hojas dispersas* (San Salvador, 1924).

[83] Año 46, nos. 218–19, July–Dec. 1958.   [84] Año 13, no. 130, Sept. 1958.

[85] ix, Jan.–Dec. 1958.

try, with a mid-twentieth century revival of somewhat smaller scope counteracting the comparative negligence of the first century of independence.

The early history of San Salvador as a state in the union provided a mixture of anti-clerical legislation and attempts to win a separate bishopric. Once the latter objective was achieved in 1842 one might have expected harmony, but church-state relationships were seldom smooth. A concordat with the papacy in 1862 lasted only nine years, when with the liberal revolution of 1871 relations were broken and El Salvador became constitutionally a nation of religious freedom. She has remained so ever since.

The bishopric of San Salvador in 1913 was raised to the rank of an archdiocese; at the same time the first bishops of San Miguel and Santa Ana were appointed. San Vicente became a bishopric in 1943, and in 1954 Santiago de María in the department of Usulután. El Salvador has a total of 733 churches served by 277 priests, a number which, at one priest for each 7,600 Catholics, compares quite favourably with that of Guatemala.[86] Nearly half the priests are members of religious orders. Five Franciscans and one Salesian in El Salvador from the United States account for only a small portion of the work carried on by these two groups in Central America. The importance of European Catholic missionary endeavour in the isthmus is illustrated most amply by the fact that the Salesian province of Central America, from a beginning made in El Salvador in 1897, now includes 304 workers, of whom only this one is from the United States.[87]

Though El Salvador has nearly five-sevenths the total population of Guatemala, she has only about half as many Protestants. Only eight Protestant churches have entered El Salvador, though (owing mostly to the efforts of one denomination) they serve more than 1,000 places of worship.[88]

The Pentecostal doctrine is widespread in this nation. After campaigns by a Canadian evangelist, the Assemblies of God sent workers in 1929. The field took on a strongly indigenous tone at the outset: '. . . Three months after the Williamses arrived in the country, twelve national workers . . . expressed their desire to preach and maintain the standards and doctrines set forth by the General Council. . . .'[89] In 1960 there were only 11 Assemblies of God mis-

[86] See ch. v, n. 140, p. 141.
[87] El Salvador has thirty-three religious houses for men and forty-two for women. See ch. v, n. 141, p. 141.   [88] See ch. v, n. 145, p. 142.
[89] From 'El Salvador', an Assemblies of God pamphlet.

sionaries in El Salvador, but 240 national ministers and 683 lay workers. The membership constituted well over one-half of the country's Protestant population.

The non-denominational Central American Mission sent the first Protestant missionaries to El Salvador in 1896, this being the last of the Central American republics to become a field of Protestant endeavour. Today the Central American Mission maintains only 12 workers in El Salvador compared to its 52 in Guatemala. This is a sizable effort, however, as are those of the American (Northern) Baptists who came in 1911; the Seventh-Day Adventists, whose work is now largely indigenous; and the National Baptist Convention, which in the United States is a Negro body.

Three other bits of Protestant activity are associated with the Missouri Synod Lutherans and California Friends who work in Guatemala, and the Protestant Episcopal Church which (as in three of the other Central American capitals) has English-language services in San Salvador. There were also 38 Mormon missionaries active in El Salvador in 1961, though their work was less than ten years old. [90]

Probably with all the work of Catholics, Pentecostals, other Protestants, and Mormons the standards of private morality are not greatly different for most Salvadorans now from what they were at the end of the colonial period. A mid-twentieth century report concerning church expectations might give church authorities little more comfort than the one of 1768–70. [91] Furthermore, there is little sign that whatever new impressions are being made among manual labourers have their counterparts among the leaders of society. There is good reason to believe that, unless the situation changes, El Salvador's way into the future will be charted by persons of other than conventional religious inspiration.

[90] See ch. v, n. 149, p. 144.   [91] See ch. iv, n. 26, p. 74.

CHAPTER VII

HONDURAS

For a moment in her colonial history (the decade of the 1540's) Honduras had seemed destined to lead the whole of Central America in Spanish civilization and authority. The gold discovered then and the silver found later, however, did not match in final value the agricultural wealth of Guatemala, El Salvador, or Nicaragua. At the end of the colonial period, Honduras seems to have ranked fourth rather than third in population among the new states, with less than one-fifth of a million persons included in her borders. This total reached the 1 million mark only in the 1930's, though by that time Honduras had taken third place from Nicaragua.[1] The mid-1958 estimate of Honduran population stood at 1,828,000—little over half of that of Guatemala, which has a smaller area. Honduras had then but 42 persons to the square mile, the second lowest population density of Central America. Though her over-all rate of growth since 1821 must be rather close to that of El Salvador, Honduras in nearly every corner is empty by comparison. Since the very incomplete road system makes no contact with several areas where people do live, the visitor by land is impressed by the great solitude of the country about him.

A 1945 census with a query concerning racial ancestry indicated that 90 per cent of the people of Honduras were racially mixed, that 7 per cent were persons of Indian ancestry, that 2 per cent were Negroes, and 1 per cent white.[2] This does not seem an unlikely picture. One might even hazard the guess that if the exact composition of the 90 per cent group were known, it would turn out to be roughly the same as the 10 per cent remainder—that is, that for every seven indigenous persons who contributed their blood to the amalgamated stream there were two Africans and one European. Certain it is that most of Honduras' native groups have lost their cultural identity. And certain it is too that Honduras received a large share of the stream of colonial isthmian slave traffic from Africa. These earlier immigrants were assimilated by the general population, but to them have been added the part-Negro Caribs and Miskitos of the north coast and a wave of English-

[1] See ch. v, nn. 1–3, p. 90. [2] U.N., *Demogr. Yb., 1956*, p. 260.

speaking Negroes who have moved from the British West Indies to banana plantations and the Bay Islands. Honduras' small contingent of whites includes a number of merchant families from the Near East and other immigrants from British possessions to the Bay Islands. The 1950 census showed a total of 32,939 foreign-born persons living in the republic, and 32,684 of foreign nationality. Of the latter, 29,092 were from the remainder of Central America (20,268 from El Salvador alone), 1,219 from Europe (country not specified), 849 from the United States, 382 from Asia, and 302 from Mexico.[3]

LOCAL GOVERNMENT

The largest city in Honduras is Tegucigalpa, whose population including adjacent Comayagüela (together they form the Central District) was 72,000 in 1950.[4] Tegucigalpa is the smallest of the Central American capitals but outranks all isthmian cities which are not capitals by quite a margin. Though Tegucigalpa began as a silver-mining centre, its importance is now almost wholly due to its use as the seat of national power and culture. Tegucigalpa became the permanent abode of Honduras' government only in 1880 and is unique among the capitals in not having a railway. The mass of its people are native-born of mixed Indian-African-European ancestry.

The tropical north coast of Honduras at the base of the mountains is a different land, abounding with railways and banana plantations. Here lie all the remaining centres of more than 10,000 population. San Pedro Sula, older than the capital and second to it in size with 21,000 residents in 1950, is the commercial centre for the western part of the nation. San Pedro Sula overcame its long colonial doldrums and achieved new importance only after it was reached by the railway from Puerto Cortés in the late 1860's. The next four cities of Honduras amounted to little or nothing before the development of the banana trade in the later nineteenth century and have really come into prominence only in the twentieth. La Ceiba, with 17,000 inhabitants, is port and headquarters for the

[3] Computed from departmental totals in *Detalle del censo de población por departamentos levantado el 18 de junio de 1950* (2 vols., Tegucigalpa, 1952).

[4] Urban population figures for Honduras (where population centres are not ranked officially as cities, towns, and pueblos) are from *Resultados generales del censo general de la república levantado el 18 de junio de 1950* (Tegucigalpa, 1952), pp. 35–373, using the urban count for the corresponding *municipio* or *distrito*. No attempt is made to adjust for a recognized sub-enumeration of 4·3 per cent (*An. Est.* (H.), *1958*, pt. i, p. 23). See ch. v, n. 8, p. 92.

Standard Fruit and Steamship Company, whose founders came here in 1899. Tela (13,000) and Puerto Cortés (12,000) are both United Fruit Company ports, the latter serving also as entrance depot for most of Honduras' imports from abroad.

Aside from Tegucigalpa, San Pedro Sula, and La Ceiba, most of Honduras' eighteen departmental capitals are rather small in size. (Tela and Puerto Cortés do not serve in this capacity.) In the population range from 8,000 to 6,000 in 1950 were Choluteca and Santa Rosa; from 6,000 to 4,000 Comayagua and Nueva Ocotepeque; from 4,000 to 2,000 La Paz, Nacaome, Santa Bárbara, Juticalpa, Trujillo, and Yoro; less than 2,000, La Esperanza, Gracias, Yuscarán, and Roatán. Puerto Lempira, smallest and youngest of all the departmental capitals on the isthmus, is a hamlet on the Caratasca Lagoon in Mosquitia designated as the head of Gracias a Dios in 1957. Comayagua, most generally the capital of Honduras until 1880, is now smaller than in colonial days and her glory greatly diminished. Ill-fated Trujillo revived for a time in the twentieth century when nearby Puerto Castilla was used as a banana shipping-point, but was isolated again when disease struck the plants in its area. Other colonial settlements, including Choluteca, La Paz (1792), Nacaome, Santa Bárbara (1761), Juticalpa, and Gracias, have gained little if at all since independence. A few of the capitals are of post-independence formation but lie close to older centres which they have partly supplanted; Nueva Ocotepeque was founded in 1934 when flood destroyed its namesake. Honduras in 1950 had only one community in the 10,000–8,000 range which was not a capital (El Progreso on the banana coast), none from 8,000–6,000, and only two from 6,000–4,000. Amapala (2,900) is an island port on the Gulf of Fonseca. Except for the banana area and the capital Honduras is clearly a nation without genuine urban development.

Honduras has 275 *municipios* for local government (1959) besides the Central District.[5] In them, officers hold approximately the same responsibilities as in Guatemala. There is democracy on the local level to the extent allowed by public interest, which in the larger centres is considerable. Local democracy is almost a novelty, however, since this system has been operating only since 1957. Before 1940 Honduras had *municipios* with nominal self-government but the reality was lacking owing to lethargy and indifference. There were also *distritos*, each including several *municipios*, but they

[5] *División político territorial: 1959* (Tegucigalpa, Dir. Gen. Est. y Censos, 1959).

were of little consequence. Starting in 1940 the word *distrito* was used for a new type of government which supplanted that of the *municipio* in all the major population centres.[6] The new unit was larger in area than the *municipio* but replaced it entirely, substituting action by officials appointed in Tegucigalpa for that of persons locally chosen. In 1950 there were 240 *municipios* and thirty-one districts.[7] Since 1957 all have returned to the former designation save the area about Tegucigalpa and Comayagüela called the Central District, which like the *municipio* holds elections.

While district government was thriving in Honduras, departmental government was declining, since departmental officials held jurisdiction only in the more rural areas where the *municipio* survived. Since 1957, however, departments play the same role in Honduras as they do in El Salvador and Guatemala. There are eighteen of them in all; they have evolved from an original seven (in 1825). Gracias a Dios was created in 1957 in the north-eastern corner; much of its territory was claimed by Nicaragua until late 1960. Colón, just west along the Caribbean shore, was cut to about one-third of its former size when Gracias a Dios was formed. Their density of population combined is 5 persons per square mile.[8] Large Olancho, with a density of 12, lies just south of these two in a world of its own, with only the aeroplane and one poor road to connect it with the rest of Honduras. Gracias a Dios, Colón, and Olancho together constitute well over two-fifths of the nation's territory but hold less than one-tenth of its population. South and west of Olancho lie El Paraíso, Francisco Morazán, Comayagua, and Yoro (38, 83, 46, 44); though they form the heart of the country (the Central District is in Francisco Morazán) they all hold much wilderness. The remaining eleven are all situated on the edges. Starting at the north-central and working counter-clockwise around the map, they are Islas de la Bahía or Bay Islands (106) whose white and Negro populations are Protestant and speak English; Atlántida and Cortés (55, 117) which contain most of Honduras' banana lands; Santa Bárbara, Copán, and Ocotepeque (67, 106, 94) along the Guatemalan border; Lempira, Intibucá, and La Paz (69, 62, 78) facing El Salvador, three-eighths of

[6] William Sylvane Stokes, *Honduras: an Area Study in Government* (Madison, Univ. of Wisconsin Press, 1950), pp. 151–78, deals in detail with this change.

[7] *Detalle del censo de 1950* lists them by department.

[8] Departmental population densities for Honduras are of 30 June 1958, computed from *An. Est.* (H.), *1958*, pt. i, p. 25. See ch. v, n. 12, p. 94.

whose people are considered Indian;[9] and Valle and Choluteca (146, 85) along the Gulf of Fonseca.[10]

DEVELOPMENT OF THE STATE

Honduras as a political entity territorially resembling her present self came into being in 1786, when she was made an intendancy along with San Salvador and Nicaragua. The same area had been administered as an ecclesiastical unit by the bishop of Comayagua, however, for more than 200 years. Though Tegucigalpa gave up its resident *alcalde mayor* reluctantly (a man with this title but reduced powers was appointed again starting in 1812), and though there was division between Tegucigalpa and Comayagua at the time of independence over faithfulness to Guatemala and adherence to Mexico, no permanent feud developed between the two, and Honduras rather easily assumed the stature of a state in the union. Her first constitution was completed in December 1825 in accordance with federal provisions. But while native sons of Honduras—notably José del Valle of Choluteca and Francisco Morazán of Tegucigalpa—played a most prominent role in the history of the union, the government in Comayagua during the next fourteen years was distinguished chiefly by its distressed condition in the face of violence and federal interventions.

In January 1839 Honduras became the second state of the union to set itself up constitutionally as a separate government. (Nicaragua had taken the same step two months earlier.) Provisions were made for a unicameral legislature and a two-year president. The tone of the times in Honduras after the dissolution of the union was set by militarist Francisco Ferrera, ally of Guatemalan Rafael Carrera, who held the presidential office from 1841 to 1845 (being reelected) and who continued to dominate the régime which followed. Juan Nepomuceno Fernández Lindo y Zelaya (usually known as Juan Lindo, 1847–52) later provided an intelligent administration of affairs, giving Honduras her first real peace since independence. A new constitution prepared in February 1848 under Lindo's guidance brought back a bicameral legislature and changed the presidential term to four years. When Lindo refused a new term in

---

[9] See Adams, *Cultural Surveys*, pp. 603–6.
[10] Six of Honduras' departments have the same name as their capitals. The others are Gracias a Dios (Puerto Lempira), Colón (Trujillo), Olancho (Juticalpa), El Paraíso (Yuscarán), Francisco Morazán (Tegucigalpa), Islas de la Bahía (Roatán), Atlántida (La Ceiba), Cortés (San Pedro Sula), Copán (Santa Rosa), Lempira (Gracias), Intibucá (La Esperanza), and Valle (Nacaome).

1852, there was a peaceful transition of executive power to a candidate not chosen by his predecessor, an event almost without equal in nineteenth-century Central America. The new president was José Trinidad Cabañas, one-time general under Morazán and now the ranking liberal of the isthmus. Cabañas served three years but was suffered by Carrera no longer. Santos Guardiola, who followed from 1856 until his assassination in 1862, was a strong man who cared little for constitutions. José María Medina, president 1863–8 and 1870–2, ruled under a new constitution after September 1865 —one designed to give the executive most of the power, though also bringing back for good the simpler one-house legislature. This constitution was the first to call Honduras a republic rather than a state waiting for a union.

Guatemalan interventions came again in 1873 and 1876, this time to ensure government by liberals and friends of Justo Rufino Barrios. A new constitution prepared in December 1873 was discarded by Ponciano Leiva (1873–6), who in April 1874 returned to the 1865 document. Marco Aurelio Soto (1876–83) brought to Honduras a real renaissance of both order and learning. Ramón Rosa, the minister of state, a scholar and admirer of José del Valle of a generation now past, was only one of several men attached to Soto's government who were genuine liberals and enthusiasts for democracy.[11] Their devotion to democratic principles, it would seem, was somewhat greater than that of Justo Rufino Barrios who had made their advent to power possible. The constitution issued by these men in November 1880 was one dedicated to the maxims in which they believed. Though several of the rights of the citizen there enumerated have yet to be granted Hondurans in actual practice, the legislature was made important again by this document in a way that was meant to be permanent, the purse-strings of the government being left in its hands. There is every reason to believe that Soto would have finished out his second term in the spirit of the new document had he not become involved in personal

[11] Rosa perhaps better than anyone else in later nineteenth-century Central America expressed the intellectual tragedy that had befallen the isthmus after the coming of independence. In speaking of the federal elections of 1834, in which it seems that Morazán was prepared to give way to Valle after the latter's victory at the polls, he said, 'What a glorious epoch that in which a true soldier, a most celebrated hero, respected and appreciated his rival, a civilian, who had no other force than that of his idea! What a glorious epoch that in which a man of letters could confront, without fear of having his dignity trampled upon, a man of the sword. . . .' See Ramón Rosa, *Oro de Honduras: antología* (Rafael Heliodoro Valle and Juan Valladares R., eds., Tegucigalpa, 1948), p. 95.

difficulties with his patron Barrios. When Soto resigned in discouragement Luis Bográn, another close friend of Barrios, held office for two terms (1883–91) during which Honduras continued her peaceful development. Bográn was the only Central American chief outside Guatemala to accept Barrios' proclamation of unity in 1885; he managed to survive the debacle which followed.

Real political life typical of a democracy seemed ready to blossom in Honduras in the year 1890 when a formal Liberal party was organized. The interplay of personalities remained a more dominant force than the expression of political philosophies, however, for at least another thirty years. The Liberal party, defeated in the elections of 1891, found an ally in President José Santos Zelaya of Nicaragua, who now assumed at least part of the role in Honduras formerly played by Justo Rufino Barrios. Policarpo Bonilla, with the aid of Zelaya, proclaimed himself president in 1893, published a new liberal constitution in October 1894, and began a four-year term under its provisions in 1895. This constitution established a record in Honduras for longevity by lasting for thirty years save for one two-year suspension. If it had been followed faithfully Honduras would have become an outstanding democracy; but with presidential re-election under its terms forbidden, military struggles at least once every four years remained habitual. Terencio Sierra (1899–1903) was put into office by Bonilla but was driven out after the expiration of his term in the midst of a three-way struggle. Manuel Bonilla, who followed (1903–7), wrote a new constitution (September 1904) which took effect in 1906 but was terminated in February 1908 by Zelaya-supported Miguel Dávila (1907–11). After new conflict in which the United States played a mediatory role, Francisco Bertrand served as chief executive provisionally (1911–12), as a vice-president (1913–15) upon the death of his superior Manuel Bonilla, and finally in his own right (1916–19) after a free election which revealed his popularity. New violence, in the causation of which Bertrand was not blameless, brought in Rafael López Gutiérrez (1920–4). The formation of a new National party in 1923, dedicated primarily to the principle of national unity to put an end to administrative chaos, now brought a real change in the nature of Honduran politics. Tiburcio Carías Andino, the Nationalist candidate, won a substantial plurality of the votes in 1923 but was denied presidential office through the refusal of his opponents to provide a quorum in the Congress which would have completed his election. A civil war having failed to decide the impasse, new mediation by the United States brought in a provisional régime, fresh elections, and the writing of Honduras' ninth constitution.

Genuine democracy was at work in Honduras from November 1924 until March 1936 while the ninth constitution lasted. Miguel Paz Baraona, president 1925-9, had been the running-mate of Carías Andino, who lent his support to the Paz régime. Paz provided a stable administration modelled on the platform of the National party, which was conservative only in its insistence upon stability coupled with progress. Congress was important under the new constitution, having the duty to elect the supreme court and the right to censure and force the resignation of cabinet ministers. The presidential campaign of 1928 was in keeping with the new spirit of democracy. Vicente Mejía Colindres, candidate of a reorganized and revitalized Liberal party, won the top position, though the Nationalists retained a majority in Congress. Carías Andino, the defeated National party candidate for the presidency, lived up to the high ideals of his own party, urging those who had supported him in the campaign now to support his victorious rival. Carías won much popularity in Honduras because of this attitude. Mejía Colindres served out most of his term (1929-33) in peace. His party was sharply split, however, when some of its leaders refused to accept the clear election of Carías in 1932 in the same spirit that Carías had manifested four years earlier. Their revolt was put down by Carías, who assumed office on the appointed date in February 1933.

Whether more honourable behaviour on the part of the rebels in 1932 would have set a determining pattern for 1936 no one can know. As matters worked out, the very fair elections of 1924, 1928, and 1932 (the latter marred only by the unsuccessful revolt) were followed by no elections at all for the office of the presidency until 1948, a whole sixteen years later. Instead, a new constitution in March 1936 (Honduras' tenth) extended the presidential term to six years and that of Carías to 1 January 1943; and Congress amended the constitution in 1939 to extend the latter extension to 1 January 1949. The 1939 decision by Congress was the practice known as *continuismo* in its rawest form, though the practical consequences were no different from those in Guatemala under Ubico and in El Salvador under Hernández Martínez (both 1931-44). Opponents of Carías' continued rule had no recourse except to arms. Revolts led to crushings of revolts in 1936 and 1937, and for a time the jails were full of political prisoners while many Liberals fled into exile. Uprisings were less common later as the nation accepted Carías' military dominance, and with fewer rebellions the government took a more lenient attitude toward its opponents. Carías slowly developed a reputation for tranquil government and for more gentlemanly dictatorship, though there was little basis for enthusiasm concerning his positive accomplishments. The new roads and schools which banana revenues now made possible were built very slowly, Honduras remaining an almost entirely undeveloped land outside the banana concessions. Congress lost its effective voice in the government by the end of Carías' long term, and the tradition of democratic elections, nervously but steadily nurtured during the 1920's, was completely shattered.

MID-TWENTIETH CENTURY POLITICS: TRAVAIL OF LIBERALISM

As might have been expected when Tiburcio Carías Andino decided to give up the reins, the National party candidate for the presidency succeeded him. Juan Manuel Gálvez, an able lawyer and friend of Carías, won by an easy margin when his Liberal opponent Angel Zúñiga Huete withdrew from the race before the elections. Gálvez, who took office for a six-year term on 1 January 1949, sought neither to repudiate nor to emulate his predecessor's régime. An income-tax law of 1949 and the institution of a National Development Bank in 1950 indeed gave promise of a new vigour in Honduras' administration. One might say that under Gálvez' leadership the National party stood again for what was originally intended to be its programme—peaceful and orderly government with gradual progress toward a better life for the nation. The progress was distressingly slow, however, with old habits in public life persisting and with no real intention on the part of Gálvez to bring other badly needed changes into the Honduran economy. Three years after the Gálvez régime had ended there was considerable justification for the placards hung in government offices staffed by Liberal party members. 'Be brief', they said. 'We have lost twenty-five years. We must recover them.' The twenty-five years ran from early 1933 into late 1957.

Perhaps the most notable event of the Gálvez administration was the presidential campaign permitted toward its close. There were three parties in the field, each having nominated its candidate for president by April 1954. The situation was complicated by the decision of the ageing Carías Andino to run again on the Nationalist ticket. A large faction in his party preferred a younger and more active person; one was available in Abraham Williams Calderón, who had been Carías' vice-president. This faction broke loose from the National party after Carías' nomination and created the Movimiento Nacional Reformista or Reformist party which supported Williams. The Liberal party, torn by internal dissension since 1932, rallied around Ramón Villeda Morales, a physician who had remained in the country at times when other Liberals had fled. Villeda Morales disclaimed any extreme leftist tendencies in politics but took a friendly stand toward the working-man at a time when labour remained unrecognized by the Honduran government. The Liberal party had not been oriented towards the working-man in its beginnings. The year 1954 proved the start of a trend in that direction.

From May to July 1954 Honduras experienced her first great labour crisis. The emergency arose, oddly enough, before most of the workers involved had become organized. Since Communist personalities were playing a public role in Guatemala during that May and June, foreign observers were quick to blame a developing Honduran strike on Communist instigation. The real trouble seems to have been terms of pay and labour which had become quite outmoded by 1954 but were still prevalent along Honduras' north coast. A quite spontaneous protest broke out on Sunday, 10 April, when dock labourers in Tela refused to load a United Fruit ship without provision for Sunday double-time pay. After a slow start, the strike spread widely until it included 50,000 workers of United Fruit, Standard Fruit, and several other concerns. Local labour spokesmen contended for leadership, a few men of Communist orientation losing out in their bid for power and others quite clearly non-Communist holding on. The settlement came in mid-July, the strikers gaining most of their demands after the fruit companies had lost considerable money through the non-movement of bananas. Most important for Honduras, labour had won recognition of its place in the sun and would probably not again be forgotten.

The very free and active presidential campaign of 1954 was carried on during and after the north-coast strike. The elections on 10 October gave Villeda Morales a clear plurality but left him 10,000 votes short of topping his combined opponents. Carías Andino ran second and Williams Calderón third. The votes for Congress, which now had the responsibility of choosing the president, gave the

Liberals 24 seats, the Nationalists 23, and the Reformists 12 in that body. President Gálvez, whose steady hand had sustained fairness to this point, was stricken with illness in November. When he left the country to seek medical attention, Vice-President Julio Lozano Díaz took his position (16 November). On 3 December, the date set for Congress to convene, only the Liberals came to occupy their places. The Nationalists and Reformists, unable to concur on a candidate of their own, had agreed to block Villeda through refusing to constitute a quorum. Lozano Díaz, basing his authority on a clause in the 1936 constitution which covered such an impasse as had occurred, assumed dictatorial power in Honduras on 6 December.

No one could have been sure in early 1955 that Lozano intended to do anything more as provisional president than find a peaceful solution for what was admittedly a difficult problem. Villeda would have had no constitutional claim to the presidency if his Congressional opponents had combined to defeat him; on the other hand their inability to agree with each other certainly gave him a prime moral right to their support, at least to the extent of lending their physical presence to establish a quorum. Lozano was nearly seventy years old himself, a business man and long-time member of the cabinet but not the type of personality one would have expected to harbour despotic ambitions. Honduras' first labour code, decreed in February 1955, made Lozano seem amazingly liberal. Only with the passage of time, during which ostensibly the registration books were being corrected in anticipation of new elections, did patiences begin to wear thin and questions begin to be asked about the sincerity of his intentions.

In October 1955 a new party was formed. This was the Partido Unión Nacional (PUN) organized to support the policies and person of Julio Lozano Díaz. When Williams and his party of Reformists decided to join PUN the plan became fairly obvious. Lozano, far from being a neutral anxious to see justice prevail, was intending to stay in office, leaning for support on a cordon of personal friends and the party which had run third in the 1954 elections. Neither Liberals nor Nationalists were happy about the new turn of events, and tensions mounted to fever height. When the Liberals held a convention in late May 1956, delegates from outside the capital were not allowed to attend. On 9 July of the same year Villeda Morales was deported from the country, allegedly for the crime of attempting to organize a strike in the banana area. Scattered violence followed, and on 1 August unsuccessful revolt by a portion of the army. With elections for a constitutional convention announced for 7 October, some hope for an honest count arose when Lozano himself became ill in September and was replaced for three weeks by his predecessor Gálvez. Lozano returned, however, a few days before the elections. The National party abstained from voting. PUN by official count won all fifty-six of the seats in the assembly. But the violent and fraudulent means by which such unanimity was accomplished had not had their equal in Honduras since very early in the 1920's.

Lozano soon found that he had gone too far. Two weeks after this election a group of young army officers insisted on his resignation. Lozano left the national palace on 21 October 1956 as quietly as he had come in two years earlier, despite all the turmoil that had transpired since; his death came on 20 August 1957, in Florida. The junta of three officers who took his place, led by General Roque Rodríguez, set about doing what Lozano had only pretended to do, preparing for honest elections to provide a representative body which would write a new constitution and return the country to legal normalcy. Rodríguez, an older man, was eliminated from the junta in July 1957, but the two remaining members (Héctor Caraccioli and Roberto Gálvez Barnes, the latter the son of Juan Manuel Gálvez) went ahead with plans for the elections on 21 September 1957. The campaign was a free one. Villeda Morales, after service for the junta as ambassador to the United States, took a vigorous part. His cause was more popular than in 1954 because he had been persecuted by Lozano. The Reformist party was most unpopular because it had supported Lozano. The system of proportional representation plus a fair count of the votes gave every segment of opinion an opportunity to express itself. The outcome was a constitutional convention composed of 36 Liberals, 18 Nationalists, and 4 Reformists. On 21 December 1957 Ramón Villeda Morales, choice of this body, was inaugurated as president. His term was to run until 21 December 1963.

Honduras' eleventh constitution took effect on the same day Villeda became president. This document, like the 1956 constitution of Guatemala and that of 1950 in El Salvador, specifies a six-year presidential term with no immediate re-election, a unicameral legislative authority (in this case called the Congress), and a judiciary chosen by the legislature. There is similarity with El Salvador but variance from Guatemala in the lack of legislative control over a cabinet officer once appointed (a step backward from Honduran practice of the 1920's) but also in the inclusion of both men and women over the age of eighteen in the popular suffrage. Four other elements present a clear distinction between the new Honduran constitution and both of the others just mentioned: (1) The entire Honduran Congress is elected at one time for six years whereas the whole Legislative Assembly in El Salvador and half the Congress in Guatemala are renewed every two years. (2) The Honduran charter stipulates that legislative elections must be in conformity with the principle of proportional representation, while in El Salvador and Guatemala that matter is determined by the electoral law. (3) The chief of the armed forces in Honduras is made an important, almost an autonomous, individual chosen by the Congress for a term of six years and given the right to dispute a president's orders. Article 319 says only that orders given by the president of the republic to the armed forces *through* their chief must be obeyed. (4) The Congress is given the right of final decision in the event of such a dispute arising.

Memories of the disgraces of the Lozano period and the role of the army in removing Lozano from office doubtless inspired the clauses of this constitution dealing with the position of the chief of the armed forces. In this one case (and indeed in some others in Spanish America during the same decade) the armed forces seemed clearly on the side of decency and fairness; in such circumstances, constitutional authorization for this check upon presidential tyranny could prove desirable. The provision is an odd one, and was not adopted without argument. It should be noted, however, that the chief of the armed forces is not given any power beyond that of the president but only the right of interposition before a final decision by Congress. Should such an emergency arise and be handled in the manner prescribed, Honduras would be brought close to parliamentary government of a type little known in the Americas.

One other difference between the latest Honduran constitution and those of El Salvador and Guatemala may be sensed in slight variations in construction. Reference may be made to the opening articles of each chapter on labour. That of El Salvador says, 'Labor is a social function, it enjoys the protection of the State, and is not regarded as an article of commerce. . . . Suitable measures shall be enacted to prevent and suppress vagrancy.'[12] The Guatemalan

[12] PAU, *Constitution of El Salvador, 1950*, p. 37.

approach is more blunt: 'Labor is a right. Every person has the obligation to contribute to progress and social well-being through
work. Vagrancy is a punishable offense.'[13] The Hondurans left
something out of their introductory article, which reads in full:
'Every person has the right to work, to choose his occupation freely,
and to give it up, under equitable and satisfactory labour conditions, and to protection against unemployment'.[14] All three of
these constitutions, like most of those written in the mid-twentieth
century, go on to provide many protections and guarantees for the
worker and his family. The difference between the Honduran
wording on the one hand and that of El Salvador and Guatemala
on the other is the avoidance of the vagrancy concept so widely
used just twenty years ago to provide cheap labour for the landowners who demanded it. Though there is undeniably a vagrancy
problem in the whole of Central America, the framers of the Honduran constitution showed themselves sympathetic to the labour-
ing class by not mentioning vagrancy in the same breath with the
declaration of a man's right to work.

The Villeda Morales régime in its first three years in office continued to court the working man, to uphold constitutionality, and
to support moderation, often against tremendous odds. Schools and
public health received special attention. The chief labour legislation was passed in 1959, when a new and very liberal labour code
was enacted and provision made for a social-security system. (Honduras was the last of the Central American nations to provide for
the latter.) Villeda had averted a serious stoppage of work on the
north coast the year before through conciliation between fruit
companies and employees. Whether the Liberal leadership is willing to proceed rapidly enough in the poor man's defence to maintain its position as Honduras' only left-wing party remains to be
seen. Forces on the north coast and in the university are very interested in more radical reform inspired by the Castro revolution in
Cuba, and have portrayed the Villeda régime as one which promised much but delivered little. Villeda has countered such criticism by vigorous personal action—a private talk with students who
opposed him; an official investigation of charges he denied, with
those who made the charges appointed a part of the board entrusted with their investigation; an amicable solution for the plight
of farmers in Choluteca department evicted from lands which they

[13] PAU, *Constitution of the Republic of Guatemala, 1956* (Washington, 1956), p. 24.
[14] PAU, *Constitution of the Republic of Honduras, 1957* (Washington, 1958), p. 15.

had peacefully but unlawfully occupied. Nevertheless, in the lack of equally vigorous action by his majority in Congress, the field for propaganda is tremendous; the eventual formation of a political group far to the left of the existing three parties, if it occurs, should not seem surprising. President Villeda Morales must have had this possibility in mind when he pointed out at the end of his second year that the state owned great tracts of land adequate for agriculture, and that there were also large districts in the possession of a few private persons, in the very sectors of the country where demand for soil was the greatest. He spoke of the small farmer's need for land in some areas as a problem which the government intended to resolve.[15] The president's ability to lead his party in the direction of agrarian reform, though the land crisis is not as critical in Honduras as in El Salvador and Guatemala, seems vital to its future.

Most of the real threats to Villeda's retention of power have come not from the left but from the right. Throughout its second year in office, this administration was plagued with revolts engineered by an unhappy army colonel named Armando Velásquez Cerrato. Velásquez initiated his activities by broadcasting attacks upon the Villeda régime from a radio transmitter located probably outside the country. A revolt which began under his direction in Santa Bárbara in February 1959, though it early proved ineffective, simmered and sputtered until on 12 July of that year there was very determined fighting, with several persons killed, in the nation's capital. Velásquez lacked popularity and his movement proved a failure. Other plots have been announced since (often at the rate of one every two months), though the opposition maintains that some are only manufactured by the government. Whatever the truth of these charges, there is no doubt that the constructive work in which this elected régime is interested has suffered from its having to guard so closely against those who are resolved to unseat it by force.

Much of the criticism of Ramón Villeda Morales has stemmed from his own moderation. Though he has stood for the cause of the worker, he has refused to seek popularity through denunciations of the United States, often pictured in hostile propaganda as the working-man's enemy. Though he has clung to democracy at home

<hr />

[15] *Informe que el Excelentísimo señor Doctor Ramón Villeda Morales, Presidente Constitucional de la República, presenta al Soberano Congreso Nacional, noviembre 21 de 1959* (Tegucigalpa 1959), pp. 65–66.

he has denied the use of Honduran soil to those who would over-throw his less democratic neighbours. Nicaraguan President Luis Somoza Debayle, who himself has been protected by Villeda's insistence that 'freedom-loving' Nicaraguans must not use Honduran soil as a take-off point for their endeavours, made matters as difficult as he could for Villeda when he decided in November 1960 against prompt compliance with a World Court decision awarding disputed territory to Honduras. The National party, still Villeda's chief opposition, screamed for immediate possession of the land, by force if necessary, and strong elements of the army and university declared they were ready to march. The president insisted there was a better way, the way of pacific mediation. He has even insisted that a dispute revived in 1960 over the ownership of the Swan Islands off the Honduran coast can be resolved through gentlemanly talks with the United States. If President Villeda Morales can hold on until the end of 1963, as is his right, and then pass on his mantle to a person chosen in elections as fair as those by which he came to power, he will have completed a record unequalled in complexities and perhaps in accomplishments in all his nation's history.

BOUNDARIES AND BUDGETS

The difficulties under which constitutional government has laboured in Honduras have not been made lighter by the fact that some ten thousand square miles of her territory were also claimed until very recently by her neighbour Nicaragua. As has been mentioned already, the Honduran border with Guatemala was settled in 1933, while that with El Salvador remains un-negotiated but presents few serious problems. Honduras' most difficult early territorial question was that with Great Britain, which again in the 1830's (as in the 1740's and 1790's) began to take an interest in the settlements on the Bay Islands. After the Clayton–Bulwer Treaty of 1850, which the United States government interpreted to mean that the British would abandon all pretensions to rule in these islands, the British government instead raised them to the rank of a British colony in 1852. Further talks, however, brought a treaty in 1859 between Great Britain and Honduras whereby Britain renounced all claims to the Bay Islands and to whatever part of the Mosquito Coast lay within Honduras.[16] The argument which has

---

[16] Adams, 'The Antillean Populations of the Bay Islands', in his *Cultural Surveys*, pp. 634–44, shows how the British heritage dominated life in the islands in 1955.

continued, and which has brought Honduras close to international war within recent years, lies between Honduras and Nicaragua as to the line at which the old Mosquitia should be divided between them.

Honduran–Nicaraguan boundary agreements drawn up in 1870 and 1888–9 were not approved by the Honduran government. A treaty drawn up in 1894 was ratified by both governments, however, and the ratifications exchanged on 24 December 1896. This treaty was to be in force for ten years. Under its terms, a boundary commission would settle the less controversial portion of the border and leave the remainder to arbitration. The treaty said that 'the arbitral decision, voted by a majority, whatever it may be, shall be considered a perfect, obligatory, and perpetual Treaty . . . and shall not admit of any appeal whatever'. The arbitration panel was to be composed of a representative of each of the two countries and 'a member of the foreign Diplomatic Corps accredited to Guatemala, chosen by the first two or drawn by lot from nominees proposed one by each party'. In case no diplomat in Guatemala would agree to serve, the election might fall, 'by agreement of the commissioners of Honduras and Nicaragua, on any foreign or Central American public personage'.[17]

The boundary commission finished its part of the work in 1904, agreeing on the line from the Pacific about one-third of the way across the isthmus. From there on, Honduras claimed the Coco (or Segovia, or Wanks) River as the true boundary for some distance, and then a large plot of land on the lower right bank of that river, reaching to Sandy Bay, as Honduran territory; while Nicaragua insisted that the Patuca River to the north and west should be the division line, with a large plot on its lower left bank, reaching to Cape Camarón, pertaining to Nicaragua. The Honduran and Nicaraguan representatives on the arbitration panel then chose, at their very first meeting, King Alfonso XIII of Spain as the third member of the panel, whose opinion would be decisive. Two years later, and only one day before the expiration of the treaty (that is to say on 23 December 1906), the arbitral award was given. The line was drawn at the Coco River, not the Patuca, but with the entire right bank of the river, including the village of Puerto Cabo Gracias a Dios at its mouth, being retained by Nicaragua. Both governments accepted this decision, or so it seemed at the moment, with President Zelaya of Nicaragua congratulating President

[17] Text of the treaty as translated in Ireland, pp. 133–4.

Bonilla of Honduras on having 'won' the case. But in 1912, after sharp change in the Nicaraguan régime, objections were voiced by the Nicaraguan government. Contrary to the original treaty, though by executive agreement of the two governments concerned, Alfonso XIII had been chosen as arbiter before an attempt was made to find a person in the Guatemalan diplomatic corps for the task. Besides, there were a few vaguenesses and irregularities in the wording of the award. Because of these objections, another half century passed with the boundary in contention, Honduras now claiming only the land to the Coco River in accordance with the award, but Nicaragua still arguing that land to the Patuca and beyond lay within her northern border. *De facto* authority was wielded by Honduras in the Patuca valley but by Nicaragua on both sides of the Coco.

The only excitement caused by this controversy until 1957 came with the publication from time to time of new maps showing the border to the dissatisfaction of one or the other party. On 21 February of that year, however, Honduras for the first time took steps to govern all the area she claimed as hers, establishing the new department of Gracias a Dios to extend all the way to the Coco River. Military moves and counter-moves then followed until 5 May, when the Organization of American States was able to arrange a cease-fire and the retirement of both sides from contact. Two more months of talks in OAS and ODECA, with a great deal of friendly mediation brought to bear, arrived at agreement to request a decision from the International Court of Justice as to the validity of the arbitral award of 1906. Hearings began on 15 September 1960, with lawyers of international fame representing each side. The judgment rendered two months later (18 November) upheld the award of 1906 in every detail and thus substantiated Honduras' claim. Though the Somoza régime in Nicaragua made no quick move to comply, and insisted instead that time would be needed to remove Nicaraguan citizens to the right bank of the Coco, there was every evidence with the passing of the months in 1961 that this decision had been accepted. The Swan Islands, two bits of land each less than 2 miles in length lying 170 miles northeast of Trujillo, are considered by Honduras part of the land thus adjudged as rightfully Honduran. The same two islets were claimed by the United States in 1863, occupied by a United Fruit radio station in 1907–27, and by a United States-operated anti-Castro transmitter in 1961. Honduras submitted a protest to the United

States government concerning its activities in the Swan Islands in August 1960, and two months later repeated the protest in the United Nations.[18]

The energy which has characterized the Villeda administration in both boundary and internal matters necessitates government spending. Nothing illustrates the comparative lethargy of the administrations before 1957 better than the small growth of their budgets. Receipts in the calendar year 1939 were 9 million lempiras or $4·5 million (1 lempira equals 50 cents U.S. since 1931); in 1944, they were $6·5 million; 1949, $14 million; 1953, $22 million; 1956, $29·5 million.[19] In the year 1955, government receipts in Guatemala amounted to about $23 for each person in the country, those in El Salvador about $30, and in Honduras only $15, with expenditures little higher. Tariff duties bring in a large but diminishing proportion of Honduras' budget (64 per cent in 1939, 50 per cent in 1956), nearly all of this amount stemming from imports rather than exports. Consumption taxes, chiefly on beer and tobacco, added to the profit from the government's liquor monopoly, make up 31 per cent of the total. An income tax first levied in 1949, along with a very small property tax on business establishments, provided 15 per cent of the government's financial resources in 1956.[20]

United States government grants have been made more sparingly to Honduras than to any other Central American country except El Salvador. The amounts were $1·5 million in 1946–50, $4 million in 1951–5, and increasing from $1 million a year to $3 million a year since; the 1946–60 total was $18 million. Of this sum, $11 million was for economic and technical assistance, $2 million for food, including famine relief in the middle 1950's, and $4 million (granted mostly since 1956) for the building of roads.[21] United Nations technical-assistance and children's-relief grants amounted to $1 million in 1954–8.[22] Only since the advent of Villeda Morales to power has Honduras arranged sizable loans from the United States and other international sources. Her highway programme was furthered when on 12 May 1961 a small grant and $2,500,000 loan from the new Inter-American Development Bank were arranged in company with a $9,000,000 loan from the International

---

[18] See ch. vi, n. 24, p. 160.
[19] U.N., *Stat. Yb., 1951*, pp. 482–3; *1959*, p. 499, Figures are converted to the nearest $million.
[20] See ch. v, n. 43, p. 111.   [21] See ch. v, n. 44, p. 111.
[22] U.N., *Stat. Yb., 1959*, p. 423.

Development Association, the first transacted by the latter organization anywhere in the world.[23]

Actual fiscal operations for the central government of Honduras amounted to $45,116,600 in 1958. Accounting procedures placed 20 per cent of the expenditure in the realm of Development and 19 per cent in Public Credit. Eight of the nine executive ministries spent most of the rest: Public Education 13 per cent, Defence 11 per cent, Health and Beneficence 8 per cent, Economy and Finance 7 per cent, Natural Resources 5 per cent, Government and Justice 4 per cent, Foreign Relations 2 per cent, and Labour and Social Welfare 1 per cent.[24] Recent expenditures for health, social welfare, and education compare quite favourably with the low emphasis placed on such matters through most of the Carías Andino régime; together they made up but 11 per cent of the money spent in 1939. The army, at a low of 11 per cent in 1958, consumed nearly one-fourth of the budget all the way through the Carías period.[25] The Villeda Morales régime, were it to drop the army entirely, could not hope from Honduras' own financial resources as presently constituted even to tie her many departmental capitals together with all-weather roads.

SUBSISTENCE AGRICULTURE

The meagreness of Honduras' economic development until the late 1950's is readily visible in her most general agricultural statistics. Honduras in 1950 was an *overwhelmingly* agricultural nation, with *five-sixths* of the economically active population engaged in farming pursuits.[26] Yet only 4,244,000 acres, or less than one-sixth of the national territory, was being used in 1952 for pasture or cultivation.[27] Honduras is known abroad as a 'banana republic' and exports a growing quantity of coffee. But more than eleven-twelfths of her active farm land is engaged in providing immediate needs for herself and (to a much smaller extent) her close neighbour El Salvador.

Maize was harvested from 741,000 acres or 17 per cent of Honduras' active farm land in 1952.[28] The average yield per acre in

[23] *New York Times*, 13 May 1961.
[24] Communications and Public Works, the remaining ministry, presumably spent most of the money designated as Development. See *An. Est.* (H.), *1958*, pt. i, pp. 130–1.
[25] U.N., *Stat. Yb.*, *1959*, p. 499.
[26] *Resultados generales del censo de 1950*, pp. 25–26.   [27] *Estruct. agr.*, p. 132.
[28] Acreages given for individual Honduran crops are computed from *An. Est.*

1959 was only 650 lb., but the total acreage grew during the 1950's to the point where fair quantities of maize could be sent to El Salvador. Maize is grown very widely, a second crop annually amounting to one-seventh of the first. Sorghum was harvested from 154,000 acres in 1952, with nearly half the country's production coming from the southern departments of Choluteca and Lempira. Its production increased only slowly during the 1950's until it dropped to third place among the crops in space occupied.[29] About three-fifths of Honduras' maize and sorghum were raised on farms of less than 10 hectares or 24·71 acres each in 1952, a fraction somewhat smaller than that of either El Salvador or Guatemala though large enough to indicate the subsistence nature of the operation. In Honduras, with its greater area per capita, only 75 per cent of the farms were smaller than 10 hectares each in 1952, while in El Salvador 88 per cent were of this size and in Guatemala 88 per cent were smaller than 10 *manzanas* (or 17·26 acres) each in the year 1950.[30]

Beans, harvested from 134,000 acres in 1952, have since come to occupy more space than sorghum. They are grown in all parts of the country in two roughly equal crops per year. Sugar-cane was found on 57,000 acres in 1952, though Honduras alone of the isthmian nations imports fair quantities of sugar. The next two ground crops were rice (28,000 acres), widely distributed through the country, and tobacco (19,000 acres), over half of which is grown in the department of Copán. Other ground crops grown in some quantity (in decreasing order according to the space devoted to their cultivation) were cassava, cotton, cabbage, wheat, potatoes, melons, tomatoes, garlic and onions, sesame, henequen, and peanuts. Cotton for export assumed a more significant role, passing cassava in acreage, in the late 1950's.[31] Most of the wheat which Honduras consumes is imported.

Tree and bush crops occupied 441,000 acres in Honduras in 1952, a proportion of the nation's area roughly equal to that of the same crops in Guatemala. Honduran cultivation is less concerned

---

(H.), *1958*, pt. i, pp. 116–19, using the 1951 line for 1952 (compare *Bol. Est.* (H., Dir. Gen. Est. y Censos), Primer Semestre 1959, pp. 17–18). Acreages published in Honduras' *Primer censo agropecuario: 1952* (San Salvador, 1954) were generally somewhat lower. No allowance is made for acreage duplication in the two harvests of maize and beans.

[29] *An. Est.* (H.), *1958*, pt. i, p. 116; *Prim. cens. agr.: 1952*, pp. 46–47. See ch. v, n. 51, p. 113 and above, n. 28.

[30] *Estruct., agr.*, pp. 28, 30–31, 188.

[31] *An. Est.* (H.), *1958*, pt. i, pp. 116–19; *Prim. cens. agr.: 1952*, pp. 47, 49. See above, n. 28.

than that of Guatemala with coffee, though space occupied by coffee in Honduras has grown considerably from the 169,000 acres reported in 1952. Bananas occupied 140,000 acres in 1952, only half of them of the type for the export trade, and their cousin plantains were raised on another 22,000 acres. Both the plantains and the Honduran-preferred types of bananas are grown widely in all departments of the country. Other tree and bush crops in 1952 (in decreasing order according to the acreage involved) were mangoes, oranges, coconuts, abacá, the African oil-palm, pineapples, avocados, *zapotes*, and cacao.[32]

Some 2,032,000 acres of pasture land were reported by Honduran farmers in 1952, in addition to a great deal of area at rest or in fallow.[33]

The counts of domestic animals were as follows: 1,147,000 cattle; 525,000 pigs; 192,000 horses; 74,000 mules; 37,000 goats; 28,000 donkeys; and 7,000 sheep. There were also 3,493,000 chickens; 76,000 ducks; and 75,000 turkeys.[34] Cattle and pigs are exported to El Salvador in considerable numbers, though not at such a rate as to create a major industry. Honduras has a greater number of pigs, horses, mules, and donkeys than any other country on the isthmus.

EXPORTS AND IMPORTS

The cochineal from Guatemala and the indigo from El Salvador the sale of which abroad meant so much to those nations' economies in the first half of the nineteenth century had no real counterpart in Honduras. It was indeed quite late in that century before Honduras began a substantial export trade of any kind. In the 1860's occasional sailing vessels began to pick up bunches of bananas along the north coast for financially hazardous transit to New Orleans. The hazard arose chiefly from the ever-present possibility that a whole cargo might become ripe before making port. With the passage of a few decades and the development of a larger banana market in the United States, steam vessels were used by traders from New Orleans who visited the north coast of Honduras on regular runs to buy the fruit from independent local producers.

[32] *Estruct. agr.*, pp. 132, 238; *An. Est.* (H.), *1958*, pt. i, pp. 117–19; *Prim. cens. agr.: 1952*, pp. 54–55. See above, n. 28.

[33] *Estruct. agr.*, pp. 132–3. The 1,049,000 acres shown on p. 133 as the total 'Barbecho o descanso' appears to be a high figure, since the total in the adjacent column 'Cultivos transitorios' is considerably less than a comparable total shown on p. 188. Possible explanations for the discrepancies involved are found in *Prim. cens. agr.: 1952*, p. xvii.

[34] *Estruct. agr.*, p. 290.

Vaccaro Brothers and Company came from New Orleans to La Ceiba in 1899 to grow bananas for their own markets. The business they established became known in 1924 as the Standard Fruit and Steamship Company, now the second largest firm in Honduras. A banana railroad built in 1902 from Cuyamel to Veracruz on the coast near the Guatemalan border came into the hands of Samuel Zemurray of Mobile, Alabama. In 1911 Zemurray organized the Cuyamel Fruit Company, whose concessions eventually included the land about Puerto Cortés. Two years later (1913) the United Fruit Company organized subsidiaries in Tela and Trujillo with concessions so extensive that there remained few banana lands on Honduras' north coast not managed by United States firms. In 1929 United Fruit purchased Cuyamel, thus reducing the number of managements and putting United in first place; within four years the enterprising Zemurray was managing director of United Fruit. But in the meantime, through the investments of Cuyamel, United, and Standard together, Honduras had risen to become the world's foremost exporter of bananas, surpassing Jamaica. She held this position quite consistently from the mid-1920's into the late 1940's, after which Ecuador took the lead. Except for a few bad years, Honduras has since kept second position.

Bananas are very important to Honduras, their value in the period 1956–9 amounting to 55 per cent of her total exports.[35] The combined forces of two fungi, however, have conspired to make them less of a bonanza than they were. The affliction called *siga-toka* (originally *Singatoka*, a banana valley in the Fiji isles) travelled half-way around the world from its place of origin in a few decades and hit Honduras forcibly, beginning in 1935. United fought *siga-toka* by spraying, Standard by specializing in a somewhat less popular type of banana which *sigatoka* does not attack. The 'Pan-ama disease', which arrived as much as twenty years earlier, ravaged United and Standard plantations alike, attacking the plant roots and eventually making it impracticable for banana operations to continue in any one area. United quit operations at Trujillo in the late 1930's while Standard developed new fields in the upper Aguán valley around Olanchito, maintaining rail service between there and La Ceiba. Severe flooding of the Ulúa valley in 1954 and the extensive strike of the same year caused other diffi-culties—United Fruit in 1960 instituted the practice of turning ac-tual production in its area over to smaller enterprises—but the

[35] U.N., *Yb. Int. Trade Stat., 1959*, i. 257.

Honduran banana industry is not being abandoned. Relatively small portions of three adjacent departments—Cortés, Yoro, and Atlántida—provide three-fourths of the nation's bananas of the types used for export.[36] The nation could ill do without them.

Friction between the fruit companies and the government in Honduras has been relatively slight, though criticism of the fruit companies is abundant. There has been much disappointment over the failure of both United and Standard to implement promises to build railways from the coast to interior cities. Samuel Zemurray won ill will by obtaining special privileges for both Cuyamel and United (for which he played a strong hand in Honduran politics) but neglecting in certain instances to obey the terms of his own contracts and the national law. Angel Zúñiga Huete, the Liberal candidate who unsuccessfully opposed both Carías in 1932 and Gálvez in 1948, was a critic of the fruit companies. Carías, Gálvez, and Lozano, like all of Carías' predecessors, were friendly and co-operative. Villeda Morales, while assuming a pro-labour stand, has not taken any action denoting hostility toward the companies' interests. Banana revenue is so important to Honduras, and her competitive position in the banana world so vulnerable, that the Honduran government is likely in most instances to continue to seek new advantages for labour and nation through non-sensational devices. The companies have followed increasingly humane policies with the passing of each decade, with more attention to their own employees' welfare and the economy of local areas. Any wider obligation of the fruit companies in Honduras to lift that whole nation's economy to a level near that of the country in which most of the bananas are sold has been given little attention by either producer or consumer.

Coffee is the second largest export item from Honduras, making up 18 per cent of the total value of exports in 1956–9.[37] Coffee culture was little known in Honduras in the nineteenth century. Like cotton-growing in El Salvador, it has really come into its own only since the Second World War, with nearly ten times as much shipped abroad in 1958 as twenty years earlier. Santa Bárbara department in the north-west grew nearly one-fourth of the nation's production in 1952, other leaders in the industry being the interior departments of Comayagua, Yoro, Olancho, and El Paraíso.[38]

---

[36] *Prim. cens. agr.: 1952*, p. 54.   [37] U.N., *Tb. Int. Trade Stat., 1959*, i. 257.
[38] FAO, *Tb. of Food and Agriculture Statistics, 1948*, p. 94; *Trade Tb., 1959*, p. 154. Also see *Prim. cens. agr.: 1952*, p. 56.

Non-agricultural exports are more important to Honduras than to Guatemala or El Salvador, wood amounting to 10 per cent and silver to 3 per cent in 1956–9. Of the miscellany comprising a remaining 14 per cent during that period, Honduras sold cattle worth more than $1,500,000 a year; cotton worth over $2 million a year after 1958; abacá over $1 million a year until 1958; and maize and vegetables over $1 million each in 1959. Honduras' total exports in 1955–8 averaged $63,300,000 annually, going 66 per cent to the United States, 8 per cent to El Salvador, 6 per cent each to Germany and Canada, and 3 per cent each to Cuba and Venezuela.[39]

Honduras' imports, chiefly from Great Britain in the nineteenth century, now come largely from other sources. In the period 1955–8 they averaged $61,800,000 annually, derived 64 per cent from the United States, 7 per cent from Germany, 6 per cent each from Japan and the Netherlands Antilles (the latter petroleum products), 4 per cent from El Salvador (chiefly sugar and textiles), 3 per cent from the United Kingdom, and 2 per cent from Belgium-Luxembourg. The 1959 imports, divided according to the Standard International Trade Classification, were as follows: Manufactured goods made up 31 per cent, including over $3 million each for synthetic fabrics and metal manufactures; over $2 million for cotton fabrics; and over $1 million each for iron and steel, for paper products, and for rubber manufactures. Machinery and transport equipment comprised 24 per cent, with over $4 million for road motor vehicles; over $2 million for electric machines and appliances; and over $1 million each for tractors and for construction and mining machinery. Chemicals constituted 13 per cent, with medicinal and pharmaceutical products over $2 million and fertilizers over $1 million. Food was 11 per cent of the total, with cereals over $2 million and sugar over $1 million. Manufactured articles other than machinery and transport were 10 per cent, with over $1 million for clothing. The last significant category was fuels and lubricants (9 per cent), including over $4 million for petroleum products.[40]

NON-AGRICULTURAL OCCUPATIONS

That small segment of Honduras' economically active population (only one-sixth) which was not at work on the land in 1950 was engaged, according to the census, in manufacturing to the extent of 5·8 per cent of the total, in service occupations only 4·4 per

[39] U.N., *Yb. Int. Trade Stat., 1959*, i. 257–8.   [40] Ibid. pp. 255–6, 258.

cent, in trade only 1·3 per cent, in transport 1·1 per cent, and in construction 1·0 per cent.[41] An industrial census of 1958 counted 20,128 persons working in 623 manufacturing establishments. Of these, 8,468 were employed in 218 food-processing plants; 4,683 worked in 64 lumber shops; and the footwear-apparel and beverage industries accounted for more than 1,000 workers each. Another 3,032 persons were engaged in the construction of buildings.[42] A census of 1950 included a large number of other shops of very small size. The average worker's wage in manufacturing in Honduras was reported as amounting to $35·85 per month in 1957.[43]

Honduras' two mining companies employed 1,712 workers in 1950, more than any one of the manufacturing industries of that time.[44] The colonial interest in silver mining, especially in the vicinity of Tegucigalpa, was revived late in the nineteenth century when United States capital became engaged. The quantities of silver exported, however, have not constituted a major industry; even less so a much smaller production of gold and lead. Honduras' woods are more important, her mahogany having interested exporters in the nineteenth century and her pine proving an attraction for business men today. Pine lumber is an important item on Honduras' export list, mahogany and cedar are also shipped, and a pulp and paper industry to be established with an expectation of wide isthmian markets seems one of Honduras' brightest prospects. The possibility of the existence of petroleum around Caratasca Lagoon in the north-east was surely not forgotten in the recently revived and solved boundary controversy with Nicaragua. If Honduras someday develops an iron industry, as some of her leaders believe possible, or finds petroleum, and in addition builds the communications and power networks she so sorely needs, the aspect of the country will have changed considerably.

Roads have been built more slowly in Honduras than in any other country on the isthmus. Only in the 1920's were earth roads constructed to connect the capital with the south coast, with boats on Lake Yojoa, and the short northern railway. An all-weather

[41] *Resultados generales del censo de 1950*, p. 25.
[42] Table in Frederick J. Tower, *Basic Data on the Economy of Honduras* (U.S. Bureau of International Programs, 1961), p. 8, based on *Investigación industrial: 1958* (Tegucigalpa, 1960).
[43] *Yb. Lab. Stat., 1959*, p. 289.
[44] Table in *Investment in C.A.*, p. 199, based on *Estadísticas industriales: 1950* (Tegucigalpa, 1953).

road connecting Tegucigalpa and San Pedro Sula was completed in 1944, but until the very late 1950's paved roads were virtually unknown. Honduras' present section of the Inter-American highway, receiving its first coat of asphalt in 1960, is only 90 miles long, passing by Nacaome and Choluteca on its way from El Salvador's La Unión department to Nicaragua's Madriz. A 75-mile side road, paved mostly in 1960, leads to Tegucigalpa and forms part of a planned trans-isthmian highway from San Lorenzo (Amapala's mainland subsidiary on the Gulf of Fonseca) through Comayagua and San Pedro Sula to Puerto Cortés. A re-routing of the Inter-American highway is projected to include Honduras' capital on its main thoroughfare. All-weather roads now connect nine of the nation's eighteen departmental capitals. Nueva Ocotepeque can also be reached in all seasons, but at present only by a long detour through El Salvador. At the end of 1960 Yoro, Santa Bárbara, Santa Rosa, and Gracias were available to adventurous drivers in dry weather only. La Ceiba is in touch by rail. Trujillo and Puerto Lempira (like Roatán, which has better reason to be so) remain practically isolated except by sea or air. Honduras licensed only 1,300 passenger cars and 1,900 commercial vehicles in 1950; in 1957 registrations had risen to 4,200 cars and 4,300 commercial vehicles.[45] Recent administrations have recognized the need for better transportation facilities, and the picture is likely to change with rapidity. A good road from San Pedro Sula to Puerto Cortés will make truck or bus transportation possible from ocean to ocean in Honduras, a dream that was dreamed more than a century ago for steam locomotives.

Ephraim George Squier, who wrote the first extensive description of Honduras ever published, was the very practical dreamer who wanted to build a railway across this part of the isthmus in the early 1850's. Squier indeed obtained a contract with the government for the railway's construction (1853), but completion of an easier line across Panama (1855) caused the Honduran project to be abandoned. The government then borrowed money in the late 1860's and built a railway 59 miles from Puerto Cortés through San Pedro Sula to the village of Potrerillos along Squier's route. Financial problems forced a termination of the project at this point. From 1920 to 1958, this short stretch was managed by fruit interests (Cuyamel and United); the government, in charge again since 1958, is now planning extensions. United and Standard connexions

[45] U.N., *Stat. Yb.*, *1959*, p. 333.

make it possible today to travel by rail along the coast from Puerto Cortés to Tela and La Ceiba, and circuitously from there to Olanchito in Yoro department. But all of Honduras' railways except the Puerto Cortés–Potrerillos line were built for the banana trade—so exclusively thus that rail connexions which once existed between La Ceiba and Trujillo were abandoned when the banana plantations about Trujillo became unprofitable. Promises made by both Standard and United when they obtained their original concessions that they would build railways into the interior to develop the country's economy were later re-negotiated to relieve the companies of these obligations. Tegucigalpa remains the only isthmian capital—and very nearly the only national capital in the world—without the sound of a rail locomotive.

Ships of the fruit companies serve northern Honduras, most goods for the capital being carried by rail from Puerto Cortés to Potrerillos, where they are loaded into trucks. Other ships stop at Amapala on its island in the Gulf of Fonseca, where their merchandise is transferred to lighters for the shallow-water ride to San Lorenzo, where once again the trucks take over for the drive to the capital. With such meagre overland facilities, Honduras has developed much reliance on air transport for cargo which must go through promptly. TACA, the regional airline now incorporated in El Salvador, originated in Tegucigalpa in 1932 as the first locally controlled airline on the isthmus, offering both domestic and international flights. Domestic service is now chiefly handled by a company called SAHSA (Servicio Aéreo de Honduras, S. A.). Locally owned TAN (Transportes Aéreos Nacionales) also provides international service as far as Florida and Peru.

The Honduran government operates telephone systems in the capital and San Pedro Sula, and telegraph offices throughout the country. The electric-power supply outside the banana zone is very deficient, even the capital city being poorly provided by a government-owned concern. Nearly the whole nation will be benefited by the completion of a long-discussed project to utilize the waters of Lake Yojoa as a source of hydro-electric power. A total of 46 million kilowatt hours of electricity was produced in 1950, and 75 million in 1957. Honduras' 23 per cent of urban homes lighted by electricity in 1949, the lowest proportion on the isthmus, included few residences away from the capital and the fruit companies' concessions.[46]

[46] U.N., *Stat. Yb.*, *1954*, p. 258; *1958*, p. 532; *1959*, p. 283.

Honduran banking was in private hands until 1950. The largest bank, called Banco Atlántida, was formed by United States capital and associated with Standard Fruit. The creation of the lempira and its stabilization at half the United States dollar in 1931 ran parallel to measures of 1926 and 1934 in Guatemala and El Salvador, but the lack of a central bank put Honduras for some time at a disadvantage in matters of finance. This lack was remedied in 1950 by the creation of two institutions, the Banco Central de Honduras as a bankers' bank, and the Banco Nacional de Fomento. The latter not only lends money to private agricultural enterprises but invests a measure of government revenue in projects deemed serviceable to the public but in which private capital has not been interested. Besides the Banco Atlántida, Honduras has four banks which are privately financed and three savings institutions.[47]

ECONOMIC OUTLOOK: RESOURCES WASTED OR UTILIZED?

'Honduras' riches—all underutilized, some wasted and being destroyed, others perhaps yet unknown. . . .' With these phrases begins a chapter of a recent study of Honduras' economic development.[48] Economic opportunities, as the study points out, abound in this republic. Yet a nation with Honduras' level of poverty was clearly not taking advantage of them. In 1950 only 31 per cent of the people wore shoes, only 6 per cent ate wheat bread, and only 5 per cent slept on beds with mattresses.[49] Honduras does not share to a high degree the race and land problems of Guatemala or the population problem of El Salvador; her one big need is simply development. If she is to undertake that activity with any degree of alacrity, her government, foreign agencies, and home capital will all have to take an interest. The process may well be one which defies classical economics.[50] President Villeda Morales has given

[47] See ch. v, n. 71, p. 123.
[48] Vincent Checchi and associates, *Honduras: a Problem in Economic Development* (N.Y., Twentieth Century Fund, 1959), p. 49.
[49] *Resultados generales del censo de 1950*, pp. 30–32. The low number of persons sleeping on beds with mattresses is not explained by a preference for hammocks. Though most available mattresses in the country are uncomfortable enough by an outsider's standards, 73·5 per cent of the people according to the census slept on beds with harder mats, 10 per cent on canvas cots, 7 per cent on ground mats, 1·5 per cent on the ground itself, and only 3 per cent in hammocks.
[50] David F. Ross, whose unpublished doctoral work on Honduran economic development is mirrored in 'Economic Theory and Economic Development: Reflections Derived from a Study of Honduras', *Int. Am. Econ. Aff.*, xiii/3 (Win-

every indication that he intends to see such a transformation take place.

The government of Honduras, which seemed little interested in the economy of the republic until 1950, has taken several pertinent steps since. In the old days (before Gálvez) far too many men in government had been willing to sell their own country short for personal advantage. It is their fault as much as anyone's that the railways which were promised and planned were never built, leaving Honduras the only nation on the isthmus without a workable land-transportation network. The building of highways to fill in this lack, the provision of power facilities, and attention to the health and literacy requisites of the masses are very basic activities tackled earnestly only since 1957. Honduras' social-security system was still in planning stages through 1960. No miminum wage had been set by the end of that year. Labour unions, allowed after Carías' time, were encouraged only under Villeda Morales, when they began to make headway. A Trade Union Federation of North Coast Workers of Honduras was organized in San Pedro Sula in 1957, and a Central Federation of Syndicates of Free Workers of Honduras in Tegucigalpa in 1958. Fourteen labour unions belonged to the former and sixteen to the latter by 1960. The North Coast Federation is affiliated with the International Confederation of Free Trade Unions with which the Central Federation also carries on friendly relations. The largest union is that of the United Fruit workers, belonging to the San Pedro Sula federation; employees of Standard Fruit are divided in their allegiance to a similarly affiliated group and an independent union.[51] But workingmen's associations in general are just beginning to feel their strength. The Villeda régime, in addition to its basic programmes, is moving toward the occupation and exploitation of the whole north-eastern part of the country now so empty.[52] Years will be required to bring so much unused territory into the national economy, but the government plans far ahead.

The foreign agencies in the best position to help develop the

---

ter 1959), 21–32, points out four classical assumptions which cannot safely be applied to Honduras.

[51] The problems of Honduras' infant unions are discussed in U.S. Bureau of Labor Statistics, *Labor Law and Practice in Honduras* (Washington, USGPO, 1961), pp. 16–22.

[52] A glimpse of the potentialities and problems of this and other areas in Honduras is provided in C. L. Dozier, *Indigenous Tropical Agriculture in Central America* (Washington, Nat. Acad. of Sci., 1958), pp. 7–48.

Honduran economy are the United States government and the fruit companies. The Washington government has long sought to render assistance through various co-operative programmes (which exist everywhere on the isthmus) providing technical information. By 1960 it was already thinking in terms of more far-reaching projects in which its aid would be crucial for success. The fruit companies have for many years furnished housing, medical care, and some education for their employees, and now pay wages better than most in the country though low by the standards of their customers. In times past, one of the company practices which hurt Hondurans the most was the abandonment of all interest in a local area when banana production there became unprofitable. Now when the companies are faced with a loss of banana acreage they tend to look for other crops which the people might grow for a profit. In their tropical research interests, indeed, the companies have looked far beyond the banana to other sources of wealth for both themselves and their former employees. United Fruit's decision to place banana production in the hands of other parties has caused some economic dislocation and insecurity in the early 1960's. But both fruit companies, if they so choose in time to come, may well lead the way toward a truly prosperous Honduras built upon a varied agriculture.

Native private enterprise had done little for Honduras by the end of the 1950's. Even merchandise shops in the cities are more often than not run by first- or second-generation outsiders. Most wealthy Hondurans, unlike the society of El Salvador, have chosen to invest in foreign concerns considered more safe, or not to invest at all. The general practice in trade in Honduras (certainly not unknown in the rest of the isthmus) is to gain as much as possible from each transaction and retain a great percentage of gross profit for oneself. Hondurans who have money need to put it to work in a more enlightened manner. Once highways and power are available some may choose to do so for the nation's welfare.

Whether or not the present holders of wealth care to join in the ventures, it seems certain that someday the country *will* be developed and its resources better utilized. As agriculture, forestry, and mining make their contributions, manufacturing will play a larger part as well. And somewhere along the way, Honduras will have more than centavos to piece out among her hungry inhabitants.

LEARNING

The torch of learning burned very dimly in Honduras during the early years of independence. Talented sons possessing some financial endowment went elsewhere to do their studying. José del Valle, most distinguished of the first generation of scholars of republican Central America, came from Choluteca but went to Guatemala City to school and stayed most of the rest of his life. José Trinidad Reyes (1797–1855), less well established in material things, studied in León, Nicaragua, and returned to his native Tegucigalpa winning renown as Franciscan priest and poet. Before Tegucigalpa became the capital of the state, Reyes founded there (1845) a school soon called the Academia Literaria de Tegucigalpa. Juan Lindo (1790–1857), whose parents lived in Comayagua, studied in Mexico. In 1841 he found himself president of El Salvador for one year; he provided part of that country's impetus for its Colegio de la Asunción. In 1847, when the latter institution became the University of El Salvador, Lindo, now president of Honduras, raised Tegucigalpa's Academia Literaria to the level of a university, now called the University of Honduras. Latin, civil and canon law, and philosophy were for some time the chief advanced courses.

A reform of 1882, under the enlightened Soto administration, brought contemporary science into the classroom. The Faculties of Legal and Social Sciences and of Medical Sciences established at that time continue in existence. To them have been added Engineering (1923), Chemical Sciences and Pharmacy (1935), Economic Sciences (with a branch in San Pedro Sula), and Odontology. Altogether, there were 1,584 persons living in Honduras in 1950 who had attended university classes. The total enrolment of the national university in 1959 was 1,164 men and 146 women.[53]

Mass education in Honduras has taken a big leap forward with the administration of Villeda Morales. In 1950, according to census count, 35 per cent of the population over the age of ten could read and write. There were 2,207 primary schools in the republic that year; seven years later (1957) the number had grown only to 2,417; but in another two years (1959) it was 3,048. Similarly, the number of primary students increased from 104,031 (1950) to 146,551 (1957) to 192,495 (1959). In the latter year there were still

---

[53] *Resultados generales del censo de 1950*, pp. 19–22; *Estadísticas Educacionales 1959*, p. 149. A history to 1930 is given in Esteban Guardiola Cubas, *Historia de la Universidad de Honduras en la primera centuria de su fundación* (Tegucigalpa, 1952).

only 14,215 persons in secondary schools, over two-thirds of them in Francisco Morazán and Cortés departments.[54]

An official gazette served as Honduras' first newspaper beginning in 1830. There has been one most of the time since. Many other papers have come and gone, including dailies since the late nineteenth century. The two most widely circulated now are *El Día* (founded 1948), a conservative sheet, and *El Pueblo* (1950) which speaks for the Liberal party. There were six dailies in Honduras altogether in 1957, having a total circulation of 44,000 or only 25 papers for every 1,000 inhabitants.[55]

Medical work has progressed to the point in Honduras where the death-rate in 1958—110·9 per 10,000 inhabitants—was lower than that of both Guatemala and El Salvador. Among the principal causes were malaria (11·0 deaths per 10,000 inhabitants); pneumonia and bronchitis (5·3); worms (3·6); whooping-cough (3·4); gastro-enteritis and colitis (3·4, but with nearly four times as many related but poorly defined cases); infections of infancy (3·1); influenza (2·4); measles (1·7); and malignant tumours (1·5). Twenty hospitals with 3,421 beds and cradles functioned during that year. Six (with 1,762 beds and cradles) were in the Central District, 1 in nearby Tamará, 10 in seven departmental capitals, and 1 each in United Fruit's La Lima, Siguatepeque in Comayagua department, and El Mochito (a mining town) in Santa Bárbara department. In 1957 there were 365 physicians (nearly 1 for every 4,800 persons, a ratio considerably better than that of El Salvador or Guatemala) but only 63 dentists.[56]

The Soto régime sponsored Honduras' first historical writing, a treatment of both province and republic by Antonio Ramón Vallejo (1844–1914).[57] Rómulo Ernesto Durón y Gamero (1865–1942), judge, statesman, and teacher, made several studies of his nation's history, leaving behind him a published synthesis covering colonial and republican epochs and valuable unfinished manuscripts.[58] Honduras boasted a historical-geographical review be-

[54] *Resultados generales del censo de 1950*, pp. 19–22; *Estadísticas Educacionales 1958*, Introducción; *1959*, pp. 5, 19, 92.

[55] U.N., *Stat. Yb.*, *1959*, p. 578.

[56] Ibid. *1958*, p. 541; *An. Est.* (H.), *1958*, pt. i, pp. 24, 47–56, 82.

[57] *Compendio de la historia social y política de Honduras* (2 vols., Tegucigalpa, 1882–3; 2nd ed., Tegucigalpa, 1926).

[58] His son Jorge Fidel Durón when rector of the University of Honduras began publication of the latter as *Historia de Honduras*, i (Tegucigalpa, 1956), covering the 1820's. The former is *Bosquejo histórico de Honduras* (San Pedro Sula, 1927; 2nd ed., Tegucigalpa, 1956).

fore any other country on the isthmus, published from 1904 to 1909 and re-established in 1927 as the organ of the newly founded Sociedad de Geografía e Historia de Honduras (1926).[59] Rafael Heliodoro Valle (1891–1959), Honduran journalist and intellectual who passed much of his life in Mexico and the United States, was a true bibliophile whose files contain the elements of a vast Central American bibliography. Late in life he produced a biography of Cristóbal de Olid as his doctoral work and a comprehensive and provocative summary of twentieth-century Central American ideas.[60]

Three outsiders contributed significant studies of Honduras in the 1950's. William Sylvane Stokes, professor of political science at the University of Wisconsin, wrote a treatise concerning constitutional development and government.[61] Robert Stoner Chamberlain, working as an historian chronologically on the fringe of Maya studies, meticulously narrated the events of the first half of the sixteenth century, leaving few stones unturned in his search for documentation.[62] Doris Zemurray Stone told Honduras' story from the conquest to the end of the nineteenth century, providing fresh insights from her own intimate knowledge of the country; her father was Samuel Zemurray.[63] Other outsiders dealt with Honduras as a part of Central America.[64] Other historical works by Hondurans cover topics in narrower scope.[65]

The Pan American Agricultural School subsidized by United Fruit, founded in 1943 at Zamorano near the capital, besides training young men from several Latin countries publishes a natural-history journal named *Ceiba*.[66] Honduras' university review, published 1909–22 and starting again in 1948, contains articles on a variety of topics showing promise for the future.[67]

[59] *R. del Archivo y Biblioteca Nacionales de Honduras*, vi/1, 30 June 1927; xxxiii/5–12, Nov. 1954–June 1955; *R. de la Sociedad de Geografía e Historia de Honduras*, xxxiv/1–9, July 1955–Mar. 1956; xxxix/4–6, Oct.–Dec. 1959.

[60] *Cristóbal de Olid, conquistador de México y Honduras* (Mexico City, 1950); *Historia de las ideas contemporáneas en Centro-América* (Mexico City, 1960). For a selected bibliography of R. H. Valle's published works, which included a number of valuable bibliographies, see Lota M. Spell, 'Rafael Heliodoro Valle (1891–1959)', *HAHR*, xl (1960), 425–30.

[61] See above, n. 6.

[62] *The Conquest and Colonization of Honduras, 1502–1550* (Washington, Carnegie Inst., 1953).

[63] *Estampas de Honduras* (Mexico City, 1954).   [64] See ch. v, nn. 100–1, p. 132.

[65] See ch. v, n. 99, p. 132; and Rafael Heliodoro Valle, 'Bibliografía historio-gráfica de Honduras', *R. Interamericana de Bibliografía*, ii (1952), 7–14.

[66] No. 1, 1950.

[67] *R. de la Univ.*, i/1, 15 Jan. 1909; xiii/1, Jan. 1948; xviii/16, June 1955; *Univ. de Honduras*, Año 3, nos. 26–27, Sept.–Oct. 1960. See ch. v, n. 116, p. 134.

Honduras

ART

Even in the middle 1950's it was a rare evening in Tegucigalpa, Honduras, which offered more than billiards, the cinema, and a military-band concert for public diversion. There are sports events with domestic and international competition as in the other Central American countries, but all on a reduced scale as befits an urban centre of smaller population. There is a national theatre, but one little used for theatre representations. A renewed interest in music and the visual arts is of very recent origin.[68] Much of Honduran folk music bears the stamp of old Spain, though modern Caribbean rhythms are also popular. There are 21 radio stations, 10 of them in the capital, and since late 1959 a single television transmitter.[69]

Hondurans are justly proud that their literary record begins with José Cecilio del Valle (1780–1834). Valle won a place in history through politics, but his writings had their separate importance. He is given proper credit as an early apostle of inter-American unity and as an assiduous thinker on nearly every theme of his day.[70] Ramón Rosa (1848–93) of the Soto epoch was great, one is tempted to say, if only because he so clearly recognized Valle's greatness.[71] In the mid-twentieth century, interest in Valle's ideas has experienced another renaissance.[72]

Since José del Valle, a large share of Honduras' literary effort has taken the form of poetry. The historian Rómulo Durón wrote some poems, translated others, and made selections from poets of the entire nineteenth century.[73] Honduras' best-known poet is Froylán Turcios (1878–1943), who published several volumes of stories and verse as well as a few short novels.[74] One of Turcios'

[68] See ch. v, n. 120, p. 136; also Guillermo Bustillo Reina, ed., *El libro de Honduras: Directorio y guía general de la republica*, i (Tegucigalpa, 1957), pp. 117–33.
[69] See ch. v, n. 118, p. 135. Honduran call letters have the prefix HR. No radio station uses more than 1,000 watts power.
[70] For his *Obras*, see ch. iv, n. 29, p. 77.
[71] See above, n. 11. Rosa's biography of Valle, first published in 1882, is given with comments by Jorge del Valle Matheu in *Obras de José Cecilio del Valle*, i. vii–cxvi. It is also available as *Biografía de don José Cecilio del Valle* (Tegucigalpa, 1943) and in Rosa, *Oro de Honduras*, pp. 33–100.
[72] Rafael Heliodoro Valle, *Bibliografía de don José Cecilio del Valle* (Mexico City, 1934); Eliseo Pérez Cadalso, *Valle, apóstol de América* (Tegucigalpa, 1954); Rubén Leyton Rodríguez, *Valle, padre del panamericanismo* (Guatemala, 1955).
[73] His translations of Byron and Poe were published in 1917; the 2nd ed. of his *Honduras literaria: Poesía* in 1957 (3 vols., Tegucigalpa).
[74] *Mariposas* (Tegucigalpa, 1895) were written at an early age; *Cuentos del amor y de la muerte* (Paris, 1930) through a lifetime; at least five publications of similar nature came between.

P   215

enterprises was the editing of the poetry of his talented friend Juan Ramón Molina (1875–1908) who had died of an overdose of morphine.[75] Rafael Heliodoro Valle, of more recent fame, before he became a noted journalist and bibliophile also established a reputation with poetry.[76] *Honduras Rotaria* founded in 1943 is essentially a literary magazine which reflects both the poetry and prose efforts that continue.[77]

RELIGION

The role of organized faith in republican Honduras has been weak. Catholic churches have increased in number, and more Protestant agencies have entered Honduras than any other Central American republic. But one cannot speak of a twentieth-century renaissance of religion in this country until more persons have been affected. The humble Honduran may call himself *católico*, as in most instances he does, but the precepts of the church worry him but little unless he is the exceptional one. In most instances he is not in effective contact with his own church or any other.

Comayagua was a bishopric when independence came, but from 1819 to 1842 there was no bishop. The man first proposed for the position, educator José Trinidad Reyes, was actually chosen by the Pope, but lost the opportunity when a false report was sent to Rome that he had died, and another was chosen in his stead. The Catholic church was favoured constitutionally in Honduras, and by concordat after 1861, until 1880, when the Soto régime established the complete religious freedom which has existed since. The comparative apathy with which Hondurans have treated religion is, oddly enough, all the more guarantee of this freedom on the popular level.

The see of Comayagua was transferred to Tegucigalpa in 1916 and raised to the rank of an archdiocese. Santa Rosa was set up as a bishopric in the same year and San Pedro Sula made separate as a vicariate apostolic for missionary work. A small prelacy with its seat in Juticalpa, Olancho, but subject to Tegucigalpa, was organized in 1949. Honduras has now a total of 632 Catholic churches staffed by 156 priests. This means one priest for each 9,950 Catholics, the poorest ratio in Central America outside of Guatemala.[78]

As in Guatemala, nearly two-thirds of the Honduran Catholic clergy are members of religious orders. Jesuits from St. Louis and

[75] *Tierras, mares y cielos* (Tegucigalpa, 1911; 5th ed., Guatemala, 1947).
[76] *Anfora sedienta* (Mexico City, 1922) is a collection.
[77] Año 18, no. 202, Sept.–Oct. 1960.   [78] See ch. v, n. 140, p. 141.

Milwaukee (19 in number) are doing the same type of work in Yoro department that the Maryknollers are doing in Huehuetenango. These Jesuits came to Yoro only in 1946. They have been assisted since 1952 by the School Sisters of Notre Dame, now half a dozen. Nineteen Franciscan friars, 5 School Sisters of St. Francis, and 3 Sisters of Mercy of the Union from the United States also work in Honduras; the Franciscan Sisters have been in Tegucigalpa since 1932.[79]

Though 19 Protestant churches and agencies are at work in Honduras, they maintain only a few more than 500 places of worship, about one-half of the number in either El Salvador or Guatemala. The total Honduran population is about three-fourths of that of El Salvador, but Honduras has only half as many Protestants.[80]

Honduras received her first Protestant community through the British relinquishment of the Bay Islands in 1859. Though Catholicism at that time was the religion of the state, the islanders were guaranteed their own religious preferences. The Methodist faith was predominant and has remained so since, though in the nineteenth century pagan rites from Africa still held an attraction for some members. Connexions are with British Methodism through the church in Belize. Methodist work on the northern mainland of Honduras, begun in 1883, has since come under the care of the Wesleyan Methodists of the United States.

The non-denominational Central American Mission entered Honduras in 1896. Its present staff of 41 is by far the largest group of Protestant missionaries in Honduras; 15 of them serve in Siguatepeque where the Mission operates the hospital. Eight more Protestant bodies carry on sizable efforts. They are an informal group whose roots in Honduras go back to 1903, supported by Christian Missions in Many Lands, a British agency; the California Friends, who spilled over the border from Guatemala in 1909; the Evangelical and Reformed Church (of German background, now merging into the United Church of Christ), which came to San Pedro Sula in 1921 and has now organized a Synod of Honduras including 22 missionaries; the Seventh-Day Adventists (1928) with the second largest membership; the Moravians, who have been working among the Indians of Honduran Mosquitia since

[79] Honduras has 29 religious houses for men and 19 for women, the lowest total in Central America. See ch. v, n. 141, p. 141.
[80] See ch. v, n. 145, p. 142.

1930 after their much earlier establishment in Nicaragua; the Assemblies of God, who came from El Salvador in 1940; the World Gospel Mission of the National Holiness Missionary Society from the United States, which started only in 1944 but has 19 missionaries at work; and finally the Church of God, with the largest membership.

The International Church of the Foursquare Gospel came to Honduras in 1952 and the Southern Baptists in 1954. Two other Baptist organizations work on the Bay Islands and the north coast; the United Brethren in Christ have churches in Atlántida; the Protestant Episcopal Church is represented but weakly; so are two more groups from the United States. In addition, there are 18 Mormon missionaries at work.[81]

Could Honduras, so little reached by organized religion despite all this activity, have anything to offer the world in matters of faith and principle? A lack of concern for one's fellows, seeming to permeate society, suggests a quick negative reply. But one who has travelled Honduran byways is brought to the question, 'What is it which makes Honduran people attractive?' There is a certain primitiveness of character, more discernible here than in most parts of the isthmus, which seems to provide the answer. Persons of this nature are led to accept others as equals and to live non-ostentatiously in their surroundings. The spirit expresses itself in dress which avoids both pomp and prudishness, and in many traits of thought, speech, and action. Such a disposition may be accompanied by apathy or even lamentable behaviour stemming from poverty, ill health, or ignorance. But one wonders if the Honduras of the future, as she overcomes these problems, must lose her pristine quality. Might she not instead reveal to the world, through the medium of some *aficionado*, the importance of being natural?

[81] See ch. v, n. 149, p. 144.

CHAPTER VIII

NICARAGUA

A 'Mahomet's paradise', Nicaragua was called in colonial times, according to a seventeenth-century traveller.[1] A paradise for the Spanish inhabitant, that is, who had nature and the Indians to provide him with a comfortable life without labour. Nicaragua became something less than a paradise in the nineteenth century, as internecine conflict laid barren the countryside and stunted the growth of population. With probably more people than Honduras (though also below a fifth of a million) at the time of independence, Nicaragua has since trailed behind, ranking fourth of the states of the isthmus. Her 1 million mark was not reached until 1947.[2] In mid-1958 the estimated total was 1,378,000—but this was only 26 persons per square mile (not counting the two great lakes), the lowest national population density in Central America. The visitor who comes to the more settled western coast is likely to get a different impression. It is well to remember that this is the part which inspired the label 'Mahomet's paradise' over 300 years ago, and that much of Nicaragua, then as now, was a trackless wilderness.

There is no census information concerning the ancestry of the Nicaraguan people. The great majority of those in the western portion are of mixed blood, with a proportion of Indian, Negro, and European inheritance such as that suggested for Honduras not unlikely. There are no large numbers of any of the three groups which have remained separate. In the eastern portion of the country, besides a scattered remnant of Indians there are the mixed Indian-Negro Miskito peoples, a few whites and orientals, and some English-speaking Negroes who have moved here from the Caribbean islands and British Honduras.[3] Nicaragua in 1950 had the smallest number of foreign-born residents of any country on the isthmus. Only 10,193 were counted in the census, and 7,129 of these were from the other Central American countries. Of the remainder,

---

[1] Thomas Gage, *The English–American: a New Survey of the West Indies, 1648* (A. P. Newton, ed., London, 1928), p. 341.

[2] See ch. v, nn. 1–3, p. 90.

[3] Nicaragua's *Censo general de población* of 1950, xvii. 126, lists 10,399 persons in the country above the age of six who spoke English in the home and 21,496 who spoke some Indian dialect. See ch. iii, n. 28, p. 51.

the United States contributed 535, China 487, and no other country more than 250.[4]

LOCAL GOVERNMENT

Nicaragua's urban centres of population in 1950 included 33 cities, 15 towns, and 77 pueblos.[5] First and by far the largest is the city of Managua, third largest capital of Central America, with a 1950 population of 109,000. (By the end of 1958, the figure had reached an estimated 184,000.)[6] Managua was only an Indian pueblo until 1819, when its reputation for loyalty to the Spanish crown brought it the designation of *villa*. The rank was changed to *ciudad* in 1846. Rivalries between León and Granada led to adoption of Managua as a compromise capital, the chief executive first taking up residence here in 1852. Since then the city has grown tremendously despite a succession of disasters, including earthquake and fire which destroyed thirty-six blocks in 1931. Rebuilding since the latter date has given Managua a rather modern appearance. Its population has shifted from an Indian base to the customary Indian-African-European mixture but also contains a majority of the foreigners who live in the country. Managua is important industrially and commercially, as well as for its government services, but unlike the other Central American capitals is not the exclusive seat of the national university.

León, with 31,000 inhabitants in 1950 (46,000 in 1958), has grown more modestly. Its use as a capital, common though not consistent through the colonial period, became more spasmodic after independence when its tendencies toward 'liberalism' often involved it in bitter controversy with more conservative Granada. Finally losing its national governing position, it kept a main part of the university which had been founded in 1812 and has remained the most important in the country. Cotton has recently become important to León. Granada, with 21,000 people in 1950 (30,000 in 1958) and a situation on Lake Nicaragua, has retained a commercial position which it first developed as a point of departure for the Caribbean and Europe via the lake and the San Juan River. Granada was burned by adventurer William Walker in 1856 but did not lose its colonial character; its history as a Spanish city with-

---

[4] *Censo general de población*, xvii. 103–4.   [5] Ibid. pp. 429–31.

[6] City and town population figures for Nicaragua are from ibid. pp. 77–81, and (given only for those above 10,000 in 1950) 31 Dec. 1958 estimates from the *Bol. de Est.* (N.), Epoca 3, no. 8 (Sept. 1960), 5–6; in both cases using the urban count of the corresponding *municipio*. See ch. v, n. 8, p. 92.

out change in location is the oldest of any on the isthmus. Nearby Masaya (17,000 in 1950; 28,000 in 1958) is Nicaragua's fourth-largest city, and Chinandega (13,000; 18,000) and Matagalpa (10,000; 14,000) follow in order. All three of these have progressed from the status of colonial pueblo to their present position on the strength of the rich agricultural lands about them.

There are ten departmental capitals in Nicaragua besides the six just mentioned. Of these, Bluefields had 8,000 inhabitants in 1950; Jinotepe 7,000; Estelí, Rivas, and Jinotega from 6,000 to 4,000; Juigalpa, Boaco, Ocotal, and Somoto from 4,000 to 2,000. San Juan del Norte, with only 307 persons in the census year, was but a pueblo in rank and at that time the tiniest departmental capital on the isthmus; Puerto Cabo Gracias a Dios, head of the separate *comarca* or territory of Cabo Gracias a Dios, is also very small. San Juan del Norte was once more important than today, having served in very late colonial times (it was founded in 1796) as a trans-shipment point for goods moving to and from Granada. In the 1850's (when it was called Greytown) it was used as a base for trans-isthmian passengers travelling from New York to California. Bluefields, founded by buccaneers in the seventeenth century and named for a Dutch Captain Bleeveldt, was the head-quarters of the British-protected territory of Mosquitia in the nineteenth century. Ocotal was founded in 1803 as the successor to the colonial 'city' of Nueva Segovia. The other departmental capitals were once colonial pueblos and have grown but slowly since. Apart from these administrative centres, Nicaragua had but one urban community in 1950 with more than 6,000 inhabitants, and five in the range 6,000–4,000. The latter include Corinto, which in 1858 took the place of old Realejo as the chief port on the Pacific; and Prinzapolka and Puerto Cabezas, more isolated ports on the Caribbean. San Juan del Sur and Puerto Somoza, other entry points on the Pacific, are very small. As in the other Central American republics, urban growth outside the capital has been quite slow in Nicaragua compared to the increase of population in the country as a whole.

There are 122 *municipios* for local government in Nicaragua (1958) besides a National District.[7] The chief officials of the *municipios* and the National District are appointed by the nation's president, so that the element of local autonomy found elsewhere on the isthmus is missing. The sixteen departments of Nicaragua play the

[7] See above, n. 6.

same governmental role as those of Guatemala, El Salvador, and Honduras, with the chief administrative officials in Nicaragua still known as *jefes políticos*. Originally Nicaragua had but four departments and a claim to the east coast. Zelaya department now comprises most of the old Mosquitia which was 'protected' by the British until 1860 and then held as an autonomous Indian reservation until 1894. Zelaya holds scarcely more than 3 persons to each square mile of its area. The territory of Cabo Gracias a Dios to the north along the coast (population density 3·7, with more than two-thirds of its people Miskito) will be reduced by more than half when the expected adjustment is made on the border with Honduras. Río San Juan (density 4·1), on the southern extremity of the same shore but stretching inland to Lake Nicaragua, added to Zelaya and the remnant of Cabo Gracias a Dios make up over one-half of the nation's land area with about one-sixteenth of its population.[8]

West of Zelaya (from north to south) lie Jinotega, Matagalpa, Boaco, and Chontales (11, 46, 28, 32), each of which includes a large expanse of the same wilderness. Nueva Segovia, Madriz, and Estelí (22, 78, 72) are west of Jinotega, the latter two being traversed by the Inter-American highway from Honduras. Chinandega and León (61, 70) are west of this highway along the Pacific. Rivas (75) is on the southern end of the Pacific frontage, squeezed between the ocean and Lake Nicaragua. Between Rivas and León, occupying the land between the two lakes and much of that about Lake Managua, lie Granada, Carazo, Masaya, and Managua (125, 194, 423, 186) holding between them less than one-twentieth of Nicaragua's land area but over one-third of its population.[9]

DEVELOPMENT OF THE STATE

When the old province of León was recognized as an intendancy in 1786, it was the second most important focus of power in the entire audiencia. Circumstances surrounding the earliest struggles for independence, however, rendered Nicaragua impotent for the isthmian role which might have been hers as a free nation. Nica-

---

[8] Departmental population densities for Nicaragua are of 31 Dec. 1958, computed from *Bol. de Est.* (N.), Epoca 3, no. 8, p. 1. See ch. v, n. 12, p. 94. In regard to Cabo Gracias a Dios, see *Censo general de población*, xvii. 76, 128; and '34 escuelas nicaragüenses pasarán a poder de Honduras', *La Prensa*, 21 Nov. 1960.

[9] All of Nicaragua's departments have the same name as their capitals except Zelaya (Bluefields), Chontales (Juigalpa), Nueva Segovia (Ocotal), Madriz (Somoto), and Carazo (Jinotepe).

ragua showed an independent streak in late 1811, when citizens of León deposed the governing intendant and the people of Granada sought a complete change of régime. Differences between these two groups of citizens hardened rapidly, however, when the colonial administration used force against Granada with the sanction of León. The feud which developed between the two cities has scarcely yet been forgotten.

When Guatemala City declared Central America's independence from Spain on 15 September 1821, León countered thirteen days later with an act of independence from Guatemala. Granada followed with a decision to adhere to Guatemala rather than León. During the impasse which ensued, no one could be sure that the Spanish régime in Nicaragua had come to an end.[10] Both León and Granada accepted union with Mexico in 1822–3, but afterwards entered upon a new series of conflicts which lasted until 1830. In one short interlude of quiet, a constitutional congress was able to complete a charter for the new state (April 1826), the last of the five of Central America to be organized. Federal intervention finally brought a few years of relative calm under Honduran Dionisio Herrera (1830–4), during which Nicaragua took on the liberal look then prevalent on the isthmus. In 1838, after renewed travail, Nicaragua became the first state to secede permanently from the Provincias Unidas (30 April) and the first to write a constitution (November) providing for separate government.

Under the new régime, which lasted after a fashion for twenty years, Nicaragua had a bicameral legislature and a 'supreme director' elected for a two-year period. Directors seldom served out their terms, as both local and isthmian conflict continued spasmodically to ravage the countryside. Though neither alignments nor ideologies were consistent in such matters, León's families in the 1840's called themselves 'liberals' while those of Granada were considered 'conservatives'. To the feeling between them, not even the placing of the capital in Managua in 1852 proved an immediate solution. When a new constitution was prepared in Granada in April 1854 but only partially accepted, blood was shed with renewed vigour until the intervention of *yanqui* adventurers finally brought a reconciliation.

Nicaragua became the object of international attention when

[10] See the account of Orlando W. Roberts' trip to León in 1822, in his *Narrative of Voyages and Excursions on the East Coast and in the Interior of Central America* (Edinburgh, 1827).

gold was discovered in California in 1848 and thousands of people began looking for passage from the east coast of the United States to where the gold lay. The Accessory Transit Company organized by Cornelius Vanderbilt of New York from 1851 to 1856 provided transportation up the San Juan River to Lake Nicaragua and a 12-mile stage-coach ride from there to San Juan del Sur on the Pacific. Atlantic steamers brought the passengers to Nicaragua from New York, and their Pacific counterparts (which could not always accommodate the crowds) carried them on to California. Such traffic could proceed across the isthmus even while warfare raged about Granada, Masaya, and Managua. Complications arose when the liberals of León invited William Walker of Tennessee and a band of followers to assist them in their battle against the conservatives. Walker captured Granada for the liberals in 1855 but made himself president of Nicaragua in 1856 to the dismay of all parties. Walker had Nicaragua's strategic international importance well in mind, and hoped principally to further his own ambition. He quickly conspired to take over the transit business. In the contention which followed, the Nicaraguan parties (now allied together) received the gathering support of all the Central American governments and of Cornelius Vanderbilt. Walker was forced out of the country in 1857, and was shot in Honduras in 1860 on a second attempt to return.[11] For a few months after his first departure, the top liberal and conservative generals ruled Nicaragua jointly. But late in 1857 conservative Tomás Martínez was recognized as sole president, and Nicaragua entered a new period in her history.

A new constitution was adopted in August 1858. Nicaragua was for the first time declared a republic. Its government was to be entrusted to a president elected for four years and a bicameral legislature. Martínez served two terms under this constitution, it being held that a provision for no re-election did not apply to him, but stepped aside in 1867 after ten years in office. He was followed by a regular succession of men from Granada which lasted twenty-two years: Fernando Guzmán (1867–71), Vicente Quadra (1871–5), Pedro Joaquín Chamorro (1875–9), Joaquín Zavala (1879–83), Adán Cárdenas (1883–7), and Evaristo Carazo (1887–9), the last-named dying in office. Nicaragua suffered little turmoil under these

[11] The centennial observance of the Walker episode brought a dozen publications on the subject, including a series of booklets by a Costa Rican Comisión de Investigación Histórica de la Campaña de 1856–1857 and two larger works, Rafael Obregón Loría, *La campaña del Tránsito, 1856–1857* (San José, 1956) and Ildefonso Palma Martínez, *La guerra nacional* (Managua, 1956).

men, who arranged peaceful transitions of power from one to the other. There was progress of a sort (the first railway in the early 1880's, for example) and prosperity for a few, but little advance for the masses except relief from continual butchery. Only the forms of democracy were observed, with a few families of Granada making all the final decisions. The circle was broken when Carazo's death brought Roberto Sacasa to the presidency. Sacasa was a conservative like his predecessors, but came from León. He began a term of his own in 1891 but was overthrown two years later in a flare-up of the old city rivalry within the confines of his own party. The liberals of León took advantage of the dissension to place one of their own group in power, where he remained for the next sixteen years.

José Santos Zelaya was president from 1893 to 1909. A constitution prepared for him in December 1893 provided for a four-year term and a unicameral legislature. Zelaya was 're-elected' twice under its provisions. A new constitution of March 1905 gave him another six-year term which he was unable to complete, and continued the single chamber. Parliamentary life meant little under Zelaya, however, as he carefully picked his own associates in government. His was not such a do-nothing administration as that of his contemporary Estrada Cabrera of Guatemala, since Nicaragua under his lead continued to make some economic advances. The country was nevertheless ruled for Zelaya and his friends alone, and the administration had no compunction about using arbitrary methods against those who disagreed with its policies. Zelaya also intervened in the affairs of his neighbours; it was these interventions, especially after the Washington Conference of 1907 to which the United States lent her signature, which eventually led to his downfall. When revolution broke out against him late in 1909 the United States government openly showed its sympathy for the rebels. Zelaya's resignation in favour of a widely respected citizen named José Madriz (president 1909–10) brought no softening of the big power's attitude. The rebels were, in fact, protected in their base at Bluefields by United States forces and were finally able (August 1910) to take Managua.

Quarrels within the ranks of the rebels made the position of the new government difficult. Juan José Estrada (1910–11) had to resign as provisional president within a year. Adolfo Díaz (1911–17) would never have lasted without the firm support of United States forces; in September 1912 these deployed along the railway from

Corinto to Granada and took several cities by force. At the request of the United States government, private New York bankers lent money to the republic of Nicaragua in 1911, with arrangements for important financial controls to be placed in their hands until the money was repaid. A new constitution prepared in November of that year provided for a return to bicameralism and a four-year presidential term after democratic elections, but the 'election' of Díaz in 1912 was unanimous (among those allowed to vote) after his designation by the United States minister. The bulk of the Nicaraguan populace (both conservative and liberal) was unhappy about this state of affairs, but the presence of one United States warship at Corinto and 120 United States marines in Managua steadied Díaz' position. The Bryan–Chamorro Treaty, signed in 1914 and ratified in 1916, brought some solace in the form of a $3 million payment to Nicaragua from the United States; though in exchange the United States was given the right in perpetuity to construct a trans-isthmian canal through Nicaraguan territory, a 99-year lease of Nicaragua's tiny Corn Islands in the Caribbean, and the privilege for 99 years of maintaining a naval base on the Nicaraguan shore of the Gulf of Fonseca. United States interests managed the customs collections, the national bank, and the national railway of Nicaragua until 1924. Emiliano Chamorro Vargas, leader of the conservatives and choice of the United States, was president from 1917 to 1921; a relative, Diego Manuel Chamorro, then held the office until his death in 1923.

As the time approached when the United States banking interests would be fully repaid, their government expressed its desire to see free elections in Nicaragua after which the marines would be withdrawn. Bartolomé Martínez, president 1923–5, did not hold free elections, but the marines left Nicaragua after Carlos Solórzano (Martínez' candidate) took office. Solórzano was forced out by Chamorro Vargas a year later (January 1926). The United States, having agreed with the Central American countries in 1923 to abstain from recognition of any isthmian régime established by force, brought about the substitution of Adolfo Díaz for Chamorro in November 1926. Then, when it became clear that Juan Bautista Sacasa, Solórzano's vice-president and a liberal, would not accept such a settlement, United States troops returned in greater numbers than before. A compromise arrangement secured by Henry L. Stimson of the United States State Department brought an end to Díaz–Sacasa warfare in 1927 with the provision that Díaz would remain as president until January 1929. But United States forces remained in Nicaragua again through the elections of 1928 and 1932.

It is an odd circumstance that this second intervention in Nicaraguan affairs by the United States government brought upon the latter more reproach than the first. In the first, though fewer troops were involved, the United States quite clearly picked the Nicaraguan leadership, refusing to consider the claims of any liberal who had supported Zelaya. In the second, United States force was used to supervise three fair elections (two of them presidential) which the liberals won. One dissident general named Augusto César Sandino continued to protest against the presence of United States troops on Nicaraguan soil, no matter who won the elections. His depredations upon his own people as well as upon any North Americans he could find attracted much attention in Latin America, where Sandino was widely regarded as an anti-*yanqui* man of valour. The National Guard trained by United States officers during the presidency of José María Moncada (1929–33) was unable to catch Sandino, who operated on the fringes of the settled country. Sandino himself made peace when Juan Bautista Sacasa took office and the last of the United States forces were withdrawn in January 1933.[12]

Neither Sacasa nor Sandino, as events worked out, was to decide the future of the new interventionless Nicaragua. Nor were the people of the country to have much of a say in the matter through the medium of continued fair elections. With Sandino at peace, the National Guard which had unsuccessfully fought him remained the supreme force in the country. Sandino was murdered by members of the National Guard on 21 February 1934, after he had dined that evening with the president himself. President Sacasa intended to punish the murderers, but found that his hands were tied by his nephew by marriage, General Anastasio Somoza García, head of the National Guard. Somoza had the presidency in mind, though both his relationship to Sacasa and his position with the Guard made him constitutionally ineligible for consideration. In September 1935 he made the assertion that he would 'eliminate' all other candidates who barred his path to this position. Then, backed by most of the old liberal party and a group called the

[12] Joseph O. Baylen, 'American Intervention in Nicaragua, 1909–33: an Appraisal of Objectives and Results', *Southwestern Social Sci. Q.*, xxxv (1954), 128–54, reviews this operation and its extensive bibliography.

Nationalist Conservatives, he pressured his uncle into resigning the high office in June 1936, quit his own commandancy of the National Guard in November, was elected president (with his only opponent in exile) on 8 December, resumed his Guard position on 20 December, and began his first term as chief executive on 1 January 1937. Somoza had much in common with his contemporaries Ubico of Guatemala, Hernández Martínez of El Salvador, and Carías of Honduras. Ubico and Hernández were deposed in 1944; Carías survived until 1949; Anastasio Somoza García, with but slight interruption, ruled until his death in 1956.

MID-TWENTIETH CENTURY POLITICS: THE SOMOZA DYNASTY

The first long presidential tenure of Anastasio Somoza García was made possible by a new constitution prepared in March 1939 which granted him a 'transitory' term until 1 May 1947 without further referendum with the people. The two-chamber Congress continued to seat some 'Traditionalist Conservatives' opposed to Somoza during this period, but their number was always less than one-fifth of the total membership. A minority of the Conservatives and most of the Liberals supported Somoza, who was constitutionally endowed with the power to detain persons whom he might hold responsible for any 'menacing' of the public tranquillity, and to restrict or suspend many guarantees which would ordinarily protect such persons from government persecution. During his first ten years in office Somoza built such a solid network of power for himself and his family, both in politics and the business world, that by the end of his term it seemed obvious that no one could dislodge him against his will without resort to dangerous violence.

The constitution made a president ineligible to succeed himself. Somoza said the National Guard, with himself at its head, would be loyal to the person elected in 1947. Leonardo Argüello, a 70-year-old whom he must have thought he could control, was his own candidate for the position and won it without difficulty. Argüello took office on 1 May 1947. Twenty-five days later, after dismissing a few of Somoza's relatives from their positions, he was forced to seek refuge in the Mexican embassy while the National Guard assumed control of the country. The régime of Benjamín Lacayo Sacasa established by this coup, with General Somoza in the cabinet, was recognized by few other nations. A new constitutional convention called to circumvent this difficulty made Víctor

Manuel Román y Reyes president on 15 August 1947. Román y Reyes was another elderly individual, but the uncle of Anastasio Somoza and unlikely to behave like Argüello. For a time Somoza seemed satisfied with the new arrangements, which were further legalized by the adoption of a new constitution in January 1948. Its terms, save for the transitory ones making provision for the years immediately ahead, varied but little from those of its predecessor.

Unexpected developments took place in 1949 and 1950. Emiliano Chamorro Vargas, president from 1917 to 1921 and still the recognized leader of the old-line Conservatives, returned home from exile and met Somoza. As though President Román y Reyes and the population of the country were but incidentals in the matter, these two principal actors made an agreement to write still another constitution to make possible new early elections. In April 1950 the date of 21 May was chosen, when both the president and the constituent assembly (which would become the new Congress) would be selected. The elections were to be fair ones, and the party which lost would be accorded fixed representation in Congress by the new basic charter. But on 25 March ailing President Román y Reyes moved to a hospital in Philadelphia; on 4 April he underwent surgery for ulcers and cancer; and on 6 May he died. Anastasio Somoza García was chosen by the old Congress to fill out the term. Somoza also won the elections a fortnight later; Chamorro Vargas was the losing candidate of the Conservatives. The constitution embodying the agreement between the two candidates took effect on 6 November 1950. Somoza was installed in office for the last time on 1 May 1951.

The 1950 constitution of Nicaragua (the tenth or, if the one of 1854 is counted, the eleventh) is most notable for its guarantee of a fixed minority representation in each house of Congress. This consists of one-third of the seats in the Chamber of Deputies and roughly one-third of those in the Senate. (The count is complicated in the Senate by seats allotted to ex-presidents of the republic and the person receiving the second highest vote for president in the last election.) This system hardly matches the proportional representation of Guatemala and Honduras, but is certainly more fair than the one-party arrangement common in El Salvador. Nicaraguans over 21 years of age, plus those from 18 to 21 who are literate and married, plus those under 18 who hold academic degrees, are given the suffrage, with the provision that women must wait until the enactment of a special law governing their franchise (such a law was passed in 1955). Various social guarantees are also provided in this constitution, though nothing of a sweeping nature is included. Minimum-wage provisions and other protections for the labourer had entered Nicaraguan constitutional law in 1939, earlier than anywhere else on the isthmus, but were little implemented. Added in 1950 was provision for a social-security system, but this was little spelled out.

The constitution of 1950 provided that the president of Nicaragua, like those of Guatemala, El Salvador, and Honduras, would serve for six years and might not be re-elected. Neither might a person be elected to the office 'who has exercised the Presidency of the Republic temporarily during any portion of the last six months of the term', nor 'relatives of the President . . . within the fourth degree of consanguinity or affinity'.[13] Once in office, however, the Nicaraguan president is constitutionally endowed with powers which go beyond those of any other president in Central America. When Congress is not in session, he may be delegated authority to enact laws 'in the fields of Development, Police, Social Welfare, Public Health, War, Public Education, Agriculture and Labor, Finances and Economy', though he may not impose taxes in peacetime.[14] He may, 'whenever in his opinion the public tranquillity is threatened . . . order the detention of persons presumed responsible, interrogate them and hold them in custody for ten days. . . .' He may suspend certain constitutional guarantees 'whenever due to any . . . circumstance it is required for the protection, peace, or security of the Nation or of its institutions or form of government.'[15] Needless to say, he appoints and removes his own ministers at will as the presidents of El Salvador and Honduras do, with Congress having no rights in the matter. As in Honduras, the Congress is elected all in one body and serves the same six-year term as the president. The national judiciary is chosen by the Congress.

The pact between Anastasio Somoza and Emiliano Chamorro which produced this constitution lasted at least two years. In July 1952, when Somoza returned from a visit to the United States, Chamorro Vargas was among the group who welcomed him home. In 1953, however, when the press reported that the Nationalist Liberals (as Somoza's party had come to be called) envisaged changes in the constitution to permit the presidency to remain in the Somoza family, all the old passions were revived. Press criti-

[13] PAU, *Constitution of the Republic of Nicaragua, 1950* (Washington, 1954), p. 32.
[14] Ibid. p. 25.   [15] Ibid. p. 38.

cism brought a new press law restricting the right to criticize the president. Nicaragua became a tense and sullen place, which she has remained ever since. On 3 April 1954 a serious attempt was made to assassinate President Somoza. The attempt failed, but accusations and tempers reached a new high pitch. The country was placed under a state of siege which lasted a whole year. Twenty-five fighter planes were purchased from Sweden. Emiliano Chamorro Vargas and Pedro Joaquín Chamorro Cardenal, owner of the chief opposition newspaper, were convicted along with others of complicity in the plot and sentenced respectively to exile and imprisonment. President José Figueres of Costa Rica was denounced too, as one who had encouraged the attempt, and international relations on Nicaragua's southern frontier became very strained.

The sentencing of the Chamorros came early in 1955. The tension with Costa Rica reached its greatest climax at the same time, when an invasion army which Somoza had permitted to train on Nicaraguan soil launched an attack along the border hoping to unseat the Figueres régime. Intervention by the Organization of American States brought an end to this affair. But Anastasio Somoza had decided by this time to continue not just his family but even his own person in the presidency he had already so long occupied. In April he signed a constitutional amendment to repeal the clauses dealing with re-election and family succession (a majority vote in Congress was all that was necessary to amend the constitution), and in November announced his intention to 'run' again. As his decisions became clear, a group of 'Independent Liberals' declared itself against re-election while the Conservatives quarrelled among themselves as to whether they should continue to participate in the Congress and the forthcoming campaign.

In 1956 agreements with Costa Rica quieted the storm on that frontier, and the two Chamorros returned to their homes. Basic resentments in Nicaragua, however, remained just the same. Anastasio Somoza still wished to retain the presidency; and this being the case, while he lived no other candidate was likely to be elected.

On 21 September 1956 one man named Rigoberto López Pérez chose to sacrifice his own life in order to change the situation. President Somoza that day received the official nomination of the Nationalist Liberals; that night he was shot four times by López Pérez, who himself was then shot dead. The president was taken to Gorgas Hospital in the Panama Canal Zone for surgery, but survived only eight days. Luis Somoza Debayle, at thirty-four years of age the elder of two sons, having already been chosen by Congress as first-designate for the high office, succeeded as acting president on 28 September to serve in his father's incapacity, and the next day fell heir to the office to fill out the term. Anastasio Somoza Debayle, the younger brother, assumed his father's previous role with the National Guard. Luis was soon designated the presidential candidate of the Nationalist Liberals. Never in the history of independent Central America had there been so direct an approach to the idea of hereditary rule.

The trial for those accused of complicity in the elder Somoza's murder was held in January 1957. Chamorro Cardenal, again among those convicted and imprisoned, was soon able to escape jail and country. In February Luis Somoza Debayle was elected president for his own term, receiving 89 per cent of the votes as against 11 per cent for his 'Nicaraguan Conservative' opponent Edmundo Amador Pineda; the Traditionalist Conservatives had refused to participate in the voting. Inauguration of the new term on 1 May 1957 brought conciliatory gestures from the new president, who stated one year later that he would retire in 1963. This declaration has been repeated each April in the annual presidential message, and came nearer reality when a reform of the constitution in August 1959 restored the articles regarding the succession which were repealed in 1955. These measures and promises of free elections in the future were not enough to quiet the passions of the Conservative opposition, who understandably found it difficult to believe that the Somoza family would really give up the reins when the moment finally arrived. An attempt to unseat Luis Somoza Debayle came in June 1959 when Nicaraguan groups led by Enrique Lacayo Farfán (himself an Independent Liberal) entered their country from Costa Rica by land and by air. The operation had no initial success and was hindered from developing over a period of time by President Mario Echandi of Costa Rica out of respect for treaty obligations. Nicaraguan exile groups continued strong in Costa Rica, their anti-Somoza ambitions winning the sympathy of many Costa Rican liberals despite the fact that the exiles themselves were more often than not ideologically conservative.

The Somoza 'dynasty' has lasted so long that it has taken on the appearance of an old-fashioned dictatorship surrounded by nations which have evolved past that stage. The personal aspects of the régime and of its pre-1961 association with the United States give every backing to that characterization.[16] The Anastasio Somozas, father and son (they are popularly referred to as 'Tacho' and 'Tachito'), both stand accused of taking personal delight in the persecution of their victims. Régimes in Costa Rica and Honduras, on either side of Nicaragua, were elected after campaigns in which free play was allowed for opposition sentiment, while the Somoza family's record of imposing its will on the nation is notorious. Still it is an error to think of the Somoza rule in Nicaragua as the equivalent of the do-next-to-nothing régime of Carías in Honduras, or of the hold-the-lines-tight-against-reform administrations of Ubico and Hernández Martínez in Guatemala and El Salvador. The Somozas' stand for office as liberals (Nationalist Liberals in the 1950's) was not entirely without meaning, though they often denied to their people the basic rights generally associated with even nineteenth-century liberalism. In particular, the Somozas have brought to Nicaragua some of the social legislation which has been introduced by more revolutionary régimes in other isthmian countries. A Nicaraguan labour code was adopted in 1944, during Somoza García's first long term; an income tax in 1952, during his second. A National Development Institute (Instituto de Fomento Nacional or INFONAC) was created in 1953 and a National Institute of Social Security (Instituto Nacional de Seguridad Social or INSS) finally in 1956. A Nicaraguan Housing Institute (Instituto Nicaragüense de la Vivienda or INVI) was founded in 1959, and President Somoza Debayle in the same year suggested an Office of National Lands to accumulate data which might be useful in the establishment of a National Agrarian Institute, which would 'search for a solution to all the problems of the countryside',[17] Even a long-overdue political reform was mentioned in 1960, when the president proposed that the ruling boards of Nicaraguan *municipios*, like those of the rest of the isthmus, be elected rather than appointed.

The Traditionalist Conservative opponents of the Somoza régime have signified some willingness to wait for a test of their strength in the 1963 presidential elections if the fairness of those

[16] Confirmation comes from both critical and friendly observers. See for example Marvin Alisky, 'Our Man in Managua', *The Reporter*, xxiii/11 (22 Dec. 1960), 26–27, which deals with the role of U.S. Ambassador Thomas Whelan; and Patrick McMahon, 'Somoza of Nicaragua', *American Mercury*, lxxviii (April 1954), 132–6, which lauds Somoza García.

[17] *Mensaje que el presidente de la república, Ingeniero Luis A. Somoza D., dirige al Honorable Congreso Nacional al inaugurar su noveno período constitucional de sesiones ordinarias* (Managua, 1959), p. xxxv.

elections can be assured through their supervision by foreign and neutral observers. President Somoza Debayle has rejected the latter idea, thus throwing himself open to charges that he intends to choose his own successor. There is every reason to believe that, if the campaign is a free one, both the president and his traditional opposition will find themselves hard pressed by forces of new inspiration. Within the Conservative party, younger members have expressed dissatisfaction with the continued power of such old men as Emiliano Chamorro Vargas. The group of Independent (anti-Somoza) Liberals has been increasingly active. Other groups have formed farther to the left; most notably the Juventud Patriótica Nicaragüense, somewhat inclined toward friendship with the Castro régime in Cuba. In the mid-term year of 1960 the youth of the country were the most active in their expressions of anti-Somoza sentiment. But when one of their number was killed on 5 September (Ajax Delgado López, eighteen years of age) ostensibly while trying to escape after imprisonment, 20,000 persons visited the cemetery to witness his burial. When the Somoza rule is ended, the Traditionalist Conservatives and Juventud Patriótica will find they have little in common. While the Somozas last, they do share one chief ambition, the political elimination of a family which has too long pretended omniscience and exercised omnipotence in Nicaraguan affairs.

BOUNDARIES AND BUDGETS

Not the least of the concerns of President Luis Somoza Debayle has been the controversy with neighbouring Honduras over Nicaragua's northern border, detailed in the chapter on Honduras. Because of the inclusion within her territories of the San Juan River and so much of Mosquitia, Nicaragua has also carried on long territorial contention with three other states, Colombia, Great Britain, and Costa Rica. The dispute with Colombia stemmed from a decision by King Charles IV of Spain in 1803 (made official but little implemented) to grant the viceroy in Bogotá jurisdiction over the San Andrés islands (east of Nicaragua) and the Mosquito Coast as far as Cape Gracias a Dios. It was settled in 1928 when Colombia gave up her claim to Mosquitia but retained the San Andrés archipelago. Great Britain for several decades had a more effective voice concerning the Mosquito Coast through her re-establishment in 1816 of association with the Miskito peoples of the area whose territory the British had promised in 1783 and 1786 to evacuate. A

Miskito 'kingdom' was both recognized and protected by the British government with increasing vigour until the years 1848–50, when Great Britain took and held San Juan del Norte (then called Greytown) by force in the name of the Miskito king. The Clayton–Bulwer Treaty of 1850 between Great Britain and the United States stated that neither nation would 'assume or exercise any dominion' over the Mosquito Coast or any part of Central America. Though the British government maintained that this wording did not apply to the Miskito protectorate arrangement, Greytown was given up in 1850 and Nicaraguan jurisdiction over the Mosquito Coast recognized in 1860. The last British intervention on this coast (at Bluefields and San Juan) came in 1894, when the Nicaraguan government persuaded the Miskito to give up the autonomy which had been granted them. A treaty in 1906 relinquished the last shreds of British interest.

Nicaraguan frontier controversy with Costa Rica has gone through long periods of dormancy but remains alive to the present. The transfer of Guanacaste province to Costa Rica in 1825 was not accepted by Nicaragua for some time, but is no longer a matter of contention. That and other territorial disputes were tentatively settled in 1858, when the boundary was established substantially as it has since remained—a straight line across the narrow neck of land between the Pacific and Lake Nicaragua, a line following the southern shore of Lake Nicaragua but two miles south so as to give Nicaragua control over the entire lake, a similar line following the San Juan River one-third of its distance to the Caribbean, and then the San Juan itself the remainder of the way but along the right bank rather than its centre. This arrangement has since been accepted only as a *modus vivendi* by Nicaragua through a complicated series of negotiations involving several unratified treaties.[18] Costa Rica during the course of these negotiations has been interested chiefly in protecting her own rights in agreements Nicaragua has made concerning an interoceanic canal. The last great protest on this score arose when Nicaragua signed the Bryan–Chamorro treaty in 1914, the subsequent controversy being that which brought about the collapse three years later of the Central American Court of Justice.

The growth of the Nicaraguan budget has been of the undramatic character of that of Honduras on the other frontier before 1957. In the fiscal year ending 30 June 1949 government receipts

[18] See ch. vi, n. 24, p. 160.

amounted to 78 million córdobas or $15 million; in 1954, they were 183 million córdobas or $26 million; in 1959, $35 million.[19] Tariff duties, chiefly those on imports, accounted for about three-fifths of the nation's revenue in 1953–4. Another fifth came from consumption taxes, principally those on liquor and tobacco. The income tax established in 1952 together with a tax on capital levied four years earlier amounted to 10 per cent of the total by 1959.[20]

The tradition of monetary assistance from the United States government to Nicaragua in return for friendly considerations may be said to have begun in 1916 with the Bryan–Chamorro Treaty. One world war later, in 1942, it was strongly in evidence when $4 million was found to assist Nicaragua in the building of a road to Rama on the Escondido River, a project which remains unfinished though large sums have since been added.[21] Nicaragua received $5 million in assistance in 1946–50, $5 million in 1951–5, $2 million in 1956 and again in 1957, and nearly $4 million a year in 1958–60, making a 1946–60 total of $27 million. A large portion of this amount, some $18 million, was for the building of roads; $7 million for economic and technical assistance; and the largest sum on the isthmus, nearly $1·4 million, for military purposes.[22] Another $1 million was received from the United Nations in technical-assistance and children's-relief programmes in 1954–8.[23] Substantial loans came during the same period from the International Bank for Reconstruction and Development.

The Somoza family, while adopting various social measures to keep up with the times, has modified with reluctance one spending characteristic from the *caudillo* generation of the 1930's. Its Ministry of War, Navy, and Aviation (including the nation's postal, telephone, and telegraph services) was granted 18 per cent of the expenditures in the 1960–1 general budget, a portion topped only by the Ministry of Development and Public Works (which had also 18 per cent, the difference being slight). The budget total was 246,337,239 córdobas or $34,941,452 (at 7·05 córdobas to the dollar). The Ministry of Public Education was apportioned 14 per cent, Public Health 10 per cent, Finance and Public Credit 10 per

[19] *Bol. de Est.* (N.), Epoca 3, no. 7 (June 1959), p. 83; no. 8, p. 89. Figures are converted to the nearest million dollars at 5·29 córdobas to the dollar in 1949 and 7·05 in 1954–9.
[20] See ch. v, n. 43, p. 111.
[21] J. Fred Rippy, 'State Department Operations: the Rama Road', *Int. Am. Econ. Aff.*, ix/1 (Summer 1955), 17–32, dwells upon the weaknesses of this particular project.
[22] See ch. v, n. 44, p. 111.   [23] U.N., *Stat. Yb., 1959*, p. 423.

cent, Government 9 per cent, Foreign Relations 4 per cent, Agriculture and Livestock 4 per cent, Economy 2 per cent, and Labour 1 per cent. The public debt was assigned 5 per cent and the judicial system 2 per cent.[24] Whatever contribution the Somozas have made to their country, it might be argued, lies in the field of the economy rather than in public finance.

SUBSISTENCE AGRICULTURE

The Nicaraguan agricultural economy changed more rapidly in the 1950's, and in any event is considerably more varied in its emphases, than that of any other nation in Central America. Yet basically Nicaragua's agriculture retains the same characteristics as those of Guatemala, El Salvador, and Honduras. Two-thirds of Nicaragua's economically active citizenry were engaged in farming in 1950.[25] Only 5,863,000 acres, or one-sixth of the nation's area, was reported in the 1952 agricultural census as marked off in farms, including land not useful for farming.[26] Nicaragua exports a considerable amount of coffee, and in recent years has sent out of the country a cotton harvest fully as important. Nevertheless it seems likely that nine-tenths of her active farming area is used for immediate subsistence.[27]

Maize is the preponderant crop in Nicaragua as elsewhere on the isthmus, but not in the overwhelming proportion of Guatemala, El Salvador, and Honduras. It was harvested from 321,000 acres in 1952, roughly 5 per cent of the land included in Nicaraguan farms and barely two-thirds of the space per capita occupied by maize in the three other countries mentioned.[28] The yield was only 700 lb. to the acre in 1959, a second harvest annually amounting to about one-half of the first, but production has been sufficient in most years to match national consumption. Both the amount and location of the maize acreage varied considerably during the later 1950's owing to the impact of the cotton crop, but in 1959 the maize harvest remained important in all parts of the country. Sorghum is also a major ground crop in Nicaragua, its 100,000 acres in 1952

[24] *Presupuesto general de ingresos y egresos de la república, 1960–61* (Managua, 1960), p. 61. Without the postal, telephone, and telegraph services, the allotment for the military remains at 14 per cent, easily the highest in Central America.

[25] *Censo general de población*, xvii. 341–2.   [26] *Estruct. agr.*, p. 136.

[27] Nicaragua's failure to separate waste lands from pasture lands in the 1952 agricultural census makes a more careful reckoning impossible. There exists also an uncertain factor of land used in raising cattle for export to Peru.

[28] *Bol. de Est.* (N.), Epoca 3, no. 8, p. 81. A lower census figure was reported earlier and appears in *Estruct. agr.*, p. 198.

giving it third place among crops of this sort in space occupied. Sorghum is grown widely except in the Caribbean departments of Zelaya and Río San Juan, but in 1959 well over half the harvest came from the central departments of Chontales and Matagalpa plus Managua and León.[29]

Nicaragua's important harvest of cotton for export, second in area among the ground crops in 1952 with 116,000 acres, occupied less than one-third of that space in 1950. In 1958 the harvest was nearly eight times what it had been just eight years earlier. Competing with sorghum for third place in 1952 was rice (99,000 acres), some of which was exported. About three-fifths of that acreage continued to be grown in the late 1950's, with Granada and Carazo departments on the Pacific side and Zelaya in the east contributing over half the production. Beans (86,000 acres in 1952 and varying widely in quantity since that time) are grown in every department, but over half of them in 1959 were raised in Matagalpa and Managua. Sesame (57,000 acres in 1952) and sugar-cane (47,000), both of which figure in the export trade, conclude the list of important ground crops. Almost all the sesame in 1959 was grown in the four departments of Managua, Granada, Chinandega, and León, while half the cane was raised in Chinandega alone. Other ground crops grown in some quantity (in decreasing order according to space devoted to their cultivation in 1952) were cassava, tobacco, henequen, potatoes, wheat, tomatoes, onions, and peanuts.[30] Most of Nicaragua's wheat consumption is imported.

Tree and bush crops were reported as covering 315,000 acres in 1952, with coffee occupying 140,000 acres of the lot. Bananas and plantains, though not of importance in the export trade, were reported on 117,000 acres. Other crops of this sort (in decreasing order according to space occupied) were coconuts, cacao, oranges, pineapples, and limes.[31]

Nicaragua reported 1,574,000 acres of cultivated pasturage in 1952 and 369,000 acres of land at rest. There was in addition a great amount of natural pasture land, not separated from waste lands in the census. The inventory of domestic animals ran as follows: 1,182,000 cattle; 234,000 pigs; 135,000 horses; 25,000 mules;

---

[29] *Bol. de Est.* (N)., Epoca 3, no. 8, pp. 81, 84–85. See ch. v, n. 51, p. 113.

[30] Ibid. pp. 81–83; *Estruct. agr.*, pp. 198, 243. The acreage for the 1952 bean harvest is taken from the more recent, and higher, figure of two not in agreement.

[31] *Estruct. agr.*, pp. 136, 243. The total acreage for tree and bush crops is computed from 'Tierras con cultivos permanentes', p. 136, less 'Henequén', p. 243.

and 5,000 donkeys. Only 963,000 barnyard fowl were counted of all classes. Nicaragua has more cattle than any other isthmian nation; some are exported to Peru. In 1957 a new inventory revealed a total of 1,331,000 cattle, one for each human being.[32]

EXPORTS AND IMPORTS

The history of independent Nicaragua's export trade is not a long one. Like Honduras, she sold no product to the exterior in the first half of the nineteenth century that could compare with Guatemala's cochineal or El Salvador's indigo. This was true in spite of the fact that colonial Nicaragua had done its share of isthmian trading; the long years of civil conflict were a depressant economically as well as in politics. When the banana trade roused Honduras' north coast in the later nineteenth century, Nicaragua remained without an export matching in volume those of the remainder of the isthmus. The picture began to change in the 1920's, and more recently has been modified radically. In 1958 Guatemala exported merchandise worth $30 for each one of her inhabitants; the comparable figure in Honduras was $38; in El Salvador $48. Nicaragua had by this time surpassed Guatemala and Honduras, and, with a figure of $46 per capita, had approached El Salvador's position.[33]

In the 1920's the Standard Fruit and Steamship Company, with a lively business established in Honduras, attempted banana operations in the vicinity of Puerto Cabezas. These plantations were abandoned by the early 1940's because of plant diseases, though United Fruit maintains a very small operation (inherited from Cuyamel) near Bluefields. In the early years of the Second World War interesting quantities of gold were exploited in the hinterlands of the same department and in Chontales and León, but production soon levelled off and after fifteen years became insignificant. Coffee was first developed as a large-scale harvest in post-war years, as in Honduras. And in the 1950's cotton cultivation, developed by the Somoza family and friends to a greater extent than in any other isthmian nation, became a greater earner of money than coffee.

Cotton accounted for 46 per cent of Nicaragua's export trade

[32] Ibid. pp. 136, 293; *Bol. de Est.* (N.), Epoca 3, no. 7, p. 76.
[33] The figures are computed from the mid-1958 population estimates (see ch. i, n. i, p. 2) and 1958 total exports from U.N., *Tb. Int. Trade Stat., 1959,* i. 185, 250 (Table 4), 258, 392. The 'córdoba oro' quoted in the latter publication, pp. 390–2, unlike the ordinary córdoba, is on a par with the dollar.

value in the period 1956–9, raw cotton making up 40 per cent and cottonseed another 6 per cent. Its cultivation occupied the attention of wealthy families, with almost the entire production in 1959 coming from the three Pacific departments of Chinandega, León, and Managua. Since these three departments are also prime producers of other harvests, the excitement caused by the new industry in this part of the country has been considerable. Even a manpower shortage developed in this limited area, and some machine methods have been employed. But despite Nicaragua's greater total volume of cotton exports, her production per acre in 1959 was only 10·0 *quintales oro* (460 kilograms) per *manzana* to compare with El Salvador's 13·7 (632 kilograms) of the year before.[34]

Coffee, the extensive cultivation of which in Nicaragua is not much older than that of cotton, has continued as the nation's second most valuable export after losing the lead in the middle 1950's. In 1956–9 coffee accounted for 36 per cent of the total trade value, though production did not increase during that period. Roughly one-fourth of the coffee is harvested in the tiny Pacific department of Carazo, nearly as much in the larger department of Matagalpa, and significant amounts in adjacent Managua and Jinotega.[35] Wood made up 5 per cent of the country's exports in 1956–8; and in 1956–9 growing amounts of live cattle and sesame seed each accounted for 3 per cent. A remaining miscellany of 7 per cent included only one other item, sugar (also on the increase), which sold for more than $1 million a year. Nicaragua's total exports in 1955–8 averaged $64,400,000 annually, going only 35 per cent to the United States, 20 per cent to Germany, 14 per cent to the Netherlands, 10 per cent to Japan, 4 per cent each to the United Kingdom and Belgium, and 2 per cent each to France, Peru, and Canada.[36]

Nicaragua's imports have risen on the same scale as her exports. Incoming trade in the period 1955–8 averaged $74,300,000 annually, coming 60 per cent from the United States, 8 per cent from Germany, 7 per cent from the Netherlands Antilles (petroleum products), 4 per cent from the United Kingdom, 3 per cent each from Belgium, Japan, and Panama, and 2 per cent each from El

[34] U.N., *Yb. Int. Trade Stat., 1959*, i. 391; *Bol. de Est.* (N.), Epoca 3, no. 8, p. 82; *An. Est.* (El S.), *1958*, i. 256.
[35] U.N., *Yb. Int. Trade Stat., 1959*, i. 391; *Bol. de Est.* (N.), Epoca 3, no. 8, p. 82.
[36] U.N., *Yb. Int. Trade Stat., 1959*, i. 391–2. See above, n. 33. Wood was not reported for 1959; its inclusion might have modified slightly the commodity percentages for 1956–9.

Salvador and Canada. The trade from Panama and El Salvador consisted of small manufactures. The 1958 imports, listed by the categories of the Standard International Trade Classification, were as follows: Manufactured goods accounted for 27 per cent of the total, including textile fabrics worth more than $7 million; metal manufactures of value over $4 million; iron and steel over $2 million; and rubber tires and tubes over $1 million. Machinery and transport equipment comprised 24 per cent, with road motor vehicles over $5 million; electric machines and appliances over $3 million; and agricultural machinery, tractors, and power-generating machinery over $1 million each. Chemicals added up to 19 per cent, with insecticides over $5 million; medicinal and pharmaceutical products over $4 million; and cosmetics and soaps over $1 million. Fuels and lubricants were 10 per cent, with petroleum products over $7 million. Food (8 per cent) included cereals over $3 million; manufactured articles other than machinery and transport (7 per cent) included $1 million for clothing.[37]

NON-AGRICULTURAL OCCUPATIONS

The one-third of Nicaragua's economically active population not involved in agriculture in 1950 were distributed occupationally, according to the census, in a manner not far different from those of Guatemala and El Salvador. Of the total of this group, 11·4 per cent were reported in manufacturing, 10·6 per cent in services, 4·6 per cent in trade, 2·6 per cent in construction, and 1·8 per cent in transport. Another 1·0 per cent engaged in mining constituted the highest proportion in Central America for that activity.[38]

Nicaragua's first census of industrial activity covers the year 1953. Altogether, 18,899 persons were counted working in 1,575 manufacturing establishments. Food-processing industries were by far the most important, employing 10,590 people in 810 shops. The production of footwear and wearing apparel occupied 2,311 workers in 288 places of business. The lumber industry was the only remaining one which engaged more than 1,000 persons. Of the 18,899 individuals involved in manufacturing activity, 1,518 were proprietors; 1,179 were administrative and technical employees whose earnings averaged $1,239 for the year; 15,267 were production workers and apprentices whose year's wages averaged $380; 178 were workers in the home who averaged $255; and 757 were

[37] Ibid. pp. 390–2. See above, n. 33.   [38] *Censo general de población*, xvii. 341.

relatives who worked without remuneration.[39] The compensation figure for production workers was higher than that for El Salvador in 1956 but lower than that for Guatemala in 1953.

Since the census of 1953 the production of cottonseed oil and of cotton textiles has grown rapidly.[40] There is a cement plant near San Rafael del Sur in Managua department. The gold shipped from Zelaya, Chontales, and León departments in the 1940's, accompanied by a much smaller value of silver, proved eventually (as gold and silver had before in Honduras and Nicaragua) not worth the cost of extraction; though the exploitation of Nicaragua's mineral resources may yet prove a boon to her economy. Exploration for petroleum is expected. Nicaragua, like Honduras, shipped out mahogany from her Caribbean coastlands in the nineteenth century and is exploiting her pine, cedar, and mahogany in the twentieth.

A fairly adequate road system in Nicaragua's western portion is almost entirely the product of the last two decades. The Inter-American highway, much of it covered with asphalt by the end of 1960, passes from the Honduran department of Choluteca through or by Somoto, Estelí, Managua, Jinotepe, and Rivas to Costa Rica's Guanacaste. Short paved or all-weather connexions with Ocotal, Jinotega, Matagalpa, Masaya, and Granada make this route a real funnel for the nation's domestic commerce, besides which it skirts the great lakes, offering excellent views of volcanoes. In the late 1950's another route, all paved, was finished from Managua to León, Chinandega, and the port of Corinto, running through a rich and well-settled district important since earliest colonial times. Paved strips reach the Pacific at Puerto Somoza and the resort village of Poneloya, and a good road at San Juan del Sur. A road from Managua to Rama, under construction since the early 1940's, provides all-weather connexions to Boaco and Juigalpa and has some paved stretches, but at the end of 1960 had not yet achieved its goal of providing a river-road route from Bluefields to the capital.[41] Eventually, it is expected that goods from the Caribbean will ascend the Escondido River to Rama and be carried from there by truck to western cities. An all-weather lumber road connects Puerto Cabezas on the Caribbean to the head of navigation

[39] *Bol. de Est.* (N.), Epoca 3, no. 7, pp. 108–9. Conversions are at 7·05 córdobas to the dollar.

[40] 'Producción industrial de Nicaragua por años 1952 a 1959', typewritten document provided by the Nicaraguan Dirección General de Estadística y Censos.

[41] See above, n. 21.

on the Coco River. There are no road connexions of any kind, however, with Puerto Cabo Gracias a Dios, Prinzapolka, Blue-fields, or San Juan del Norte, the entire eastern coast thus remaining isolated from the rest of the country save for the San Juan River and the air. Nicaragua licensed only 800 each of passenger cars and commercial vehicles in 1948, but by 1957 the numbers had advanced to 7,800 and 5,700 respectively.[42]

The railways of Nicaragua, like her highways, are concentrated in the west. In the 1880's lines were constructed from Corinto to the western tip of Lake Managua and from Managua to Granada, to provide cross-country communications via these railways, the lakes, and the San Juan River. The line from Corinto was then extended to Managua, to eliminate the smaller of the lakes, and a branch built from Masaya to Jinotepe and nearby Diriamba. Other branches were constructed in the 1930's to the inland community of El Sauce in the department of León and to Puerto Mora-zán in Chinandega. The latter is a riverside hamlet which maintains launch connexions across the Gulf of Fonseca with La Unión in El Salvador, making it possible for the independent traveller on the Salvadoran rail line (with its connexions all the way from Canada) to continue his journey by train southward to Granada. Another short line was laid in the 1930's to connect San Juan del Sur through Rivas with the edge of Lake Nicaragua, in the vicinity long discussed as most likely for a trans-isthmian canal. Steamer service on Lake Nicaragua unites the big and little systems, and is owned and operated like the railways by the Ferrocarril del Pacífico, a government concern.

The San Juan River trade channel, now little used, has been the subject of trans-isthmian canal speculation ever since Nicaragua's independence from Spain. The first extensive survey to determine the feasibility of a Nicaragua canal was performed by John Baily, an Englishman who made Central America his home.[43] In the second half of the nineteenth century and until the very eve of the digging of the Panama Canal, the proponents of the Nicaraguan route were many, and controversy over the advantages of the two sites waxed loud and long.[44] The idea has been revived, particular-

[42] U.N., *Stat. Yb.*, *1959*, p. 333.
[43] Baily was the translator of the first comprehensive volume on Central America published in English; see ch. iv, n. 14, p. 68. His surveys are reported in Stephens, i. 406–13, and in his own *Central America* (London, 1850).
[44] Periodical indexes list more than 140 articles dealing with the proposed Nicaragua canal in the decade 1891–1900.

ly since 1945 when new threats of the atomic age seemed to render the security of the Panama route less certain. Though many arguments were raised against the practicability of the Nicaragua canal when rival passages were under consideration, the feasibility of a waterway through Nicaraguan soil now seems beyond question. Developments in air transport and in world politics hold the key as to whether the matter will again be considered at government level.

Nicaragua, whose old port of Realejo was the scene of shipbuilding activities as early as the sixteenth century, became recently the first isthmian nation to own an ocean shipping company. The Marina Mercante Nicaragüense or MAMENIC line, as it is called, was organized in 1953 to operate between the two coasts of the nation and ports in the United States and Europe. Domestic air service in Nicaragua, on the other hand, is less developed than in any other isthmian country save El Salvador. There is one company, Líneas Aéreas de Nicaragua (called LANICA) which provides better service to foreign investors than to the nation itself, though it does also fly to Florida.

Nicaraguan telephone and telegraph facilities, along with the postal service, are controlled by the nation's military arm. As is customary in Central America, outside the capital telegrams are more common than telephone messages. The government also owns and operates the electric-power industry of Managua, which has far greater capacity than that of all the remaining public plants in the country. Most of Nicaragua's power is generated by thermal units, although hydro-electric resources are available and plans have been made to tap them. A grand project on the Tuma River promises to supply much of the country's needs in the future. In the year 1940, only 12 per cent of Nicaragua's homes were lighted with electricity, including 31 per cent of those in urban areas and less than 1 per cent of those classified as rural. The production of electric power increased, however, from a total of 77 million kilowatt hours in 1948 to 128 million in 1957. Over half of this production was private.[45]

Central-banking arrangements came to Nicaragua before any other country in Central America, as a consequence of the first intervention by the United States. The Banco Nacional de Nicaragua, formed in 1912 by United States interests (when also the córdoba was created), was turned over to the government in 1924 and (with reorganizations in 1940 and 1961) has been managed by

[45] U.N., *Stat. Yb.*, *1959*, pp. 284, 545.

the state ever since. Traditionally it has operated to favour the agriculturists of the nation whose holdings were already plentiful, but the latest reorganization is intended to establish contact with more needy sectors of the economy. INFONAC, organized in 1953, has already created some new impetus in both agriculture and manufacturing in its attempt to encourage the development of the nation's resources. Nicaragua has also four private banks and five small savings institutions.[46]

ECONOMIC OUTLOOK: TERMINATION OF PRIVATE DOMAIN

When Anastasio Somoza García died in September 1956 there was much speculation on the size of his estate. One news magazine in reporting on his activities said,

Meanwhile, by 'buying from heirs' Somoza acquired coffee *fincas* and cattle ranches, parlayed them into a fortune estimated at $60 million. . . . He reputedly owned one-tenth of the country's farmland, plus interests in lumber, liquor, soap, cement, power, textiles, cotton-ginning, sugar-milling, air transport, merchant shipping, even a barbershop—an estimated 430 properties. 'You'd do the same thing yourself if you were in my place', he used to explain.[47]

Speaking of the same enterprises another observer wrote,

Although nobody knows just how much all these properties are worth, the Somoza wealth is estimated as high as 200 million dollars. . . . If you ask local people how this fortune was built, most of them will tell you that, for years, the only way to get ahead in Nicaragua has been to do business with General Somoza.[48]

Concerning son Luis Somoza Debayle, three years later a visitor commented: 'Dr. Guillermo Urbina Vásquez, a leftist, asserts that the personal fortune of Luis is no less than $300,000,000. Nicaraguans who have been close to the Somoza family have given me even higher figures'.[49] Another statement on the subject the same year said, 'The fortune of the Somoza family is conservatively estimated at some 150 million dollars'.[50]

---

[46] See ch. v, n. 71, p. 123.
[47] 'The Champ is Dead', *Time*, lxviii/15, 8 Oct. 1956, p. 43.
[48] 'Trouble for Another U.S. Neighbor', *U.S. News & World Report*, xli, 5, Oct. 1956, p. 64.
[49] James L. Busey, 'Mission to Somozaland', *Nation*, cxc (1960), 187–9.
[50] Charles W. Anderson, 'The Political Future of Nicaragua', *Canadian Forum*, xxxix (1959), 107–9.

Whatever the precise size of the sum, most visitors would agree that such wealth in a country as poor as Nicaragua is unconscionable. While the president and his family and friends live lavishly, the workers for whom they express concern earn wages of less than $500 a year.[51] The prices the workers paid in Managua in December 1959, far from being commensurate, ran at 9·4 cents U.S. per lb. of beans or second-class rice, 4·0 cents per lb. for maize, 9·6 cents for potatoes, 28·0 cents for beef, 40·6 cents for pork, 98 cents for a work shirt, $2·29 for a pair of work pants, and $4·96 for a man's pair of shoes.[52] The Nicaraguan agricultural economy, it has already been observed, changed more rapidly in the 1950's than any other in Central America. Exports more than doubled during the decade.[53] Yet it is obvious that the benefits from the new production have gone almost exclusively to the Somoza family and friends. The most immediate economic problem affecting the Nicaraguan public is how to terminate this private domain.

This is not to say that the Somoza governments have done nothing for labour. INSS, created in 1956, counted 9,000 contributors to sickness and maternity benefit plans and old-age pensions by 1957.[54] Somoza García himself helped to start a national labour organization in 1944 at the time when he issued his labour code. Called the Confederation of Workers of Nicaragua, it fell—oddly enough—under Communist dominance and was dissolved in 1948 after the Communists turned anti-Somoza. A new General Confederation of Labour (1949) sought affiliation with the Peronist hemisphere labour movement—the Agrupación de Trabajadores Latino Americanos Sindicalizados—until that group became defunct in 1955. The General Confederation had eleven unions as members in 1960; an offshoot of 1953, now called the National Confederation of Workers of Nicaragua, had forty-four. Also nationally organized are the transport workers (since 1952), numbers of white-collar workers (1959), and the teachers (1947). None of the five national associations is now internationally affiliated.

Labour associations, like all other components of the Somoza-revived economy, work within circumscribed limits. The awakening of agricultural enterprise itself is closely confined, since it chiefly affects the west coast. Most of central Nicaragua, like so much of Honduras, has simply never been developed, while the

[51] See above, n. 39, for 1953 manufacturing earnings.

[52] *Bol. de Est.* (N.), Epoca 3, no. 8, pp. 139–40. Prices are averages of those quoted, converted at 7.05 córdobas to the dollar.

[53] Ibid. p. 148.   [54] *Yb. Lab. Stat., 1959,* p. 454.

situation in eastern Nicaragua has through most of the twentieth century actually deteriorated.[55] Despite the vigour shown by agricultural statistics even before his death, the elder President Somoza cannot be said to have concerned himself with the nation's economy except as that seemed to him identical with his personal interests. The younger Somoza executive has at least talked in terms of the national welfare. But only an unlikely self-divestment of the gains of two and a half decades would make his words ring with sincerity.

Economically as well as politically, the big question in Nicaragua is how to bring about that divestment. In 1950–1 a study of this country indicated 'that more than 25 per cent of the national income accrues to about 1 per cent of the population. . . . Little of the tax burden falls upon the upper 1 per cent. Most of it is borne by the remaining 99 per cent, whose average income, after taxation, is probably less than $100 per year'.[56] At the time those words were written, there was no clear political alternative. Emiliano Chamorro Vargas and his Conservatives were then co-operating with father Somoza. Even when they quarrelled, while Chamorro would have liked to change the composition of the affluent 1 per cent of the population there was no sign of his caring to change its status. With the passage of ten years after 1951, the income tax probably made some dent in the statistics, though not much. Social security will make the dent larger; Somoza-sponsored agrarian reform could bring further betterment. But alternatives to the Somoza family-fortune anachronism, even a dented one, are now clearly visible. As plainly as in other countries at other times, if the fortune is not terminated by peaceful means it will be terminated more dramatically. Only when that change occurs, through whatever set of circumstances, will the people of Nicaragua have a real chance to prosper by the fruits of their own economy.

LEARNING

At the dawn of independence Nicaragua was the only Central American state other than Guatemala to boast a degree-conferring institution of higher learning. This rank had come to the seminary in León only in 1812. It and a rival institution in Granada (whose first roots went back to 1804) functioned in spasmodic form as uni-

[55] See the first-hand economic and social descriptions of San Juan del Norte, Bluefields, and their vicinities in Dozier, pp. 88–102.

[56] IBRD, *The Economic Development of Nicaragua* (Baltimore, Md., Johns Hopkins Press for IBRD, 1953), p. 75.

versities through most of the nineteenth century. The national capital joined the competition in 1895 with a school of law, the third in the country. In 1941 the school in Managua was declared the Central University of Nicaragua, and all three with a paucity of resources attempted to teach both law and medicine. In 1947 a logical reorganization was made, setting up one national university, but ignoring the feelings of those who were proud of Granada's long independent record. Five faculties were recognized—in León Law and Notary, Medicine and Surgery, Pharmacy and Chemistry, and Odontology; in Managua, Engineering. According to the census, 2,492 men and 341 women living in Nicaragua in 1950 had attended university classes, numbers significantly higher than in Honduras. But the total university enrolment in the subdued atmosphere of 1958 was only 916.[57]

The régime of the 1950's took steps to further elementary education. In 1950 the census showed that 34·5 per cent of the population over the age of six and 37·4 per cent over the age of ten (including only 38·6 per cent of those between fifteen and nineteen) could read and write. The low achievement level of many of those who were literate was attested by the fact that only 25·5 per cent of the children aged between six and fourteen were attending school in the same year. Matriculation in primary schools operated by the national government, however, increased from 68,130 in 1951 to 117,921 in 1958. In the latter year municipal and private schools on the same level had an enrolment of 14,668. Registration in secondary schools is slight; it increased in the national schools from 1,632 in 1952 to 2,751 in 1958, private schools in the latter year accounting for 2,706.[58]

An official gazette has been published in Nicaragua in most years since 1847. Daily papers appeared in the major cities by the late nineteenth century. *Novedades* (founded 1937) is the most widely read in the country and a Somoza mouthpiece. *La Prensa* (1926), the Conservative sheet of Pedro Joaquín Chamorro Cardenal, is permitted considerable liberty to criticize the government and to publicize unwanted facts.[59] Though the other papers do not share

[57] *Censo general de población*, xvii. 202; *Bol. de Est.* (N.), Epoca 3, no. 7, p. 44.

[58] *Censo general de población*, xvii. 176–7, 187–8; *Memoria* 1952–53 of the Nicaraguan Ministro de Educación Pública, pp. 8–9; *Bol. de Est.* (N.), Epoca 3, no. 8, pp. 42–43, 46.

[59] Marvin Alisky, 'La Prensa Leads the Fight against Nicaragua Censorship', *The Quill*, xlix/3 (March 1961), 15–16, 19, calls this permission an example of 'showcase democracy'.

these traits, people seem to read more newspapers in Nicaragua than in Honduras, Guatemala, and El Salvador. There were ten dailies altogether in 1957 with a total circulation of 120,000, a good 90 papers for every 1,000 inhabitants.[60]

Nicaragua's registered death-rate—94·9 per 10,000 inhabitants in 1958—is the second lowest in Central America. Among the chief causes of death in 1958 were gastro-enteritis and colitis (12·7 deaths per 10,000 inhabitants), malaria (6·7), worms (5·2), pneumonia and bronchitis (3·9), infections of infancy (3·5), measles (3·0), and whooping-cough (1·8). There were hospitals in all but two of Nicaragua's departments in 1958, but more than one-third of the patients assisted were in Managua. In 1955 there were 477 physicians in the country (nearly one for every 2,600 persons, the highest ratio in Central America) and 95 dentists.[61]

Nicaragua's significant republican historiography begins with an excited book by William Vincent Wells portraying William Walker as a hero.[62] Walker himself before his death made a more careful attempt to tell his own story.[63] Jerónimo Pérez (1828–84), Nicaraguan secretary to General Tomás Martínez, resolving that the war's backgrounds should not be lost with the destruction of the nation's documents, produced Nicaragua's first great historical work during the next several years.[64] Historian William Oscar Scroggs of the United States has dealt ably with the subject since.[65]

The work of Pérez was soon followed by that of two more comprehensive historians. Tomás Ayón (1821–87) sorted out the accounts of colonial Nicaragua from the more general printed sources, living only to finish his work to 1821.[66] José Dolores Gámez (1851–1918) covered the same ground more briefly and carried through to 1860, making a serious attempt to write good history.[67] No work on the same scale has been attempted since; for details of Nica-

[60] U.N., *Stat. Yb.*, *1959*, p. 578.
[61] Ibid. *1958*, p. 541; *Bol. de Est.* (N.), Epoca 3, no. 8, pp. 1, 10, 15, 26. The death-rates for gastro-enteritis and colitis and for worms are interpolated from more general categories, using figures from Honduras as a guide.
[62] *Walker's Expedition to Nicaragua* (N.Y., 1856).
[63] *The War in Nicaragua* (Mobile, 1860).
[64] *Memorias para la historia de la revolución de Nicaragua y de la guerra nacional contra los filibusteros, 1854 a 1857* (2 vols., Managua, 1865–73); reproduced in *Obras históricas completas* (Managua, 1928).
[65] *Filibusters and Financiers* (N.Y., Macmillan, 1916).
[66] *Historia de Nicaragua* (i–ii, Granada, 1882–7; iii, Managua, 1889; 2nd ed., 3 vols., Madrid, 1956).
[67] *Historia de Nicaragua* (Managua, 1889; 2nd ed., Madrid, 1955).

ragua's history in later decades (often unavailable) one looks instead to outsiders and their more general treatment.[68]

A historian, Isaac Joslin Cox, and a journalist, Harold Norman Denny, wrote accounts of the United States involvement in Nicaragua in the twentieth century.[69] Accounts from Latin points of view are so passionate they can hardly be called studies.[70] Spain has made two significant contributions to Nicaraguan biography.[71] Nicaraguan Sofonías Salvatierra (b. 1882) broke new ground when he studied his country's colonial history in the archives at Seville in 1934.[72] Andrés Vega Bolaños (b. 1890) more recently has collected documents from Spain on a grand scale, publishing seventeen volumes on the first half of the sixteenth century.[73] Salvatierra, Vega Bolaños, and a handful of other men have supported an Academia de Geografía e Historia de Nicaragua founded in 1935, which publishes a small review.[74] The journalist and politician Pedro Joaquín Chamorro y Zelaya (1891–1952), first editor of this review, in 1951 published the isthmus' most extensive history of Central America's period of federation.[75]

The best general descriptions of Nicaragua were written a century apart, by Ephraim George Squier (1852) and the International Bank for Reconstruction and Development (1953).[76] But there are some signs that less than another century will elapse before Nicaraguans take to analysing their own country in writing.[77]

ART

The development of mass recreation in Nicaragua is little different from that of El Salvador. Nicaraguan enthusiasm for baseball

[68] See ch. v, nn. 99–101, p. 132; also Carlos Molina Argüello, 'Bibliografía historiográfica de Nicaragua', *R. Interamericana de Bibliografía*, iv (1954), 9–22.

[69] Cox, *Nicaragua and the United States, 1909–1927* (Boston, 1927); Denny, *Dollars for Bullets* (N.Y., 1929).

[70] See for example Máximo Soto Hall, *Nicaragua y el imperialismo norteamericano* (Buenos Aires, 1928); and Rafael de Nogales, *The Looting of Nicaragua* (N.Y., 1928).

[71] Marqués de Lozoya, *Vida del segoviano Rodrigo de Contreras, gobernador de Nicaragua (1534–1544)* (Toledo, 1920); Pablo Alvarez Rubiano, *Pedrarias Dávila* (Madrid, 1944).

[72] See his *Contribución a la historia de Centroamérica: monografías documentales* (2 vols., Managua, 1939).

[73] *Colección Somoza* (Madrid, 1954–7).

[74] *R. de la Academia de Geografía e Historia de Nicaragua*, i/1, 15 Sept. 1936; xviii–xix/1–4, Jan.–Dec. 1959, all in one issue.

[75] *Historia de la Federación de la América Central, 1823–1840* (Madrid).

[76] See ch. iii, n. 32, p. 53, and above, n. 56.

[77] *Cuadernos Universitarios*, founded in 1954 (no. 14, Dec. 1959), is a beginning. See ch. v, n. 116, p. 134.

is perhaps greater than elsewhere in Central America—it extends to the point where the 'big leagues' in the United States are much followed in news reports. Nicaraguan folk music retains more Indian characteristics than that of Honduras. Nicaragua and Guatemala are the only two Central American countries offering distinctive popular music. This small republic has 38 radio stations, the record number in Central America, with exactly half of them located in Managua.[78] There is also one television transmitter.

Luis Delgadillo (b. 1887), Nicaragua's best-known musician, was educated in Italy and has composed music of varied character and inspiration. His *Sinfonía Centroamericana*, first performed in 1921, is based on isthmian themes.[79] A stirring of interest in the visual arts during the last few decades has brought attention abroad to two leaders of the movement, the painter Rodrigo Peñalba and the sculptor Genaro Amador Lira.

The genius of one of her sons has brought Nicaragua fame in the world of literature. He was born in 1867 in a village of Matagalpa department now named Darío in his honour; it is situated on the Inter-American highway. Rubén Darío, as he named himself, spent his youth in Nicaragua and El Salvador; he was also probably acquainted with the connecting corner of Honduras.[80] He moved to Chile in 1886 (earning half a living henceforward by newspaper work) and two years later published *Azul*, a book of stories and poems which brought him attention. He returned to Central America, then travelled to New York and Paris, and lived five years (1893–8) in Buenos Aires. In 1896 appeared his celebrated *Prosas profanas*, which set the standards for Spanish America's first distinct literary movement. Darío himself, conscious of his role, gave the new style the name *modernismo*. The verses he contributed to set the pace have been described as 'aristocratic sentiment, disdainful toward the reality of its time . . . in a poetry exotic, cosmopolitan, reminiscent of art and nostalgic towards historical epochs'.[81]

The frivolous tone, the hedonist tone, the erotic tone prevalent in *Prosas profanas* were typical of Darío's works. The reflective tone then also apparent revealed itself more plainly in his later produc-

[78] See ch. v, n. 118, p. 135. Nicaraguan call letters have the prefix YN. Three stations use 10,000 watts power.
[79] See ch. v, n. 120, p. 136.
[80] Thomas B. Irving, 'San Marcos de Colón', *Univ. de San Carlos*, no. 34 (July–Sept. 1955), 79–92, tells of the traces he found there of Darío.
[81] Enrique Anderson Imbert, *Historia de la literatura hispanoamericana* (Mexico City, 1957), p. 273.

tions.[82] Darío moved on to Paris, where he lived a dissolute life. But from there issued his famed *Cantos de vida y esperanza* setting forth a philosophy of life: 'Art is an adventure in the absolute: . . . almost a mystical mode of knowledge. And the artist, a hero, a demigod suffering in his loneliness.'[83] Darío returned to Nicaragua in 1907, a much imitated and highly praised writer. From there he went to Spain, continuing his writing; years later he travelled to New York. In that city he contracted pneumonia; a few months later, back in Nicaragua again (1916) he died of acute cirrhosis.[84]

Santiago Argüello (1872–1942) was Nicaragua's leading stay-at-home *modernista* following in Darío's footsteps. Argüello was a most prolific writer of both poetry and prose, his first volume of verse appearing in 1897, a review of French literary trends in 1899, a three-act drama in 1906, and a multi-volume collection later in life when he lived in Guatemala.[85] Gustavo Alemán-Bolaños (b. 1884) has written some poetry but is better known for his short novels and pro-Sandino, anti-Somoza writings.[86] Salomón de la Selva (b. 1893), who lived for some time in the United States, translated some of Darío's poems into English and later contributed his own verse in two languages.[87] Hernán Robleto (b. 1892) has tried his hand at several novels from the *yanqui* intervention, through the times of the Second World War, to the recent Somoza period.[88] To the Somoza family, as to the *yanqui* intervention, he is opposed.

RELIGION

The religious situation of western Nicaragua is not unlike that of El Salvador, where a mid-twentieth century revival of interest has

[82] The four 'tones' are presented in Imbert, *Historia de la literatura hispano-americana.*

[83] Ibid. p. 274.

[84] The 8th edition of Darío's *Poesías completas* (Madrid, 1954) is fuller than any of the first seven. See also his *Cuentos completos* (Mexico City, 1950); his *Autobiografía* (5th ed., Madrid, 1945); Arturo Torres Ríoseco, *Vida y poesía de Rubén Darío* (Buenos Aires, 1944); Henry Grattan Doyle, *A Bibliography of Rubén Darío* (Cambridge, Mass., Harvard University Press, 1935); and Julio Saavedra Molina, *Bibliografía de Rubén Darío* (Santiago de Chile, 1945).

[85] *Primeras ráfagas; Siluetas literarias; Ocaso;* all published in León. Vol. 8 of his *Colección guatemalteca* was printed in 1935.

[86] For example, *El país de los irredentos* (Guatemala, 1927); *Los pobres diablos, 1937–1947* (Guatemala, 1947); *La factoría; novela de un américo-hispano en Nueva York* (Guatemala, 1925).

[87] *Eleven Poems of Rubén Darío* (N.Y., 1916); *Tropical Town, and Other Poems* (N.Y., 1918).

[88] *Sangre en el trópico* (Madrid, 1930); *Don Otto y la niña Margarita* (Managua, 1944); *Cárcel criolla* (San José, 1955), in part documented.

taken on only moderate proportions. In the old Nicaraguan Mosquitia on the east coast the picture is quite different, with Protestantism strong and both Catholic and Protestant mission stations hard at work. Altogether, 95·9 per cent of the nation's population was counted Catholic in the 1950 census.[89] But for many in Nicaragua both the labels Catholic and Protestant must be taken in a loose or general sense.

Nicaragua remained officially close to the Catholic church through most of the nineteenth century. The most notable difference between the conservatives who ruled here until 1893 and their liberal contemporaries after the 1870's in Guatemala, El Salvador, and Honduras was the unwillingness of the Nicaraguans to break with the church. Even the Jesuits expelled from Guatemala in 1871 were given refuge here until ten years later when a quarrel led to their expulsion from Nicaragua. A concordat with the papacy reached in 1862 was violated by the Zelaya régime after 1893. The Catholic faith was given special mention in the conservative constitution of 1911, but the free exercise of other cults was guaranteed. The constitutions since 1939 have dropped the special reference, leaving the state officially a secular one like Guatemala, El Salvador, and Honduras.

The Nicaraguan Catholic hierarchy was reorganized in 1913, when Managua became the seat of an archdiocese covering the western two-thirds of the republic. The old bishopric of León was continued under Managua's jurisdiction and a new one added at Granada. A separate vicariate apostolic was established in the same year at Bluefields. A bishopric at Matagalpa was added in 1924. There are 387 Catholic churches in the whole of Nicaragua served by 222 priests. Here there is one priest for every 4,550 Catholics, a far higher ratio than in Guatemala or Honduras and nearly as high as the isthmian record in Costa Rica. Nearly half the priests are members of religious orders.[90]

The Catholic missionary work of the vicariate apostolic of Bluefields has been entrusted since its inception to the Capuchin order of friars. Spanish personnel managed the enterprise from 1913 to 1938, when Capuchins from the United States took over; there are now 28 of them in the field. They are assisted in school work by the Christian Brothers, who have been active in western Nicaragua since 1903. Spaniards were once prominent in the work of the Christian Brothers as in that of the Capuchins, but of the 62 now

[89] *Censo general de población*, xvii. 138.   [90] See ch. v, n. 140, p. 141.

in the field 20 are from the United States and others from various countries. United States Catholic enterprise in Nicaragua also includes 8 Maryknoll Sisters, 6 Carmelite Sisters of the Divine Heart of Jesus, and 6 Sisters of St. Agnes.[91]

Obvious historical circumstance accounts for the fact that while 4·0 per cent of the population of Nicaragua was counted Protestant in 1950, Protestants constituted 36·8 per cent of the people of Zelaya department and 63·6 per cent of those in the *comarca* of Cabo Gracias a Dios.[92] Though the primary motive of the British 'protection' of the Mosquito Coast until 1860 was not the missionary one, Moravians from Germany began work here in 1849. They continued until the First World War, when their North American counterparts took their place. Roughly half of Nicaragua's Protestants are Moravians; 24 missionaries are in the field. Recent reports may read like one from the Sandy Bay district: 'We have had our disappointments as well this year. Quite a number of the people fell under the spell of a sorceress, whom they paid to bless their cassava plantations. . . .'[93] But the more amazing fact is the quite full sense in which many of the Miskito people have become distinctively Moravian.

Ten Protestant churches and agencies have come to Nicaragua since the Moravians, bringing the total of Protestant places of worship to a little over 400.[94] The more sizable efforts are those of the Protestant Episcopal Church, succeeding the Anglicans who came to Bluefields in 1900; the Seventh-Day Adventists, who arrived in 1904; the American Baptists, who came in 1917 and whose work is the strongest on the west coast; the Assemblies of God, whose entry into Nicaragua in 1926 was their first on the isthmus; and the more recently arrived National Baptist Convention and Church of the Nazarene (the latter with 17 missionaries). Also represented are the non-denominational Central American Mission (which was first on the west coast in 1900 but has fewer workers here than in any other Central American republic), the Church of God, the Church of the Foursquare Gospel, and one other small mission from the United States. There were also 14 Mormon missionaries active in this land in 1961.[95]

---

[91] Nicaragua has 21 religious houses for men and 41 for women. See ch. v, n. 141, p. 141.

[92] *Censo general de población*, xvii. 138.

[93] Board of Foreign Missions of the Moravian Church in America, *The Gospel under Palm and Pine: 1960 Annual Report*, p. 18.

[94] See ch. v, n. 145, p. 142.   [95] See ch. v, n. 149, p. 144.

Nicaragua's religious future is as uncertain as her leadership. The Conservative opposition to Somoza still speaks in terms of a renewal of close ties between Nicaragua and the Roman Catholic church. Other forces which might take over when Somoza rule is ended would likely treat Catholics and Protestants alike, even if the treatment were unfriendly. The possibility that sweet reason and morality will prevail during the cutting of the Somoza hold on the nation now seems *only* a possibility.

CHAPTER IX

COSTA RICA

THE 'rich coast' of the south-easterly end of Central America was conspicuously the poorest part of the isthmus in colonial times both in economic resources and in population. Had not the population grown considerably in the eighteenth century, Costa Rica would scarcely have been prepared at the declaration of independence to have assumed her role as one of five juridically equal states.[1] With only 60,000 or 70,000 people upon the assumption of statehood (not much more than one-third of the number in Honduras or Nicaragua) Costa Rica has always remained the smallest of the Central American states in population. Her rate of growth has been the most rapid of all, however, bringing the Costa Rican total to 1 million in 1956 and an estimated 1,076,000 in mid-1958.[2] Three-fourths of Costa Rica's population live in an area measuring 25 miles by 75 about the capital, often called the Meseta Central.[3] But the remainder of the country is so sparsely inhabited that the national population density in mid-1958 was only 55 persons per square mile.

The ancestry of the Costa Rican people is quite different in ratio from that of the other Central American republics but consists of the same basic elements. Less than one-half of 1 per cent of the people were counted as Indians in the 1950 census, nearly 2 per cent as Negroes, and well over 97 per cent as white or mixed.[4] In the highland basins about the capital a great majority of persons are European in stock—wholly so in some instances, in others only preponderantly so with a trace of Indian or Negro also present. In Guanacaste province the Indian strain predominates, as in Nicaragua to which Guanacaste once pertained. On the Caribbean coast a bilingual Negro element is important because of migration

[1] Presumably some of the eighteenth-century increase in population was due to Spanish immigration. The problem raised by the fact that church censuses of the time show a diminution of 'Spaniards' in the province is discussed by Bernardo Augusto Thiel, 'Monografía de la población de la república de Costa Rica en el siglo XIX', pp. 1–52 of *Costa Rica en el siglo XIX* (San José, 1902), p. 9.

[2] See ch. v, nn. 1–3, p. 90.

[3] Robert E. Nunley shows how this came about in *The Distribution of Population in Costa Rica* (Washington, Nat. Acad. Sci., 1960).

[4] *Censo de población de Costa Rica: 22 de mayo de 1950* (San José, 1953), p. 34.

from the British islands and Panama. Of the 33,251 foreign-born residents of Costa Rica counted in 1950, 20,507 came from the remainder of Central America (18,904 from Nicaragua alone), 3,947 from British possessions (chiefly the West Indies), 2,064 from Panama, 1,107 from Spain, 956 from the United States, 610 from Colombia, 586 from China, 564 from Italy, 522 from Poland, 409 from Germany, and 253 from England and Wales.[5]

LOCAL GOVERNMENT

Costa Rica's capital city of San José, second smallest of Central America, held 87,000 residents in 1950 and an estimated 110,000 in mid-1960.[6] Though settlement began in San José only in 1736, its growth was such that it held the largest concentration of people in Costa Rica by the time of independence. San José was made a city in 1813; one year later it became the seat of the educational institution which was to develop into the nation's university. The capital was switched here from Cartago in 1823, but not permanently so until fifteen years later. San José led the other three provincial capitals of the Meseta Central (Cartago, Heredia, and Alajuela) by only a small margin of population until late in the nineteenth century, when its number of inhabitants began to grow rapidly. Public buildings erected at that time tend to set the atmosphere of the heart of the city today; until very recently there were few grand governmental structures such as have characterized the other Central American capitals. San José is today the centre of the republic's commerce and finance as well as its government, and provides a home (together with its several suburbs) for a broad representation of the country's varied population as well as for a large percentage of her foreign residents.

Situated on either side of San José so that a traveller on the Inter-American highway reaches them all in a 30-mile drive are three other cities of Costa Rica. Alajuela with a population of 14,000 in 1950 (18,500 in 1960) is the first encountered as one approaches from the north-west; Heredia (12,000 in 1950; 17,700 in 1960) comes next; then San José; and last Cartago (13,000; 17,800).

[5] Ibid. pp. 88–89.

[6] Urban population figures for Costa Rica are from ibid. pp. 49–55, and 30 June 1960 estimates for the provincial capitals from *Principales Hechos Vitales Ocurridos en Costa Rica* (Dir. Gen. Est. y Censos), no. 22 (1st semester, 1960), p. 15. Costa Rican population centres are not ranked officially as cities, towns, and pueblos. Four *distritos* are considered the city of San José, and two make up Cartago. For the others, the urban count of the corresponding single *distrito* is used. See ch. v, n. 8, p. 92.

Each of these four is a provincial capital whose province spreads far away from this central nestling-place into very primitive country. Cartago, badly damaged by earthquake in 1910, still contains many reminders of the two hundred years when it was the only city of Costa Rica. Heredia founded in 1707 and Alajuela in 1782 are flavoured by the more immediate past, but give no more of an impression than Cartago of mid-twentieth century modernity. All three are based on the agricultural wealth of the country about them, with coffee very important to Alajuela and Heredia.

About the same size as Alajuela, Cartago, and Heredia is Puntarenas (13,000; 18,300), Costa Rica's chief port on the Pacific. Puntarenas, situated at the end of a 4-mile sand spit in the Gulf of Nicoya, was first used as a port in the early nineteenth century; since 1909 it has been connected with San José by railway. Limón, sixth city in size (11,000; 16,000) and the chief port on the Caribbean, was founded in the early 1870's as the terminus for the railway to that coast which was finished in 1890. In the first three decades of the twentieth century, Limón was important as a shipping point for bananas. Puntarenas and Limón are both provincial capitals, as is Liberia, the seventh and smallest in the nation (3,000; 6,000). Liberia developed from a colonial pueblo to take the place of Nicoya as the administrative head of Guanacaste but grew little until the Inter-American highway was finished through the province in 1955. Besides her seven provincial capitals, Costa Rica had in 1950 one urban centre of over 8,000 population, two from 8,000–6,000, and five from 6,000–4,000. All of these save two in the last category were immediate suburbs of San José. The two exceptions were Turrialba, on the railway to Limón, and Golfito, United Fruit shipping point on the Pacific close to the republic of Panama. Another United Fruit port on the Pacific, Quepos, is somewhat smaller than Golfito.

The basic unit of local government in Costa Rica is the *cantón*, roughly the equivalent of the *municipio* in the remainder of the isthmus though somewhat broader in its conception. The *cantón* is divided into *distritos*, there being eleven of the latter in the central *cantón* of San José, for example, only four of which are considered a part of the city. Altogether there are sixty-five *cantones* and 326 *distritos* in the country (1959).[7] Councilmen for the *cantones* are elected locally, but the budgets for all are approved by an officer of the national government.

[7] *An. Est.* (C. R.), *1959*, pp. 14–21.

In place of the department as a midway unit of government, Costa Rica has seven *provincias* or provinces, each one ruled by a governor appointed by the president of the republic. Population densities of the central four Costa Rican provinces are somewhat deceiving because of their geographical lay-out. San José and Cartago, having more of the Meseta Central and less of the outlying wilderness within their borders, rank as the most thickly settled of the country, with 182 and 137 persons to the square mile respectively.[8] Heredia and Alajuela (61, 56) are also densely populated at their southern extremes but contain large expanses of almost uninhabited land extending to the border with Nicaragua. Guanacaste and Puntarenas (32, 30) occupy the Pacific coast from Nicaragua to Panama. Puntarenas consists of two nuclei of territory (one about the Gulf of Nicoya, the other near Golfo Dulce) connected by a strip of ocean frontage nearly 100 miles long and only 6 wide. As in Nicaragua and eastern Honduras, the Caribbean side of the nation with its heavy rainfall is the least populated, Limón province containing only 16 persons to the square mile. One-third of Limón's population were counted as Negroes in 1950 and nearly the same percentage listed English as their mother tongue.[9] Five of Costa Rica's provinces were constituted in 1825. Puntarenas and Limón have been set aside since, first as *comarcas* and then on a par with the others.[10]

DEVELOPMENT OF THE STATE

Costa Rica as a whole, though but a *gobierno* late in the colonial period when Nicaragua, Honduras, and San Salvador had all achieved higher rank, enjoyed an isolation which gave her much freedom of movement at the dawn of independence. Faced with the declarations of Guatemala (freedom from Spain) and of León (freedom from Guatemala), Cartago in October 1821 decided not to hurry its own decisions, but on 1 December issued a 'Social Pact' which provided Costa Rica's first provisional government of her own making. The central cities split ideologically in 1822–3, Heredia and Cartago leaning toward union with imperial Mexico while San José and Alajuela preferred federation with the new

---

[8] Provincial population densities for Costa Rica are computed from population estimates for 31 Dec. 1958, from ibid. *1958*, pp. 11–19, and areas from ibid. *1959*, p. 4. See ch. v, n. 12, p. 94.

[9] *Censo de población: 1950*, pp. 34–35.

[10] All of Costa Rica's provinces have the same name as their capitals except Guanacaste (Liberia).

republic of Colombia to the south. This disagreement led to a battle, through which San José won the capital from Cartago; but in 1823 all parties agreed to co-operate with the new Provincias Unidas del Centro de América. Costa Rica was the second state of the five to organize her own government, her constitution being finished in January 1825. Juan Mora Fernández served as the first *jefe* from 1824 to 1833; none of the other original chiefs of state in Central America lasted beyond 1827. Costa Rica was not rich. Many Costa Ricans were not happy. But while civil war raged elsewhere, this southernmost appendage of the union remained undisturbed. Costa Rica actually seceded from the troubled union in April 1829 but rescinded her action just nine months later.

Tranquillity was put aside in 1835, but for purely local reasons. A decision the year before had assigned the capital to all four cities of the Meseta Central taking turns a year at a time. A new president, Braulio Carrillo (1835–7, 1838–42), preferred to keep the capital in one place (San José), but to gain his point had to rout in battle those who disagreed. Carrillo ruled Costa Rica firmly and arbitrarily, bringing order out of the chaos that had developed and establishing a stable economy based on coffee production, but paying slight regard to the ideals of liberalism on which the Costa Rican state had been built. His second rise to power (1838) was by force. A constitutional convention declared Costa Rica out of the union in November of that year, and in March 1841 Carrillo made himself dictator for life under a 'Plan' which replaced the original constitution.

The lifetime dictatorship lasted just one year, but was followed by a period of confusion from which emerged another *caudillo*. Francisco Morazán, ex-president of the Provincias Unidas, was the person who brought an end to Carrillo's rule in April 1842 and restored the 1825 constitution, but Morazán was executed in September of the same year by forces opposed to his using Costa Rican soil as a base for military operations to restore the union. A new constitution in April 1844 continuing the office of *jefe* came in the middle of a rapid succession of provisional chief executives. Unrest continued through the adoption of two more basic charters, one in January 1847 setting up the office of president with a term of six years, the other in November 1848 designating Costa Rica a republic. Juan Rafael Mora, who rose to the presidency in 1849 to fill out a term, stayed on as chief executive for ten years, re-establishing order and maintaining the forms of democracy without much of the spirit. Mora played a prominent role in the Central American war against William Walker's band in 1856–7, which has made him a national hero. But soon after his third inauguration in 1859 Mora was deposed. Attempting an invasion of his homeland a year later, he was executed eighteen days after the man from Tennessee had met the same fate in Honduras.

Costa Rica had thus far followed two cycles from constitutionality to chaos to dictatorship, and was now entering her third. There is a difference from this point on, however, in that each step backward after 1859 carried with it some gain in the breaking of the pattern. The first achievement was stability in government with an orderly succession of presidents for eight years under a constitution of December 1859 establishing a three-year term. The family of José María Montealegre (president 1859–63) remained dominant during this period, but chose men for office who in the long run were more powerful than the family. The writing of another constitution in February 1869 came on the heels of a political 'double play' by which the Montealegre power was eliminated. (The family supported a coup to oust its own choice, only to have its new candidate turn against it.) Another change in 1870 brought Tomás Guardia to power, himself a dictator at heart, but one who supported the kind of material changes which during his time interested liberals in Guatemala, El Salvador, and Honduras. Under Guardia a new constitution was prepared in December 1871, which had the longest life (seventy-five years, not counting one two-year interruption) of any such document on the isthmus. By its terms, Guardia could not succeed himself in 1876, but he remained as chief military commander, reassumed the presidency in 1877, and held power as he pleased until he died in 1882. The constitution nevertheless survived, as did the railways Guardia built despite powerful opposition. Upon his death, with old family alignments broken, new forces were in a position to take over.

Constitutionalism (a four-year presidential term and a one-house Congress half of whose members were renewed every second year) prevailed for thirty-five years after 1882, though the margin by which it survived was often a very narrow one. Credit for the establishment of the pattern can be given to Bernardo Soto, a nineteenth-century liberal in the European rather than the very restricted isthmian sense, who became president in 1885 on the death of his predecessor and started his own four-year term in 1886. It was Soto's Minister of Education Mauro Fernández who provided the

impetus for the system of free and compulsory public education
which has since gone far toward removing Costa Rica from the
drag of illiteracy. Though Soto was tempted to pave the way for a
successor who would continue his liberal policies, and doubtless
had the power to do so, both he and Ascensión Esquivel (the man
he had chosen) made the decision to step aside when the free vote
they encouraged in 1889 went against them. Thus Costa Rica experienced her first genuine election in which the people at large
took part and her first peaceful transition from a group in power to
the opposition. Only Honduras of the other Central American
countries has ever experienced the latter phenomenon in her history. José Joaquín Rodríguez (1890–4), conservative in sentiment,
ruled Costa Rica without his liberal Congress after 1892, and im-
posed Rafael Iglesias as his successor. Iglesias (1894–1902) had a
subservient Congress change the constitution to make his re-
election possible in 1898, but to avoid catastrophe in 1902 made
an agreement to support liberal Ascensión Esquivel as his successor (1902–6). In a five-way race in 1906, which ended with no
candidate having a majority, Congress declared Cleto González
Víquez elected. González Víquez had the highest number of popular votes, but his election came only after Esquivel had exiled three
candidates who were legally joining forces to prevent González
Víquez from winning. Ricardo Jiménez Oreamuno won by a clear
majority in 1910. But in 1914, when no one of three candidates had
a majority, Jiménez out-manoeuvred all three and managed the
selection by Congress of Alfredo González Flores, who had not even
been in the running. González Flores did not finish his term, but
his five predecessors had completed theirs and in doing so had
brought a degree of soundness to the Costa Rican economy (based
on coffee and bananas) quite unknown in other parts of the isthmus. Short-lived political parties operated quite freely during this
period of Costa Rican history, generally having rather full opportunity to criticize the government though they were often denied
justice at the polls. Most important of all for the eventual triumph
of democracy, though the wealthy class continued definitely in control, the education of the poorer classes in cities and towns was
steadily expanded.

President González Flores, in a weak position from the beginning, took two steps which weakened it still further. One was towards reform of the tax system so as to place a heavier burden
upon the rich; the other was his attempt to control the mid-term

elections to Congress. In January 1917 he found himself out of office as a result of rebellion by his Minister of War Federico Tinoco Granados. Soon Tinoco was elected president and a new constitution prepared (June 1917). Tinoco lacked popularity, however, and failed to win recognition by the United States government. After much difficulty he resigned his office, the 1871 constitution was restored (September 1919), and Julio Acosta García, one of several leaders who had opposed Tinoco by force, became president in his place (1920–4).

The era from 1924 to 1936 in Costa Rican history may be characterized in three fashions: (1) It was the age of 'don Ricardo' and 'don Cleto' of which conservative Costa Ricans still speak with great affection. Ricardo Jiménez Oreamuno served as president from 1924 to 1928, Cleto González Víquez the following four years, and 'don Ricardo' again from 1932 to 1936, their successions marred only by a brief revolt by an unsuccessful candidate in 1932. Both men had served their first terms earlier in the century. Both of them respected the democratic traditions and both supported progressive measures within the framework of nineteenth-century society.

(2) The years from 1924 to 1936 were also the time when dissatisfactions of the mass of the people first showed themselves plainly. The poor life which most Costa Ricans shared with other peoples of the isthmus had slowly become coupled in this land with an awareness of possibilities for change. Forty years of educational effort on the part of the Costa Rican government had borne its natural fruit. Quickest to sense the new public spirit were the Communists, who were organized in Costa Rica in 1929 by a 19-year-old named Manuel Mora Valverde. Five years later, the Communists were strong enought to elect two members of Congress and to lead a strike in the banana zone of Limón province which brought a minimum-wage provision for the workers of that area higher than that prevailing in the rest of the country.

(3) This was likewise an age when some old-time leaders recognized that a new day was dawning. The most important of these men was President Jiménez Oreamuno himself. In 1924, the very first year of his second term, Jiménez sponsored the creation of a National Bank of Insurance (since 1948 called the National Institute of Insurance) to give Costa Ricans better protection than they had enjoyed before, while helping to keep funds within the country. The Bank was given a monopoly of the sale of the various types

of insurance as it deemed itself ready to handle each business. In 1933, during Jiménez' third term, Costa Rica's first minimum wage was set. In 1935 Jiménez received a donation from the United Fruit Company of 250,000 acres of land to be distributed in 50-acre plots to landless farmers. Jiménez had no intention to reorganize Costa Rica's economy, to be sure; but the tone of these actions contrasts quite sharply with actualities of the 1930's in the four other republics of Central America, where *caudillos* who neither understood nor cared for the change such programmes suggested were busy ensconcing themselves in power.

Costa Rica was rapidly maturing politically, to the point where her traditionally ephemeral political groupings (formed only to support one candidate in one campaign) would no longer suffice. The Communist example of continuing political activity between elections was followed by the National Republican party after its formation to support 73-year-old Jiménez in 1932. In 1936 the National Republicans won a clear majority in the presidential contest under the lead of 53-year-old León Cortés Castro, who served for four years while introducing moderate reforms (government stabilization of prices began under Cortés, for example), making arrangements for a new Pacific-coast banana industry, and 'changing the guard' to a generation of younger men enthusiastic for the future. In 1940 the National Republican candidate was Rafael Angel Calderón Guardia, 40-year-old physician with the common touch, who swept the country in a landslide vote.

The contributions of the Calderón régime to Costa Rican public welfare were notable. The radical quality of the new administration frightened many who had supported its rise to power, including ex-president Cortés who now organized the Democratic party in opposition. As he lost some of the support of the moneyed class, Calderón turned toward co-operation with Manuel Mora and his Communist associates who gave him every encouragement. In 1943 the Communist party was dissolved to make way for an organization called the Popular Vanguard (Vanguardia Popular) designed to include Communists and other working-class groups. Such alliances were common in those days when Russia, Central America, the United States, and Great Britain were all engaged in the war against the Axis powers. Even Archbishop Víctor Manuel Sanabria y Martínez said he could not condemn the Popular Vanguard in 1943 or find any objection to Catholic workers joining the organization. President Calderón and Archbishop Sanabria both approved a new section of social guarantees added to the constitution in that year, beginning with these words: 'The State will work for the greatest wellbeing of Costa Ricans, protecting in a special way the family, the basis of the Nation; assuring aid to mothers, children, the aged, and the destitute ill, and organizing and stimulating production and the most adequate distribution of wealth.'[11] Before the end of 1943, Costa Rica had a social-security system and a labour code legislated into existence as beginning steps in implementing the new guarantees.

MID-TWENTIETH CENTURY POLITICS: TRIUMPH OF DEMOCRACY

The working coalition between the small Popular Vanguard and the much larger National Republican party won the presidency in the term beginning 8 May 1944 for Teodoro Picado Michalski, friend of Calderón Guardia prepared to follow through with Calderón's policies. The defeated candidate of the Democratic (conservative) party opposition was León Cortés Castro. The Congress elected in 1944 consisted of 28 delegates from the National Republican party, 13 Democrats, and 4 from the Popular Vanguard. Though the latter were but a small minority, Vanguard members played an active role in the administration of social and labour programmes, attracting much public attention. Opposition to Communist influences in the Picado régime brought about the formation of two new political groupings to contest Congressional elections in 1946—the National Union party of conservative sentiment and the Social Democratic party, which spoke of a Second Republic for Costa Rica, more free and more honest than the first and dedicated to the interests of the mass of its people. The National Union party revolved about the person of Otilio Ulate Blanco, publisher of the *Diario de Costa Rica*, long an enemy of *calderonismo* for its social-action programmes as well as for its alleged ties with Moscow and frauds perpetrated in the 1944 elections.

Prominent in the new Social Democratic organization was José Figueres Ferrer, well-to-do but self-made agriculturist. (His physician-father and teacher-mother had migrated from Spain not long before his birth.) Figueres had lived in Mexico for two years after being forced to leave Costa Rica in 1942, and during this period had shaped a philosophy. Antagonism toward Calderón had brought on his expulsion; in a radio speech, Figueres had attacked

[11] Fitzgibbon, p. 208.

the régime's handling of the war (a United Fruit steamer had been torpedoed by a German submarine at the dock in Limón only four days earlier), its co-operation with Communists, and its proclivities towards spending. Wartime price-fixing and the proposed social security he seemed to ridicule, though perhaps he meant to indicate vexation with their inadequacy rather than alarm concerning their boldness: 'My peons do not have shoes, nor clean sheets, nor milk for their children, but Social Security guarantees them an old age without privations. *Señores del Gobierno:* let us finish the comedy; assure the *costarricenses* a good burial, and let them die of hunger.'[12] Less than a year later Figueres wrote a letter from Mexico City in more positive vein. Highest on a list of objectives for his country which he cited to friends were honesty in government and liberty for the people. Number 3 on the same list was the use of professional civil servants in public administration. Number 4 was 'to give the country a social orientation; to have the state assume gradually . . . the direction of all economic activity, with these objectives: a greater production of wealth and more equity in its distribution'.[13]

The National Union and Social Democratic parties won only one Congressional seat each in the elections of 1946, while Popular Vanguard annexed one more for a total of 5, the National Republicans held 26, and the Democrats 13. After these elections León Cortés Castro made overtures to President Picado for a new alignment of political forces which would isolate the Vanguard party from the government. When Cortés died in the midst of these negotiations, however, opposition to the Picado régime focused on the person of Otilio Ulate Blanco and talk of accommodations with the régime in power ceased. The passage of an income-tax law late in 1946 did not enhance Picado's popularity with the wealthier classes, and the feeling between the party in power and its varied opposition became unusually bitter. Early in 1947 the Democratic, Social Democratic, and National Union parties joined forces with Ulate as leader; that December they decided to go to the elections all under the National Union banner with Ulate the sole opposition candidate for president. Calderón Guardia had decided to seek a second term on the National Republican ticket, and the campaign shaped up as a very turbulent one. Even before the candidates

[12] Arturo Castro Esquivel, *José Figueres Ferrer: el hombre y su obra* (San José, 1955), p. 33.
[13] Ibid. pp. 52–53. The letter was written on 29 March 1943.

were officially chosen, enthusiasts for both sides were clashing in the streets.

In Cartago and San José, on 20–21 July 1947, anti-Calderón demonstrations were dispersed by the police with brutality. The economic life of the nation was then paralyzed by a general stoppage of work called the 'strike of fallen arms' in which very large numbers joined. After nearly two weeks the Picado régime (in a document signed also by the National Republican leadership) agreed to the demands of the strikers, placing the police of the country under the control of the National Electoral Tribunal for any matter pertaining to the campaign, and promising to respect as definitive the decision of this Tribunal as to the outcome of the poll. Elections took place on 8 February 1948. For twenty days the country waited for the Tribunal's decision. Then it was announced that two members had agreed that Ulate had won the presidency by 54,931 votes as against 44,438 for Calderón; the third member of the group contended that still more time was necessary to scrutinize the ballots.[14] Two days later, on 1 March, despite the solemn promises made the previous August, the National Republican majority in Congress by a vote of 27 to 19 decided to annul the elections.

This act was indeed a brazen one, explicable only when one considers the deep bitterness of the epoch. At the end of the meeting of Congress, government forces arrested Ulate and his party chiefs and fatally wounded the physician in whose home Ulate had taken refuge. But the Picado régime did not have the force to impose its will upon an enraged citizenry. After one week during which Ulate was released and Archbishop Sanabria vainly attempted mediation, fighting broke out between the opposing forces. From La Lucha, the country estate of José Figueres on the far side of Cartago, sallied forth a group of armed men to capture San Isidro del General in south-eastern San José province and to conduct sporadic operations against government troops holding the Meseta Central. Figueres' men were fighting for justice to Otilio Ulate Blanco, but under a motto which Ulate had not created: 'We will found the Second Republic!' Finally a group of them called the Caribbean Legion, operating by sea and air, entered the port city of Limón on 11 April. The next day they held Cartago, and on 13 April a cease-fire was arranged so that peace talks could take place to secure a peaceful transition of power. With Figueres' forces surrounding

[14] *New York Times*, 2 Mar. 1948.

the capital and only irregulars following the command of Manuel Mora Valverde still disposed to fight against them, the third-designate for the presidency, Santos León Herrera, succeeded to the position of Picado on 19 April, while the latter and his mentor Calderón Guardia fled to Nicaragua. Figueres entered the cabinet of Herrera on 24 April, and a Founding Junta of the Second Republic took charge of the nation on 8 May. Figueres and Ulate had agreed that the junta would rule with Figueres as its president during the writing of the constitution for the Second Republic, but that the junta would request the constituent assembly to acknowledge Ulate as president of the nation for four years without further election.

The Founding Junta of the Second Republic governed for eighteen months, from 8 May 1948 to 8 November 1949. In December 1948 it had to contend with an invasion force which had been prepared on Nicaraguan soil under the aegis of Calderón Guardia, Picado, and Anastasio Somoza García. With the help of a prompt and thorough investigation by a commission of the Council of the Organization of American States, this conflict was soon ended. The Inter-American Treaty of Reciprocal Assistance under which the investigation was carried out had come into force with Costa Rica's ratification only eight days before the study was requested.[15] In April 1949 there was a short-lived domestic rebellion, handled by the junta alone. Figueres and his companions were interested in much more than preserving the peace, however. Before these two threats arose, in fact, they had dissolved the Costa Rican army, leaving only a police force for protection. The real tone of their civic orientation was shown in the nationalization of Costa Rican banks as one of their first measures.

Fundamentally, [said Figueres] it is the banks which distribute and administer the financial resources by which agriculture, industry, and commerce are fed. . . . The administration of money and credit ought not to be in private hands, any more than the distribution of drinking water or the services of the post office. It is the State, political organ of the Nation, to which correspond these vital functions of the economy. . . . This is a public service, and public should be the ownership of the institutions which manage it.[16]

---

[15] This incident provided not only the first action of the OAS Council under the Treaty, but also the first two articles for the new OAS publication *Américas* in March 1949. They were Hernane Tavares de Sá, 'Test Tube for Peace', i/1, pp. 2–8; and 'How the Río Treaty Works', ibid. pp. 9–11, 47.

[16] Castro Esquivel, pp. 165–6. The speech was made on 19 June 1948.

At the same time as the bank nationalization the junta levied an extraordinary 10 per cent tax on private capital to rehabilitate the nation's administrative structure. A National Council of Production was organized as a separate institution (the name had been used before) to stimulate agricultural activity and stabilize all prices. A state-owned Electric Power Institute was designed to develop the nation's power resources, though private firms in this industry were not eliminated. The Figueres junta likewise prepared a draft of a constitution to serve as the basis of the Second Republic, one which expressed the junta's sentiment for a revision of Costa Rican society. But the *first* bywords of this régime were honesty and liberty, not social reform, and these two concepts in 1949 actually worked temporarily to defeat the more far-going programme that the group had in mind.

Ulate, scheduled to be first president of Costa Rica's 'second republic', had been elected under the banners of the first. The constituent assembly chosen by the people in December 1948, while the junta ruled, was distinctly pro-Ulate rather than pro-Second Republic. The National Union party, in fact, held 33 seats, two other friendly groups 8 seats between them, and the Social Democrats, to whom Figueres belonged, only 4. The constitution suggested by the junta was rejected in March. The one which was written in its stead—the tenth for Costa Rica—took effect on 7 November 1949. Oddly enough, it is since 1957 the oldest of the five constitutions in force in Central America. It says nothing of a second republic, and goes but little beyond the sentiment and even the wording of the charter (as amended in 1943) which preceded it.

New in the 1949 document were sections specifying the absolute control of elections by a Supreme Electoral Tribunal, tightening controls over public finance, and mentioning the existence of autonomous institutions (specifically the state banks and insurance company) and plans for a civil service. Costa Rica's traditional four-year presidential term, interrupted in regularity only twice since the year 1886, was preserved, with the stipulation that the president to be elected in 1953 would serve an extra half-year in order to bring the inauguration date back to a time-honoured 8 May. An article forbidding presidential re-election until eight years had passed has since been amended to cut that waiting period in half. A provision that, in the absence of a majority vote, the president and two vice-presidents are elected by a plurality over 40 per cent is intended to help solve the problem posed by multiple candidates. A Legislative Assembly elected in one body for the four-year term takes the place of the old Congress, half of which was renewed every two years. (The system of proportional representation is followed in elections to the Assembly, though the constitution itself does not require it.) The magistrates of the Supreme Court are chosen by the Legislative Assembly for eight-year terms, and are automatically continued in office unless the Assembly by a two-thirds vote chooses to replace them. The voting age for both men and women, without other qualification, is twenty years. Though the constitution of 1949 is not a revolutionary one by twentieth-century standards, it does (as amplified by the electoral code passed in 1952) provide the apparatus whereby the people can have what they want in government. Under it, Costa Rica has remained remarkably devoted to the real spirit of political democracy. The precedent for the new age had been set by the Founding Junta of the Second Republic, when it accepted gracefully the verdict of the people in December 1948 that further innovation could wait.

Elections for the Legislative Assembly to serve four years concurrently with President Otilio Ulate Blanco were held in October 1949 before the constitution took effect. Ulate's National Union party captured 33 seats as it had in the constituent assembly, while the Social Democrats took 3 and others 9. Ulate took office as scheduled on 8 November 1949. Though the ideas for the innovations of 1948–9 were not his, and though he did not favour the nationalization of the banks, Ulate had in his hands the administration of the programmes which had been adopted. His emphasis in governing was to do well what had to be done rather than to look for new avenues of service. The national economy prospered under his rule, though most Costa Ricans remained very poor. When Ulate presented his last annual message to the Assembly in May 1953, he expressed particular pride in having ruled with complete respect for the legislative authority. He stated too, taking his words from a Chinese expression, that his desire had been to end his term with 'the sabre rusty, the plough bright, the prison idle, and the granary filled'.[17] Without doubt his greatest pride was the table appended below these words and his signature, which showed how Costa Rica's national treasury had enjoyed a modest surplus of revenue from 1936 to 1939, how it had then suffered a deficit every

[17] *Mensaje del señor Presidente Constitucional de la República don Otilio Ulate presentado a la Asamblea Legislativa el 1º. de mayo de 1953* (San José, 1953), pp. 30–31.

year from 1940 through 1948, and how, beginning in 1950, the surplus had reappeared and mounted to heights far above those known previously. It cannot be argued that Ulate as president was a failure in matters which to him seemed important, nor that constitutionalism and democracy were to him a bore.

The group of men about José Figueres Ferrer, most of whom had fought for the right of Ulate to succeed to the presidency in 1948, were not content with the direction politics had taken after their success in battle. Their dedication to the concept of social change, as evidenced by the orientation of the ruling junta in 1948–9, was matched in all Central American history only by that of the Arévalo and Arbenz régimes in Guatemala. The small Social Democratic party which had expressed their goals from 1946 to 1949 was now put aside, as a new Party of National Liberation was formed to fight for the presidency. Figueres stated the general position of the group before it was formally initiated:

Within a hundred years, Americans . . . will not understand . . . how we, in the middle of the twentieth century, with our natural resources, with the present advance of science, and with two thousand years of Christianity, maintained the greater part of our population at an intolerable level of misery. But they will not be able to accuse the men of the Movement of National Liberation of Costa Rica, if some meticulous historian reaches the point of mentioning us, of having been retrogressive. We endure the present economic and social situation of the world, under protest.[18]

Figueres publicly announced his candidacy for the position of president in March 1952, sixteen months before the elections. The following month, when the National Union party of Ulate nominated Mario Echandi Jiménez for the post, dissidents re-formed the Democratic party, which had once constituted the chief opposition to Calderón and Picado, and chose Fernando Castro Cervantes as a third nominee. Echandi had been the foreign minister in Ulate's cabinet; Castro was a wealthy 68-year-old businessman.

As the early campaign progressed through 1952, the pro-Figueres sentiment of the country became obvious. In December his opponents decided to combine forces. Echandi withdrew his candidacy so that the National Union party could support Castro Cervantes. They were joined by the National Republican group of Calderón (who was still outside the country) and eventually by an 'Independent Progressive' group which was excluded from the

[18] From 'Tres años después . . .' published in *La República*, 11 Mar. 1959, as quoted in Castro Esquivel, pp. 265–6.

ballot counting because its rolls included many from the old Popular Vanguard. (This action was taken by the Assembly over the protest of President Ulate.) The campaigning continued through the first half of 1953, with the National Liberation party depicting a series of far-reaching goals toward which it intended to work on both the domestic and international fronts, and the opposition favouring a much more conservative approach.[19] With lines of divergency thus made entirely clear, the Costa Rican people on 26 July gave Figueres nearly twice the vote they accorded Castro Cervantes. Candidates for the Legislative Assembly were chosen in the same proportion, 30 seats going to the National Liberation forces (including the nation's first three women deputies) and just half that number to the combined opposition. The Democratic party won 11 of the seats, the National Republicans 3, and the National Union only one, a notable come-down from their previous majority. Fernando Castro Cervantes conceded his defeat with grace, as the Figueres enthusiasts had conceded in the assembly elections four and five years earlier.

The Figueres régime which administered the country from 8 November 1953 to 8 May 1958 proved a moderate one. Moderate, that is, measured by the fears of those who had fought its coming to power most vehemently; moderate as measured by the set of goals enunciated during the campaign, many of which could only be proposed as goals and not as immediate measures; moderate even when held up against its own beginnings, for the Figueres junta of 1948–9 and the first year of the new régime were far more earth-shaking than that which followed. The pace had been set in 1948 by the nationalization of the banks. It seemed to be just as fast in 1954, when the nation's contract with the United Fruit Company was re-negotiated greatly to the nation's advantage; when a National Institute of Housing and City-Planning (Instituto Nacional de Vivienda y Urbanismo, or INVU) was set up to tackle urban problems; and especially when the top income-tax rates were doubled and action taken to raise minimum wages. Invasion from Nicaragua in January 1955 and severe floods the following October, however, brought on financial difficulties not easy to handle. The years after 1955 were devoted largely to an implementation of programmes already undertaken.

---

[19] Details of the campaign are presented by Harry Kantor, quite sympathetic to the Figueres candidacy, in *The Costa Rican Election of 1953: a Case Study* (Gainesville, Univ. of Florida Press, 1958).

Altogether, it was the hardest-working and heaviest-spending administration Costa Rica had ever known, propelled in many offices by a very high tone of national pride and ambition. There were problems, including that of land reform, which by 1958 the régime had hardly begun to tackle. But those which were treated first were certainly among the most basic. The opposition from moneyed families was strong even on most elementary matters. After the raising of wages (though new minima remained at a very low level) President Figueres felt constrained to point out 'that the prognostications of conservative people that the raising of daily wages would result in a greater sale of liquor have not been realized. On the contrary, the consumption of milk and meat has grown, of rice and beans, bread, eggs. . . .'[20] But opposition on such a plane was only an indication of the tremendous problems a régime such as this one faces if it is to act realistically in lifting the level of a nation. The financial standards of the régime, which left no deficit to burden future generations, made its task all the more difficult.[21]

At the end of his period Figueres indulged in some modest self-congratulation: 'The economic level of Costa Rica has risen more than in comparable countries. Meanwhile the prices of articles of popular consumption have risen less. . . . We have succeeded in keeping our currency stable. . . .'[22] Yet well over half his final message to the Legislative Assembly dealt with problems which remained unsolved: 'We leave owing to the country one institution more: the Institute of Lands and Colonies. . . . Costa Rica cannot avoid the agrarian conflicts which have scourged other countries, if she does not count with the mechanism which can bring justice to landless *campesinos*. . . .'[23] Whatever the human frailties of the men and women who composed the government during his term, an amazing number of them shared their leader's spirit. The second republic, it might be said, had experienced a spiritual birth even though it had missed its baptism.

Costa Rica by 1955 had counted three elections in a row (1948, 1949, and 1953) in which the group in executive authority had bowed to the success of another party. Ample room had been made

[20] *Mensaje del señor Presidente de la República don José Figueres . . . 1º. de mayo de 1955* (San José, 1955), pp. 11–12.

[21] Expenditures rose from 165 million colones in the fiscal year 1952 to 289 million in 1957, but receipts at the same time rose from 189 million to 298 million. See the *Memoria Anual* of 1959 of the Ministerio de Economía y Hacienda, p. 52.

[22] *Mensaje del señor Presidente de la República don José Figueres . . . 1º. de mayo de 1958* (San José, 1958), p. 4.

[23] Ibid. p. 7.

in the electoral combat of 1953 even for the followers of Rafael Calderón Guardia, who had stepped out of politics so ungracefully in 1948. The *calderonistas* in fair contest in 1953 won only 3 seats out of 45 in the Legislative Assembly. Yet on 11 January 1955 a group of them were bold enough to appear on Costa Rican soil only 35 miles from the capital in open rebellion against the established régime. They had come from Nicaragua. The Council of the Organization of American States voted three days later to 'condemn the acts of intervention of which Costa Rica is victim and call attention to the grave presumption that there exist violations of international treaties in force'.[24] The party (who was not named) guilty of the violations (which did exist) was Anastasio Somoza García, president of Nicaragua and friend of Calderón Guardia, who had given the latter much assistance in the preparation and launching of the invasion. Action of the investigating committee of the Council in requesting planes to be used for field observation brought a quick end to danger to the Figueres régime; the committee then continued its work until hostilities were ended along the boundary.[25] The handling of this case by the Organization of American States, it may be noted, differed substantially from its lack of prompt action half a year earlier when Guatemalan insurgents invaded Guatemala.

Even without military invasion and the disastrous floods which came later in the same year, the Figueres régime needed more than one term to pursue its programme of reform. Figueres himself favoured as his successor in the chief executive position a lifetime friend and companion, Francisco José Orlich, his Minister of Public Works. Unfortunately for the success of Orlich at the polls, the position was also coveted by Jorge Rossi Chavarría, Figueres' Minister of Finance. The rift which developed between Orlich and Rossi during the year 1956 encouraged division in the National Liberation party between those who spoke most of continued reform after the next election and those who stressed that more time was needed to implement measures already taken. Figueres and Orlich placed themselves on the left wing during this discussion, while Rossi headed the more conservative faction. In March 1957, after Figueres had made his support for the candidacy of Orlich

[24] 'Costa Rica–Nicaragua Situation', *Ann. OAS*, vii (1955), 141–60, 233–5, p. 157. This report is concluded in 'Situation between Costa Rica and Nicaragua', ibid. viii (1956), 183–90.

[25] An account is given in 'Costa Rica and the Invasion: Difficulties of a Central American Democracy', *World Today*, xi (1955), 129–38.

very plain, Rossi and three other ministers resigned from the cabinet and organized the Independent party to contest both presidential and Assembly elections.

In January 1957, more than a year before the elections, the National Union party which had done so poorly in 1953 chose Mario Echandi Jiménez as its candidate. Echandi had played the same role for National Union in 1953 until he withdrew in favour of Castro Cervantes. A man of wealth and aristocratic lineage, he had served as foreign minister under Ulate and as a member of the opposition in the Legislative Assembly during Figueres' term. His personal distaste for the latter administration was so strong that in 1955 he sympathized with the invasion by Calderón to the extent that he was charged with treason. The *calderonistas* in the campaign of 1957–8, while running their own slate of delegates (now under the name Republican) for the Assembly, chose to back Echandi for president. Three tiny parties did the same, while most of the Democratic party active in 1953 remained entirely inside the National Union fold. Echandi spoke during the campaign of his faith in private enterprise and of his preference for a partly denationalized banking system, but he did not propose to undo most of Figueres' programme.

Thus in the presidential contest held on 2 February 1958, the Costa Rican voters could choose between Echandi's mild opposition to the programme of reform, Rossi's mild support, and Orlich's planning for its extension. The campaign had been conducted with a remarkable lack of recrimination.[26] President Figueres set a precedent by inviting three outsiders from a list suggested by the United Nations (a law-school dean from Halifax, Nova Scotia; a newspaper publisher from Stockholm; and the president of the Supreme Electoral Tribunal of Uruguay) to observe the elections. Of 354,779 persons registered to vote, 221,549 voted for a candidate for president—102,851 for Echandi; 94,788 for Orlich; and 23,910 for Rossi. Of the ballots cast for party lists for the Legislative Assembly, National Liberation captured 86,081; the Republican party 46,171; National Union 44,125; the Independent party 20,314; a small group called the Revolutionary Civic Union 6,855; and the three tiny parties a total of 2,970.[27] Because of Rossi's defection from National Liberation ranks, Echandi had won the

[26] Paul P. Kennedy, observer for the *New York Times*, wrote (2 Feb. 1958): 'The oldest observers cannot remember an election in which so little bitterness and so few physical clashes have been noted.'

[27] Figures provided by the Costa Rican Tribunal Supremo de Elecciones.

presidency with 46·42 per cent of the total vote. (The Orlich percentage was 42·79.) In the Assembly, National Liberation held 20 seats compared with 11 taken by the Republicans and 10 by National Union. The balance of power, as long as party discipline would prevail, clearly rested with the 3 seats held by the Independents of Rossi and the one taken by the Revolutionary Civic Union. Whatever the outcome of the balloting, with the concession of defeat made by Orlich on 8 February democracy in Costa Rica had won another triumph. The *New York Times* was led to comment editorially:

The elections for President and the Legislative Assembly in Costa Rica were a model of what democratic elections can and should be. This was a splendid example for Latin America as a whole and one that we could expect from such a democracy as Costa Rica and such a confirmed champion of liberty as President José Figueres.[28]

President Mario Echandi took office on 8 May 1958. Two years later he could say: 'Another year has passed in the life of the Republic without its democracy suffering eclipse or retrocession; on the contrary, it has lived more than ever strengthened and in full function. . . . One year more of free institutional movement. . . .'[29] Because of his own weak position in the Assembly, his difficulties had been many. Deficits in the budget, caused by continuing high expenditures at a time when receipts (owing to causes beyond Echandi's control) were lower, made for particular troubles. Only slowly, because of statutory regulations concerning their autonomy, was Echandi able to gain control over several of his own governing institutions. Civil service had become a reality and posed its own problems as many government employees remained loyal to the president's opponents. But Echandi had accepted the Costa Rican government organization as he had found it, and was willing to abide by the rules. By late 1959, through some changes in sympathy, he could often command 23 of the 45 votes in the Legislative Assembly, and by 1960 he was coming into control of various governing boards as older members rotated out of office. He did not move toward a denationalization of the banking system; instead he surprised observers by moving briefly at one point toward a more complete nationalization of the nation's power resources. His general policies have been simply to administer that which he found;

[28] 5 Feb. 1958.

[29] *Mensaje del señor Presidente de la República Lic. don Mario Echandi presentado a la Asamblea Legislativa el 1°. de mayo de 1960* (San José, 1960), p. 3.

in doing so he has brought progress to Costa Rica. Despite much criticism, he has made it difficult for Nicaraguan refugees to use Costa Rican soil in attacks against the neighbouring government. To defend this policy he has only to point to many international agreements. His position in the matter is weakened only by the preference he showed for the invaders of his home country in 1955 who were acting in contravention of the same agreements.

Costa Rica is the only nation of the five in Central America which allows its presidents to serve only four years. One year out of every four seems destined to be devoted to straight politics. In January 1961 ex-president Otilio Ulate Blanco became the presidential candidate of National Union for the elections of February 1962. One month later Francisco José Orlich received the nomination of National Liberation; the party contest was lively, with Orlich (now the more moderate of two choices) catching only three votes for each two going to Daniel Oduber Quirós. The 1958 split in National Liberation appeared to be healed. The Republican party was slower to decide its course of action. On the occasion of a visit to Costa Rica by a distinguished statesman in February 1960, President Echandi had sat at dinner with ex-presidents Figueres, Ulate, and Calderón Guardia, a most remarkable combination. The dinner was no augury of tranquillity through the 1961 campaign, which instead promised to be a determined one. But it was difficult to believe as this campaign began that it could terminate in anything more or less than the free verdict of a people as to which persons and policies should prevail for another four years of administration.

BOUNDARIES AND BUDGETS

Costa Rica's frontier with Nicaragua, which separates régimes so very unlike, is settled on a *modus vivendi* basis only, as was explained in the chapter on Nicaragua. Costa Rica's other short frontier, that with Panama, was settled by treaty between the two countries in 1941 after more than a hundred years of spasmodic negotiation. At the break of independence, the government in Colombia (of which Panama was then a part) had a paper claim to the whole of Costa Rica, based on the decision of King Charles IV of Spain in 1803 to include the Mosquito Coast in Bogotá's jurisdiction. Colombia gave up claim to virtually all land now included in Costa Rica as early as the first boundary treaty (of 1856) between them. Details concerning sections of land on the Caribbean coast held up full agreement, however, through other unratified treaties and arbitration, until Panama in 1903 inherited Colombia's side of the dickering. Thirty-eight more years were needed for the final solution. Little Coco Island (3 miles by 5) lying 300 miles south-west of the isthmus at 5° 30′ North Latitude and 87° West Longitude is recognized as Costa Rican territory by both Colombia and Panama. Coco has but few people.

Costa Rica's less stable boundary, that on the north with Nicaragua, separates her from a régime as dissimilar in budgets as in general management. Costa Rica's government revenue has for some time been the highest per capita of all Central America. Receipts in the calendar year 1939 were 43 million colones or $8 million; in 1944, $9 million; in 1949, $22 million; in 1954, 234 million colones or $35 million; in 1958, $48 million.[30] Customs duties contribute a very important part of this money (55 per cent in 1939, 60 per cent in 1958), a ratio of 9 : 1 prevailing between import taxes and export taxes in 1958. Costa Rica's income tax, levied in 1946, and a property tax together brought in 18 per cent of the revenue in 1958. Levies on coffee processing and liquor consumption accounted for a great deal of the rest.[31]

United States aid to Costa Rica has been generous. In 1946–50 it reached a total of $3 million; in 1951–5, $9 million; in 1956 alone, $2 million; 1957, $5 million; 1958 and again 1959, $8 million; in 1960 it dropped to $3 million. The total for the period 1946–60 was $39 million, the highest for any of the Central American countries except Guatemala. A very large share of this ($27 million) was for highways, chiefly the Inter-American. Another $11 million was for economic and technical assistance, and only $9 *thousand* for the military.[32] Technical-assistance and children's-relief programmes of the United Nations brought Costa Rica $1 million in 1954–8.[33] At the same time, she received loans from the International Bank for Reconstruction and Development and the United States Export–Import Bank.

The Costa Rican national budget planned for the year 1961 amounted to a total of 345,750,900 colones or $51,992,617 (at 6·65 colones to the dollar). By far the largest allotment direct to one of the ten ministries was the 22 per cent planned for the Minis-

[30] U.N., *Stat. Yb.*, *1951*, pp. 476–7; *1958*, p. 469; *1959*, p. 496. Figures are converted to the nearest million dollars at 5·65 colones to the $ in 1939–49 and 6·65 in 1954–8.
[31] See ch. v, n. 43, p. 111.   [32] See ch. v, n. 44, p. 111.
[33] U.N., *Stat. Yb.*, *1959*, p. 423.

try of Public Education. The other ministries with their portions were in turn as follows: Public Works 8 per cent; Government, Police, Justice and Ecclesiastical Affairs 5 per cent; Economy and Finance 5 per cent; Public Security 4 per cent; Public Health 3 per cent; Agriculture and Livestock 2 per cent; Foreign Relations 1 per cent; Labour and Social Welfare 1 per cent; and Industries less than one-half of 1 per cent. Other large allotments in this budget were 14 per cent for the public debt, 6 per cent for subventions to the municipalities, 5 per cent for the judiciary, 4 per cent to cover as an extra the additional salary granted public servants early in the term of Figueres, 3 per cent to the University of Costa Rica, 2 per cent to the Supreme Electoral Tribunal, and 2 per cent to INVU, which was busy building houses.[34] Expenditures for education, health, and social-welfare programmes in Costa Rica rose from 20 per cent of the budget in 1938 to 45 per cent just twenty years later. Those for defence dropped in the same period from 7 to 4 per cent.[35] Recent differences in budget emphasis between Costa Rica and her Central American neighbours are simply startling. While the others have moved generally in the same directions, the most advanced of them all has demonstrated how far they have yet to go in state assistance to their needy populations.

SUBSISTENCE AGRICULTURE

The changes taking place in Costa Rica's social structure have been mirrored only to a small extent in her basic industry, agriculture. Costa Rica has a smaller proportion of her economically active population engaged in farming than any other nation on the isthmus, the figure in 1950 being 54 per cent.[36] Yet some 2,427,000 acres, or one-fifth of the national territory, were reported as devoted to active farming in the agricultural census year 1950, a fraction not far different from that of Guatemala, Honduras, and Nicaragua.[37] And though Costa Rica is known for both her coffee and bananas sent abroad, and also ships a lively export of cacao, nine-tenths of her active farming area until very recently was devoted to immediate subsistence needs, as elsewhere in Central America.[38]

Costa Rica differs from her neighbours in her comparative lack

---

[34] *Ley de presupuesto ordinario de la república, para el año 1961* (San José, 1960), pp. 3, 45, 47–52, 55.
[35] U.N., *Stat. Yb., 1959*, p. 496.   [36] *Censo de población: 1950*, pp. 45–46.
[37] *Estruct. agr.*, p. 115.
[38] Since 1954 the subsistence ratio has changed somewhat owing to a developing export of cattle.

of interest in maize. This crop was raised in Costa Rica in 1950 on only 136,000 acres or 6 per cent of the nation's active farm area, barely one-half of the space per capita reported from Nicaragua and one-third that of Guatemala, El Salvador, and Honduras. An agricultural census of 1955 showed that the area devoted to maize had dropped to 124,000 acres, somewhat less than the space occupied by Costa Rican coffee. The maize yield in 1955 was less than 850 lb. to the acre. Neither is the crop as widespread as elsewhere on the isthmus, almost two-thirds of it in 1955 being grown in three provinces, Guanacaste, San José, and Puntarenas. Nevertheless maize remains the most important ground crop of the nation, a second harvest annually amounting to about one-fifth of the first.[39]

Costa Rican beans occupied 68,000 acres or half the space devoted to maize in 1950, and 83,000 acres or two-thirds of the maize holdings in 1955. Well over half the bean crop is raised in the two provinces of San José and Puntarenas, the two harvests a year in the country being about equal. Rice is also a major crop, covering 57,000 acres in 1950 and 63,000 in 1955. Two-thirds of the rice is grown in Puntarenas and Guanacaste, a second harvest amounting to one-fifth of the first. Sugar-cane is important (49,000 acres in 1950; 48,000 in 1955), almost all of it being grown in Alajuela, Cartago, and San José. Other ground crops of some consequence (in decreasing order according to space devoted to their cultivation in 1955) are cassava, potatoes, tobacco, sesame, cotton, tomatoes, peanuts, cabbage, onions, and garlic.[40] Cotton is less important to Costa Rica than to any of the other nations of Central America.

Costa Rican tree and bush crops covered 328,000 acres in 1950 and 385,000 in 1955. Coffee alone was found on 121,000 acres in 1950 and 139,000 in 1955. Bananas of types preferred in Costa Rica plus the plantains of the country were grown on 103,000 acres in 1955, almost half of them in San José and Alajuela, where the plants are used for shade for coffee. Bananas and cacao for export occupied another 58,000 and 49,000 acres respectively in 1955. Other tree and bush crops (in decreasing order according to the acreage

[39] *Estruct. agr.*, p. 170; *Censo agropecuario de 1955* (San José, 1959), pp. xxxix, 26, 28, 30, 46. One *fanega* of maize in Costa Rica is 768 Spanish lb. or 778·75 lb. avoirdupois. No allowance is made for acreage duplication in the two harvests of maize or where maize is interplanted with other crops.

[40] *Estruct. agr.*, p. 170; *Censo agropecuario de 1955*, pp. 18, 20, 22, 24, 32, 34, 52, 170–8, 185–90. No allowance is made for acreage duplication in the two harvests of beans and rice or where these two are interplanted with other crops.

involved in 1955) are coconuts, oranges, avocados, pineapples, and papayas.[41]

Costa Rica reported 928,000 acres of natural pasturage in 1950, another 619,000 acres of cultivated pasturage, and 216,000 acres of other farm land at rest. The following counts of domestic animals are for 1950 and 1955 respectively: cattle 608,000 and 705,000; pigs 115,000 and 102,000; horses 78,000 and 88,000; mules 8,000 in both censuses; goats and sheep 2,000; and donkeys less than 500. Some cattle have been exported in recent years to Peru and Colombia. In 1950 the barnyard inventory included 901,000 chickens; 17,000 ducks and geese; and 14,000 turkeys. There were also 16,000 swarms of bees.[42]

EXPORTS AND IMPORTS

Costa Rica like Guatemala and El Salvador, and unlike Honduras and Nicaragua, grew a crop for export early in her separate history. She was unique furthermore among the Central American nations in developing the same export crop in the first half of the nineteenth century that provides her chief source of foreign exchange today. That item was coffee; and though both Guatemala and El Salvador surpass Costa Rica in total coffee production, neither sold as much per capita as did Costa Rica in 1958. Costa Rica has a strong lead among the Central American nations in total trade per capita, her exports in 1958 amounting to $85 for each person as compared with a figure of $38 for the other four republics combined.[43]

Coffee was known in Costa Rica before the end of the colonial period. It was first exported in the 1830's, three decades before El Salvador began the practice and four before Guatemala did. Braulio Carrillo during his second presidency (1838–42) encouraged the industry by offering land for coffee growing. Shipments to Europe by way of the passage around Cape Horn in South America began in the 1840's. The trade grew quite steadily until the 1870's, spurted again when the railway was completed to the Caribbean in 1890, and increased rapidly starting in the 1920's. Coffee accounted for 51 per cent of the total value of Costa Rica's exports in the period 1956–9.[44]

[41] *Estruct. agr.*, p. 221; *Censo agropecuario de 1955*, pp. 8, 38, 46, 52, 54, 209–17, 260–2, 264–6, 270–2. Abacá is also grown but was not reported in the census.

[42] *Estruct. agr.*, pp. 116, 283; *Censo agropecuario de 1955*, pp. 56, 63, 65, 67.

[43] U.N., *Yb. Int. Trade Stat., 1959*, i. 153, 184, 250, 258, 392. See ch. viii, n. 33, p. 239.

[44] Ibid. p. 153.

The large coffee estate is important in Costa Rica as in El Salvador. In 1955, the *fincas* of 100 *manzanas* (172·6 acres) or more, being 7·2 per cent of the number growing coffee, reported 44 per cent of the total production. Farms from 50 *manzanas* (86·3 acres) to 99·9 in area made up 9·3 per cent of the total number and provided 13 per cent of the production. A more important role than in El Salvador is played by the farmer with 10 *manzanas* (17·26 acres) to 49·9 who grew 25 per cent of the coffee in 1955, and by the still smaller farmer who grew over 17 per cent. Almost all the coffee is grown on the Meseta Central, San José province contributing more than one-third of the total, followed in turn by Alajuela, Cartago, and Heredia.[45] Coffee cultivation in Costa Rica has always been in the hands of native families, while banana, cacao, and abacá exports, developed more recently, are controlled to a large extent by foreigners. Since the coffee harvest comes almost exclusively from the four provinces which touch the Meseta Central while the bananas, cacao, and abacá for export are derived from the soils of Puntarenas and Limón, provincial statistics provide some measure of the economic opportunities for workers employed by their countrymen on the one hand and those employed by outsiders on the other. The average farm worker in Heredia province who had employment two or more days during the week before the agricultural census of 1955 received $1·49 U.S. for his week's labours; in San José province $1·50; in Alajuela $2·10; in Cartago $2·78.[46]

The organized sale of bananas, like the export of coffee, began in Costa Rica before it extended to other parts of the isthmus. Though some bananas were shipped from Costa Rica to New Orleans as early as the 1870's, their cultivation on a large scale was started by Minor Keith in the following decade as a project to make the railway he was building from Limón to the Meseta Central a profitable venture. The banana company formed by Keith was one of those merged to form the United Fruit Company in 1899, and Keith himself became vice-president of United Fruit. Banana exports from Costa Rica rose quite steadily until 1913, by which time the Panama disease had become a scourge in the area about Limón. Production then declined until the 1930's, when United Fruit began developing new properties in Puntarenas about the ports of Quepos and Golfito. The Golfito district and another small area

[45] *Censo agropecuario de 1955*, pp. 46, 230.
[46] Ibid. pp. 322–4. Conversions are made at 6·65 colones to the dollar.

on the Caribbean end of the Panama border (the latter serviced by railway to Panama) enable Costa Rica to maintain third place among banana exporting nations of the world today, surpassed only by Ecuador and (in most years) Honduras. In the good year 1958, with bananas as with coffee, Costa Rica's export per capita was the highest in Central America. In the period 1956–9 bananas and plantains accounted for 33 per cent of Costa Rica's total value of exports.[47]

While other Central American nations have in recent years developed sizable exports of cotton, Costa Rica has been entering the market for cacao. Twice as much cacao was sold from here in 1959 as in 1956, the total for the period 1956–9 amounting to 6 per cent of Costa Rica's exports. Virtually all of the cacao is grown on lands formerly devoted to bananas in Limón province, the United Fruit Company having taken the initiative in the new enterprise both on its own lands and through assistance to independent farmers. A declining quantity of abacá has also been sent out in the 1950's from Limón by United Fruit and Standard Fruit (which has purchased some of United's properties), amounting to more than $1 million a year until 1959. The United Fruit Company in Costa Rica, though it has been involved from time to time in labour difficulties and in controversy with the state, has made decisions sufficiently liberal in each case to provide a new *modus vivendi* and a better deal for both its workers and the nation at large. President Figueres in 1953 spoke of the possibility of the government's purchasing United's properties, but in 1954 he settled for a larger payment of income tax by the corporation (setting a precedent for other isthmian states), for fewer special privileges for the company than were formerly allowed, and for the transfer to the state of many of United's welfare enterprises. Farm workers who were employed two or more days in the week before the census of 1955 in Puntarenas province, from which come most of Costa Rica's exported bananas, earned an average of $6·34 during the week; those in Limón, from which are derived some bananas, most of the cacao, and all the abacá, earned $7·49. These figures compare quite favourably (there being no comparable difference in prices) with the averages of $1·49 to $2·78 in the other five provinces, though for a people who buy over half their imports from the United States of America they are certainly not extravagant.[48] The dis-

[47] U.N., *Yb. Int. Trade Stat., 1959,* i. 153, 257.
[48] Ibid. p. 153; *Censo agropecuario de 1955,* pp. 260–2, 322–5. See n. 46 of this

parity between agricultural wages paid in Limón and Puntarenas on the one hand and in the other five provinces on the other seems an indication of two factors in the Costa Rican economy: (1) the combined forces of government and strong labour unions, together with a growing enlightenment in Boston headquarters, have during the last thirty years brought some real improvement in living standards to Costa Rican United Fruit families and the areas in which they reside. (2) The same forces have not been equally brought to bear upon wealthy Costa Rican employers, especially in the coffee industry, who have been reluctant to pay a living wage to their own countrymen.

Costa Rica's miscellany of minor exports after coffee, bananas, and cacao, amounting to 10 per cent of the total, includes besides abacá the item of livestock, which sold for over $2 million in 1957 and 1958. Costa Rica's total exports in 1956–9 averaged $83,100,000 annually, going 49 per cent to the United States, 25 per cent to Germany, 6 per cent to Canada, 3 per cent to the Netherlands, and 2 per cent each to Italy, Belgium-Luxembourg, and Peru.[49]

Nineteenth-century predominance of Great Britain in Costa Rica's import trade has given way, as in the remainder of Central America, to the lead of other countries, though the portion remaining for the United Kingdom is slightly higher than elsewhere on the isthmus. Costa Rican imports in 1956–9 averaged $99 million annually, coming 52 per cent from the United States, 10 per cent from Germany, 6 per cent from the United Kingdom, 4 per cent each from Japan, the Netherlands Antilles (petroleum products), and the Netherlands, 3 per cent from Canada, and 2 per cent each from Belgium-Luxembourg, France, and Italy. The imports of 1959, as reckoned by the categories of the Standard International Trade Classification, were roughly the same in nature as those of the rest of Central America: Manufactured goods made up 29 per cent of the total, with more than $9 million spent for textile fabrics; over $4 million each for metal manufactures and for iron and steel; over $3 million for paper products; and over $1

chapter. The earnings figure for Guanacaste is $1.58. *Indice de Precios al por Menor* (Dir. Gen. Est. y Censos), no. 102 (Dec. 1960) shows food and clothing prices considerably *lower* in the vicinities of Golfito, Quepos, and Limón than in the capital. Food prices in the three coastal zones are roughly equal to an average on the Meseta Central and clothing prices somewhat higher, but far from the difference in wages.

[49] U.N., *Yb. Int. Trade Stat., 1959*, i. 153–4.

million each for rubber manufactures and cement. Machinery and transport equipment comprised 25 per cent, with over $6 million for road motor vehicles; over $5 million for electric machines and appliances; over $2 million for tractors; and over $1 million each for construction and mining machinery, for power-generating machinery, and for aircraft. Chemicals amounted to 15 per cent, with over $4 million each for fertilizers and for medicinal and pharmaceutical products, and over $1 million each for cosmetics and soap and for insecticides. Food was another 15 per cent, with over $6 million for cereals, and over $1 million each for animal feeds, margarine and shortenings, dairy products, and fruits and vegetables. Lesser categories were manufactured articles other than machinery and transport (8 per cent) with over $2 million for clothing; and fuels and lubricants (6 per cent) with over $5 million for petroleum products.[50]

NON-AGRICULTURAL OCCUPATIONS

The fact that 45 per cent or nearly half of Costa Rica's economically active population in 1950 was not engaged in farming does not indicate the existence of other major industries. Manufacturing accounted for only 11·0 per cent of the group in 1950, a somewhat smaller proportion than in Guatemala, El Salvador, and Nicaragua. Costa Rica surpassed the others significantly, however, in service occupations (14·8 per cent), trade (7·9 per cent), construction (4·3 per cent), and transport (3·5 per cent).[51]

A manufacturing census taken in 1951 included 3,247 establishments with 18,491 employees. Nearly half the number of both (1,445 businesses with 8,955 workers) were engaged in the processing of foodstuffs—chiefly wheat, coffee, and sugar, but with canneries and dairies more important than in the remainder of the isthmus. There were 663 plants and 2,713 people engaged in the footwear and apparel industry. The lumber industry was the only other one involving more than 1,000 people. The average salary paid for the year to all the employees included in the 1951 census was only $265.[52] A selection of 36 food and beverage plants in 1958 paid an average of $1,826 for the year to 61 persons classified as technical personnel, $1,303 to 243 administrative employees, and $551 to

[50] Ibid. pp. 152–4. [51] *Censo de población: 1950*, p. 45.
[52] *Investment in C.A.*, p. 69, with data based on *Censo de comercio e industrias de 1952* (San José, 1954). See above, n. 46.

1,500 remaining workers and apprentices.[53] The latter sampling seems in accord with an average of $44·56 per month reported earned in manufacturing in Costa Rica in 1957, and is not remarkably higher than a comparable figure of $35·85 for Honduras in the same year.[54]

Gold, rather widespread in the form of ornaments in fifteenth-century Costa Rica, is little found today, though gold and magnesium are among the few minerals Costa Ricans have worked. This end of the isthmus lacks the pine forests of Honduras and Nicaragua, and cuts wood mainly for its own use. The first exciting oil strike in Central America was made in Costa Rica in January 1956 at the hamlet of Cocoles, on the Caribbean side and very near the Panamanian border. For several months the well held forth some promise of providing a 'rich coast' of which Columbus never dreamed. But by the end of the year the flow of petroleum had become a trickle, and enthusiasm had dwindled correspondingly.

Costa Rica's highway system has developed in two stages. Asphalt connexions between the four cities of the Meseta Central were developed as early as any on the isthmus. Their age is betrayed today by their inadequacy; they are much travelled but narrow and tortuous. Plans are made for a modern highway to ease their load through the area. It was not until May 1955, however, that Costa Rica's north-western section of the Inter-American highway was completed, giving all-weather road access for the first time to the remainder of Central America. A paved strip now runs from Nicaragua's department of Rivas by Liberia and Puntarenas to Alajuela, Heredia, San José, and Cartago. From Cartago to Panama's Chiriquí the road was not finished at the end of 1960, but was in advanced stages of construction. When completed, it will be the last link to be put into place of a through passage-way for cars, trucks, and buses from Canada and the United States to the Panama Canal. Except for several more short roads on the Meseta Central and one all-weather connexion into part of the Nicoya peninsula, the remainder of the nation is almost roadless in wet weather. Limón is connected only by rail at present; a highway to that destination is expected soon. Costa Rica's road structure until 1955, though it included two paved highways for tourists up

---

[53] *Encuesta industrial: 1959* (San José, Dir. Gen. Est. y Censos, 1960), pp. 3–5. The twelve-month period covered ended on 30 Sept. 1958. The number of technical personnel is taken from Cuadro 2 (Sept. 1958); the numbers of the other two categories are averages from Cuadro 4. See above, n. 46.

[54] *Yb. Lab. Stat.*, *1959*, pp. 288–9. See above, n. 46.

the sides of intriguing volcanoes, provided an excellent illustration of the isthmian isolation of four centuries of life on the Meseta Central.[55] Costa Rica licensed only 1,900 passenger cars and 800 commercial vehicles in 1937. Twenty years later the numbers had risen to 12,800 and 8,500 respectively, nearly twice as many per capita in both categories than had any other state in Central America.[56]

The first railway in Central America operated in Costa Rica, on a 14-mile track between Puntarenas and the village of Esparta. It was opened in 1854, just three years after the first line in South America and one year before the completion of track-laying all the way across Panama. The Tomás Guardia régime, in 1871, approved a contract whereby United States-born Henry Meiggs, who had already proved his mettle at difficult railway construction in Chile and Peru, would build a line to connect the cities of the Meseta Central with the Caribbean at Limón. Meiggs turned the work in Costa Rica over to his nephew Henry Meiggs Keith, who in the next two years built both ends of the line, Alajuela to Cartago and Limón to Matina (the latter only 22 miles), leaving a large gap between. The gap was filled in during the years 1886–90 by Minor Keith, a brother, who raised bananas to make the line pay for itself before it was finished. The British interests which backed Keith financially have a 99-year lease on this line called the Northern Railway (though its track lies east of the Meseta Central), after which it will become the property of the Costa Rican government. The United Fruit Company rented the line from 1905 to 1941 and built several branches of its own in Limón province, which are now a part of the Northern Railway system. From 1897 to 1909 the Meseta Central obtained its first good contact with the Pacific, when another rail line was built from San José to Puntarenas. The state already administers this western line, which is called the Ferrocarril Eléctrico al Pacífico, being electrified from one end to the other. Even with the completion of highway connexions to the territory of isthmian neighbours, these two railways with their affiliated port facilities will presumably continue to handle the bulk of Costa Rican imports. Private United Fruit lines leading to Golfito

[55] San José during a two-months' residence at the end of that year, through most of which (because of wash-outs) it would have been impossible to have retraced the path the author's family had travelled from Nicaragua, seemed still in much closer contact with Europe than with Nicaragua or Panama on either side.

[56] U.N. *Stat. Yb.*, *1951*, p. 317; *1959*, pp. 332–3.

and Quepos, and to Almirante on the Caribbean coast of Panama, handle a large share of the exports.

A variety of shipping lines call at both Limón and Puntarenas. Costa Rica is also well served by international airlines as well as several of her own. The most important of the latter is the company called Líneas Aéreas Costarricenses (LACSA), which maintains flights as far as Florida and Mexico in addition to covering the country. Smaller domestic lines specialize in service to particular regions.

Costa Rica's telegraph lines are managed by the government, but most of the telephone service is handled by a subsidiary of the United States-owned American & Foreign Power Company, which also provides the electricity used in San José. There was much talk of expropriation of the properties of this concern in Costa Rica as early as the 1930's but the move has never been made. Development of new hydro-electric resources, however, has been in the hands of the Instituto Costarricense de Electricidad (ICE) formed by the Figueres provisional government in 1949. ICE, in the belief that Costa Rica's demands for power will grow and that the country's short but fast-flowing streams should be harnessed for the benefit of the whole nation, is proceeding with large plans and projects. Electricity is inexpensive in Costa Rica, and as a result much more common than in the rest of Central America. In 1949, 82 per cent of Costa Rican dwellings in urban zones were provided, contrasting with the figure of only 39 per cent in El Salvador and Guatemala. In the short period 1952 to 1956, production by plants supplying public power alone increased from 190 to 290 million kilowatt hours.[57]

There is little doubt that in the 1950's Costa Rica was better served by its banking facilities, almost entirely state-owned, than any other nation on the isthmus. The Banco Nacional de Costa Rica, organized by the government in 1937, developed three special departments to give encouragement to small farmers, to investors in manufacturing, and to co-operatives as well as to wealthier agricultural interests. The Banco Central de Costa Rica, the functions of which were separated from those of the Banco Nacional only in 1950, serves as a bankers' bank. Three private banks (Banco de Costa Rica, Banco Anglo-Costarricense, and Banco de Crédito Agrícola de Cartago) were nationalized in 1948, leaving only one small private bank in the country. There is also a small mortgage

[57] U.N., *Stat. Yb.*, *1959*, pp. 283, 543.

institution owned by the government, called the Crédito Hipotecario de Costa Rica, and a system spread through the country of
Juntas Rurales de Crédito served by the Banco Nacional. Credit is
extended, and saving encouraged, on a scale not yet experienced
in the other Central American countries, even where state-owned
facilities have become available.[58]

ECONOMIC OUTLOOK: PROSPERITY THROUGH CO-OPERATION?

Costa Rica is the only republic of Central America with an annual per capita income of more than $200. But per capita income
is a poor measure of economic well-being unless one can compare
buying preferences and prices. In an effort to measure the material
prosperity of the Central American nations in the mid-1950's, the
United States Department of Commerce employed sixteen other
indices. These were selected on the basis of their being 'representative of goods and services whose consumption shows important increases as personal incomes rise'. They were the registration
of automotive vehicles, the number of radios in use, the number of
telephones in use, motion-picture-theatre seating capacity, the circulation of daily newspapers, and imports of automotive vehicles,
gasoline, radios, newsprint, kraft paper, structural steel, flat glass,
refrigerators, sewing-machines, watches, and typewriters. It is significant that on every index Costa Rica was ahead per capita. On
all but the number of radios in use, imports of typewriters, and (in
the case of Nicaragua alone) motion-picture-theatre seating capacity, Costa Rica was far, far ahead.[59]

That Costa Rica rates so high among isthmian states in the realm
of material comforts is due almost entirely to the low rating of the
others. There is not really much money per capita in this country,
nor is it well distributed. One can only say that there is a little more
wealth than in the rest of Central America, and that what there is
is somewhat better distributed. A sampling taken in the metropoli-
tan area of San José in 1958 suggested that 23·9 per cent of the
families had incomes of less than $60 per month; 36·1 per cent be-
tween $60 and $120; 16·4 per cent between $120 and $180; 9·1
per cent between $180 and $240; and 14·5 per cent above $240.
The 'families' included 'guests' and servants, 19 per cent of those in
the sample (including 21 per cent of those in the bracket $60 to
$120) having eight members or more.[60] In such circumstances,

[58] See ch. v, n. 71, p. 123.   [59] *Investment in C.A.*, p. 34.
[60] *Ingresos y gastos de las familias del área metropolitana de San José según encuesta*

and at prices paid in San José, only the 14·5 per cent above $240 may be said to live at all comfortably. It is the size of this group, small though it be and unrepresentative of much of the rest of the country, which differentiates Costa Rica from the remainder of Central America.

What is the reason for the difference? Without much doubt, the greatest factor is Costa Rica's size-of-farm gradation. In Costa Rica 19·87 per cent of the farms in 1955 were of 50 *manzanas* (86·3 acres) or more extension; 9·17 per cent were of at least 100 *manzanas*. Compare this with the 1950 picture in Guatemala, where only 2·17 per cent of the farms were of 64 *manzanas* or more but these covered 72 per cent of the nation's farmed area. Costa Rica like all other Central American states has a land-distribution problem—her 19·87 per cent of farms of 50 *manzanas* or more covered over 81 per cent of her total farm area—but the much higher percentage of landowners with enough land makes a real difference in the economy.[61] This is not, general evidence would indicate, a very new situation.

Costa Rica, with her higher degree of literacy, has for one generation worked on new avenues toward mass prosperity through national co-operation. Moves in this direction began in 1924 with President Jiménez' plan for national insurance. In 1933 wage minima were set—low ones, to be sure, but the first on the isthmus. In 1943 social security was introduced. Fourteen years later 83,000 Costa Ricans contributed to sickness and maternity benefit plans and 23,000 toward old-age pensions.[62] Under the labour code adopted in 1943 Costa Rica has developed a few strong unions. The income tax arrived in 1946. The banks were nationalized in 1948; the Electric Power Institute formed in 1949. Five years later INVU was founded. While more conservative administrations did not move ahead on these fronts, neither did they undo progress already made in this direction. Costa Rica's social legislation works toward the equalization of benefits from the wealth the nation produces. The benefits themselves remain sharply limited, however, by the inadequacy of the wealth to be distributed.

It is interesting to note that the people of the Meseta Central

---

preliminar de 1958 (San José, 1960), pp. 31, 33, 35. An average of 1·7 persons per family contributed to the income. Conversions are made at 6.65 colones to the dollar.

[61] *Censo agropecuario de 1955*, p. 121. See ch. v, n. 78, p. 127.

[62] *Yb. Lab. Stat.*, *1959*, p. 453. Protection against employment injury in 1953 included 133,000.

have not led the way in Costa Rican economic advancement. Vigorous trade-union activity has been one of the elements producing a higher standard of living in the provinces of Limón and Puntarenas. The whole nation sat up and took notice when Communists led a successful strike in Limón in 1934. Unions formed on the Meseta Central in the early 1930's were generally weak. In 1943 the Confederation of Workers of Costa Rica was organized in close association with the Popular Vanguard, lasting until it was dissolved by the Figueres junta in 1948. The same junta included as its Minister of Labour and Social Welfare, however, the person of Padre Benjamín Núñez, then the secretary-general of the Costa Rican Confederation of Labour 'Rerum Novarum', also founded in 1943. This group, affiliated to the International Confederation of Free Trade Unions since 1949, now counts 38 labour unions as members (1958). The General Confederation of Costa Rican Workers (36 unions) was founded in 1953; it is affiliated with the Communist-led World Federation of Trade Unions. A small National Confederation of Workers (14 unions) belonged to the Peronist labour movement for a year after its founding in 1954. Banana workers in the Golfito zone have since the 1940's been the object of solicitude on the part of both Communist and non-Communist leadership; a union merger there in 1960 was to the advantage of the Communists.

The spirit of working together for mutual benefit has only slowly pervaded the nation. But Costa Rica is a small country, quite literate, and not overpopulated. Students and teachers of her national university, quite representative of the country at large, tend to think of their nation's destiny as their own personal problem.[63] Through the university such thought habits may well come to pervade the whole nation. Despite the present narrowness of life for most of the people, there is growth and a readiness to tackle the difficulties which lie ahead. If personal privilege is put aside and the whole people permitted to move forward, Costa Rica may soon find the way to become genuinely prosperous.

LEARNING

The stress which Costa Rica has put upon education in the twentieth century was not evident at the time of independence,

[63] The degree to which government and university relate is typified by *La actual situación: temas económicos de la actualidad costarricense* (San José, 1959), a study presented by Raúl Hess Estrada, ex-Minister of Economy and Finance, to the Association of Graduates of the School of Economic and Social Sciences.

when even elementary training was rare. Like Honduras and El Salvador, the tiny state nevertheless felt compelled to create a separate university when political ties with the rest of the isthmus were broken. The University of Santo Tomás in San José was created in 1843 (an elementary school of that name had existed since 1814) offering advanced courses in theology, law, and medicine. In the 1870's and 1880's, through a series of decisions, the university ceased to function. Emphasis was placed instead on the secondary level; an 1888 decision to close what remained of the university was made by none other than Mauro Fernández, the nation's greatest enthusiast for public education. Instruction in law continued, and as time went by other centres of high-level teaching were added.

In 1940 the University of Costa Rica was organized. It was composed of the existing Faculties of Law (1843), Fine Arts (1897), Pharmacy (1897), Education (1914), and Agronomy (1926), and new Faculties of Engineering, Philosophy and Letters, and Sciences. To these were soon added Odontology (1942) and Economic and Social Sciences (1943). A reform of 1957 brought into being a Department of General Studies, offering first-year courses obligatory for all university students. This work is taught by a new Faculty of Sciences and Letters; while from the dust of the old Faculty of Sciences have been constructed those of Microbiology and Medicine.[64] A new university city is being developed on the edge of San José. The Costa Rican census showed in 1950 that 1·15 per cent of the population had attended university-level classes one year or more—9,210 persons, far more than in any other country of Central America. The total enrolment of the University of Costa Rica in 1959 was 2,280 men and 1,392 women—figures very high (for the isthmus) in ratio to population and much more nearly balanced than others between male and female.[65]

The results of sixty years of real effort in Costa Rican elementary education were shown by the census of 1950, which counted 78·76 per cent of the people over the age of ten as able to read and write. This was twice the percentage of El Salvador, which had the second-best record of Central America. In Guanacaste province the figure was 67·50 per cent; in Heredia, 88·28 per cent. The 1950's saw further strengthening of the system. There were 1,131 primary schools in 1953; 1,540 in 1960. There were 123,939 chil-

---

[64] *Estatuto orgánico: Universidad de Costa Rica* (San José, 1957); *Reforma académica: la Facultad de Ciencias y Letras* (San José, 1957).

[65] *Censo de población: 1950*, p. 40; *An. Est.* (C.R.), *1959*, p. 113.

dren in primary school in 1953; 188,927 in 1960. There were 32 secondary schools in 1953; 63 in 1960. There were 9,135 students in secondary schools in 1953; 27,491 in 1960.[66]

The first printing-press to operate in Costa Rica was set up in 1830. The first newspaper appeared early in 1833. A government gazette has been published quite regularly, though under a variety of names, since 1842. Dailies appeared as elsewhere on the isthmus in the late nineteenth century. Those most widely read at present are *La Nación* (founded 1946) and *La República* (1950). *La Nación* (independent but essentially conservative) is probably the most informative paper on the isthmus in presenting its own nation's news, though like all the others it omits important items from opposition politics. *La República* is the mouthpiece for the National Liberation movement. There were only five dailies in Costa Rica in 1957, but with a total circulation of 95,000 or 92 papers for every 1,000 inhabitants.[67]

In medical practice as in education Costa Rica has led the way among the Central American countries. In 1928 her death-rate was 236 per 10,000 inhabitants, not far above that of Guatemala thirty years later. By 1938 it had fallen to 177, by 1948 to 132, and by 1958 to 90·1. Among the chief causes of death in the latter year were gastro-enteritis and colitis (11·5 deaths per 10,000 inhabitants); malignant tumours (8·3, by far the highest figure in Central America for this item); pneumonia and bronchitis (7·3); worms (2·9); tetanus (2·1); and infections of infancy (1·7). Each provincial capital had a general government hospital in 1959, besides which there were 6 smaller hospitals of the same type in six other communities, 13 rural health centres with beds, 6 specialized institutions for medical care, and 10 private hospitals and clinics. Altogether they provided 5,746 beds, of which 3,063 were in San José. There were 379 physicians in 1957 (nearly one for every 2,700 persons) and 113 dentists.[68]

Boundary contentions provided the impetus for Costa Rica's first extensive work in history. León Fernández (1840–87) interested himself in the whole history of the small nation as he collected boundary documents from Costa Rica, Guatemala, and finally Europe. Five volumes of them were published before his early death by violence, and five posthumously by his son Ricardo

[66] *Censo de población: 1950*, p. 42; *An. Est.* (C.R.), *1953*, pp. 58, 65, 67; *1960*, pp. 108, 111.

[67] U.N., *Stat. Yb.*, *1959*, p. 578.

[68] Ibid. *1958*, p. 541; *An. Est.* (C.R.), *1958*, pp. 11, 37–50; *1959*, pp. 118–19.

Fernández Guardia (1867–1950),who also edited his father's history of Costa Rica in the colonial epoch.[69] Manuel María de Peralta (1844–1930) spent most of his adult life in Europe as Costa Rica's ambassador to various capitals, and collected another notable series of documents.[70] In the meantime, Francisco Montero Barrantes (b. 1864), a teacher back at home, wrote the nation's first history dealing with both colonial and republican periods, bringing his narration all the way to 1890.[71] A public servant, Francisco María Iglesias, had ferreted out valuable documents concerning Costa Rica's independence which Montero used and which were later published.[72] At the end of the nineteenth century, as though to celebrate her new-found literacy, Costa Rica published a commemorative volume containing contributions on Costa Rican civilization by several of her scholars.[73]

Ricardo Fernández Guardia set the pace for historical studies in the twentieth century. His distinction sprang from quality rather than magnitude of output. In dealing with the Spanish conquest, independence, the events of the early 1840's, and a host of small episodes, he shattered legends and reproduced the real life of the times.[74] One of his historical works had the rare distinction for an isthmian book of being translated into English.[75]

Fernández Guardia, as director of the national archives, began publication of a historical review, since continued by his successors Jorge Volio Jiménez (1882–1955) and José Luis Coto Conde; its contents are chiefly documents.[76] Luis Dobles Segreda (b. 1890) compiled a most comprehensive and well-organized Costa Rican bibliography.[77] But the only Costa Rican to write details of his

[69] *Colección de documentos para la historia de Costa Rica* (i–iii, San José, 1881–3; iv–v, Paris, 1886; vi–x, Barcelona, 1907); *Historia de Costa Rica durante la dominación española* (Madrid, 1889).

[70] The series began with *Costa Rica, Nicaragua, y Panamá en el siglo XVI* (Madrid, 1883) and continued with other titles in 1886, 1890, 1891, 1898 (two), 1899, and 1900. The last three were published in French and used directly in frontier-arbitration proceedings.

[71] *Elementos de historia de Costa Rica* (2 vols., San José, 1892–4).

[72] *Documentos relativos a la independencia* (3 vols., San José, 1899–1902).

[73] See above, n. 1.

[74] *Historia de Costa Rica: el descubrimiento y la conquista* (1905); *Crónicas coloniales* (1921); *La independencia y otros episodios* (1928); *Cosas y gentes de antaño* (1935); *Morazán en Costa Rica* (1943); all published in San José. All but the last have been printed in more than one edition.

[75] *History of the Discovery and Conquest of Costa Rica* (N.Y., 1913).

[76] *R. de los Archivos Nacionales*, Año 1, nos. 1–2, Nov.–Dec. 1936; Año 24, nos. 1–6, Apr.–June 1960.

[77] *Indice bibliográfico de Costa Rica* (9 vols., San José, 1927–36).

nation's twentieth-century history was Tomás Soley Güell (1875–1943), author of a pioneering economic study.[78]

Costa Rica has of course been included in the studies of outsiders dealing with the whole of Central America.[79] Outsiders have also contributed an analytical study of the country at large;[80] a sociological treatise dealing with daily life;[81] an analysis of the Costa Rican economy;[82] and a sociological case study of the changing community of Turrialba and its nearby countryside.[83]

Turrialba is the seat of the Inter-American Institute of Agricultural Sciences, founded in 1944 as a co-operative venture of all the American republics. The Institute serves as an active centre of research. Costa Rica's capital is the seat of the small Escuela Superior de Administración Pública América Central (1953) sponsored by the five Central American republics. The National Liberation party of Costa Rica joined with like-minded groups in nearly all the Latin American countries to create in October 1960 a new Institute of Political Education designed to prepare democratic leaders for the hemisphere.[84] The same political grouping, characterized by the names of José Figueres, Rómulo Betancourt of Venezuela, and Víctor Raúl Haya de la Torre of Peru, has published in San José since 1958 the magazine *Combate*, a significant campaigner for liberal causes in the whole hemisphere.[85] Costa Rica's basic structure of literacy is thus evidenced by her attraction to and for new ideas. One can feel a new world growing in San José, especially in the university.[86] There seems every likelihood that this institution, essentially new itself, is already on the way to intellectual advances hitherto unknown in Central America.

ART

The national theatre of San José, inaugurated in 1897, is a symbol of Costa Rica's cultural advancement. This is too small a na-

[78] *Historia económica y hacendaria de Costa Rica* (2 vols., San José, 1947–9); see ch. v, n. 99, p. 132.   [79] See ch. v, nn. 100–1, p. 132.
[80] Chester Lloyd Jones, *Costa Rica and Civilization in the Caribbean* (Madison, Univ. of Wisconsin Press, 1935).
[81] John and Mavis Biesanz, *Costa Rican Life* (N.Y., Columbia U.P., 1944).
[82] Stacy May and others, *Costa Rica: a Study in Economic Development* (N.Y., Twentieth Century Fund, 1952).
[83] Charles P. Loomis and others, *Turrialba: Social Systems and the Introduction of Change* (Glencoe, Ill., The Free Press, 1953).
[84] The Institute, Apartado 1030, San José, publishes a *Newsletter* (i/11, Jan. 1962).   [85] No. 13, Nov.–Dec. 1960.
[86] *R. de la Universidad de Costa Rica*, founded in 1945 (no. 20, Mar. 1960) reflects the new era. For other current periodicals, see ch. v, n. 116, p. 134.

tion to have contributed a great deal that is original to the world of art. But wealthy Costa Ricans have for some time enjoyed the music and drama of Europe, with which likewise the people at large are now making contact.

The mass recreation picture in Costa Rica during the last few decades differs little from that of the remainder of the isthmus. The bull-fight has remained on the scene more than in Nicaragua, Honduras, and El Salvador, but has followed its own evolution to become a popular sport in fiesta season. Already by the New Year's celebration of 1931 it was common for spectators to enter the arena. One paper commented, 'Someone pointed out to us that bulls were being run with sharp-pointed horns, which constitutes a great danger, since those who enter the ring are not experts and at times do not act in sane judgment.'[87] Popular music in Costa Rica is very cosmopolitan, though the country possesses a dance of its own, the *punto guanacasteco*. It is interesting that Guanacaste province, most typically Central American in its population make-up but rather atypical in many Costa Rican traits, has provided most of the nation's native musical inspiration. The dance tunes and songs of virtually the entire hemisphere may be heard on Costa Rica's 37 radio stations, 22 of which are in her capital—surely a near record for a city of its size.[88] Because of a conflict over commercial television Costa Rica was the last country on the isthmus to develop a television station.

Religious music used by both Catholics and Protestants was composed by Alejandro Monestel (1865–1951) who began and ended his career in Costa Rica but lived thirty-five years in the United States. Costa Rican folk music provided themes for Monestel in other pieces, as it did for Julio Fonseca (1885–1949) and for Julio Mata (b. 1899).[89] San José has a symphony orchestra which performs for schoolchildren as well as adults, and an *a cappella* chorus. In recent years interest in the visual arts has begun to match that in music and foreign drama. Max Jiménez (1900–47) was both sculptor and painter, and did much to encourage the new trend.

Costa Rica's literacy has led to a production of literary works far outmatching in quantity those of the other Central American

[87] *D. de C. R.*, 1 Jan. 1931.
[88] See ch. v, n. 118, p. 135. Costa Rican call letters have the prefix TI. Two stations use 10,000 watts power.
[89] See ch. v, n. 120, p. 136.

republics.[90] Many Costa Rican authors are well known on the isthmus, and a few throughout Spanish America, though none has begun to reach the fame of a Rubén Darío. Their writings began to appear only late in the nineteenth century and early in the twentieth.

A first cluster of birth dates in a selected list of sixteen stretches from 1861 to 1867. Justo Facio (1861–1931), born in Panama, came to Costa Rica while young and made an impression with his verse.[91] José María Alfaro Cooper (1861–1939) untouched by *modernista* influences wrote a three-volume life of Christ in poetry.[92] Carlos Gagini (1865–1929) made a painstaking study of the Costa Rican language and composed short stories, novels, and dramatic works including a play about the founder of the Bethlehemite order, the Marqués de Talamanca.[93] Aquileo Echeverría (1866–1909) is called the 'national poet' of Costa Rica—Rubén Darío first made the designation—for his verse in popular language dealing with the life of his country.[94] Ricardo Fernández Guardia of fame as an historian also wrote well-liked short pieces of fiction and made translations of the works of foreigners who had visited the isthmus.[95]

Four more authors of the selected list were born between 1874 and 1878. The best-known of these was Roberto Brenes Mesén (1874–1947), who studied in Chile and for some time taught Spanish American literature in the United States. Brenes Mesén did much to determine the twentieth-century orientation of primary education in Costa Rica. He also wrote poetry and essays of a philosophical bent, and performed a few highly praised translations.[96] Alejandro Alvarado Quirós (b. 1876) wrote literary and critical

[90] In Henry Grattan Doyle, *A Tentative Bibliography of the Belles-Lettres of the Republics of Central America* (Cambridge, Mass., Harvard U.P., 1935) Costa Rican items take up 59 pages, Guatemalan 31, Salvadoran 18, Honduran 15, and Nicaraguan 10. To the last must be added, however, 25 pages from Doyle's *A Bibliography of Rubén Darío*.

[91] *Mis versos* (San José, 1894).   [92] *La epopeya de la cruz* (San José, 1921–4).

[93] *Diccionario de costarriqueñismos* (San José, 1919); *El marqués de Talamanca; zarzuela en tres actos y en verso* (Santa Ana, 1905).

[94] One collection called *Concherías* (San José, 1905) included all his poems published during his lifetime. See Georgina Ibarra Bejarano, *Aquileo J. Echeverría: estudio crítico-biográfico* (San José, 1946).

[95] *Cuentos ticos* (San José, 1901) were translated into English under the same title (Cleveland, 1905; 3rd ed., 1925) and into French as *Contes et poèmes de Costa-Rica* (Paris, 1924), pp. 5–217. The most remarkable translation was *La guerra de Nicaragua, escrita por el general William Walker* (San José, 1924).

[96] *En el silencio* (San José, 1907), his first book of poems, stamped Brenes Mesén a *modernista*. Others followed throughout his life. His best-known translation is that of *L'oiseau bleu* by Maeterlinck.

articles which attracted attention.[97] Lisímaco Chavarría (1877–1913) wrote poetry of distinct regional flavour, which he at first published under his wife's name.[98] Claudio González Rucavado (1878–1929) wrote three novels on Costa Rican themes.[99]

A new cluster of birth dates occurs from 1881 to 1884, containing only three names. Joaquín García Monge (1881–1958) was known throughout Spanish America for his vigorous and cultured editing of *El Repertorio Americano*, one of the hemisphere's leading magazines from 1919 until the death of its maker.[100] The literary appeal of *El Repertorio Americano* sprang as much from its thought content as its style; it was a true child of the twentieth century. García Monge himself wrote articles, short stories, and short novels of local inspiration. Rómulo Tovar (b. 1883) contributed short stories, thoughtful essays (including a long one on a speech by the president of United Fruit before the Bond Club of New York), and a translation of a well-known Spanish American literary history from the English language.[101] José Fabio Garnier (b. 1884), who studied in Italy, wrote literary criticism and dramatic works, the latter in both Spanish and Italian.[102]

A final group of four from the selected list of sixteen Costa Rican authors are considerably younger, their birth dates ranging from 1890 to 1895. The work of two of them showed appreciation for what had gone before. Luis Dobles Segreda, before he began his able career as a bibliographer, had attracted attention with his stories, particularly of the city of Heredia.[103] Rafael Cardona (b. 1893) composed poetry of acknowledged merit.[104] Rogelio Sotela (1894–1943) wrote much verse and commented upon the writings of others, particularly those of his own country.[105] Moisés Vincenzi

[97] His first collection, *Bric-a-brac* (San José, 1914); his last in this genre, *Nuestra tierra prometida* (San José, 1925).

[98] For example, *Nómadas* (San José, 1904); his wife was Rosa Corrales de Chavarría.

[99] *El hijo de un gamonal* (1901); *Escenas costarricenses* (1906); *Egoísmo* (1914); all published in San José.

[100] Año 36, l/5, May 1958; one more issue (no. 1186) was published in 1959.

[101] *Un discurso y una campaña* (San José, 1928); Alfred Coester, *Historia literaria de la América española* (Madrid, 1929).

[102] His chief book of criticism, *Perfume de belleza* (Valencia, 1909); a comedy, *A la sombra del amor* (San José, 1921); a drama, *Con toda el alma* (San José, 1929).

[103] *Por el amor de Dios* (San José, 1918) depicts five humble *heredianos; Caña brava* (San José, 1926) is an Heredia miscellany.

[104] *Oro de la mañana* (San José, 1918), though brief, is the only collection.

[105] *Rimas serenas, 1914–1934* (San José, 1935); *Escritores de Costa Rica* (2nd ed., San José, 1942).

(b. 1895) has written short novels and essays of philosophic reflection.[106]

Rogelio Sotela said of Luis Dobles Segreda and his arduous accomplishments in bibliography, 'His constancy merits a eulogy, especially here where we are a little indolent.'[107] The Costa Rican record of authorship seems to deserve no such censure. Dobles Segreda's own collection of the books listed in his extensive but unfinished bibliography is evidence enough that in three generations of literacy this tiny republic has contributed its share of good reading to the Spanish-speaking world. Three novels by Fabián Dobles in the 1940's are an indication of continuing ability and interest.[108] When the remainder of Central America with its greater population follows suit to Costa Rica in the matter of mass education, the isthmus will attract continual attention in the literary world without the necessity of a Darío in every generation.

RELIGION

In the realm of religion Costa Rica has remained closer to the Roman Catholic faith than any other Central American republic. Costa Rica is indeed the only one of these where intolerance of other beliefs exerts notable influence on the national level. Though Protestants in Guatemala were free in 1957 to celebrate their seventy-fifth anniversary with a massive parade through the capital, those of Costa Rica were refused permission to do likewise on a seventieth anniversary in 1961. Despite some handicaps written into the statutory law and constitution, however, Protestantism also flourishes in this quite religious country.

Costa Rica's early constitutions stated that only Roman Catholicism would be tolerated. San José became a bishopric in 1850, and Costa Rica joined Guatemala two years later in her early formalization of relations with Rome. Other faiths were allowed by the constitution of 1872, and the concordat was broken in 1884 before that of Nicaragua. The charter of 1949 reads concerning matters of faith, 'The Apostolic Roman Catholic Religion is that of the State, which contributes to its maintenance, without impeding the free exercise in the Republic of other worship that is not opposed to universal morality or good customs.'[109]

In 1921 the archdiocese of San José was created, with a suffragan

[106] *Diálogos filosóficos* (San José, 1924).   [107] *Escritores de Costa Rica*, p. 354.
[108] *Ese que llaman pueblo* (1942); *Aguas turbias* (1943); *Una burbuja en el limbo* (1946); all published in San José.
[109] PAU, *Constitution of the Republic of Costa Rica, 1949* (Washington, 1951), p. 11.

bishop in Alajuela and a vicariate apostolic (subject to San José) established in Limón. Another bishop was added in 1954 at San Isidro del General. There are 679 Catholic churches in Costa Rica served by 246 priests—one priest for every 4,200 Catholics, the highest ratio on the isthmus.[110] Nearly half the priests are members of religious orders. There are 24 Franciscan missionaries from the United States, working chiefly in the banana areas of Puntarenas, where they have been located since 1946. There are also 9 School Sisters of St. Francis doing educational work, though this order appeared on the scene only in 1957.[111]

Some 300 Protestant places of worship are not by themselves a true measure of Costa Rican Protestant activity.[112] San José has, in fact, become an informal sort of headquarters for Protestant evangelization in the whole of Spanish America. This is due to the location here of two schools—one a language school for missionaries whose mother tongue is English, the other the Seminario Bíblico Latinoamericano training native pastors from many countries and denominations. The seminary, the roots of which go back to 1923, is a project of the Latin America Mission, which carries out mass-evangelization campaigns in the hemisphere and maintains 16 missionaries in Costa Rica.

The non-denominational Central American Mission came to Costa Rica from Texas in 1891. It was the Protestant-less state of this small republic at that late date which attracted the attention of Cyrus Ingerson Scofield, the noted Biblical scholar and Congregationalist who provided the impetus for the movement.[113] The five more sizable Protestant endeavours other than the Latin America Mission and the Central American Mission are those of the Methodist Missionary Society of Great Britain, active in Limón since 1900; the Protestant Episcopal Church, carrying on Anglican work begun in Limón early in the century; the Methodist Church of the United States, which arrived in 1918 and now has 18 missionaries; the Seventh-Day Adventists (1927), with the largest membership and 12 missionaries; and the Southern Baptist Convention, on the scene only since 1947. Smaller programmes are carried on by the Assemblies of God, the Church of the Foursquare Gospel, the Pentecostal Holiness Church, the Church of God of Prophecy (all four of these with Pentecostal orientation), and a

[110] See ch. v, n. 140, p. 141.
[111] Costa Rica has 34 religious houses for men and 54 for women, the highest total in Central America. See ch. v, n. 141, p. 141.
[112] See ch. v, n. 145, p. 142.   [113] See ch. v, n. 147, p. 143.

distinct Church of God with Indiana headquarters. Fourteen Mormon missionaries also labour in this country.[114]

The Costa Rican Catholic church, still clearly in the ascendancy over all these new movements, bears the mark of both eighteenth and twentieth centuries. Its high interest in imagery and grudging disposition toward dissenters match attitudes of the days before independence. But the church has taken up modern lines which give it influence in national life far exceeding that exercised by religious groups in other Central American republics. There is real meaning in the fact that Archbishop Sanabria y Martínez approved membership for Catholics in the Popular Vanguard of 1943, whatever the subsequent history of that organization. There is significance too in the fact that a Costa Rican Federation of Labour is named Rerum Novarum and that Padre Benjamín Núñez, well known internationally, is the head of the new Institute of Political Education, the training-school for democracy in San José. Whatever its hesitations on freedom of religious propaganda and practice, the Catholic church in Costa Rica has shown its interest in justice in other spheres. In so doing, it has taken a step toward public righteousness, which in the rest of the isthmus seems almost to have been abandoned by the religious organizations to the more materialistic creeds.

[114] See ch. v, n. 149, p. 144.

CHAPTER X

A NEW DECADE

HEADLINES for the entire western hemisphere were provided by John Fitzgerald Kennedy, president of the United States, on 13 March 1961. At a reception for Latin American delegates in Washington he proposed an Alliance for Progress. 'A vast effort', he called it, 'unparalleled in magnitude and nobility of purpose, to satisfy the basic needs of the American people for homes, work and land, health and schools—"techo, trabajo y tierra, salud y escuela".' Looking toward 'economic progress' and 'social justice', the effort would be made 'by free men working within a framework of democratic institutions'. There would be a 'ten-year plan for the Americas—a plan to transform the Nineteen Sixties into an historic decade of democratic progress'. Success would mean that 'the close of this decade will mark the beginning of a new era in the American experience'.[1]

More than one-fourth of the delegations President Kennedy addressed represented the five nations of Central America. Barely two weeks had passed when (on 28 March) the representatives of eighteen parties from thirteen Latin American countries signed a Declaration of San José (Costa Rica) affirming their support of the Alliance for Progress. They likewise avowed their own interest in social reform and their desire to bring about social justice. The Declaration of San José was signed by five Central Americans—Fernando Agüero for the Conservatives and Enrique Lacayo Farfán for the Independent Liberals of Nicaragua; José Mejía Arellano for the Liberals of Honduras; Mario Méndez Montenegro for PR of Guatemala; and José Figueres for National Liberation of Costa Rica.[2]

Subsequently, as planning for the alliance progressed, all the régimes of Central America approved the broad principles of the programme, as did most of the hemisphere. Many of the requirements laid down for this bold march into the future have been discussed through the pages of this book. As final touchstones for the

---

[1] *New York Times*, 14 Mar. 1961.
[2] This Declaration, though it speaks for political elements, was used by the United States Information Service in its pamphlet 'Alianza para el Progreso'.

possibilities of success for the undertaking on the Central American isthmus, it seems pertinent to inquire into the politics of each Central American republic during the year after the alliance was proposed, and finally to examine (through the medium of six isthmian headlines gathered just before President Kennedy's speech) some underlying attitudes and habits.

POSTCRIPT ON POLITICS

The government of Miguel Ydígoras Fuentes of Guatemala began the decade of the 1960's in quite open co-operation with the Central Intelligence Agency of the United States, aimed at the downfall of the Castro régime in Cuba. Many of the Cubans who participated in the unsuccessful invasion of their own republic on 17 April 1961 had received their training in Guatemala. The programme of preparation for the attack was accompanied by repeated denials from the United States and Guatemalan governments that such an invasion was afoot. The preference shown by the planners for those Cuban refugees who were opposed to social reform showed that the attempt was inspired by factors other than pure anti-Communism, and raised the ghosts of the Guatemalan affair of 1954 by which Castillo Armas had become president. In both instances the power of the United States and the influence of Ydígoras Fuentes, for whatever it counted, seemed to be on the side of those most vocal in their denunciations of Communism rather than with those whose reform inclinations might have produced a viable alternative.

Ydígoras' reputation for unconstructive conservatism, thus enhanced, gained all the more during the year 1961 from his failure to induce his own majority backing in Congress to adopt an income tax. His dedication to the democracy of which he had spoken so often was questioned most severely during violence which followed the Congressional elections of December; accusations of widespread fraud led to demands for the president's resignation. However, as had happened before, decisions made by the courts provided remedies for some of the gravest complaints, and room remained in Guatemalan public life for opposition sentiment. When Congress convened in March 1962 Ydígoras found that he could count on fewer votes than in the previous session. Redención and MDN together held 41 seats out of 66, only 2 more than four years earlier. Other major news items—such as Ydígoras' decision to sell the Fincas Nacionales back to private ownership—fell under the

long shadow of the forthcoming presidential campaign. One poten-
tial candidate was Juan José Arévalo, who, despite his authorship
of anti-*yanqui* literature very popular in Cuba, made statements in
1961 disassociating himself from the Cuban swing to Marxism.
Permission for Arévalo to run would signify more clearly than ever
that democracy in Guatemala is still alive.

In El Salvador, Lt.-Colonel Julio Adalberto Rivera and a new
Partido de Conciliación Nacional (PCN) appeared on the scene in
1961 in a manner reminiscent of Major Oscar Osorio and PRUD
in 1949. The Directorio Cívico Militar became more military than
civic when two of its civilian members (Rodríguez Porth and Valiente) resigned without replacement after but two and a half
months in office. The remaining directorate drew cries from the
aristocracy by passing a series of small measures to aid the farm
labourer. Then, in September, Rivera resigned, PCN was formed,
and a new electoral law was issued, followed by a decree raising the
percentages on high-level income taxes. Thus a reputation for leftist reform was established—Osorio had accomplished the same result with his early introduction of social security. A short campaign
was conducted until 17 December 1961, when PCN won 54 of the
54 seats in the new Assembly. PRUD in its day had managed the
same percentage.

Yet the election was a regular one in the sense that the electoral
law was followed. Less than half the registered voters cast ballots,
but those who did gave PCN a majority while a coalition ticket
supported by PAR, PSD, and PDC and a separate effort by PAC
did very poorly. The elected body took office as a constituent assembly and on 4 January 1962 proclaimed a new constitution to replace that of 1950. Few changes appeared in the new document,
but among them was a provision for a five-year presidential term
beginning on 1 July to replace the six-year term beginning on 14
September. Lawyer Eusebio Rodolfo Cordón, chosen as provisional president, replaced the directorate on 25 January, one year after
it had assumed office. In February PCN nominated Julio Adalberto Rivera as president for the term from 1 July 1962 to 1967. In
the election of 29 April it was obvious that Rivera would win; no
other candidate opposed him. Rivera expressed strong support for
the Alliance for Progress. Like Osorio and Lemus, he posed as an
enthusiast for social action. Even agrarian reform, he said, would
be on his agenda. There seemed little real prospect, however, that
a régime with such a beginning as that of Rivera could aid the cause

of democracy. The army remained in charge of this republic in 1962—nor was there any real sign that the aristocracy would lose its governing influence.

The decade opened quietly for the régime of Ramón Villeda Morales of Honduras. Armed insurrections came less often though criticism flowed freely. While higher income-tax rates were discussed and agrarian reform studied, politicians were thinking ahead to the 1963 campaign. While several presidential hopefuls jousted for position within the Liberal party, the Nationalists and Reformists made plans to reunite their forces. Villeda Morales remained a moderate between distracting extremes, but continued to move toward a new Honduras.

Luis Somoza Debayle in Nicaragua co-operated in the April 1961 invasion of Cuba by permitting the Cuban assault forces to group and embark from the Puerto Cabezas area on Nicaragua's east coast. The Corn Islands leased to the United States were, according to report, also involved in the operation. Nicaraguan expressions of bitterness in 1961, however, had little to do with this episode. They came from parties unconvinced that the Somoza family would yield its power on 1 May 1963 when a new presidential term would begin. The Traditional Conservatives made an early nomination of Fernando Agüero Rocha for the presidency, in January 1962. Traditional Conservatives and Independent Liberals were united in the demand that there must be outside supervision of the elections to maintain honesty. President Somoza replied that neutral observers might be allowed, but that neutral supervision would be beneath Nicaragua's dignity. The Nationalist Liberal party of Somoza Debayle conducted talks on electoral reform with the Nicaraguan Conservative party, but the real opposition was not present. Liberals and Conservatives vied with one another in suggesting plans for agrarian reform. But most important of all was the enduring likelihood that the Nationalist Liberal candidate would be a close friend of the Somoza family backed by all their power.

Politics provided the dominant theme in the last presidential year of Mario Echandi Jiménez of Costa Rica. Echandi stayed out of the campaign as old rivals engaged forces. Candidates Otilio Ulate Blanco (National Union) and Francisco José Orlich (National Liberation) were joined in September 1961 by Rafael Angel Calderón Guardia, nominee of the Republicans, and Enrique Obregón Valverde, choice of Acción Democrática Popular, a new group friendly to Cuba's Castro. The elections in February 1962 gave Orlich a majority of the popular vote, making him president for the term 8 May 1962 to 1966. Calderón Guardia held second place, Ulate a poor third, and Obregón Valverde an almost inconspicious fourth. National Liberation also gained a majority of the seats in the Assembly, their total of 30 comparing with 19 for the Republicans and 8 for National Union. Thus in 1962 Costa Rica witnessed her fourth transition in a row (1949, 1953, 1958, 1962) from a political régime in power to its elected opposition.

Costa Rica has proved, it might be argued, that democracy in government is possible on the Central American isthmus. Through education, public-health programmes, and social reform Costa Rica has already moved towards the new era of which President Kennedy spoke in 1961. Costa Rica will move farther, as will her four neighbours to the north-west, with a massive programme of aid from the United States. But there are six underlying attitudes and habits which—if they persist—can negate all the advantage the aid brings. Four are the responsibilities of Central Americans, two of outsiders. All may be recognized, in various forms and patterns and placed in sundry contexts, as the responsibilities of other peoples throughout the human world.

'LO QUE HICIMOS EN GUATEMALA'

This striking headline—'What We Did in Guatemala'—appeared in a Salvadoran newspaper over a column of Salvadoran authorship.[3] The immediate words, more correctly stated as 'what we did *with* Guatemala', were those of Vice-President Richard Nixon of the United States as he was campaigning for the presidency in 1960. His opponent John Kennedy had spoken in favour of government aid to Cuban anti-Castro forces which would amount to anti-Castro intervention. Vice-President Nixon said,

Now let's just see what this means. We have five treaties with Latin America, including the one setting up the Organization of American States in Bogotá in 1948 in which we have agreed not to intervene in the internal affairs of any other American country. . . . Now, what can we do? Well, we can do what we did with Guatemala. . . . We quarantined Mr. Arbenz. The result was that the Guatemalan people themselves eventually rose up and they threw him out.[4]

The Salvadoran comment read in part as follows: 'The phrase of

[3] *El Diario de Hoy*, 10 Nov. 1960.   [4] *New York Times*, 22 Oct. 1960.

Nixon—"what we did in Guatemala"—will stand in the history of political debates as a true jewel of ingenuousness and imprudence.'

The simple fact, as Vice-President Nixon knew, was that the United States had done more to get rid of Mr Arbenz as president than to quarantine him. The United States in 1954 had renewed an isthmian practice widely thought to have been abandoned when the last marines withdrew from Nicaragua in January 1933. The intervention came at a time when United States business interests felt threatened, and when (as was explained in the chapter on Guatemala) there was no clear-cut issue between democracy and Communism, both of these elements lying at the moment more on President Arbenz' side.

This is the only instance since the inception of the Good Neighbour Policy when outside pressure has been exerted so directly in so weighty an isthmian affair. It is not, however, the only instance of outside influence carrying the predominant role in decision-making. The co-operation of the Ydígoras and Somoza régimes in the anti-Castro exercise of April 1961 serves as a case in point. The *New York Times* puts the matter plainly when it says editorially,

Guatemala is a protégé of the United States.... Since ... 1954 the United States has played a dominant role in Guatemalan politics and economics. When it was necessary to find a place to train Cuban exiles to invade Cuba, Guatemala was the chosen country. Consequently, we have a special interest in its stability.[5]

A similar role for Nicaragua, it may be noted, extends back to 1912. Recent relationships between the United States and the other three republics have been far more subtle.

The danger in the continuance of this system is that the nations of Central America, with enough problems of their own, thus become involved as pawns in a game which need not include them. There may be droplets of benefit to be derived from the game (though these—as in the case of reassigned sugar quotas—more often accrue to private individuals than to the nation), but no one can argue that Central America is well off today through her long association with rich neighbours. Central America can and should be assisted by the United States, with whose economy the isthmus is linked so intimately; but such assistance should be rendered without the accompaniment of political arrangements, until the day comes when these are undertaken voluntarily by the whole

[5] 24 Mar. 1962.

people on both sides. Otherwise the real interests of the isthmus are likely to be overlooked in the pursuit of what are considered more far-reaching international objectives. In the meantime, the small Central American republics should find sufficient leeway for the expression of their own international sentiments through the Organization of American States and the United Nations.

'HONDURAS NO ES UN TRAMPOLÍN'

A *trampolín* is of course a trampolin, recently become popular in juvenile sport. The statement that Honduras is *not* a trampolin or springboard for the invasion of other nations came from President Villeda Morales himself, in an interview with a Guatemalan reporter.[6] It was a response to a query concerning the possibility of an attack upon the Ydígoras régime by some Guatemalan military personnel who had taken refuge in Honduras after an earlier adventure of theirs had failed. The words were not idle ones. The sincerity of Villeda's intention to prevent the use of Honduran soil for attacks upon neighbours has been tested several times. In staying with his principle, he is breaking new and important ground for isthmian development.

With fairness many people associate the very name of the Caribbean with the concept of international conspiracy. It seems that the dwellers on all sides, once they have found a good thing, are not content until all other peoples bordering on the sea share their good fortune; or on the other hand that other dwellers on all sides, having seen their neighbours fall a prey to known dangers, cannot rest until they have delivered them from their perils. A well-known Stanford University publication painted the picture thus in its first words on isthmian affairs in 1948:

Political observers have felt for some time that trouble was brewing in the Central American region, with an alignment taking place that would eventually create a very tense military situation. Those suspicions were at least partially confirmed recently by an announcement from General Anastasio Somoza, head of the armed forces of Nicaragua. In a formal statement, he warned the nations of the world that peace was being threatened by the 'communist' governments of Cuba, Guatemala, and Venezuela, aided by Costa Rica, who were planning and preparing a revolutionary movement against the governments of Nicaragua, Honduras, and El Salvador. General Somoza referred to evidence. . . .[7]

The evidence is seemingly always there, whether or not there is

[6] *Imp.*, 26 Dec. 1960.   [7] *Hispanic World Report*, i/1 (Nov. 1948), 5.

really a conspiracy. But the conspiracies themselves happen often enough to validate the impression made upon outsiders.

The practice began on the isthmus when men like Carrera, Justo Rufino Barrios, and Zelaya used quite open force or intrigue to attain their own goals in the various capitals. Armies marched unabashedly across borders in the earlier days when the whole region was a sort of battleground between liberals and conservatives. After the time of Zelaya intrigue became generally a bit more subtle. The overthrow of an established régime lay now in the hands of persons disaffected from their own government who would use a neighbour's soil for the training of men and the collection of munitions and supplies. But as the character of intrigue became more restricted, its geographical horizons broadened. Nineteenth-century Carrera's influence reached as far as Nicaragua. A Figueres, a Somoza, or an Ydígoras may be interested in Cuba, the Dominican Republic, or Venezuela.

General Somoza, in the words quoted from him in 1948, spoke of a situation which had begun to take shape four years earlier. The 1944 success of anti-Ubico forces in Guatemala had been matched, it was thought at the time, by that of the revolutionary party of Cuba to which Fulgencio Batista had deferred after eleven years in power (1933–44). In 1945 Venezuela escaped from the lengthened shadow of tyrant Juan Vicente Gómez (dictator 1908–35) into the hands of the popular Democratic Action party of Rómulo Betancourt. The Figueres junta installed in Costa Rica in May 1948 was most friendly to Betancourt. What more natural than that these four newly fashioned régimes should encourage volunteers of their own and surrounding nations to prepare to attack the régime of Castaneda, betrayer of the 1944 revolution in El Salvador, or Carías and Somoza, champions of *continuismo* in Honduras and Nicaragua? Somoza might have added (save for the delicacy involved in expressing concern for an extra-isthmian government) that the same revolutionary forces were out to get the régime of Rafael Leonidas Trujillo Molina, lord of the Dominican Republic (1930–61).

The group organized to carry out the ambitious programme of ridding the area of dictators was called the Caribbean Legion. A group by the same name had aided the Figueres cause at Limón in April 1948. Though it was Somoza who expressed apprehension, the first move in the game after his statement was the invasion of Costa Rica from Nicaraguan soil in December 1948. The Legion made its only warlike move, an unsuccessful one, from Guatemala to the Dominican Republic in June 1949. When this happened, its own backing was already crumbling. Counter-revolution in Venezuela had ended the rule of Democratic Action in November 1948. Ulate, less interested than Figueres in revolutionary fervour, became president of Costa Rica in November 1949. The Cuba of Ramón Grau San Martín and Carlos Prío Socarrás, in any event more revolutionary in name than in actuality, returned to Batista's hands in 1952. For a time only the sore-pressed Arbenz régime remained of the new-fashioned ones. Its 1954 demise occurred through the co-operation of the Nationalist government of Honduras and the Osorio régime in El Salvador.

Nicaragua has been involved, either as the injured or injurer, in all across-the-border movements on the isthmus since 1954. Figueres' inauguration as president of Costa Rica in November 1953 set the stage for a Somoza–Figueres feud which reached such proportions in January 1955 that Somoza challenged Figueres to a duel. Relations between the two countries improved somewhat after the Organization of American States, a few days later, helped to stop the invasion of Costa Rica from Nicaraguan soil. Troubles between Nicaragua and Honduras began in February 1957 when their border controversy was renewed through Honduras' creation of the department of Gracias a Dios. Villeda Morales inherited these troubles in December 1957; Echandi Jiménez of Costa Rica inherited some which remained on Nicaragua's other border in May 1958.

The winning of the isle of Cuba by Fidel Castro on 1 January 1959, ending the second period of Batista, once again set the Caribbean astir. For a few months mad rumours spread everywhere that remaining dictatorships would be tumbled; all conservative régimes seemed to have something to fear, whatever their mode of election. Such rumours did not materialize in Central America. Cuba engaged in propaganda activities as she could, until diplomatic relations with the Castro régime were broken by Guatemala in April 1960, Nicaragua in June 1960, El Salvador in March 1961, Honduras in April 1961, and Costa Rica in September 1961. Ydígoras and Somoza Debayle have often accused Cuba of giving aid to rebels against their régimes, but the charges remain largely unsubstantiated, in contrast to those of Cuba against Ydígoras and Somoza. Chester Lacayo, son of Enrique Lacayo Farfán, was even arrested in Cuba in 1960 for conspiratorial activity against the

Somoza régime (though it seems certain the incident occurred only after Lacayo had become injudiciously involved in a conflict of Castro and non-Castro auspices). Castro's resolute swing to Marxism in 1960–1 terminated any thought of co-operation between Cuba and more democratic reformist régimes. Indeed Castro has worked far harder to unseat Betancourt, president of Venezuela since February 1959, than he has to get rid of Somoza.

Illegal Central American border crossings of 1959–61 were chiefly those of Nicaraguans entering Nicaragua. There is little doubt that, in the series of attempts which were made, President Somoza Debayle profited from steps taken by Presidents Villeda and Echandi on either side to hamper Nicaraguan expatriate activities. Echandi began the practice after the launching of a fairly large-scale invasion of Nicaragua from Costa Rica in June 1959. His reasoning and the consistency of his attitudes have already been discussed. Neither Echandi nor Villeda has prevented all armed forces from entering the country between them, but both have tried, arresting groups about to move even though the arrests were unpopular in their own countries. Villeda's position has been simple, clear, and constant. It is not a stand of friendship for dictatorship or tyranny. It is only a recognition of Central America's need to stop an old comedy.

The cry of fraud has been raised in nearly every Central American election. It usually has substance, one may quickly agree, but the *extent* of fraud or in whose favour the truth lies is most often uncertain. Who is to decide the credentials of a nation's leadership when the nation cannot trust its own electoral system? One certainty is that among the least qualified to make judgements are the leaders of neighbouring régimes. Villeda's policy is an acknowledgment of that principle.

'¡ MÁTENME A MI; NO A LOS MUCHACHOS!'

'Kill me; not the boys!' shouted Santiago Delgado, or words to that effect, on 9 September 1960, in a Managua street.[8] His own boy, Ajax Delgado López, had been killed four days earlier by Nicaragua's National Guard, ostensibly while attempting to flee from prison. The father's remarks were occasioned by continued street turbulence between various young people of the city and the Guard during the days while religious services were being held for the son. There was of course a reason why Ajax Delgado died

[8] As reported in *La Prensa*, 11 Sept. 1960.

rather than his father, and why the Guard was faced with boys rather than men in the streets. The men of Nicaragua had learned the futility of protest against the Somoza régime without proper cover. The boys had yet to learn; the shooting of Ajax was indeed one of their lessons.

The plain fact seems to be that administrations as recent as those of Picado in Costa Rica, Somoza Debayle of Nicaragua, Lozano of Honduras, Lemus of El Salvador, and Ydígoras of Guatemala have not learned to get along—in moments of local crisis—without brutality to their more vociferous opponents. Each has allowed freedom in various ways; never has the rule been totalitarian. Yet time after time when interests have clashed, civilians have been needlessly injured. Those who are hurt most often, because they protest most often, are university students.

Central America's five universities are her greatest bastions of freedom. By tradition and legal standing they all have privacy through autonomy. But in times of emotional crisis student excitement pours out onto the streets. The students may be fair or unfair in their judgements, mature or immature in their thinking. As a rule they *are* idealistic, and most critical of a present administration. Their protests begin peacefully but increase in intensity when demands are not met. All too often tension builds up between students and soldiers until dozens of students are in prison, or perhaps a few dead on the streets. At this point one stops to inquire, 'How did it all happen?' And one knows the answer is that a régime which did not want to kill its own people was brought to it because it had not learned how to deal with criticism.

Central American leaders need to establish closer contact with the people of their countries. They need to explain actions better—most deeds have their own rationale—and to desist riding herd on their opponents. It appears that at least Costa Rica and Honduras are coming around to the point of view that democracy cannot exist in a climate of fear, and that fear will continue where there is government-countenanced or government-sponsored violence.

'¡INMEDIATA EJECUCIÓN DEL LAUDO! ¡NADA
DE DILATORIAS!'

This cry was a motto appearing day after day on the front page of an opposition paper in Honduras.[9] In reference to the judgment made by the International Court of Justice on the border dispute

[9] *El Día*, 20 Jan.–1 Feb. 1961.

with Nicaragua, it was a plea for 'Immediate execution of the award. No delays!' A few weeks earlier, as President Villeda Morales prepared to meet President Somoza Debayle to plan a peaceful transition of power in the affected area, the cry had been 'Immediate execution of the award. No protocols!'[10] A huge headline printed in the interim announced 'EL EJERCITO LISTO' (The Army Is Ready!)—ready of course to march into the awarded territory whenever the president gave his command, and rather impatient to be at it.[11] Such journalistic enterprise represented more, of course, than the enthusiasm of national spirit. The basic intent was to embarrass the president of Honduras before a public who might not see any reason for delay on the boundary once the court's judgment had been pronounced. The delay was not of Villeda's choice, except that he preferred to treat with a losing Nicaragua in gentlemanly fashion. For this he came near being accused of treason to Honduras.

'When are they going to let Betancourt govern?' asked a Costa Rican paper in 1961, taking note of the fact that although Betancourt was president of Venezuela by popular choice, he had had to spend much of his energy and time fighting off Venezuelans who lacked respect for elections.[12] The same question might be asked of isthmian governments chosen by the people but hounded at every turn. There are many ways to work at bringing down a régime besides open armed conflict. Those members of the press or public who concentrate their energies upon terminating a popularly elected administration before its term of office has expired are guilty of mutiny against popular verdict. Their presence in every state constitutes one of Central America's greatest handicaps.

The habit of rebellion or incitement to rebellion may stem from impatience, or from extreme confidence in the popularity or rightness of one's own opinions, or from simple desire to obtain power regardless of popularity or rightness. Simple desire for power can be handled only by police action. Impatience and extreme confidence may be differently contained. The parliamentary form of government, which none of the republics has tried, would provide legal avenues for changes of régime especially designed for the impatient. Extreme confidence too could be tested in meaningful ways under this system, placing in the glare of ridiculosity all extraconstitutional efforts. Demands for quick change might become

[10] Ibid. 7–9 Jan. 1961.   [11] Ibid. 18 Jan. 1961.
[12] '¿ Cuándo van a dejar gobernar a Betancourt?', *La Nación*, 21 Feb. 1961.

313

all the more incessant under the parliamentary method. But a greater likelihood is that they would become more responsible in nature.

Chief accountability in this matter of course continues to lie with the people. A popularly elected régime, regardless of its form, deserves every right to work under the established rules during the established term of office. Costa Rica is the only one of the republics where such practice now seems standard. Education of the remainder of Central America's masses will help make them less susceptible to appeals for *immediate* action, with all the excitement and danger that entails. But what is needed most of all is respect for the laws (of a democratic state) by the already-educated citizen.

'NI IMPUESTOS NI DENUESTOS'

'Neither taxes nor insults', editorialized one of Guatemala's leading papers directed by one of Central America's leading journalists, as part of its reply to the request of President Ydígoras Fuentes for an income tax.[13] To a payer of this type of tax in another republic which gives money to Guatemala, this comment too seems irresponsible. But most comment has its own logic. The objection in this case was to publication of statements by the Ydígoras régime to the effect that the proposed income tax would fall upon a small minority of Guatemalan families:

A *peronismo* already discredited, of course. Besides which it is a mode little commendable—for a government which prides itself as democratic and is itself situated in the advanced trenches against Communism—to encourage hatred between classes: see for yourselves, gentlemen—one can read between the lines—that the plan gives opportunity for vengeance, since it will fall upon the capitalists. . . .

Further comment was to the effect that 'Guatemala is tired of taxes', and that one might wonder if the whole plan was not inspired by 'a simple desire to have more in order to spend more'. The 'insults' mentioned in the headline had appeared in the government daily, applied to the persons of two prominent lawyers who had drawn up a petition against the tax.

Most newspapers in Central America, it must be emphasized, agree with the point of view expressed by this headline. The Guatemalan case differs only in that here there is *no* private income tax, whereas elsewhere on the isthmus there is a *small* income tax. The

[13] *Imp.*, 31 Jan. 1961.

opinion printed everywhere is a straightforward expression of the reluctance of the moneyed class to give up its privileged position. Ghosts of the French, the Russian, and a variety of other revolutions would advise, if their voices were heeded, to give up before it is too late.

In what does the reluctance consist? Unwillingness to pay taxes —both before and after the passage of tax laws—to provide schools for Indians or peasants. Aversion to giving up land, even unused land—with or without compensation—which could provide a living for hungry workers, but which if retained grants power or prestige. Hesitation to invest in new industry at home when safer investments are available abroad. Refusal to pay a living wage to a countryman who has nowhere else to go. Such reluctance is short-sightedness. Its continuance will undermine the best efforts of any Alliance for Progress.

'DIEZ CENTAVOS MÁS'

Simple solutions for great problems are often judged unrealistic. Whether they *are* unrealistic usually depends upon a certain set of assumptions made by the persons who pass the judgement. *Diez centavos más* or 10 cents more for one pound of coffee would seem a rather simple solution for Latin America's economic ills. The suggestion was made by Ricardo Castro Beeche, editor of Costa Rica's *La Nación*, at a Chamber of Commerce banquet in Chicago.[14] 'What difference would it make', he said, 'if the householders of the United States were to pay ten cents of a dollar more for a pound of coffee?' Little difference to the consumer, was his theme, but much to the producer who relies upon coffee for a living. Jorge Mejía Palacio of Colombia had the same theme in mind when he pointed out a year and a half later that his country 'had lost two to three times as much foreign income from falling coffee prices as it had received in Alliance for Progress credits'.[15]

Those economists who hold that coffee and other products have a natural price determined by laws of supply and demand will judge the talk of Mejía Palacio irrelevant and the suggestion of Castro Beeche ingenuous. Despite the viewpoint of such economists, intergovernmental action is now planned to stabilize the price of coffee. But if prices of food products or raw materials in international commerce can be stabilized in this fashion, they can be raised in like manner. Then the question arises, 'Why not?' If the

[14] *La Nación*, 25 Nov. 1960.   [15] *New York Times*, 24 Apr. 1962.

prices of coffee, bananas, and cotton could be raised materially—but most especially those of coffee—Central America as one region might do much to lift herself economically towards a decent plane of existence. Is there any reason why she should not be permitted to attempt this operation on her own rather than be pauperized as a dependent?

Basically, only two factors enter into the answer: (1) Would Central American coffee, bananas, and cotton be bought if the prices were higher? The coffee would be bought, it seems certain, unless competition of similar quality in the mild flavours undercut the price. Such competition would have to be covered by far-reaching international agreements; areas in a position to compete share Central America's need for the money. Bananas might or might not sell at higher prices. Sales competition would presumably come from other fruits. Who is in a position to gauge their respective appeal to the North American or European appetite? Cotton is more deeply involved in international entanglement; its future price may depend upon mechanization and good management. If Central America can compete on these scores, her weather and soils grant her an advantage.

(2) Should Central American exports be expected to pave the way to modern life for isthmian inhabitants? An argument may certainly be made that all those in the exporting business—both management and labour—deserve as good a life as their customers as long as they remain diligent. Such a life for the many involved in coffee, bananas, and cotton would mean increased incomes for many others as well. Under these changed circumstances large segments of the population would become interested in goods never before within their reach. Whether *present* exports could revolutionize the life of the entire isthmus is a larger question. If too small a proportion of the people were affected, even under such radically different treatment, only new products or new markets could yield the aid necessary to perform the task.

To say that in such a way Central America *might* lift herself economically is not of course to say that she *would* lift herself economically. Many archaic practices mentioned in the pages of this book would have to be abandoned. Governments would have to remain progressive. Purchases abroad of materials easily produced at home would have to be terminated. Finally—and most important of all—10 or 20 cents more a pound for coffee or 5 cents more for a hand of bananas will provide no help whatsoever if the extra amount paid by the consumer goes into the pockets of those whose wants are already provided. Save for this great snare, one would be tempted to suggest advertisements reading, 'We urge you to buy at this higher price for the sake of the man in the field'.

THE NEW INDEPENDENCE

With all the underlying problems that remain, of which these headlines are an evidence, the hemispheric steps taken in 1961 may lead to a new independence for Central America. Recognition of a right, that is to say, may lead to its realization as future events unfold. Political sovereignty came within Central America's grasp in 1821; economic sovereignty seems to have come within reach 140 years later.

The 140 years after first independence were full of disappointments and failures. The union dissolved and was never refashioned; the envisaged democracy did not begin to materialize until four generations had passed by. Will the new freedom be handled better?

One may say yes—with much confidence—if Guatemala, Honduras, and Costa Rica are not handed back to the small minorities which once ruled their affairs and if El Salvador and Nicaragua can somehow escape the same domination. Popular judgement may often be unwise, and the pitfalls along the way may be grave ones. Yet the talent is there, if set free, to solve problems and to make the isthmus happy in its material lot.

If Central America does not fritter away her new independence, is there anything significant—to the rest of the world—that she can do with it? Is there anything Central America can offer the world, that is to say, *other* than high-quality coffee, bananas, and cotton? Perhaps Honduras' good-natured living will be preserved, despite all the threats to it, until some philosopher (native or foreigner) has had the time to absorb its content and study its method. Perhaps Guatemala's marimba bands will travel more widely, bringing the pleasure of their deep-throated resonance to ears which have never heard and enjoyed it. Perhaps Costa Rica's record as regards education and democracy will join with geography to bring her the capital of an ever-more-closely-united America.

In the days when the *Popol Vuh* was composed, Central America had a personality of her own. She has still, as the meeting-place of three races rather than the home of one, though some traits have changed and others lie dormant and unrecognizable. It is to be hoped that as she steps into the modern world her individuality will not be lost. If it is instead perceived and appreciated, her third and final freedom will have been won.

NOTES ON BIBLIOGRAPHY

I. MAPS

The most detailed maps of the Central American area are quadrangles published by the Dirección General de Cartografía in Guatemala, offices of the same name in El Salvador and Honduras, the Oficina de Geodesía in Nicaragua, and the Instituto Geográfico de Costa Rica. There is a series intended to cover the area of each country, the work of smaller El Salvador (scale 1 : 50,000) and Costa Rica (1 : 25,000) being already well advanced. Early sheets printed in Nicaragua (1 : 50,000) and Guatemala (1 : 25,000) show areas near the Pacific; Honduras was preparing to publish its first in 1960. These maps show topography (through the use of contour lines), a variety of vegetation coverings, and cultural detail down to individual rural dwellings. A separate series (1 : 250,000) initiated in Guatemala shows the same features except the finer cultural detail, and seems ideally suited for the surface-borne tourist who is curious concerning the country about him. The offices busy preparing these series also distribute large-scale maps of many urban zones and districts of special interest.

The only complete topographic map of Central America at present available is contained in six sheets of the 1 : 1,000,000 Map of Hispanic America published by the American Geographical Society of New York. Of these, the Tegucigalpa sheet—including virtually all of El Salvador and Honduras, over half of Nicaragua, and a corner of Guatemala—has a 1952 copyright; so does the Istmo de Tehuantepec sheet, showing the western half of the Petén. The other four—named Belize, Ciudad Guatemala, Lago de Nicaragua, and Panamá—are dated from 1928 to 1937.

The best road maps of the area are those prepared by the General Drafting Company for Esso Standard Oil (Central America), S. A. There is a separate map for each Central American country and Panama showing highways, railways, streams, volcanoes, departmental and provincial lines, and a very large number of settlements (approximately 1,200 of them, for instance, in Honduras). The scales for the first editions published (about 1948–50) were near 1 : 385,000 for El Salvador, 1 : 630,000 for Costa Rica, and 1 : 935,000 for the others. Editions of 1960 present El Salvador and Costa Rica on a reduced scale.

The two maps in this book are traced in part from the Esso map of all Central America and Panama (1 : 2,300,000) shown on the reverse side of older editions of the individual country maps. The first shows the physical features mentioned in Chapter I, including several volcanoes not included on the base map. The second shows all departmental and provincial capitals, other cities above 10,000 population in 1950, and the ports, as well as the public railways (the crosstie symbol), the paved high-ways (solid lines heavier than the river lines), and all-weather earth roads connecting the capitals (the broken lines). For patient and careful work on these maps, the author is indebted to his friend and neighbour Mr Eugene Eagle.

II. NEWSPAPERS

Central American newspapers are generally easy to obtain through direct mail subscription, though rates are quite high from El Salvador, Honduras, and Nicaragua. Packages containing the issues of a week or more are dispatched by surface mail, with an occasional one failing to reach its destination. Particular issues were missing from an opposition Honduran paper in 1960 and 1961 in such manner as to suggest government interference, but censorship difficulties were not encountered else-where during the same period of time.

The subscriber to a single newspaper from the isthmus will be disappointed (1) in its failure to give any but crisis or capsule news of the four countries other than the one where it is published; and (2) in its unwillingness to cover news of its own political opponents. Even *El Imparcial* of Guatemala City and *La Nación* of San José, in many respects the most mature news sheets in Central America, are subject to these limitations. *Diario de Centro América* of Guatemala City and *El Día* of Tegucigalpa have a Central American page and column respectively, but in both cases the isthmian coverage remains inadequate while the home reporting is most partisan.

A subscription to two or more papers from each country will provide a fair coverage. But the record remains incomplete at crucial points even if one reads every paper in the land. In moments of crisis particularly, the official 'hand-out' is relied upon as the news of the day, and 'the news behind the news' is not sought out by enterprising reporters. On such occasions, the foreigner must turn to New York or London for even a half-clear picture of what has transpired. On more humdrum days the isthmian papers will fill in with important details.

The more distinguished daily newspapers (four for each country, ex-cluding the official gazettes) are listed below. All save two are published in the respective capitals. Those which are starred are mentioned some-where in the pages of this book.

Guatemala

Diario de Centro América (*)
La Hora
El Imparcial (*)
Prensa Libre (*)

Notes on Bibliography

El Salvador

El Diario de Hoy (*)
Diario Latino (*)
La Prensa Gráfica (*)
Tribuna Libre

Honduras

Correo del Norte (San Pedro Sula)
El Cronista
El Día (*)
El Pueblo (*)

Nicaragua

El Centro-Americano (León)
La Noticia
Novedades (*)
La Prensa (*)

Costa Rica

Diario de Costa Rica (*)
La Nación (*)
La Prensa Libre
La República (*)

III. GOVERNMENT REPORTS

Government documents and statistics are easy to obtain from Central American capitals under two conditions: (1) One must expect in a large number of cases a considerable lag between the date of the report and the date of its publication. (2) One must be prepared in most instances to go and ask for the data in person. Of recurring publications, only the annual presidential messages from all five countries and the statistical publications of Costa Rica are kept regularly up-to-date and available by mail. The presidential messages (reports on the state of the nation) generally serve as guides to material spelled out in annual ministerial and agency reports, but these latter frequently wait several years for publication. A useful listing of available government reports from this area was made in James B. Childs, *The Memorias of the Republics of Central America and of the Antilles* (Washington, 1932) and in vols. 6, 10–11, and 13–14 (all Washington, 1947) of the series *A Guide to the Official Publications of the Other American Republics*, done by the United States Library of Congress.

The Dirección General de Estadística of Guatemala and the Dirección General de Estadística y Censos of each of the other four republics are very active offices which work under an impressive variety of handicaps. Considering the problems they face, the most amazing aspect of their labours is not the errors they commit but the usefulness of their projects.

All have been most courteous and generous in the provision of material used in this study. The Costa Rican office provides a checklist of its current publications through which the interested researcher may secure those which he desires by mail.

Following is a list of periodical or recent statistical publications which are of special interest. The place of publication is the respective capital in all cases but one. Most have been cited in the pages of this book.

The issuing department is the Dirección General de Estadística, or de Estadística y Censos, of each republic.

Guatemala

Boletín Estadístico.
Censo agropecuario: 1950. 3 vols., 1954-5.
Guatemala en Cifras.
Primer censo industrial de Guatemala: año de 1946. 1951.
Segundo censo industrial: 1953. 1957.
Sexto censo de población: Abril 18 de 1950. 1957.

El Salvador

Anuario Estadístico.
Boletín Estadístico.
Comercio Exterior.
Diccionario geográfico de la república de El Salvador. 3rd ed., 1959.
Hechos y Cifras de El Salvador.
Primer censo agropecuario: Octubre–diciembre de 1950. 1954.
Primer censo industrial y comercial: 1951. 2 vols., 1955.
Segundo censo de población: Junio 13 de 1950. 1954.
Segundo censo industrial y comercial: 1956. 2 vols., 1959.

Honduras

Anuario Estadístico.
Boletín Estadístico.
Comercio Exterior.
Detalle del censo de población por departamentos levantado el 18 de junio de 1950. 2 vols., 1952.
División político territorial: 1959. 1959.
Estadísticas Educacionales.
Primer censo agropecuario: 1952. San Salvador, 1954.
Resultados generales del censo general de la república levantado el 18 de junio de 1950. 1952.

Nicaragua

Boletín de Estadística.
Censo general de población de la república de Nicaragua: Mayo 1950. 17 vols., 1951-4.

Notes on Bibliography

Costa Rica

Anuario Estadístico de Costa Rica.
Atlas estadístico de Costa Rica. 1953.
Censo agropecuario de 1950. 1953.
Censo agropecuario de 1955. 1959.
Censo de comercio e industrias de 1952: 1o de octubre de 1950 al 30 de setiembre de 1951. 1954.
Censo de población de Costa Rica: 22 de mayo de 1950. 1953.
Comercio Exterior de Costa Rica.
Indice de Precios al por Menor.
Principales Hechos Vitales Ocurridos en Costa Rica.
II censo de comercio de Costa Rica: 1958. 1961.

Only in a few matters, such as the reporting of imports and exports, has there come to be a fair degree of uniformity in Central American statistical presentations from one country to the other. A bewildering array of weights, measures, and (most perplexing of all) subtly varied definitions awaits the person who dares to attempt comparisons. In this work, international compilations which have given proper thought to the problems involved prove especially useful, though their reporting of details is necessarily limited. *Investment in Central America* (United States Bureau of Foreign Commerce, Washington, 1956) and *La estructura agropecuaria de las naciones americanas: Análisis estadístico-censal de los resultados obtenidos bajo el Programa del Censo de las Américas de 1950* (Washington, Inter-American Statistical Institute, 1957) have been especially useful in this connexion. See Ch. v, n. 71, for data concerning the *World Trade Information Service*, certain numbers of which constitute a supplement to *Investment in Central America*.

Other international periodical or recent statistical publications cited in the pages of this book are as follows:

Basic Ecclesiastical Statistics for Latin America (World Horizon Reports, Maryknoll, New York).
FAO. *Trade Yearbook.*
—— *Yearbook of Food and Agriculture Statistics.*
Foreign Grants and Credits by the United States Government (United States Office of Business Economics).
International Labour Office. *Year Book of Labour Statistics.*
Protestant Missions in Latin America: a Statistical Survey. Washington, 1961.
United Nations. *Demographic Yearbook.*
—— *Statistical Yearbook.*
—— *Yearbook of International Trade Statistics.*
U.S. Catholic Overseas Missionary Personnel, January 1, 1960. Washington, 1960.
World Christian Handbook.
World Radio Handbook.

Copies of the current national budgets may be secured through the appropriate government offices in the respective capitals. Copies of the constitutions are available in English or Spanish from the Pan American Union, Washington.

IV. PERIODICALS

The only magazine which gives a wide scope of Central American affairs regular attention is the *Hispanic American Report*, founded in November 1948 as the *Hispanic World Report* (see the Preface and Ch. x, n. 7). Generally only in times of deep crisis can more complete information be found in other foreign newspapers and magazines. The *Hispanic American Report* often attempts to inquire into the meaning of things, and is seldom content with any government's proclamations.

Other periodicals cited in the pages of this book are listed below. Numbers given in parentheses refer to the chapter and footnote in the book where further bibliographical information is provided:

Guatemala

Anales de la Sociedad de Geografía e Historia de Guatemala (ii 13; iii 5, 13; iv 9, 22; v 94, 111).
Antropología e Historia de Guatemala (v 104).
Boletín del Archivo General del Gobierno (v 96).
Instituto Indigenista Nacional. *Boletín* (v 105).
Universidad de San Carlos (v 81, 115, 125; viii 80).

El Salvador

Ars (vi 85).
Ateneo (vi 83).
ECA (vi 84).
La Universidad (vi 74).

Honduras

Ceiba (vii 66).
Honduras Rotaria (vii 77).
Revista de la Sociedad de Geografía e Historia de Honduras (vii 59).
Revista de la Universidad (iii 21; v 143; vii 67).
Revista del Archivo y Biblioteca Nacionales de Honduras (vii 59).
Universidad de Honduras (vii 67).

Nicaragua

Cuadernos Universitarios (viii 77).
Revista de la Academia de Geografía e Historia de Nicaragua (viii 74).

Notes on Bibliography

Costa Rica

Combate (ix 85).
Newsletter of the Institute of Political Education (ix 84)
El Repertorio Americano (ix 100).
Revista de la Universidad de Costa Rica (ix 86).
Revista de los Archivos Nacionales (ix 76).

International and Foreign

American Anthropologist (ii 6, 30; iii 6, 26).
American Antiquity (i 10 f.; ii 8, 10, 33; iii 1 f.).
The American Journal of International Law (iv 35; v 28, 40).
American Mercury (viii 16).
The American Political Science Review (v 28).
Américas (ix 15).
Annals of the Organization of American States (iv 35; v 29; ix 24).
The Annual Register (v 39).
Archaeology (iv 17).
Bulletin of the American Museum of Natural History (i 3).
Bulletin of the Pan American Union (v 121).
The Canadian Forum (viii 50).
Carnegie Institution of Washington. *Year Book* (i 9).
Central American Bulletin (v 147).
Foreign Affairs (v 23).
Harper's New Monthly Magazine (i 6).
Hispania (v 126).
The Hispanic American Historical Review (v 20, 40, 99; vii 60).
Human Organization (v 31).
Inter-American Economic Affairs (v 58; vii 50; viii 21).
International Affairs (v 40).
International Journal of American Linguistics (iii 7).
International Labour Review (v 59, 76).
International Organization (iv 38).
Life (v 22).
Maya Research (*Mexico and Central America*) (ii 3).
Middle American Research Records (i 13).
The Nation (viii 49).
Organización de Estados Centroamericanos. *Boletín Informativo* (iv 37, 40).
The Quill (viii 59).
The Reporter (viii 16).
Revista Interamericana de Bibliografía (vii 65; viii 68).
The Southwestern Social Science Quarterly (viii 12).
Time (viii 47).
U.S. News & World Report (v 30; viii 48).
The World Today (v 22; ix 25).

V. BOOKS

A. There are twelve sections of this book containing rather compact bibliographical treatments *which are not repeated here*. The headings under which these sections fall are given below, with their chapter and footnote references:

Maya Studies (ii 14–33).
Indian Studies (iii 29–45).
Guatemala: Learning (v 88–116); Art (v 123–37).
El Salvador: Learning (vi 66–75); Art (vi 79–85).
Honduras: Learning (vii 57–67); Art (vii 70–77).
Nicaragua: Learning (viii 62–77); Art (viii 80–88).
Costa Rica: Learning (ix 69–86); Art (ix 90–108).

B. *Travel accounts*. The following is a selected list of accounts by persons who travelled in Central America, only a few of which have been cited in these pages. The list is arranged chronologically by dates of first editions or completed manuscripts, with later versions mentioned as part of the same item when they are important:

1525. Pedro de Alvarado. 1924 ed., *An Account of the Conquest of Guatemala in 1524*. S. J. Mackie, ed., N.Y.

1557. Gonzalo Fernández de Oviedo y Valdés. 1851–5 ed., *Historia general y natural de las Indias, islas y tierra-firme del mar océano*. J. Amador de los Ríos, ed., 4 vols., Madrid.

1565. Girolamo Benzoni. *La historia del Mondo Nuovo*. Venice. 1857 ed., *History of the New World*. W. H. Smyth, tr., London.

1578. Bernal Díaz del Castillo. 1908–16 ed., *The True History of the Conquest of New Spain*. G. García, ed.; A. P. Maudslay, tr.; 5 vols., London. 1933–4 ed., *Verdadera y notable relación del descubrimiento y conquista de la Nueva España y Guatemala*. 2 vols., Guatemala.

1629. Antonio Vázquez de Espinosa. 1942 ed., *Compendium and Description of the West Indies*. C. U. Clark, tr., Washington.

1648. Thomas Gage. *The English-American: his Travail by Sea and Land*. London. 1928 ed., *The English-American: a New Survey of the West Indies, 1648*. A. P. Newton, ed., London.

1735. John Cockburn. *A Journey over Land, from the Gulf of Honduras to the Great South-Sea*. London. 1740 ed., *The Unfortunate Englishmen*. London.

1809. George Henderson. *An Account of the British Settlement of Honduras*. London.

1827. Orlando W. Roberts. *Narrative of Voyages and Excursions on the East Coast and in the Interior of Central America*. Edinburgh.

1827–8. J. Haefkens. *Reize naar Guatemala*. 2 vols., The Hague.

1828. Henry Dunn. *Guatimala*. N.Y.

1829. George Alexander Thompson. *Narrative of an Official Visit to Guatemala from Mexico*. London.

1839. George Washington Montgomery. *Narrative of a Journey to Guatemala, in Central America, in 1838.* N.Y.

1841. John Lloyd Stephens. *Incidents of Travel in Central America, Chiapas, and Yucatan.* 2 vols., N.Y. 1949 ed., R. L. Predmore, ed., 2 vols., New Brunswick, N.J.

1842. Thomas Young. *Narrative of a Residence on the Mosquito Shore, during the Years 1839, 1840, & 1841.* London.

1847. Robert Glasgow Dunlop. *Travels in Central America.* London.

1850. Frederick Crowe. *The Gospel in Central America.* London.

1855. Ephraim George Squier. *Waikna; or, Adventures on the Mosquito Shore.* N.Y.

1856. Moritz Wagner and Karl Scherzer. *Die Republik Costa Rica in Central-Amerika.* Leipzig.

1857. Arthur Morelet. *Voyage dans l'Amérique Centrale, l'île de Cuba, et le Yucatan.* 2 vols., Paris. 1871 ed., *Travels in Central America.* M. F. Squier, tr., N.Y.

1857. Karl Scherzer. *Wanderungen durch die mittel-amerikanischen Freistaaten, Nicaragua, Honduras und San Salvador.* Braunschweig. 1857 ed., *Travels in the Free States of Central America.* London.

1857. William Vincent Wells. *Explorations and Adventures in Honduras.* N.Y.

1863. Wilhelm Marr. *Reise nach Central-Amerika.* 2 vols., Hamburg.

1868. Frederick Boyle. *A Ride across a Continent: a Personal Narrative of Wanderings through Nicaragua and Costa Rica.* London.

1877. John Whetham Boddam-Whetham. *Across Central America.* London.

1877. Joseph Laferrière. *De Paris à Guatémala: Notes de voyages au Centre-Amérique, 1866–1875.* Paris.

1884. Mary Lester. *A Lady's Ride across Spanish Honduras.* Edinburgh and London.

1885. Edward A. Lever. *Central America.* New Orleans.

1886. Otto Stoll. *Guatemala: Reisen und Schilderungen aus den Jahren 1878–1883.* Leipzig.

1887. Carl Erik Alexander Bovallius. *Resa i Central-Amerika, 1881–1883.* Uppsala.

1887. William Tufts Brigham. *Guatemala: the Land of the Quetzal.* N.Y.

1890. Cecil Charles. *Honduras: the Land of Great Depths.* Chicago and N.Y.

1895. Tommaso Caivano. *Il Guatemala.* Florence.

1896. Richard Harding Davis. *Three Gringos in Venezuela and Central America.* N.Y.

1897. Albert Morlan. *A Hoosier in Honduras.* Indianapolis.

1897. Karl Theodor Sapper. *Das nördliche Mittel-Amerika nebst einem Ausflug nach dem Hochland von Anahuac: Reisen und Studien aus den Jahren 1888–1895.* Braunschweig.

1898. Hezekiah Butterworth. *Lost in Nicaragua.* Boston and Chicago.

1899. Charles Napier Bell. *Tangweera: Life and Adventures among Gentle Savages.* London.

1899. Anne Cary Maudslay and Alfred Percival Maudslay. *A Glimpse of Guatemala, and Some Notes on the Ancient Monuments of Central America.* London.

1902. James Wilson Grimes Walker. *Ocean to Ocean: an Account, Personal and Historical, of Nicaragua and Its People.* Chicago.

1907. José Segarra and Joaquín Juliá. *Excursión por América: Costa Rica.* San José.

1909. Rubén Darío. *El viaje a Nicaragua, e Intermezzo tropical.* Madrid.

1909. Nevin Otto Winter. *Guatemala and Her People of To-day.* Boston.

1910. Frederick Palmer. *Central America and Its Problems: an Account of a Journey from the Rio Grande to Panama.* N.Y.

1913. George Palmer Putnam. *The Southland of North America: Rambles and Observations in Central America during the Year 1912.* N.Y. and London.

1916. Jacinto Capella. *La ciudad tranquila (Guatemala): impresiones de un viaje a través del país de la eterna primavera.* Madrid.

1922. Eugene Cunningham. *Gypsying through Central America.* London.

1922. Emil Landenberger. *Durch Central-Amerika.* Stuttgart.

1924. Morley Roberts. *On the Earthquake Line: Minor Adventures in Central America.* London.

1926. Wallace Thompson. *Rainbow Countries of Central America.* N.Y.

1928. Arthur Brown Ruhl. *The Central Americans: Adventures and Impressions between Mexico and Panama.* N.Y. and London.

1930. Franz Josef Lentz. *Aus dem Hochlande der Maya.* Stuttgart.

1931. Alfred Batson. *Vagabond's Paradise.* Boston.

1932. Carleton Beals. *Banana Gold.* Philadelphia and London.

1934. Aldous Leonard Huxley. *Beyond the Mexique Bay.* N.Y. and London.

1934. Agnes Edwards Rothery. *Images of Earth: Guatemala.* N.Y.

1936. Louis Joseph Halle. *Transcaribbean: a Travel Book of Guatemala, El Salvador, British Honduras.* N.Y. and Toronto.

1937. Erna Fergusson. *Guatemala.* N.Y. and London.

1937. Joseph Henry Jackson. *Notes on a Drum: Travel Sketches in Guatemala.* N.Y.

1937. Peter Keenagh. *Mosquito Coast.* London.

1939. Addison Burbank. *Guatemala Profile.* N.Y.

1940. Victor Wolfgang Von Hagen. *Jungle in the Clouds.* N.Y.

C. *Current affairs and conditions.* A selected list of books published since 1945. Books dealing with more than one country are included in the first group.

Central America

Adams, Richard N. *Cultural Surveys of Panama—Nicaragua—Guatemala— El Salvador—Honduras.* Washington, 1957.

Aubrun, Charles Vincent. *L'Amérique Centrale.* Paris, 1952.

Bayo, Alberto. *Tempestad en el Caribe.* Mexico City, 1950. The Caribbean Legion.

Notes on Bibliography

Carr, Archie Fairly. *High Jungles and Low*. Gainesville, Fla., 1953. Natural history.

Clark, Sydney Aylmer. *All the Best in Central America*. 2nd ed., N.Y., 1958. A guidebook.

Contreras, Agustín. *Centroamérica vista por un mexicano*. Mexico City, 1951.

Coto Romero, Rafael. *Visión de Centro América*. San Salvador, 1946. Philosophical analysis.

Dozier, Craig L. *Indigenous Tropical Agriculture in Central America*. Washington, 1958.

Gómez Naranjo, Pedro Alejandro. *Faro de cinco luces: perfiles de Centro América*. Bucaramanga, Colombia, 1950. Essays.

Guzmán, Mauricio. *La federación colegiada de las repúblicas de Centroamérica*. San Salvador, 1957. A union proposed.

Hancock, Ralph. *The Rainbow Republics*. N.Y., 1947. Description.

Herrarte, Alberto. *La unión de Centroamérica*. Guatemala, 1955.

——, comp. *Documentos de la unión centroamericana*. Guatemala, 1957.

Karnes, Thomas L. *The Failure of Union: Central America, 1824–1960*. Chapel Hill, N.C., 1961.

Krehm, William. *Democracia y tiranías en el Caribe*. Mexico City, 1949.

Martz, John D. *Central America: the Crisis and the Challenge*. Chapel Hill, N.C., 1959. A generally pessimistic country-by-country review of politics.

May, Stacy, and Galo Plaza. *The United Fruit Company in Latin America*. Washington, 1958.

Mörne, Håkan. *Den förgyllda fattigdomen: en resa i Centralamerika*. Stockholm, 1949. *Caribbean Symphony*. M. Michael, tr., London, 1955.

Navarro, Miguel. *Elementos de geografía de Centro América*. Tegucigalpa, 1950.

Organización de Estados Centroamericanos. *Primer Seminario de Integración Económica Centroamericana*. Guatemala, 1959. The proceedings.

United States, Bureau of Foreign Commerce. *Investment in Central America*. Washington, 1957.

Valle, Rafael Heliodoro. *Historia de las ideas contemporáneas en Centro-América*. Mexico City, 1960.

Viera Altamirano, Napoleón. *Las fronteras malditas*. San Salvador, 1947. Pro-union.

Wallström, Tord. *Andarín: resa i Centralamerika*. Stockholm, 1953. *Wayfarer in Central America*. M. A. Michael, tr., London, 1956.

Guatemala

Adams, Richard N., ed. *Political Changes in Guatemalan Indian Communities: a Symposium*. New Orleans, 1957.

Adler, John H., and others. *Public Finance and Economic Development in Guatemala*. Palo Alto, Calif., 1952.

Arévalo, Juan José. *Discursos en la presidencia, 1945–1948.* Guatemala, 1948.
—— *Guatemala: la democracia y el imperio.* Montevideo, 1954. 1960 ed., Havana. Relations with United States.
Asociación Nacional Cívico-Cultural. *Poemario: poetas jóvenes guatemaltecos.* Guatemala, 1957.
Bauer Paíz, Alfonso. *Cómo opera el capital yanqui en Centroamérica: el caso de Guatemala.* Mexico City, 1956.
Bianchi, William J. *Belize: the Controversy between Guatemala and Great Britain over the Territory of British Honduras in Central America.* N.Y., 1959.
Bloomfield, Louis M. *The British Honduras–Guatemala Dispute.* Toronto, 1953.
Brown, Lilian. *Bring 'Em Back Petrified.* N.Y., 1956.
Bush, Archer C. *Organized Labor in Guatemala, 1944–1949.* Hamilton, N.Y., 1950.
Cardoza y Aragón, Luis. *Guatemala: las líneas de su mano.* Mexico City, 1955.
—— *La revolución guatemalteca.* Mexico City, 1955. Communist version.
Castelló, Julio. *Así cayó la democracia en Guatemala: la guerra de la United Fruit.* Havana, 1961.
Castillo Armas, Carlos. *La realidad de un mensaje (Pláticas presidenciales).* Guatemala, 1957.
Cifuentes, José Luis. *Algunos escultores contemporáneos de Guatemala.* Guatemala, 1956.
—— *Algunos pintores contemporáneos de Guatemala.* Guatemala, 1956.
——, ed. *Algunos poetas contemporáneos de Guatemala.* Guatemala, 1956.
Comité de Estudiantes Universitarios Anticomunistas. *El calvario de Guatemala.* Guatemala, 1955.
Congreso contra la Infiltración Sovietica en América Latina. *El libro negro del comunismo en Guatemala.* Mexico City, 1954.
Córdoba, Horacio de. *Mis nueve horas con el diablo: prisión, torturas, destierro.* Mexico City, 1957. Anti-Arbenz.
Díaz Rozzotto, Jaime. *El carácter de la revolución guatemalteca: ocaso de la revolución democrático-burguesa corriente.* Mexico City, 1958. Post-Arbenz Marxist outlook.
Dodge, David. *How Lost Was My Weekend: a Greenhorn in Guatemala.* N.Y., 1948.
El Salvador, Secretaría de Información. *De la neutralidad vigilante a la mediación con Guatemala.* San Salvador, 1954.
Galich, Manuel. *Por qué lucha Guatemala: Arévalo y Arbenz, dos hombres contra un imperio.* Buenos Aires, 1956.
Gandarias, León de. *Democracia: La mejor arma contra el comunismo.* Guatemala, 1957. Government-sponsored.
García Bauer, Carlos. *En el amanecer de una nueva era: episodios de la participación de Guatemala en la vida internacional.* Guatemala, 1951.
—— *La controversia sobre el territorio de Belice y el procedimiento ex-aequo et bono.* Guatemala, 1958.

Great Britain, Foreign Office. *Report on Events Leading up to and Arising out of the Change of Régime in Guatemala.* Cmd. 9277. London, 1954.

Guatemala. *Una era de labor constructiva en Guatemala.* Guatemala, 1956. The Castillo régime.

——, Secretaría de Divulgación, Cultura, y Turismo. *Así se gestó la liberación.* Guatemala, 1956. Entirely pro-Castillo.

Hersey, Jean. *Halfway to Heaven: a Guatemala Holiday.* N.Y., 1947.

Holleran, Mary P. *Church and State in Guatemala.* N.Y., 1949.

Humphreys, Robin A. *The Diplomatic History of British Honduras, 1638–1901.* London, 1961.

IBRD. *The Economic Development of Guatemala: Report.* Washington, 1951.

Inman, Samuel Guy. *A New Day in Guatemala.* Wilton, Conn., 1951.

James, Daniel. *Red Design for the Americas: Guatemalan Prelude.* N.Y., 1954.

Jensen, Amy Elizabeth. *Guatemala: a Historical Survey.* N.Y., 1955.

Judson, Lyman, and Ellen Judson. *Let's Go to Guatemala.* N.Y., 1949. A guidebook.

Kelsey, Vera, and Lilly de Jongh Osborne. *Four Keys to Guatemala.* 2nd ed., N.Y., 1961. First published 1952.

Martz, John D. *Communist Infiltration in Guatemala.* N.Y., 1956.

Mejía, Medardo. *El movimiento obrero en la revolución de octubre.* Guatemala, 1949.

Menton, Seymour. *Historia crítica de la novela guatemalteca.* Guatemala, 1960.

Monteforte Toledo, Mario. *Guatemala: monografía sociológica.* Mexico City, 1959.

Nájera Farfán, Mario Efraín. *Los estafadores de la democracia: hombres y hechos en Guatemala.* Buenos Aires, 1956. Anti-Arbenz.

Nash, Manning. *Machine Age Maya: the Industrialization of a Guatemalan Community.* Menasha, Wis., 1958.

Reina, Ruben E. *Chinautla, a Guatemalan Indian Community.* New Orleans, 1960.

Samayoa Chinchilla, Carlos. *El quetzal no es rojo.* Guatemala, 1956.

Schneider, Ronald M. *Communism in Guatemala, 1944–1954.* N.Y., 1958.

Schwauss, Maria. *Tropenspiegel: Tagebuch einer deutschen Frau in Guatemala.* Halle, 1949.

Seminario de Integración Social Guatemalteca. *Integración social en Guatemala.* 2 vols., Guatemala, 1956–60.

Silvert, Kalman H. *A Study in Government: Guatemala.* New Orleans, 1954.

Spain, Mildred W. *'And in Samaria'.* 2nd ed., Dallas, 1954.

Suslow, Leo A. *Aspects of Social Reforms in Guatemala, 1944–1949.* Hamilton, N.Y., 1949.

Toriello Garrido, Guillermo. *La batalla de Guatemala.* Mexico City, 1955.

United States, Department of State. *Intervention of International Communism in Guatemala.* Washington, 1954.

——House of Representatives, Select Committee on Communist Aggression. *Communist Aggression in Latin America.* Washington, 1954.

Valle Matheu, Jorge del., comp. *Guía sociogeográfica de Guatemala.* Guatemala, 1956.

——*La verdad sobre el 'caso de Guatemala'.* Guatemala, 1956. Reply to pro-Arbenz arguments.

Waddell, David Alan Gilmour. *British Honduras: a Historical and Contemporary Survey.* London, 1961.

Whetten, Nathan Laselle. *Guatemala: the Land and the People.* New Haven, Conn., 1961.

El Salvador

Alvarado, Gustavo. *El alma de la patria.* San Salvador, 1951.

Cea, José Roberto, comp. *Poetas jóvenes de El Salvador.* San Salvador, 1960.

El Salvador, Ministerio del Interior. *14 de diciembre de 1951: tercer aniversario de la revolución salvadoreña.* San Salvador, 1952.

Feuerlein, Willy John. *Proposals for the Further Economic Development of El Salvador.* N.Y., 1954. U.N. study.

Fortín Magaña, Romeo. *Democracia y socialismo.* San Salvador, 1953. Essays.

Gonzáles Ruiz, Ricardo. *El Salvador de hoy.* San Salvador, 1952.

Hoselitz, Berthold Frank. *Industrial Development of El Salvador.* N.Y., 1954. U.N. study.

Lardé y Larín, Jorge. *Guía histórica de El Salvador.* San Salvador, 1958. First published 1952.

——*El Salvador: historia de sus pueblos, villas y ciudades.* San Salvador, 1957.

Lemus, José María. *Mensajes y discursos.* 5 vols., San Salvador, 1957–60.

Mertens, Robert. *El Salvador: biologische Reisen im Lande der Vulkane.* Frankfort on the Main, 1952.

Osborne, Lilly de Jongh. *Four Keys to El Salvador.* N.Y., 1956.

Turner, George P. *An Analysis of the Economy of El Salvador, April 1961.* Los Angeles, 1961.

Ventocilla, Eleodoro. *Lemus y la revolución salvadoreña.* Mexico City, 1956.

Wallich, Henry C. and others. *Public Finance in a Developing Country: El Salvador—a Case Study.* Cambridge, Mass., 1951.

Honduras

Bustillo Reina, Guillermo, ed. *El libro de Honduras: directorio y guía general de la república,* vol. i. Tegucigalpa, 1957.

Checchi, Vincent, and others. *Honduras: a Problem in Economic Development.* N.Y., 1959.

Helbig, Karl Martin. *Die Landschaften von Nordost-Honduras, auf Grund einer geographischen Studienreise im Jahre 1953.* Gotha, 1959.

Notes on Bibliography

Honduras, Oficina de Cooperación Intelectual. *Obra material del gobierno del doctor Gálvez: dos años y medio de administración pública.* Tegucigalpa, 1951.

Leyton Rodríguez, Ruben. *Honduras ilustrada.* Tegucigalpa, 1951.

Stokes, William Sylvane. *Honduras: an Area Study in Government.* Madison, Wis., 1950.

Vásquez, José V. *Album cívico hondureño.* El Progreso, 1952. Current biography.

Nicaragua

Castro Silva, Juan María. *Nicaragua económica.* Managua, 1949.

Chamorro Cardenal, Pedro Joaquín. *Estirpe sangrienta: los Somozas.* Buenos Aires, 1959.

Cuadra Downing, Orlando, ed. *Nueva poesía nicaragüense.* Madrid, 1949.

IBRD. *The Economic Development of Nicaragua.* Baltimore, 1953.

Mejía Sánchez, Ernesto. *Romances y corridos nicaragüenses.* Mexico City, 1946.

Tweedy, Maureen. *This is Nicaragua.* Ipswich, 1953.

Costa Rica

Barahona Jiménez, Luis. *El gran incógnito: visión interna del campesino costarricense.* San José, 1953.

Castro Esquivel, Arturo. *José Figueres Ferrer: El hombre y su obra.* San José, 1955.

Cortés Chacón, Rafael. *Necesidad de una reorganización del sistema educativo costarricense.* San José, 1957.

Fallas Monge, Otto. *La medicina social y la dignidad humana: la subgerencia médica en la Caja Costarricense de Seguro Social.* San José, 1958.

Kantor, Harry. *The Costa Rican Election of 1953: a Case Study.* Gainesville, Fla., 1958.

Liga Espiritual de Profesionales Católicos. *Costa Rica, un estado católico.* San José, 1955.

Loomis, Charles P., and others. *Turrialba: Social Systems and the Introduction of Change.* Glencoe, Ill., 1953.

May, Stacy, and others. *Costa Rica: a Study in Economic Development.* N.Y., 1952.

Nunley, Robert Edward. *The Distribution of Population in Costa Rica.* Washington, 1960.

Soley Güell, Tomás. *Historia económica y hacendaria de Costa Rica.* 2 vols., San José, 1947-9.

D. *Other items cited.* Other books particularly useful in this study, of an historical or reference nature, will be found cited in conjunction with the subjects of which they treat.

The Central American Republics

E. *Bibliographies.* By far the most useful treatments of Central American bibliography are offered by Robin A. Humphreys, *Latin American History: a Guide to the Literature in English* (see my Preface) and by William J. Griffith, 'The Historiography of Central America since 1830' (see Ch. v, n. 99, p. 132). Among the several listings available, the most extensive in scope is Henry Grattan Doyle's *A Tentative Bibliography of the Belles-Lettres of the Republics of Central America* published in 1935 (see Ch. ix, n. 90, p. 297). Items from 1935 to the present are described briefly in the *Handbook of Latin American Studies* published annually (no. 1, 1936; no. 23, Gainesville, Univ. of Florida Press, 1961). For a description of current bibliographical enterprise in Central America itself, see Helen F. Conover, 'Records of Current Publishing in Latin America', in *Handbook* no. 22, pp. 327–34; and Peter de la Garza, 'Records of Current Publication in Bolivia, Ecuador, and Honduras', in *Handbook* no. 23, pp. 408–13.

ABBREVIATIONS[1]

AJIL	*American Journal of International Law.*
Am. Anthrop.	*American Anthropologist.*
Am. Antiq.	*American Antiquity.*
An. Est.	*Anuario Estadístico.*
Anales	*Anales de la Sociedad de Geografía e Historia de Guatemala.*
Bol. de Est.	*Boletín de Estadística* (Nicaragua).
Bol. Est.	*Boletín Estadístico* (Guatemala, El Salvador, and Honduras).
Carnegie Inst.	Carnegie Institution of Washington.
D. de C.R.	*Diario de Costa Rica.*
D. de Hoy	*Diario de Hoy* (El Salvador).
DCA	*Diario de Centro América* (Guatemala).
Dir. Gen. Est.	Dirección General de Estadística (Guatemala); (— y Censos in El Salvador, Honduras, Nicaragua and Costa Rica).
Estruct. agr.	Inter-American Statistical Institute. *La estructura agropecuaria de las naciones americanas* (1957).
HAHR	*Hispanic American Historical Review.*
IBRD	International Bank for Reconstruction and Development.
Imp.	*El Imparcial* (Guatemala).
Int. Am. Econ. Aff.	*Inter-American Economic Affairs.*
Int. Lab. R.	*International Labour Review.*
Mid. Am. Res. Inst.	Middle American Research Institute.
Mid. Am. Res. Rec.	*Middle American Research Records.*
PAU	Pan American Union.
Prim. cens. agr.	*Primer censo agropecuario.*
U.N., *Demogr. Yb.*	U.N., *Demographic Yearbook.*
— *Stat Yb.*	— *Statistical Yearbook.*
— *Yb. Int. Trade Stat.*	— *Yearbook of International Trade Statistics.*
Yb. Lab. Stat.	*Year Book of Labour Statistics* (ILO).

[1] Excluding such familiar abbreviations as Int.=International; J.=Journal; Mus.=Museum; Q.=Quarterly; R.=Review or Revista.

INDEX

337

Index

Index

Gainza, Gabino, 77 f.
Galich, Luis Fernando, 107
Gálvez, Juan Manuel, 83, 189, 192, 204, 210
Gálvez Barnes, Roberto, 192
Gann, Thomas William Francis, 29 f.
García Monge, Joaquín, 298
Gazeta de Guatemala, 69, 71, 75 f.
Germans, 116, 122, 144, 173
Germany, 91, 117 f., 133, 166, 173, 205, 240, 254, 257, 284
Goicoechea, José Antonio, 68, 73
Golfito, 258, 282, 283 n., 287, 291
Golfo Dulce, 6, 51, 259
Gómez Carrillo, Agustín, 131, 138
Gómez Carrillo y Tible, Enrique, 138–9
González de Avila, Gil, 45
González López, Luis Arturo, 106
González Víquez, Cleto, 262 f.
Government, 18–19, 37, 47 f.; colonial, 58–63; federal, 78, 81, 83; local: —G., 91–94; —El S., 146–8; —H., 182–5; —N., 220–2; —C.R., 257–9; national: —G., 94–95, 97–98, 105; —El S., 148 ff., 152–3, 154–5, 304; —H., 185 ff., 192–4; —N., 223 ff., 228, 229–30; —C.R., 259 ff., 263, 269–70
Gracias, 46 f., 58, 183, 185 n., 207
Gracias a Dios: Cape, 43, 234; dept., 183 f., 185 n., 198, 310
Granada, 45 f., 58, 61, 76, 220 f., 223 ff., 242 f., 247 f.; dept., 222, 238; dioc., 253
Great Britain, 61 f., 65; and G., 91, 100 n., 109 f., 118; and El S., 161, 164, 166, 177; and H., 196, 205, 217; and N., 234 f., 240, 254; and C.R., 257, 264, 284
Greytown, *see* San Juan del Norte
Guanacaste (prov.), 78, 235, 242, 256, 258 f., 280, 283 n., 292, 296; *see also* Nicoya (*alc. may.*)
Guardia, Tomás, 261, 287
Guatemala, 1 f., 4 f., 7 ff., 11, 77 ff., ch. v, 302, 303–4, 306–7, 308 ff., 312, 314, 317; antiquities, 12 ff., 25, 27, 30 f., 33 f.; Indians, 34 ff., 49–50, 52 ff.; colonial, 45 ff., 60, 62 f., 67 ff., 71 f., 74 f.; and reunification, 80 ff., 85 ff.; and El S., 145 ff., 160, 162, 164 ff., 173 ff., 177 ff.; and H., 181, 183 ff., 188, 192–4, 195 ff., 199, 201 f., 205, 209, 213, 216 f.; and N., 222 f., 225, 228 ff., 233, 237, 239,

241 f., 247, 249, 251 ff.; and C.R., 259, 261, 271, 274, 278 ff., 285, 288, 290, 293, 297 n., 299
Guatemala (dept.), 94, 107
Guatemala (dioc.), 94, 107
Guatemala City, 7, 9, 11, 35, 50; (1773–1821), 57, 66, 68 ff., 74 ff.; (since 1821), 77, 79, 91–92, 104, 119, 121 f., 129 f., 135 f., 138, 142 f., 168, 174, 212, 223
Guatuso (l. and p.), 35, 51
Guayape River, 7 f.
Guerrero, José Gustavo, 176
Güetar (l. and p.), 35, 51
Güija, Lake, 7, 155, 170
Gutiérrez, Víctor Manuel, 102

Henequen, 64, 114, 201, 238; El S., 163
Heredia, 58, 257 ff., 286, 298; prov., 259, 282, 292
Hernández de Córdoba, Francisco, 45 f.
Hernández Martínez, Maximiliano, 151–2, 156, 161, 188, 228, 233
Herrera, Santos León, 268
Hispaniola, 44 ff.
Historiography, 67–68; G., 131–2; El S., 175–6; H., 213–14; N., 249–50; C.R., 293–5
Honduras, 1 ff., 5 ff., 78 f., 90 n., ch. vii, 302, 305, 308 ff., 312 f., 317; antiquities, 12 ff., 25 f., 30, 33 f.; Indians, 34 ff., 39, 50 f., 53; colonial, 43, 45 ff., 58, 60, 62, 64, 68; and reunification, 80 ff., 87 f.; and G., 100 f., 104, 109, 112, 116, 120 f.; and El S., 147 f., 160, 164, 166, 169; and N., 219, 222 ff., 228 ff., 233 ff., 237, 239, 242, 246, 248 f., 251, 253; and C.R., 256, 259, 261 f., 279 ff., 283, 286, 292, 296, 297 n.
Honduras (dioc.), 72, 216
Honduras (int.), 60, 148, 185, 259
Honduras, Gulf of, 6
Huehuetenango, 17, 49, 92, 120; dept., 94, 141, 217

Iglesia Evangélica (G.), 143
Ilopango, Lake, 7
Imports: G., 118; El S., 166–7; H., 205; N., 240–1; C.R., 284–5
Income tax, 314–15; G., 108, 111, 303; El S., 160–1, 304; H., 189, 199, 305; N., 233, 236; C.R., 266, 272, 278, 290

341

343

CENTRAL AMERICA: GENERAL

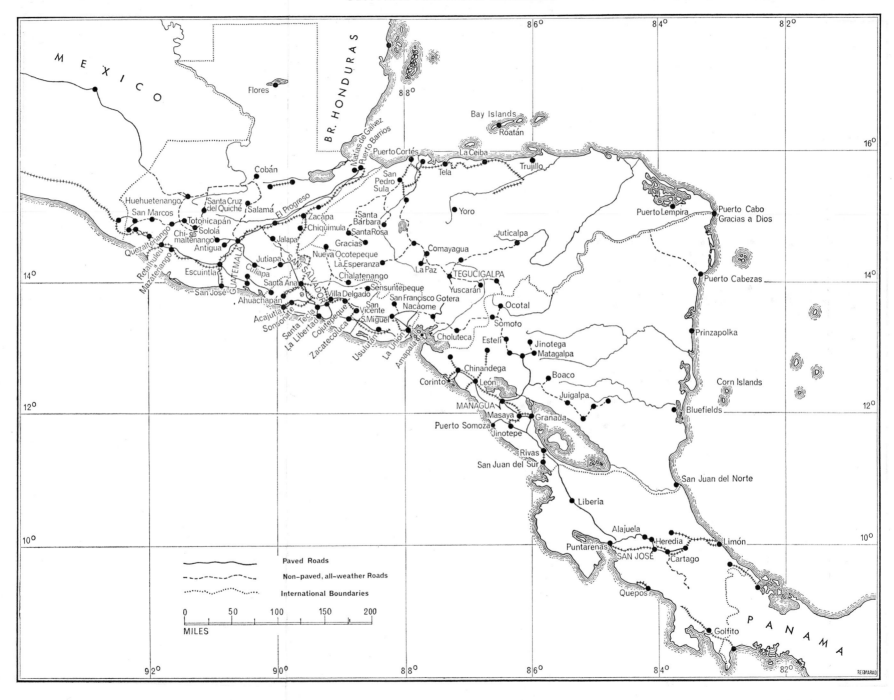

MEXICO

BR. HONDURAS

Flores

Bay Islands
Roatán

Puerto Cortés
Matías de Gálvez
Puerto Barrios
La Ceiba
Tela
Trujillo

Cobán
San
Pedro
Sula
Yoro
Puerto Lempira
Puerto Cabo
Gracias a Dios

Huehuetenango
Santa Cruz
del Quiché
Salamá
El Progreso
Zacapa
Santa
Bárbara
Santa Rosa
Juticalpa
Puerto Cabezas

San Marcos
Totonicapán
Chiquimula
Gracias
Comayagua
Quezaltenango
Sololá
Chi-
maltenango
Jalapa
Nueva Ocotepeque
La Esperanza
La Paz
TEGUCIGALPA
Retalhuleu
Antigua
Jutiapa
GUATEMALA
SAN SALVADOR
Chalatenango
Yuscarán
Puerto Cabezas
Mazatenango
Culiapa
Escuintla
Santa Ana
Sensuntepeque
Ocotal
Prinzapolka
San José
Villa Delgado
San Francisco Gotera
Ahuachapán
Santa Tecla
Villa Delgado
San
Vicente
Nacáome
Somoto
Acajutla
Sonsonate
La Libertad
Cojutepeque
S.Miguel
Choluteca
Estelí
Jinotega
Corn Islands
Zacatecoluca
Usulután
La Unión
Amapala
Matagalpa
Chinandega
Boaco
Corinto
León
Juigalpa
Bluefields
MANAGUA
Masaya
Granada
Puerto Somoza
Jinotepe
Rivas
San Juan del Norte
San Juan del Sur

Liberia

Alajuela
Limón
Puntarenas
Heredia
SAN JOSE
Cartago

Quepos

Golfito

PANAMA

Paved Roads
Non-paved, all-weather Roads
International Boundaries

0   50   100   150   200
MILES

REGMARADJ